# Unplanned Parenthood

SO-BZR-668

# Unplanned Parenthood

## The Social Consequences of Teenage Childbearing

Frank F. Furstenberg, Jr.

**THE FREE PRESS**

*A Division of Macmillan Publishing Co., Inc.*
NEW YORK

Collier Macmillan Publishers
LONDON

Copyright © 1976 by The Free Press
A Division of Macmillan Publishing Co., Inc.

All rights reserved. No part of this book may be reproduced or transmitted in any form or by any means, electronic or mechanical, including photocopying, recording, or by any information storage and retrieval system, without permission in writing from the Publisher.

The Free Press
A Division of Macmillan Publishing Co., Inc.
866 Third Avenue, New York, N.Y. 10022

Collier Macmillan Canada, Ltd.

First Free Press Paperback Edition 1979

Library of Congress Catalog Card Number: 76-8144

Printed in the United States of America

printing number

HC          3   4   5   6   7   8   9   10
SC   1   2   3   4   5   6   7   8   9   10

**Library of Congress Cataloging in Publication Data**

Furstenberg, Frank F.
    Unplanned parenthood.

    Bibliography:  p.
    Includes index.
    1.   Adolescent mothers--United States--Longitudinal
studies.   2.   Pregnant school girls--United States--
Longitudinal studies.   3.   Teen-age marriage--United
States--Longitudinal studies.   I.   Title.
HQ759.4.F87         301.41'76'463         76-8144
ISBN 0-02-911010-6
ISBN 0-02-911030-0 pbk.

*To My Parents,
who made this
study possible*

# Contents

# List of Tables

# Foreword

Life history is once again a vigorous field of inquiry in the behavioral sciences, and no stronger testimony to its renaissance can be found than *Unplanned Parenthood*, a thought-provoking longitudinal study of the effects of adolescent parenthood on the lives of young women. Not since the 1930s have we encountered such multidisciplinary interest in biographical research or more fruitful developments in ways of thinking about and studying lives through time. Over the past decade improved interviewing techniques have been employed in life-history studies by sociologists, clinical psychologists, and social historians; advances in data management have been applied to the collection and retrieval of life record information; new vitality and intellectual respectibility have been brought to studies in developmental psychology; and a life-course perspective, with emphasis on the timing and synchronization of events, has evolved from greater awareness of the diverse meanings and implications of age. Instead of viewing life histories solely in terms of the occurrence and chronology of important events, such as marriage and parenthood, this perspective also takes account of their temporal context and pattern. Frank Furstenberg employs a life-course approach to good effect in this volume by expertly tracing the process by which adaptations to teenage parenthood influence the life changes of mother and child.

All projects have careers, but the career of Furstenberg's study deserves special notice for what it tells us about problem formulation and its research significance. In these times of rapid methodological advances and readily accessible archives, one senses a general neglect of the most fundamental aspect of inquiry, that of defining and conceptualizing research problems. Elegant modes of analysis and available data may have encouraged us to bypass or short-circuit the painstaking requirements of problem formulation. In this regard, one thinks of those who come to research equipped with a favored statistical device or data set, but lacking a well-conceived problem or an understanding of it. The Early Parenthood project, as I have known it over the past decade, supplies a refreshing contrast. It is a study that evolved from a narrowly restricted evaluation design into an investigation of timing and adaptations in the life course that has theoretical significance well beyond the territory of unwed motherhood or early parenthood.

The project began in 1966 when Furstenberg was asked by the Adolescent Family Clinic of Sinai Hospital, Baltimore, to direct a short-term evaluation of a service program for teenage mothers in a section of the city with a predominantly low-income, black population. At the time, he was engaged at Columbia University in dissertation research on the transmission of social disadvantage. This line of research and the Clinic's aim of preventing unwanted pregnancies jointly influenced the etiological focus of the research; the mothers of participants in the program were to be interviewed along with the girls themselves. From such a beginning, one would be hard pressed to recognize the project before us—a six-year longitudinal study of the consequences of adolescent parenthood, the first study of its kind on this problem and one that seems destined to leave its mark on ways of thinking about life experience.

It is during the first four years that we see a shift in problem foci and analytic structure from the causes to the consequences of early parenthood and the emergence of ideas on life-course adaptations to an ill-timed event. The postponement of marriage, the rescheduling of schooling, and the control of fertility are represented as ways of managing the disarrangements, tensions, and deprivations associated with an unplanned birth at an early age. These developments in concept required an expansion of the research design to include a comparison group of adolescent girls who had not become pregnant in adolescence. School records were used to select a matched sample of the former classmates of the adolescent mothers; both groups were interviewed in 1970 and 1972.

The project's life history conveys a vivid and genuine impression of circumstances that are frequently encountered in longitudinal studies and of adaptations that enable the researcher to make the best of what he has. In the midst of graduate work and with no time for adequate preparation, Furstenberg entered an applied research program which was largely structured by his employer. But the turn of events (lack of funds to extend the service program, limitations of the program) soon created an opportunity for him to rethink the study in the light of research experience and an interest in the causes of social disadvantage. The decision to focus on the consequences of early parenthood appears to flow logically from such interests and the research advantage of an extended longitudinal study. Even so, the initial data base (up to 1969) offered little guidance or comfort on the question of whether to proceed; the early interviews were not designed with career analysis in mind. Furstenberg provides the reader with a full report of the limitations and consequences of this deficient archive.

One important element is slighted in the project's recorded history; an account of how the investigator came to place his study of early parenthood within a life-course framework. Why this approach rather than one with less emphasis on event sequences and timing? Notions of timetables and scheduling, off and on time, were not part of the active vocabulary of sociologists before the mid-1960s, and we find no evidence of this general orientation in Furstenberg's doctoral dissertation. However, by the end of the decade a number of developments had increased awareness of the theoretical significance of age and timing in the study of lives. These include the emergence of a cohort historical perspective in which age locates individuals in the social structure and in a specific historical context. The life-course implications of birth year and cohort membership stem from exposure to a distinctive slice of historical experience over the life span, and from attributes of the cohort itself—its social composition and size. Furstenberg is mindful of the potentially unique historical experience of the adolescent mothers and their classmates, all members of a single cohort from the baby-boom era. He suggests that the striking growth of adolescent cohorts between the early and mid-60s contributed to the emergence of adolescent parenthood as a social problem. In the 1960s there were more adolescent girls than ever before to give birth to a child out-of-wedlock, and an increasing proportion did so.

A second age-based development is more directly relevant to the conceptual framework of the study: an expanding interest in the social-time dimension of life patterns, the age patterning of events, role sequences, and careers. Two foci in particular may be viewed as theoretical contexts of the life-course approach in *Unplanned Parenthood:* (1) a career perspective on life events—the order of events in a natural history and events as social transitions with a sequence of phases; and (2) the patterning of event timetables by age expectations and systems of social control, a domain exemplified by the work of Bernice Neugarten and her associates. Furstenberg applies a career model to the antecedent events of unwed motherhood. He may have been influenced in this direction by the writings of William Goode (his mentor at Columbia) and of Willard Waller on social phases leading to and following divorce. The model depicts a birth out-of-wedlock in adolescence as an outcome of a particular sequence of events in a distinctive moral career: premarital sexual experience (vs. nonexperience); sex without contraceptives (vs. such protection); pregnancy (vs. not pregnant); and birth of a child out-of-marriage (vs. abortion or motherhood in marriage). At each stage in the career, the research task is to explain why some girls engage in a particular activity and others do not. A full account of unwed motherhood thus entails linking a set of explanatory models. Lines of action followed in each stage of the career require different explanations; variables that explicate premarital sexual experience differ from those which bear on the failure to use contraceptives or on the choice among options following a birth out-of-wedlock. Consistent with the earlier findings of Prudence Rains, Furstenberg employs the model to advantage in documenting the essentially "unplanned" character of adolescent parenthood, an interpretation that runs directly contrary to the still popular assumption that out-of-wedlock births are a consequence of motives that push girls toward bearing a child out-of-marriage.

Adolescent parenthood is described in this volume as one example of "distrubances in the normative schedule," of life events which are ill-timed or off schedule according to prevailing social norms. Whatever their consequences, the purely normative implications of such disturbances (between births in- and out-of-wedlock, for example) are exceedingly difficult to pin down. To be sure, some adverse effects of childbearing in adolescence are readily attributable to negative sanctions; for example, the exclusion or isolation of pregnant girls by school authorities. Other punitive sanctions are expressed more indirectly, such as through the age handicap of adolescent fathers in the labor market. But given the scant knowledge we have of age norms and enforcement measures, no single study could do justice to their influence. In any case, it is the disturbance generated by early childbearing that assumes center stage in the analysis; disturbances in the scheduling and possibilities of other career lines among the adolescent mothers—educational, marital, occupational. Apart from the approved timetable of parenthood, early childbearing is off schedule in relation to social maturation, completion of school, and self-support. Problems of synchronization and life management arise from this ill-timed event and from others which occur out of order or off schedule. These problems enter the analysis through an examination of coping strategies; judicious planning, the rearrangement of schedules, and educational aspirations played a major role in enabling some adolescent mothers to repair the damage of an early birth to their life chances.

By following the adolescent mothers into their early 20s, we discover how erroneous some of our impressions of early parenthood have been; in particular, the notion that bearing an unplanned child in adolescence leads inevitably to a life of deprivation. Diversity of histories and future prospects is one of the most striking findings of the study. Though most of the women were from black, low-income families, their life situations some five years after the birth of their first child reflect a broad range of advantage and hardship which seems to defy a simple accounting scheme. These differences are expressed in the parenting behavior of the mothers and in the development of their children.

Frank Furstenberg's skillful explication of these life paths brings fresh insights and a deeper understanding to the process and consequences of early parenthood. As might be expected, a good many questions are left unanswered, including that of the generality of the study's findings, but this fact merely serves as a long overdue reminder of how much work lies ahead in unraveling the complexities of parenthood. Such prompting and a fruitful way to proceed may well represent the most enduring contribution of this important study.

Chapel Hill, North Carolina                                  Glen H. Elder, Jr.

# Acknowledgments

In the course of a study that has spanned nearly ten years more debts are accumulated than one can possibly repay. I cannot hope to list all the people who have provided aid and comfort along the way, but neither can I fail to acknowledge the special assistance of particular individuals. My greatest appreciation goes to the participants in the study, who gave generously of themselves at times when it was painful to share a part of their lives. In interpreting their accounts, I realize that I am at a triple disadvantage, being neither black, female, nor poor. The real and self-imposed barriers created by these differences are not easily overcome, and I would regard this report as at least a partial success if the subjects felt that what I have written accurately portrays their experience in entering parenthood.

It goes without saying that this study could not have been conducted without the generous assistance of the Maternal and Child Health Service in HEW (Grant Number MC-R-420117-05-0). I wish to express special thanks to Charles P. Gershenson for his encouragement in the early phases of the study and to Gloria Wachernah for her support and patience while the research was being conducted.

I also owe a special debt to Drs. Milton Markowitz and Leon Gordis who were at Sinai Hospital of Baltimore when the study was undertaken. They initiated the research and played an important part in its early stages. At various points throughout the study, the administration and staff of Sinai Hospital were extraordinarily helpful in facilitating the project.

I greatly benefited from the professional assistance of the staff of Sidney Hollander Associates. Their cordiality and cooperation were unstinting. Marilee Considine supervised the fieldwork and helped in innumerable other ways. Shirley Blumberg rendered invaluable assistance throughout the project. It is no exaggeration to say that the research would not have been possible without her involvement.

In the development of the study a number of colleagues offered excellent advice and criticism. In the early phases, William J. Bowers offered helpful comments on the questionnaire. Joy Osofsky and Judith Porter provided consultation in developing the children's interview. Susan A. Ricketts gave indispensable assistance in part of the analysis.

Special thanks go to a group of colleagues who took the time to read the manuscript and suggest (with unusual tact and sensitivity) many helpful revisions. I should acknowledge that they were somewhat more generous in offering suggestions than I was in accepting them. Therefore, I, not they, should be held accountable for the ultimate product. These colleagues are Jerry Coombs, Glen Elder, Mel Kohn, Richard Lincoln, Jane Menken, John Modell, Harriet Presser, John Scanzoni, Jim Trussell, and Etienne Van de Walle. Evelyn Weinman made a number of editorial improvements in an early draft of the manuscript and Gladys Topkis reviewed the final copy with great skill and consideration.

Kathy Gordon Talvitie, my research assistant for the past two years, has been in a very real sense a collaborator in the preparation of this book. Her commitment and contribution to the project have been enormous.

A number of colleagues at the University of Pennsylvania and elsewhere provided helpful advice and encouragement: Digby Baltzell, Ann Beuf, Fred Block, Diana Crane, Renée Fox, Erving Goffman, Van Harvey, Carol Joffe, Judy Modell, and Vincent Whitney. I also wish to express my gratitude to the friends who nurtured me when I felt, as I often did, discouraged about the progress of the study. The Bardachs, Dalsimers, Lavins, Nathansons, and Umbargers lent support at long range, and my Philadelphia intimates Larry Gross, Sol and Tobia Worth, and especially Gino and Nina Segrè must know of my permanent obligation to them.

It is customary to reserve a final expression of gratitude for one's spouse. In most cases, if the spouse is a female, she is thanked for her encouragement and forbearance. My wife, Anne-Linda, provided these in abundance, but I am even more grateful for her willingness to discuss and exchange ideas, her tough-minded criticism of the final manuscript, and her knowledgable suggestions.

Philadelphia, Pa.                                                F.F.F.

# 1. Adolescent Parenthood in American Society

WHEN PARENTHOOD OCCURS early in adolescence, it often creates a dilemma for the young mother and her child, threatening both their immediate and their long-range interests. Teenage childbearing is thought to be associated with a wide spectrum of psychological, economic, and social problems, but the link between precipitate parenthood and events in later life is incompletely documented and poorly understood. This study seeks to elucidate this link by exploring when, how, and why childbearing before the age of 18 jeopardizes the life prospects of the young mother and her child.

In considering these questions it is useful to recognize that actions such as early childbearing belong to a more general category of social incidents that may be thought of as "disturbances in the normative schedule." In the first part of this chapter we shall show why departures from the prescribed life course typically pose problems for individuals as well as for society. Later in the chapter we shall present evidence indicating that societal reaction to early childbearing has changed in recent years. For reasons that we shall mention, teenage parenthood has become less socially acceptable at the same time that it has become more publicly visible. The response has been an upswing in social concern. Unfortunately, this surge of interest has not been matched by an expansion of information about the problem. The concluding section turns to some conspicuous gaps in existing knowledge and introduces a study undertaken from 1966 to 1972 which explored certain neglected questions about what happens to young mothers and their offspring after childbirth.

## NORMATIVE SCHEDULES AND THEIR CONSEQUENCES

All societies possess social standards that control the sequence and the tempo of important life occurrences. This normative schedule necessarily corresponds to

1

biological rhythms, but its precise structure is prescribed by cultural rules and regulated by social constraints. The form and the flexibility of normative schedules vary tremendously across societies. Some cultures explicitly specify the timing of life events; in others, members are allowed greater individual discretion. Contrasts can also be found in the sequencing of stages in social careers. Important transitions may be arranged in rapid succession or staggered so that no more than a few occur at any one point in the life course (Modell et al., 1976).

For the purposes of this initial discussion, we are less concerned with explaining the specific features of normative schedules than with accounting for their general existence. Norman Ryder (1965, 1974) has pointed out that an inevitable "demographic metabolism" requires cultural mechanisms in every society for filling social positions as they become vacant. Efficient phasing requires some degree of social preparation for both entrance into and exit from existing positions. Provision must be made for recruits as they enter new statuses and for incumbents who may be forced to relinquish familiar ones. In order to manage these movements, skills, material resources, and rewards must be allocated to ease the transition to and from social positions (Riley et al., 1972). In sum, normative schedules provide social guidelines that chart the expected course of life, putting members of a society on notice as to when and under what circumstances status transitions may occur. As Ryder (1965:856) puts it:

> Every society seizes upon the circumstances of birth as modes of allocating status, limiting the degrees of freedom of the person's path through life. Virtually every subsequent occurrence will depend on the societal plan for utilizing characteristics present at birth: sex, race, kinship, birthplace, and so forth.

In the abstract, any general statement on the social functions of normative schedules probably conveys the erroneous impression that the mere existence of timetables ensures the minimum of friction and conflict in handling transitions within society. The opposite is probably more accurate: normative schedules provide an agenda for personal and social change, but they do not offer any assurance the life course will be smooth. Timetables exist at least in part because changes throughout the life span are inherently stressful and full of conflict. Ryder (1974:45) captures the problematic element in status passage rather well:

> Society at large is faced perennially with an invasion of barbarians. Somehow they must be civilized and turned into contributors to fulfillment of the various functions requisite to societal survival. . . . That invasion can be regarded as a threat to the persistence of the system; the challenge must be faced, even if there is no guarantee of success.

# SOURCES OF DISTURBANCE IN NORMATIVE SCHEDULES

One source of systemic conflict is the lack of perfect agreement among members of a complex society as to the nature of normative schedules. Quite possibly, traditional societies experiencing little social and economic change may reveal normative schedules that are relatively fixed, but timetables in modern societies are in a continual state of flux.[1] At any given time there is probably substantial disagreement within the society over the specifics of the schedule (Riley et al., 1972: chs. 1, 10). Depending on their age, sex, and social class, individuals may be exposed to varied conceptions of the appropriate life course, and hence the child is likely to be confronted by conflicting expectations in the course of growing up (Neugarten and Moore, 1968).

There are other reasons impelling individuals to depart from a life course that is normatively prescribed. A variety of structural conditions may arise that make it difficult for an actor to conform to the idealized life course. Natural catastrophes, wars, demographic fluctuations, political upheavals, or economic collapses may upset the careers of entire cohorts (Clausen, 1972; Elder, 1974). These events—particularly if they occur over an extended period of time or affect a large proportion of society—may restructure the normative schedule. However, this redefinition may be slow in coming. In the meantime, many people experience the uncomfortable perception that their lives are departing from the expected or regular route (Elder, 1976). Personal or idiosyncratic events also may throw an individual off schedule (Thomas and Znaniecki, 1958; Volkart, 1951). Limitations in individual capacities, physical handicaps, shortages of critical resources, the absence of social support, or temporary misfortunes may produce unexpected and undesired departures in one's life course. In some instances, an individual may foresee obstacles to staying on course but be helpless to prevent them. External pressures may lead him or her to make decisions that unavoidably disrupt the normative schedule, or he or she may use discretion unwisely at certain critical junctures. Actors are not always willing or able to take future events into consideration when making decisions. These miscalculations may permanently alter the life course (Becker, 1970: pt. 3).

[1] There is little historical research on the degree of consensus on life cycle transitions in American society. Kett (1974) has speculated that in previous times the life course was less orderly than it is today. In a paper coauthored by John Modell, Theodore Hershberg, and myself (1976), we set forth a conceptual and methodological framework for examining the changing construction of the life course.

## THE CONSEQUENCES OF VIOLATING
## NORMATIVE SCHEDULES

Disturbances in the normative schedule sometimes result in premature status transition, propelling persons into positions that they are unready or unprepared to assume (Neugarten, 1968) and forcing them to relinquish statuses that they currently enjoy (Rossi, 1968). Others with whom they must interact in their new positions may be unprepared to accept the newcomers, to grant them the prerogatives of their new positions or to provide them with the support necessary to perform their new roles (Clausen, 1972). Consequently, they may perform indifferently or incompetently in the new roles they are required to play.

In other situations, schedule disturbances may have the opposite effect, retarding status transitions and locking individuals into positions from which they are unable to move (Roth, 1963; Riley et al., 1969). Immobility may lead to discontent, withdrawal, or socially rebellious forms of behavior. Alternatively, persons thus entrapped may come to feel that it is too late to catch up. The possibility of change may become threatening; they may become overly committed to their current status and unwilling to relinquish it even when opportunities for movement arise (Waller, 1940; Liebow, 1967).

While career disarrangement increases the likelihood of social disadvantage and personal stress, these outcomes are by no means inevitable. Individuals may respond effectively to the challenges of accelerated status movement or adapt creatively to prolonged status occupancy (Waller, 1930; Volkart, 1951; Elder, 1974). Indeed, these disruptions may produce detours in the life course that are subsequently viewed as "lucky breaks." Physical handicaps, illness, military draft, or unemployment can have unanticipated and favorable consequences in redirecting social careers. However, for every such case, there are undoubtedly many more instances in which a departure from the normative schedule works to the individual's disadvantage.

Although we can state as a general principle that schedule disruptions are usually disadvantageous to the "deviant," we know little about how disturbances in the normative schedule are handled—in particular, why some persons manage to escape the ill effects of an untimely life event, while the careers of others are damaged irreparably. This book addresses this question empirically. Early parenthood, especially when it occurs out of wedlock, is a prime example of a departure from the normative schedule. As such, it inevitably raises a series of problems for the young parents that must somehow be resolved after the child is born.

## THE SCHEDULING OF PARENTHOOD

When and under what circumstances parenthood is permitted varies from one culture to another, but no society leaves the scheduling of parenthood purely to biological happenstance or puts it entirely in the control of the prospective parents (Davis and Blake, 1956; Goode, 1960, 1961). Social theorists have long recognized the universal existence of cultural restrictions on reproduction. In his influential essay "Parenthood, the Basis of Social Structure," Bronislaw Malinowski (1930) argued that the institution of marriage exists in all societies not to mandate sexual relations but to regulate parenthood. Central to Malinowski's formulation is the proposition that unregulated parenthood is costly for both the child and society. Children who lack a sociological father are more vulnerable economically as well as socially for they must rely on one parent and one family instead of two for support and social connections. Unregulated parenthood also poses serious problems for society. In societies in which children are an economic liability, there may be reluctance to assist the offspring of nonmarital unions. Where children are an economic asset or a source of social repute, the question arises: Who has the right to the child's labor or social benefit? Malinowski suggested that marriage provides a means of avoiding potentially destructive conflicts by settling this issue in advance.

The assumption of Malinowski and his students that a sociological father is indispensable to the welfare of the child has been questioned by a number of scholars on the family who raise the possibility that the principle of legitimacy may rest on a hidden and unexamined patriarchal cultural bias (Stack, 1974; Caulfield, 1974; Scanzoni and Scanzoni, 1975). Regardless of one's position on this issue, pressures to regulate parenthood may arise for reasons other than the need to designate a sociological father.

In addition to safeguarding the welfare of the child, rules regulating the formation of new families protect individuals from incurring obligations that they are not yet ready to assume. Thus, the marriage ceremony not only serves as a social device for determining who may become parents but traditionally has signified the time when parenthood may commence. By establishing a culturally sanctioned sequence leading up to parenthood, a mechanism—marriage—exists for delaying (or perhaps in some instances promoting) the onset of parenthood.

Few societies permit marriage and childbearing to take place at puberty. Even in traditional social systems, in which family formation tends to occur earlier, the age at marriage is likely to be postponed beyond the point at which individuals are biologically capable of becoming parents. The scheduling of marriage and parenthood will depend on the type of kinship system, on the social and economic value of children, and probably on demographic constraints on population growth (Moss, 1964). Consequently, we can expect to find considerable variation across societies in the socially acceptable age for marriage and childbearing (Dixon, 1971).

Although empirical data are sparse, most experts agree that early marriage and childbearing—that is, family formation much before the end of the second decade of life—are universally discouraged in modernized societies (Sullerot, 1971). (There is some evidence that early childbearing is regarded with increasing disfavor and concern in the United States even though in recent years the incidence of adolescent parenthood has remained relatively stable.) Since the performance of adult responsibilities in such societies requires an extensive period of training, the acquisition of complex knowledge and skills, and a substantial investment of material resources, individuals are not considered to be "ready" to support a family until their early twenties. This constraint applies particularly to males, but it holds true for females as well since women generally have assumed an important economic role in maintaining a family.

## THE INCIDENCE OF EARLY CHILDBEARING IN AMERICAN SOCIETY

If it were somehow possible to infer cultural norms strictly from patterns of social behavior (a position to which we do not subscribe), then we would have to conclude that at no time has early childbearing been socially acceptable in American society. Contrary to popular impression, parenthood before the age of 18 has never been common in this country. Reliable data on the fertility patterns of youth prior to the Civil War are extremely difficult to come by, but scattered statistical evidence on family formation in the seventeenth and eighteenth centuries suggests that women typically married in their early twenties (Greven, 1966; Smith, 1973). Marriage prior to age 18 was unusual and generally confined to the affluent. Census data collected in the late nineteenth century reveal that teenage marriage occurred only infrequently and that the overwhelming majority of women did not have their first child until they reached their twenties (Modell et al., 1976). A special census taken in Massachusetts in 1885 reported that the total number of children ever born to females in their teens was less than 20 per 1,000 (Taeuber and Taeuber, 1971). More extensive statistics on marriage patterns confirm the impressions given by the sketchy data on early childbearing in the nineteenth century. Monahan (1951), for example, drawing on a vast number of marriage records, found that matrimony rarely took place before the late teens. State laws generally prohibited youthful marriage without parental consent (Kephart, 1964). While these laws may have contributed to a certain amount of age falsification, they also testify to the historical undesirability of early marriage.

More plentiful data on teenage childbearing are available for the period following 1915, when the government began publishing vital statistics natality figures on a regular basis. These records show a constant pattern of teenage fertility during the first half of the twentieth century. The birthrate among 15- to 19-year-olds remained essentially unchanged until the end of World War II, fluctuating between 50 and 60 births per 1,000 women. In 1910, the total number of children ever born to teenage mothers stood at 69 per 1,000. The comparable figure in 1940 was 68 (Taeuber and Taeuber, 1958).

It is difficult to tell how many of these births occurred among women who were not yet 18 since no specific information was published on this age group, an indication perhaps of how rare early childbearing was. Extrapolating from contemporary data, we suggest that no more than 90,000 of the 300,000 teenage women who gave birth in 1940 were under the age of 18.

The post-World War II period brought about some modification of this historical trend. There was a sharp rise in the rate of teenage marriages and accordingly some decrease in the median age of the mother at first birth. Even in this period of early marriage and burgeoning family size, childbearing typically did not occur until the early twenties. However, the number of teenage births did increase substantially in the postwar decade. The teenage birthrate climbed from 51.1 per 1,000 women in 1945 to 96.3 by 1957, the peak year of the baby

Table 1.1. *Fertility in U.S. Teenage Population, 1950-1970*

| Age of Mother | Total Number of Live Births | Estimated Number of Illegitimate Live Births | Illegitimacy Ratios *out of wedlock* (Ratios per 1,000) Live Births |
|---|---|---|---|
| **1970** | | | |
| Total (15-19) | 644,708 | 190,400 | 295.3 |
| Under 15 | 11,752 | 9,500 | 808.4 |
| 15-17 | 223,590 | 96,100 | 429.8 |
| 18-19 | 421,118 | 94,300 | 223.9 |
| **1965** | | | |
| Total (15-19) | 590,894 | 123,200 | 208.3 |
| Under 15 | 7,768 | 6,100 | 785.3 |
| 15-17 | 188,604 | 61,800 | 327.1 |
| 18-19 | 402,290 | 61,400 | 152.6 |
| **1960** | | | |
| Total (15-19) | 586,966 | 87,100 | 148.4 |
| Under 15 | 6,780 | 4,600 | 678.5 |
| 15-17 | 182,408 | 43,700 | 239.6 |
| 18-19 | 404,558 | 43,400 | 107.3 |
| **1955** | | | |
| Total (15-19) | 478,214 | 69,100 | 142.3 |
| Under 15 | 5,883 | 3,900 | 662.9 |
| 15-17 | 143,839 | 34,800 | 231.8 |
| 18-19 | 334,375 | 34,300 | 102.3 |
| **1950** | | | |
| Total (15-19) | 419,635 | 56,100 | 133.5 |
| Under 15 | 5,021 | 3,200 | 637.3 |
| 15-17 | 126,941 | 28,700 | 226.1 |
| 18-19 | 292,694 | 27,400 | 93.6 |

| | Birthrate (15-19) | Estimated Illegitimacy Rate (15-19) |
|---|---|---|
| *1975*   *57* | | |
| 1970 | 63.3 | 22.4   *since 1970* |
| 1965 | 70.4 | 16.7   *gone up only a* |
| 1960 *decreases* | 89.1 | 15.9   *small amount* |
| 1955 | 90.3 | 15.1 |
| 1950 | 81.6 */1000 teens* | 12.6 |

Sources: *Vital Statistics of the United States, 1970* and Clague and Ventura, 1968

boom (Clague and Ventura, 1968; Vital Statistics of the U.S., 1970). Thus, the trend in the teenage population paralleled that in other age groups except that the birthrate shot up much more rapidly for teenagers than for the rest of the population. However, births to very young women still accounted for only a small proportion of teenage fertility.. Of the 425,000 teenagers who had a child in 1950, approximately one-third, or 132,000 births, occurred among women under the age of 18. In 1960, just after the baby boom reached its crest, the number of adolescent births had risen to about 190,000 (Table 1.1).

Although the absolute number of teenage births, and in particular births among women under the age of 18, has risen since the end of the baby boom, the birthrate among teenagers has steadily and sharply declined. Today it stands at or slightly below the level prior to that at the end of World War II. As can be seen from Table 1.1, since the mid-1960s the number of teenage mothers has remained relatively constant despite an enormous expansion in the size of the teenage population. Early childbearing has leveled off. Slightly more than 230,000 births occur each year among school-age mothers.

## THE EMERGENCE OF ADOLESCENT PARENTHOOD AS A SOCIAL PROBLEM IN AMERICA

Paradoxically, it was only after the late 1950s, when teenage childbearing began to stabilize, if not actually to recede, that public concern about the problem of teenage parenthood became manifest. Although in previous times very early childbearing may have been discouraged for reasons of health, there is little evidence from historical documents (e.g., travelers' accounts, marriage manuals, and sermons) that marriage or parenthood was considered to be a problem for a female when it occurred before she was 18 (Calhoun, 1960). Perhaps this event happened too infrequently to command much notice. Nevertheless, one gets the impression from popular literature of the time that negative sanctions were not attached to youthful childbearing so long, of course, as the woman was married at the time of delivery.

If adequate historical evidence were available, we might detect a shift in the age norms for marriage and childbearing in the postwar period (Modell et al., forthcoming). Beginning in the 1950s, we find references in the writings of professionals and in the mass media on the undesirable consequences of teenage marriage (Burchinal, 1960). In a sense, these commentaries were a response to what appeared to be a growing trend toward earlier family formation. But the negative reaction toward youthful marriage and childbearing corresponded to the diminution of job opportunities for teenagers and the accompanying expansion of educational training following World War II. During this period, high school graduation, if not college training, became an essential credential for a white-collar job and for entrance into the middle class (Coleman, 1974). Limited economic opportunities and higher educational expectations ultimately helped to discourage early marriage and childbearing. Increasingly, we find signs that teenage parenthood, even when it occurs after marriage, has come to be viewed as a violation of the normative schedule.

By the early sixties, a distinctly unfavorable portrait of the adolescent parent can be detected in government and social welfare publications. "Premature parents," "school-age mothers," and "high-risk adolescent mothers" are terms liberally sprinkled throughout the child welfare, social work, and educational journals. There is no single explanation for the swell of disquietude about teenage parenthood, but we can cite a number of factors that converged during this period and served to focus interest on this group.

1. At least in part, concern was generated by the sheer growth in the number of teenage mothers in the late fifties and early sixties. As we have pointed out, this change did not reflect a tendency toward higher fertility among the very young but was due, rather, to the expanding pool of young women who were available to bear children. In the first half of the sixties, there was an increase by more than 25% in the number of females in their middle teens as the children of the baby boom entered adolescence. This sharp rise offset and obscured the decline in fertility that was taking place concurrently, conveying the false impression that women under the age of 18 actually were producing more babies than ever before. Of course, they were not; however, their share of the teenage births did rise from 31% in 1950 to 36% in 1970. Although these birthrates were no novel cause for alarm, nevertheless the increasing number of school-age mothers inevitably attracted attention to the problem of early parenthood.

2. General apprehension about overpopulation in the 1960s intensified concern about adolescent parenthood. The emergence of a "population problem" in the sixties encouraged advocates of family planning to direct their efforts toward specific groups within the population that had experienced a high incidence of unintended and unwanted births and that might yield the largest payoff, given the limited resources available. Even though among teenage mothers fertility had begun to decline in the early sixties, the decrease was occurring more slowly than it was among other age groups. Reducing unwanted births among teenagers, it was reasoned, might help to establish permanent patterns of family planning during later years of life.[2]

3. A distinctive feature of teenage births is the high proportion that occurs out of wedlock. This pattern always has been evident, but during the late fifties the "illegitimacy" ratio—the proportion of illegitimate to legitimate births—

---

[2] For an extensive bibliography of publications on the desirability of extending birth control services to teenagers, see Perkins (1974) and *Family Planning Perspectives*, vols. 1-7.

began to rise throughout the population.[3] Teenagers by virtue of their marital status, had the greatest potential for producing out-of-wedlock children, and therefore the rising ratio among this group inevitably attracted most attention. At the beginning of the decade, 15% of the births among teenage women were out of wedlock; by 1970, the last year for which complete published information is available, the proportion of illegitimate births had nearly doubled. More than one-fourth of the births among women under 20 and close to one-half of the births among women under 18 occurred out of wedlock.[4] Moreover, these statistics greatly understate the prevalence of prenuptial pregnancies since most legitimate children born to teenagers were conceived prior to their parents' marriage.

Two factors contributed to the increase in teenage illegitimacy. First, changing patterns of sexual behavior were exposing a higher proportion of unmarried adolescents to the possibility of pregnancy.[5] Second, at the same time that premarital sex was becoming more prevalent and more accepted, the appeal of early marriage was diminishing among youth (Hetzel and Cappetta, 1973). Reliable trend statistics to demonstrate this point are unavailable, but it seems likely that in the 1960s more and more teenage couples faced with a premarital pregnancy were deciding not to marry merely to avoid out-of-wedlock parenthood. The extension of education, the reduction of job opportunities for teenagers, and the negative sentiment toward early marriage that had developed in the preceding decade all contributed to a changing pattern of marital behavior in the 1960s (Sklar and Berkov, 1974; see also Cutright, 1974; and Furstenberg, 1974a).

Increasingly, then, adolescent parenthood was equated with unwed parenthood. This trend stimulated efforts to limit childbearing among the very young. By the middle of the decade, there were open appeals for birth control programs for unmarried youth. Within a remarkably brief span of time, these appeals began to receive widespread support. Judith Blake (1974) discovered from a secondary analysis of public opinion polls that public sentiment on supplying

[3]The quotation marks around *illegitimacy* indicate that the term is not one of my own choosing. In referring to some births as illegitimate, I do not intend the moral disapproval that the term sometimes implies.

[4]The illegitimacy ratio actually was increasing largely because the overall decline in teenage births among married women was not matched by an equal decline in the unmarried population. Married teenagers were having fewer children at the same time that unmarried teenagers were having more. The rate of legitimate births among teenagers declined by more than 10% during the 1960s, while the incidence of teenage illegitimacy rose by more than 40% during the same period, going from 15.3 in 1960 to 22 in 1970 (Sklar and Berkov, 1973).

[5]Although reliable data on sexual patterns of teenagers are difficult to find before 1970, there is good reason to suspect that the sixties ushered in more liberal standards of sexual behavior among youth. Several studies of college-age youth indicate a significant upward trend in the incidence of coitus during the last decade (Smigel and Seiden, 1968; Christensen and Gregg, 1970; Bell and Chaskes, 1970). No doubt the incidence of premarital pregnancies also went up; however, toward the end of the decade wider contraceptive use and the availability of abortion probably began to curb this trend.

birth control information to teenagers began to shift substantially toward the end of the decade. Throughout the sixties, there had been high opposition to family planning services for adolescents. By the early seventies, a majority of Americans said they favored the provision of contraception to teenagers who requested it.

4. In the first year of the 1960s government officials also began to take notice of the social and economic implications of teenage births. In the latter part of the Kennedy administration and in the early part of the Johnson presidency, public attention was drawn to the issues of racial and economic inequality in American society, setting off a national debate on strategies for eliminating poverty. At least in the initial phase of this debate, most discussions centered on the cultural and social barriers to social mobility that poor people encountered. How to break into the "vicious cycle of poverty" was the question that was argued repeatedly in the early writings on social policy approaches to poverty. The assumption that poverty was a social heritage naturally led to the view that modifying patterns of family life among the poor should be an important focus of programmatic attention. Promiscuous sexual behavior, illegitimacy, and early marriage were singled out as cultural elements that contributed to the maintenance of poverty (Rainwater and Yancey, 1967).

In the sixties, a series of publications by government researchers and demographers examined the incidence of teenage parenthood, in particular, illegitimacy among adolescents (Martz, 1963; Bernstein, 1963; Clague and Ventura, 1968; Haselkorn, 1966; Herzog, 1967). Most of these documents were not intended as moral tracts on the irresponsible sexual patterns of the young, the poor, or blacks. Indeed, their tone was generally careful, neutral, and judicious. Nevertheless, they provided statistical ammunition for those who advocated greater government intervention to prevent early childbearing. Increasingly, a tight causal connection was drawn between adolescent parenthood and a host of social and economic ills.

Concern over unplanned childbearing and its relationship to poverty inevitably prompted a series of intervention efforts. Under the aegis of the Children's Bureau (the Maternal and Child Health Service, as it later came to be known), a succession of programs was launched to delay the onset of childbearing and to extend services to adolescent parents. The earliest efforts concentrated on improving health services for young mothers, providing educational and vocational counseling, and offering social services during pregnancy (Howard, 1968). As the notion of family planning became more widely accepted, government funds became available for comprehensive adolescent programs, joining maternal and child health care with educational, vocational, and contraceptive service programs (Baizerman et al., 1971; Perkins, 1974). During the early seventies, the growth of programs for school-age mothers was nothing short of spectacular. In 1967, it was estimated that there were several dozen programs offering educational and medical services to adolescent parents. A recent publication recorded more than 375 such programs throughout the country in 1974, and the number is undoubtedly still growing.[6]

One effect of the increase in public programs may have been a considerable heightening of public consciousness about the undesirability of early childbearing. By publicizing the perils of teenage parenthood, the action programs helped to reinforce and promote the norms regarding the appropriate age for marriage and childbearing that were previously only implicit. Accompanying the proliferation of programs for the adolescent parent has been a greater interest in the causes and consequences of early childbearing. Practitioners frequently complain that little is known about the population for which these services are being designed.

## RESEARCH ON EARLY CHILDBEARING

The widespread conviction that early childbearing precipitates a number of social and economic problems is founded on surprisingly little evidence. In 1971, the Consortium on Early Childbearing and Childrearing, an advocacy group organized to disseminate information about the problems of adolescent parenthood, published a comprehensive review of scholarly research issued during the 1960s dealing with the antecedents and effects of early childbearing (Baizerman et al., 1971). While the review overlooked a few important published monographs and excluded unpublished material, the bibliography reflects rather accurately the state of knowledge at the beginning of this decade. A general conclusion of the research compendium was that adolescent mothers are a "particularly burdened group of women." "Ideally," the document stated, "recognition of sociological factors as contributory to adolescent pregnancy should lead to an acceptance of societal responsibility in preventing and treating the negative consequences of the phenomenon" (Biazerman et al., 1971:6).

Just what are the negative consequences? An examination of the research studies that purported to show the adverse effects of early childbearing is an exercise in frustration. Only a few of the approximately 200 items in the consortium's bibliography provided results of empirical research on adolescent parents, and most of these studies were based on clinical reports of small samples of *pregnant* adolescents. Those studies that examined the experiences of young mothers *after* pregnancy were based on samples of participants in adolescent service programs and rarely offered observations about the life experiences of

[6]These estimates are provided by *Sharing,* the newsletter of the Consortium on Early Childbearing and Childrearing. This publication was launched in 1967 under the sponsorship of The Children's Bureau to disseminate information about research, policy, and programs on adolescent parenthood. At last count, the circulation of *Sharing* had reached 8,000.

the teenage parent in general. As the organizers of the review reported (Baizerman et al., 1971:1):

> Critical and analytic reading of these studies shows that most are methodologically weak, so much so that great care must be taken by the reader lest he draw conclusions from the report which are unsubstantiated by the data contained therein.

The studies omitted from the consortium's bibliography and investigations carried out since 1970 offer little basis for revising the conclusion that systematic research on the consequences of adolescent parenthood is virtually nonexistent. The consortium's review failed to report several important studies that examined the impact of out-of-wedlock childbearing, although none of these investigations was confined exclusively to the adolescent population (Bowerman et al., 1966; Sauber and Corrigan, 1970). In addition, there have been several more careful evaluations of adolescent service programs; however, these recent studies provide little general information on the long-term postpartum experiences of young parents. Understandably, their attention is focused on assessing the impact of services provided (Klerman and Jekel, 1973; Baizerman, et al., 1974; Braen and Forbush, 1975).

The narrow scope of existing studies on the consequences of adolescent parenthood is not their most serious shortcoming. The major defect is their failure to contrast the experiences of young mothers with those of their peers who avoided early parenthood. The absence of a comparative design makes it difficult, if not impossible, to assess the manifold effects of early childbearing. Moreover, most existing research on the careers of unwed or adolescent mothers, or both, has concentrated on the immediate postpartum experience, offering little or no information on the long-range impact of the unscheduled pregnancy.

## SOME UNANSWERED QUESTIONS

One possible explanation for the lack of research on the consequences of early childbearing is that these consequences appear obvious. Virtually everyone who is familiar with the phenomenon is firmly convinced that adolescent parenthood disrupts the normal life course of the mother. For reasons mentioned earlier, it is assumed that unscheduled parenthood propels the young mother into a role for which she is only casually prepared and often feels unready to assume (Osofsky, 1968). By becoming pregnant prematurely, the adolescent mother often is removed from the sources of support and resources available to women who defer parenthood until after marriage. Moreover, precipitate entry into parenthood preempts the educational, vocational, and social experiences the adolescent would otherwise acquire to prepare her for adult roles, including motherhood.

No one has expressed this idea more cogently than Arthur Campbell (1968:238) in the following passage:

> The girl who has an illegitimate child at the age of 16 suddenly has 90 percent of her life's script written for her. She will probably drop out of school; even if someone else in her family helps to take care of the baby, she will probably not be able to find a steady job that pays enough to provide for herself and her child; she may feel impelled to marry someone she might not otherwise have chosen. Her life choices are few, and most of them are bad. Had she been able to delay the first child, her prospects might have been quite different assuming that she would have had opportunities to continue her education, improve her vocational skills, find a job, marry someone she wanted to marry, and have a child when she and her husband were ready for it.

The scenario provided by Campbell is both a succession of hypotheses and a series of conclusions about the consequences of unscheduled parenthood. While plausible enough, it tends to assume that the career route of the unwed adolescent mother is virtually fixed: "Suddenly [she] has 90 percent of her life's script written for her." Like most other observers, Campbell appears to adopt the position that having a child during early adolescence, especially out of wedlock, is such a potent event that it precludes options and adaptations that could repair the initial disadvantage created by a pregnancy. Consequently, early childbearing has the effect of negating conditions that have preceded the pregnancy and overriding contingencies that occur after the child is born. Campbell in fact probably would not want to embrace such a deterministic point of view. Even in his description, which is overstated in order to emphasize a point, he leaves the door open a crack: 10% of the adolescent unwed mother's script is unwritten. A few adolescent parents may manage to reroute their life course and escape the destiny of disadvantage that Campbell has described so well.

Even if the life course of adolescent parents were so rigidly established, it would be relevant for social practitioners to know how the lucky few are able to avoid this path. However, it is a reasonable bet that there is more latitude in the situation than is generally admitted. Just how much is an open question, directly connected to a more important problem: what kinds of conditions, events, actions, and circumstances permit some adolescent parents to escape the deleterious effects of an unscheduled pregnancy but relegate others to pathways of social failure?

In a recent discussion of social structure and personality, Glen Elder (1973:796) pointed out how poorly understood are the "chains of events and processes that connect social arrangements to the life situations and psychology of the individual." Elder argued that investigators tend to cut short their inquiries at the very point at which they should begin. Finding an association between social conditions and individual behavior is hardly a substitute for arriving at a specific understanding of how and why these phenomena are related. Elder is stating something more than the familiar assertion that correlation does not necessarily imply causality. He is claiming that social investigators have paid lip service to this assertion and have become practiced in avoiding the difficult task of exploring the factors that account for the connections between social structure and individual actions.

The writings on unscheduled parenthood serve as a case in point. Theories explaining why early parenthood might adversely affect the life chances of the adolescent mother or empirical observations of social welfare workers and researchers confirming that adolescent mothers do indeed encounter social and personal problems are not sufficient grounds for concluding that early childbearing leads to social disadvantage. To establish this proposition, it is essential, as Elder argues, to provide specific documentation on the social processes that link early parenthood to school dropout, marital instability, further unwanted pregnancies, or difficulties in childrearing. For each of these presumed sequelae (or others that we might think of), it is necessary to show not only whether but also how and why they are associated with unscheduled parenthood.

We have already alluded to several reasons why adolescent mothers (and fathers as well) might suffer social disadvantage. One explanation that figured prominently in our earlier discussion held that adolescent parents are not equipped adequately or fully socialized to handle their new responsibilities. As a result, they perform adult roles with less skill than do individuals who enter these positions later in life. Hence, problems in marriage, work, birth control, or childbearing arise because the adolescent parent is "incompletely socialized." They are denied, or fail to acquire, the experience or training necessary to perform adult roles as competently as others who delay entry into parenthood.

A variant form of this argument holds that adolescents who become pregnant are different to begin with and that their life course emanates from, and reflects, this initial difference. Though they may not elect to lead a life of social disadvantage, most women who become young mothers are destined to do so by virtue of a distinctive set of beliefs, standards, and social practices that they acquired at an early age. According to this interpretation, adolescent motherhood is the result, not the cause, of a divergent life-style and the cluster of social problems associated with it.

At the other extreme are the structural interpretations that were touched upon earlier in this chapter. These arguments locate the source of disadvantage not in the cultural origins or social training of the young mother but in the social and economic position parenthood imposes upon her. Premature entry into parenthood may mean that the adolescent childbearer is formally or informally denied the resources and support normally provided to mature mothers. The disordering of the "normal" family career removes the young mother from the systems of social and economic support upon which she has depended. At the same time, her age and social position may limit her access to alternative arrangements that could ensure economic independence. Subtle and explicit forms of discrimination may be applied to adolescent mothers by their families, their schools, or potential employers, disturbing their chances of resuming old roles or performing new ones.

Although we have treated these several interpretations as though they were necessarily distinctive and perhaps competing ways of explaining the consequences of unscheduled parenthood, they are in fact neither mutually exclusive nor entirely conflicting. In subsequent chapters, each of these general interpretations will be explored in some detail in order to elucidate the career patterns of the adolescent mothers in our sample.

## OVERVIEW OF THE BOOK

The research on which this book is based began as an evaluation of the Adolescent Family Clinic of Sinai Hospital of Baltimore, one of the first comprehensive service programs for teenage mothers. However, it quickly became apparent that it was impossible to understand the specific impact of the program without delving into more general issues of how early parenthood alters the life course of the teenage parent. Gradually, the study was transformed from a short-term evaluation of a single program into a five-year investigation of the consequences of early childbearing.

As the goals of the study expanded, we modified the design accordingly. Interviews were conducted with a control group of young women, former classmates of the young mothers. These comparative data allowed us to probe the link between adolescent parenthood and life events more systematically. A brief chronicle of the study is presented in Chapter 2, acquainting the reader with a "natural history" of the project. At the end of this chapter, we will introduce the participants in the study.

Although our analysis does not deal directly with the etiology of unscheduled motherhood, we hope that it will serve as a corrective to some of the existing studies on "why" women have children out of wedlock and will provide a framework for future research on this question. Chapter 3 describes what we have called the "process of unplanned parenthood."

Chapters 4-8 explore the impact of parenthood on subsequent transitions in the early adult life of the young mother. Most adolescents in our study faced the difficult choice of marrying or bearing a child out of wedlock. In Chapter 4 we examine the factors that affected their choice, and in Chapter 5 we consider the consequences of that decision on the marital careers of those women who decided to wed. Chapter 6 explores the subsequent history of pregnancies among the young mothers, focusing on the factors that encouraged or deterred additional unwanted pregnancies.

Family formation affects and is affected by the young mother's commitment to educational advancement. In Chapter 7 we look at the educational career of the adolescent mother to assess the impact of early pregnancy on her schooling. Chapter 8 then analyzes the effect of early pregnancy on the economic status of the young mother in early adulthood.

Chapters 9 and 10 describe the adaptation to parenthood, first from the perspective of the young mother and then from the point of view of her child. We take up the hitherto largely unexplored question of whether early parenthood adversely affects the attitudes and skills of the mother and the intellectual and social development of the child.

Chapter 11 summarizes our findings and draws some conclusions about the experiences of adolescent parents that may be of some use to those concerned with formulating policies toward establishing service and programs for, adolescent parents and their children.

# 2. The Baltimore Study

INVESTIGATORS FREQUENTLY FAIL to acknowledge the emergent character of social research, glossing over the methodological improvisations that invariably enter into the design of an empirical study. The very term *design* suggests an exaggerated notion of planfulness that is rarely accomplished in sociological studies (Hammond, 1964). It is in the spirit of fuller disclosure that this chapter provides a chronicle of the Baltimore project, reconstructing the most important decisions, miscalculations, and unforeseen events that figured into the research design. Our aim is to trace the evolution of the project from a short-term program evaluation to a five-year longitudinal examination of the career of the adolescent mother.

## THE INCEPTION OF THE STUDY

In 1964, two physicians at Sinai Hospital of Baltimore drew up a proposal for an Adolescent Family Clinic (AFC), a coordinated service program for pregnant teenagers who entered the hospital for prenatal care. About a decade earlier, Sinai Hospital had moved from the heart of the black community in east Baltimore to the center of the Jewish ghetto in northwest Baltimore. Ironically, almost immediately blacks moving out of the center of the city began to relocate in the northwest. By 1964, the outpatient clinic of Sinai was once again serving a predominantly black population, introducing the need for special programs. In certain neighborhoods within the hospital's catchment area, 1 out of every 10 females had a child by age 16. Few medical and social services were available to these young parents, and what services existed were fragmented and not well equipped to meet the special needs of the adolescent population. Finally, although it was commonly known that repeat pregnancies frequently occurred among this group, practically no assistance was offered to prevent subsequent unwanted conceptions.

19

In 1964, the federal government was reaching out to communities, urging their participation in the Great Society. Money was in greater supply than new ideas, and Washington was entertaining proposals for extending social services to impoverished areas, particularly the deteriorating urban centers of larger cities. For reasons discussed in Chapter 1, the "high-risk" mothers, (women with a strong probability of encountering medical, social, and economic problems at childbirth) had been singled out for special attention. The Adolescent Family Clinic at Sinai Hospital was an obvious candidate for government support.

The program that was designed in 1964 called for a broad range of services for the teenage parent, including child care education, nutritional advice, medical examinations, educational and vocational guidance, family counseling, and birth control information. These services were to be delivered by a team of physicians, social workers, and public health nurses. An innovative feature of the program was the intention to offer medical and family planning assistance from the time the prospective mother first registered for prenatal care throughout the early years of parenthood. The Adolescent Family Clinic received an initial grant from the Children's Bureau in 1964 and was refunded on an expanded basis in 1965.

## TIME 1: THE INITIAL INTERVIEW

Early in 1965 my mother was hired as the social worker for the AFC. In the course of her duties, she was asked to help design a questionnaire that could be administered to young women at the time they registered for prenatal services. The questionnaire would be used to determine their attitudes toward medical care in general and toward family planning in particular, their orientation toward impending parenthood, and their plans for child care after delivery. At that time I was doing graduate work in sociology at Columbia University, and my mother turned to me for assistance.

I drafted a 5-page interview schedule containing about 25 questions. Shortly thereafter, in December 1965, the program administrators invited me to the hospital to discuss a procedure for measuring the success of the AFC. One thing led to another, and soon I had agreed to take on the responsibility of evaluating the program.

While at Columbia I worked most closely with three members of the faculty: William Goode, Herbert Hyman, and Richard Cloward. Goode (1960, 1961) had been examining cross-cultural data on illegitimacy and was interested in out-of-wedlock pregnancy as an indication of normative disruption; Hyman (1959), for whom I was working at the time the study began, was pursuing a long-standing interest in the transmission of social attitudes and values; and Cloward (Piven and Cloward, 1971), with whom I was later to work, was applying to the study of the urban poor his ideas on the structure of social opportunity that had developed from his studies of delinquency. With my ongoing work in these related areas, it is not surprising that the study eventually developed into an exploration of the transmission of social disadvantage. When I first joined the project in early 1966, however, I had only a vague interest in this issue.

At the outset I regarded the study as an opportunity to explore certain ideas that I was examining in my dissertation, ideas on the transmission of social attitudes in the family. Looking back now at the initial interview schedule, I see all too clearly that it did not include many critical questions that might have been asked had my ultimate intent been better defined. At this preliminary stage, my interests were narrowly confined to the problem of the existence of a culture of poverty that sanctioned premarital sexual activity and early pregnancy. Such a cultural mandate might well undermine the efforts of the proposed family planning service. This line of inquiry thus comfortably fit both the aims of the evaluation and my intellectual interests at the time.

The study was set up to interview all adolescents under the age of 18—regardless of whether they were assigned to the special or to the regular clinic—shortly after they registered for prenatal care. Interviews would also be conducted six months after delivery and again a year later. Presumably, by comparing the women enrolled in the AFC with their counterparts in the regular clinic we could at the time of the follow-ups measure the impact of the program. After I joined the project, we decided to interview the adolescent's mother at the time of the initial contact to obtain information on the family's reaction to the pregnancy and on the degree of social support shown for the prenatal program.[1]

During the spring of 1966, preliminary interview schedules for the adolescents and their mothers were developed. The interview schedules went through several drafts and pretests in the next six months. The original list of 25 questions eventually grew to include more than 100, and with each successive revision, the scope of the study broadened. The adolescent interview focused on occupational and marital career plans, impact of the pregnancy, sexual patterns, birth control knowledge and experience, attitudes toward medical care, and information on family relations. The interview with the adolescent's mother repeated many of the questions contained in the daughter's interview and solicited more personal background material about the family and the occupational careers of the parents. Since we were operating under many of the

[1] In response to the requirement of the Children's Bureau that methods of evaluation be built into the program design, it was proposed that half of the teenagers who came to the hospital be assigned on a random basis to the AFC and the other half to the general prenatal outpatient clinic (GOC). The AFC quota was eventually enlarged to include nearly three-fifths of the incoming pregnant adolescents. In the final sample of 404 adolescents who participated in the first phase of the study, 233 (58%) were served by the Adolescent Family Clinic.

Nine others were assigned to the AFC but elected to attend the regular clinic because they did not wish to attend the weekly group meetings. When the two programs are compared in Chapter 6, these few cases are excluded from the analysis.

prevailing biases of that time, very little information was obtained about the father of the unborn child or about the adolescent's own father.

In March 1966, an interviewer with considerable fieldwork experience was hired to pretest the two schedules. The interviewer, Mrs. B., immediately demonstrated a remarkable ability to establish rapport with the adolescents. Mrs. B. had a strong tendency to volunteer advice, to offer support, and occasionally to administer motherly admonitions. Following the initial interview, she would often do little favors for the participants, take them to lunch, or intervene at the hospital on their behalf. Clearly, she violated many of the canons of professional interviewing, becoming involved, and on occasion overinvolved, with the subjects of the study. On the other hand, the young women obviously appreciated her warmth and responded to her interest in them. Her outside relationships with the respondents turned out to be a tremendous asset when it came time to conduct the follow-ups.

Taking into consideration the racial and socioeconomic composition of the population and also to insure against possible bias because of Mrs. B.'s white middle-class status, we attempted in the summer of 1966 to locate an experienced black interviewer. However, at that time only one staff member was needed to handle the work load, so the decision to hire a second interviewer was not made.

In the summer fieldwork was begun with a revised version of the interview schedule. During the next two years, every adolescent who registered at the prenatal clinic at Sinai Hospital was interviewed if she was below the age of 18 and had never been pregnant before. A total of 421 interviews was conducted, representing the entire population of adolescents who sought prenatal services at the hospital. Seventeen respondents were subsequently removed from the analysis because (1) upon further examination they turned out not to be pregnant, (2) they did not deliver at the hospital, or (3) they had been pregnant previously. An average of five school-age females registered for prenatal care each week. Each was interviewed as soon as consent could be secured from her mother. Generally, this occurred in the hospital on the first visit, when the expectant mother was accompanied by her parent.

As soon as it could be arranged, an interview with the pregnant adolescent's mother was conducted in her home. Interviews were completed with 350 (87%) of the prospective grandmothers, including almost all (96%) of the mothers of young women who were single at the time of their first visit to the hospital and 59% of the mothers of the married women. (Most of the married adolescents were no longer living with their parents, and we had less success in completing the mother's interview in these cases.) Only two mothers indicated unwillingness to participate in the study. We failed to interview 53 of the prospective grandmothers either because they were no longer living or resided in another city or because their whereabouts were not known to their daughters.

A detailed description of the women in the study appears later in this chapter, but a few comments are needed here about the adolescents who sought prenatal services at Sinai. The clinic was designed to serve those who could not afford a private physician; therefore, our population consisted almost exclusively of women residing in low-income households. Most teenagers who registered for prenatal care, especially in the early years of the program, did not know of the special services available at Sinai but came merely because it was the hospital closest to their homes. Since Sinai was easily accessible to the black community in northwest Baltimore and many blacks could not afford private medical care, the women in our study were predominantly black. But, as we shall discover later, the participants turned out not to be so very different from the sample we might have expected had it been drawn from the entire population of pregnant adolescents who delivered a child in Baltimore during the period of the study.

## TIME 2: THE ONE YEAR FOLLOW-UP

Once the fieldwork was under way, I withdrew temporarily from the study to complete my dissertation. My absence from the project made the follow-up originally planned six-months after delivery impractical, and we decided instead to schedule the first follow-up one year after the child was born.

In the proposal I submitted to the Children's Bureau requesting funding to continue the study beyond 1967, reference was made to a projected 200 interviews to be divided equally among women participating in the AFC and the GOC programs. In arriving at these estimates, however, we had not taken into account changes in the marital status of the adolescents. Approximately 20% of the adolescents were married by the time they registered in the program, and many more married shortly after childbirth. From the start, it was apparent that single and married females could not be treated together in the analysis. Since this difference between the two subgroups promised to be an important factor in determining the receptivity of the adolescents to the AFC program, we decided to augment the sample to include a sufficient number of married adolescents. Enlarging the sample meant extending the fieldwork period until we had enough eligible participants. Consequently, we were still conducting initial interviews during the preparation and administration of the one-year follow-up.

A short form for the follow-up interview consisting largely of items previously used in the initial schedule was prepared in the fall of 1966 and expanded in the spring of 1967. This reworked questionnaire was pretested and revised over the summer in order to be ready for the participants who had delivered their children the preceding fall. During this same period, arrangements were made to process the data from the initial interviews to meet the demands of the program administrators for some conclusions from the first phase of the study. Although the first phase of the fieldwork was not completed, the summer of 1967 was spent processing the nearly 200 interviews that had been completed and doing a preliminary analysis of these data (Furstenberg, 1969).

As Mrs. B. became increasingly occupied with the follow-up interviews, we looked around for a second interviewer. Our resolve to hire a black interviewer yielded to the temptation of convenience: a white staff member of the hospital was looking for a job at the time and was hired in the winter of 1967. With her assistance, the first phase of the study was concluded by the spring of 1968.

Meanwhile, the follow-up interviews were proceeding without much difficulty. Judging from prior studies, we had anticipated a fairly substantial attrition of the sample (see Hyman et al., 1954; Weiss, 1972). First, low-income families are known to be residentially mobile; second, many of the women had married after the first interview and there was reason to fear that their changes of name and address would complicate the tracing process; and, finally, we suspected that some of the women would be reluctant to participate in the follow-up because they had no particular stake in the research and perhaps wished to conceal their status of unwed mother. These possibilities notwithstanding, in the first follow-up, we reinterviewed, much to our surprise, 95% of the original population.[2]

The follow-up did present one problem. Scheduling the interview exactly 12 months after delivery was difficult since many of the women could not be located immediately. Occasionally the number of overdue follow-up interviews built up, resulting in a delay of a month or more. Half the interviews were completed at 12 months, three-fourths by the end of the thirteenth, and 90% before the sixteenth month. About two-fifths of these interviews took place in the hospital when the young women came in for pediatric appointments; the remainder were conducted in their homes.

## TIME 3:  THE THREE-YEAR FOLLOW-UP

Toward the end of 1968, I began to sense that certain changes were in store for the program. One of the administrators had been offered a position elsewhere, and the other had received a promotion within the hospital. In turn, the hospital, experiencing some financial difficulty from the rising costs of medical care, was cutting back on programs that served low-income patients exclusively.

The supplementary grant from the Children's Bureau that supported the Adolescent Family Clinic was scheduled to run out in 1969, and word was received that the application would probably not be renewed. The AFC program was slated to be merged with other adolescent services. Unless additional money

---

[2] Although the attrition rate was generally low, it was greater among adolescents who were married at Time 1 (14%) than among women who were not (4%). Married women were much more likely to have moved in the year preceding the second interview, and a higher proportion had left the city shortly after childbirth. We were also less successful in obtaining the subsequent interview in cases where we had not been able to interview the adolescent's mother at Time 1; marital status did not enter into this problem. Presumably, some of these adolescents had come to Baltimore to stay with relatives only until they delivered. In any event, the young mothers whose parents did not live in Baltimore were less tied to the city.

became available, the study would have to be concluded prematurely, and the evaluation would necessarily be compromised.

The one-year follow-up appeared to show that the program had a modest effect on fertility patterns, but it remained to be seen whether this result would be short-lived or relatively permanent. By this time, I was also beginning to sense the advantages of following the young mothers through the early years of parenthood, examining not only their fertility patterns but their parental, marital, educational, and occupational careers as well. A new proposal was written in early 1969 and was submitted both to the Children's Bureau and to the Population Council. This application reflected my growing interest in the social career of the adolescent parent and for the first time I referred explicitly to the link between unplanned parenthood and social disadvantage. However, most of the proposal dealt with a continuation of the evaluation of the family planning program. I was still not fully aware of the implications of the study; also, I felt that the prospects for continuing the research would be improved by stressing the evaluative features of the study.

After first responding discouragingly both the Children's Bureau and the Population Council approved the applications for a continuation of the study. Suddenly I was confronted with the unusual dilemma of having more funds than had been anticipated. The additional funds permitted an expansion of the study along two lines. First, an effort was made to contact as many of the fathers as could be located. Since the men did not figure prominently in the AFC (a fact that I later came to regard as a shortcoming of the program), there had been little reason to devote much attention to them in the early interviews. However, if the study sought to understand the career of the teenage parent, it would be necessary to know more about the fathers. Second, we interviewed a sample of former classmates of the young mothers, women who had not become pregnant in early adolescence, in order to have a basis for assessing the impact of an unplanned pregnancy on the career of the young mother.

As I began to weigh the repercussions of early parenthood, it soon became clear that the data I had collected were seriously deficient in one respect. How could we determine whether an early pregnancy affected the life chances of the adolescents in our study when all of the participants had had the common experience of becoming pregnant before the age of 18? Originally I had planned to get around the limitations in the research design by using certain baseline data from other studies, as well as by contrasting the primaparas and the young mothers who experienced more than one pregnancy. However, it seemed far preferable to collect data on the social careers of adolescents from similar backgrounds who had not become pregnant during early adolescence. The former classmates of the adolescent mothers were an obvious and suitable control group.

The task of contacting the fathers proved more difficult than expected. The only way of locating them was through the mothers. We explained the purpose of interviewing the fathers and asked for the women's help in locating them.

Almost all of the young mothers responded enthusiastically, and several commented that we should have talked to the fathers earlier in the study.[3] However, nearly one-third of the women either did not know the whereabouts of the father or reported that he had left town, was in the armed forces, was in jail, or was dead. Despite repeated attempts, we managed to find only slightly more than half of the 260 men for whom we had some residential information.[4] Interviews were completed for only 33% of the fathers, over half of whom were residing with the young mothers and their children when the interviews took place.

The low completion rate among the men in this study restricts the uses to which the data from the fathers can be put. However, at various points in discussing the men, we will present data from those fathers we did manage to interview. Otherwise we are compelled to rely on the information about the fathers supplied by the young mothers.

Our success in interviewing the classmates points up the special difficulty in locating the fathers. The fieldwork on the classmates was scheduled to coincide with the second follow-up of the young mothers; we planned to use a questionnaire similar to that developed for the reinterview. A sample of 415 classmates was drawn from the homeroom lists of the schools attended by the adolescent mothers. Some of names thus obtained turned out to be unusable because the addresses given were incorrect or nonexistent. Interviews were attempted with only 361 classmates.[5] Although the addresses we had for the classmates were several years old, we were able to contact more than 70% of the designated sample and to interview most of those whom we were able to locate. Only 7% of the classmates we located refused to participate in the study.

[3]It seems likely that our success in contacting the fathers would have been much greater had we interviewed the fathers initially. Yet, even if we had, the completion rate for the males would have been much lower than that for the females. After all, those fathers who had never married or who were separated from their families had a stake in remaining inaccessible; they probably feared that demands would be made upon them if their whereabouts were known.

[4]When such information was not provided by the adolescent mother, we were almost never able to locate the father. In some instances, interviews could not be carried out when the addresses supplied were not current. Among the men we were able to locate, a few (less than 8%) refused to be interviewed, and three respondents broke off the interview once it began. As is known from other studies, low-income males are particularly mobile. In the event that the man had moved, we rarely were able to find someone who could or would supply a current address.

[5]This sampling procedure was enormously time-consuming; every adolescent mother in the sample had been in a different homeroom, and the records from each school were located in different places. To make the sampling procedure more manageable, we drew a sample of 30 schools that the young mothers had attended, thus halving the original number of 60 elementary, junior, and senior high schools. From each homeroom list, we selected every ninth female. Even this simplified sampling plan took nearly two months to complete.

The additional funding provided in 1969 also permitted some modifications in the procedure for following up the young mothers. The practice adhered to earlier—the use of only one interviewer—created a number of methodological difficulties: sample attrition increased when the fieldwork was spread out over such a long period; there was a higher risk that respondents would be influenced by different external events when the fieldwork was prolonged; and the protracted fieldwork period slowed up the data analysis. In addition, I was still concerned about the bias introduced by heavy reliance on a single interviewer, and a middle-class white one at that.

In the second follow-up, we randomly assigned half the interviews to Mrs. B. and her associate, and a Baltimore research agency was engaged to hire and train eight black interviewers to conduct the other half. We presumed this arrangement would maintain continuity with past procedures while compensating for some of the weakness of the previous design. Moreover, the fieldwork could be completed much more quickly.

Almost immediately, the agency reported difficulty in assembling a staff of black interviewers with the qualifications and experience comparable to those of their usual white fieldworkers. Consequently, most of the black women who were hired to work on the study had not attended college and had little or no prior fieldwork experience. It was thought that proper training and supervision would compensate for this lack.

Pretesting began in the spring of 1970. It was soon apparent that the fieldworkers from the research agency were encountering more difficulties than Mrs. B. and her associate in locating respondents and in gaining access to their homes. In addition to their inexperience, the new interviewers lacked the advantages of prior contact with the respondents and association with the hospital program. However, the results did call into question the assumption that matching the racial characteristics of interviewer and respondent produces instantaneous rapport. In general, the quality of the interviewing was uneven. Several of the members of the agency field staff demonstrated great talent for careful and skilled questioning; others were far more casual; a few were indifferent and extremely careless.

Mrs. B. and her associate interviewed nearly all the respondents assigned to them. Eventually, they were also given the names of the respondents whom the agency interviewers had been unable to find, and they managed to locate over half of this group as well. While this practice compromised the original design, it enabled us to reinterview at the three-year follow-up slightly over 90% of the original cohort.

When the response patterns obtained by Mrs. B. and her associate on a sample of 60 attitudinal items were compared with those provided by the agency team, on all but a dozen of these items no significant differences appeared. There was more variability among the agency interviewers themselves than between white and black interviewers. In short, there was no indication that the status difference between the white interviewers and the respondents produced severe distortions in the data we collected.[6]

## Fieldwork Results

The fieldwork for the second follow-up was concluded in the fall of 1970; the data processing was completed by the end of that year. Looking at the first 12 months, we could conclude that the AFC mothers had experienced lower rates of repeat pregnancy than the GOC mothers although the differences were not large. The data from the second follow-up indicated that the effects of the program had all but vanished by three years after delivery.

As will be reported in Chapter 6, faulty implementation of the program was partly to blame for its minimal impact on the fertility patterns of the adolescent participants; more important, however, the AFC program was simply not designed to meet the particular needs of its participants. In identifying those needs, I finally came to the realization that childbearing events cannot be understood apart from other circumstances in the lives of the parents. Most of the young women's contact with the hospital was short-lived. Their experience in the program had little effect on their subsequent histories of pregnancy, especially when set against the backdrop of more consequential episodes in their lives during the early years of parenthood. It was at this point that I finally stopped thinking of the study as a specific evaluation of a family planning program and recast it into a more general exploration of the consequences of unplanned parenthood. Of course, in a certain sense it had always been both, but only in 1970, faced with the limited success of the program, was I compelled to be more deliberate in developing a framework for interpreting the data collected over the previous three and one-half years.

To account for the negligible impact of the program, I was forced to address a series of broader issues: what was the effect of unscheduled parenthood on the life course of young women? Why were some adolescent mothers more success-ful than others in negotiating the problems of early parenthood? What kinds of events, opportunities, and resources affected the capacity of the young parent to respond positively to new demands made upon her? To what extent was it possible to modify the adaptive response that followed unplanned parenthood? All these questions had a direct bearing on the more general problem of how social careers are shaped by life circumstances, personal styles, and social resources. Partly by design and partly by accident, I had gained an unusually

---

[6]There was no consistent direction to the differences that did emerge between the two teams of interviewers, with one exception. Respondents interviewed by Mrs. B. and her associate tended to display more liberal attitudes about sex and to acknowledge more sexual activity. Apparently, the previous contact these interviewers had had with the respondents increased their willingness to disclose certain types of sensitive information.

good vantage point from which to study processes of social scheduling and the organization of the life course.

## TIME 4: THE FIVE-YEAR FOLLOW-UP

### Restructuring the Study

In early 1971 I began to reconsider the data from this fresh perspective. The interview schedules reflected only partly the shift in orientation from an evaluation to a broader assessment of the social consequences of early childbearing. Consequently, there were large gaps in the information collected on the social and economic situation of the adolescent mothers and their classmates, and virtually no information was obtained on the childrearing experiences of the young parents. Moreover, the uneven quality of the fieldwork reduced the confidence we could place in the results obtained. For these reasons, a proposal for a five-year follow-up interview was submitted to the Maternal and Child Health Service in 1971. It was funded without delay and the fieldwork was carried out the following year.

We reinterviewed the young mothers, their classmates, and the children born to women in both samples who had become parents before 1969. Interviews were attempted with all the firstborn children of the adolescent mothers and with the classmates' children who were at least 42 months old in 1972. Far more information was collected in this interview than had been obtained in the previous phases of the study. The interview explored in some detail the educational, occupational, marital, and childrearing experiences and pregnancy histories of the women in the study; it also solicited a good deal of information about the father of the child and his involvement in the childrearing. The children's interview was designed to appraise the developmental status of the study children and to introduce another important criterion for assessing the long-term effects of unscheduled parenthood on family life. For the first time, the stated goals of the study were to explore the process of adjustment to unplanned parenthood and to explain the divergent life patterns that occur as a consequence of an unscheduled birth. The central question posed was why some women are able to overcome the obstacles of early parenthood while others are permanently marked by their experience.

Since the fieldwork had been a weak point in the second follow-up, a number of changes were instituted. We decided not to make a special effort to match the race of the interviewers and the respondents but merely to use the most experienced and skillful fieldworkers we could find. (As it happened, one of the six interviewers hired was black.) Rather than assemble a large part-time field staff, as had been done previously, we decided to hire a small number of interviewers on a full-time basis. The members of this team would work together closely, developing—we hoped—a strong sense of interest and involvement in the study.

The fieldwork staff was fully assembled by spring. By that time I had pretested the questionnaires in Philadelphia with families who were similar to those of the respondents in the Baltimore sample. Videotapes of these interviews were used in the training sessions that took place in Baltimore. The interviewers were given published and unpublished material on the study, background reading on low-income families, and the instruments for the pilot test.

Typically, interviewers are kept as ignorant as possible about the true aims of a study because most researchers believe that such knowledge may bias the interview situation. However, evidence also exists to support the idea that interviewers, when uninformed, formulate their own impressions of what the study is about and that these false impressions are equally likely to bias their performance. Moreover, concealing the aims of the study often can have an alienating effect on the field staff.

Consequently, an effort was made to inform the staff fully about the general purposes of the research, what the previous findings had shown, and what we hoped to learn from the current interviews. We encouraged the interviewers to discuss with the field supervisor problems that came up. Regular exchanges were a necessary part of the informal solidarity and professional commitment that we were trying to build among the staff. Moreover, we were interested in promoting a climate of trust in order to prevent staff turnover, which might reduce the quality of the fieldwork. All six staff members remained on the study for the duration of the fieldwork.

In the final grant, funds were allotted to pay the respondents a small stipend. Since the respondents derived very little in the way of immediate benefits from the research, it seemed appropriate to compensate them for the time they spent participating in the study. Discussions with the field staff indicated that the stipend had a favorable effect on the quality of the interview. Feeling that they were doing a job and been paid for it, most participants responded even more conscientiously than they had in the past. Moreover, the interviewers felt better about taking the respondents' time away from other activities.

Interviews with the mothers were conducted during the summer of 1972; with their classmates, later in the fall. Once again, we had great success in reinterviewing the young mothers. Of the 404 eligible participants who were interviewed at Time 1, we managed to reinterview 331 women, or 82% of the sample.[7]

While the mother was being interviewed, with her permission her child was given a short battery of tests by a second fieldworker, who then entertained the

[7]Eight of these respondents were removed from the final analysis because of suspected dishonesty in portions of the interview.

youngster until the mother's interview was concluded. In all but 30 families, an interview with the child was also conducted. (Half of the small group of children not interviewed were no longer alive; most of the others were living apart from their mothers.) Among the preschoolers who were interviewed, a number (especially the younger and less alert children) found it difficult to remain involved for the entire 40-minute session. Nearly one-fifth of the 303 children contacted had great difficulty completing the interview either for intellectual or for emotional reasons, and their questionnaires, or parts of them, had to be removed from the analysis.

Although the home visit did not allow time for full-scale observation of the family, a few situations were set up that were conducive to systematic appraisal of the interaction between mother and child. Before the interview started, a puzzle was given to the child and the parent was told that she could work with the youngster to put it together. At the end of the interview, the child was allowed to select a toy in the presence of the mother. The staff team was asked to record the interaction between the two and to note any other relevant situations that came up during the home visit. The observational data on the family from both the interviewer and the tester were coded by the editing supervisor into general analytic·categories describing the quality as well as the quantity of parent-child interaction.

We did not do quite so well as previously in locating the classmates at Time 4, although our completion rate was satisfactory. Of the 268 classmates who were interviewed in 1970, 75% were reinterviewed in 1972. An additional 20 interviews were obtained from classmates whom we could not locate in the previous follow-up. Of the total sample of 361 drawn two years earlier from the school records, 61% were interviewed at the time of the five year follow-up. Slightly more than one-third of the classmates interviewed had families by 1972; however, only half of these women had children who were old enough to be tested. We obtained childrearing information from the mothers whose children were over two and interviewed 37 children who were at least 42 months old by the time the mother was contacted.[8] The sample attrition over the study period is summarized in Table 2.1.[9]

The classmates were the only group in which there was serious attrition. Looking at the losses that occurred in the sample of adolescent mothers, we were led to suspect that the noninterviewed classmates would be married whites who had moved out of the Baltimore area or who had changed their name and address following marriage. Of the 18% of the young mothers whom we were not able to reinterview at Time 4, over one-third were white married women. Higher losses also occurred among blacks who were married at Time 1, although

---

[8]Three of these children had extreme difficulty in responding to the tests and were excluded from the analysis.

[9]The fathers, who are referred to only occasionally in the analysis, have not been included.

Table 2.1. *Study Design*

| Interview Schedule | Dates of Interviews | Participating Samples | Attempted Interviews | Completed Interviews[1] |
|---|---|---|---|---|
| Time 1: During Pregnancy | 1966-1968 | Adolescent Mothers | 404 | 404 (100%) |
| | | Grandmothers | 379 | 350 (92) |
| Time 2: One Year after Delivery | 1968-1970 | Adolescent Mothers | 404 | 382 (95) |
| Time 3: Three Years after Delivery | 1970 | Adolescent Mothers | 404 | 363 (90) |
| | | Classmates | 361 | 268 (74) |
| Time 4: Five Years after Delivery | 1972 | Adolescent Mothers | 404 | 331 (82) |
| | | Children of Adolescent Mothers | 331 | 306 (92) |
| | | Classmates | 307 | 221 (72) |

1. This category includes a small number of interviews that were excluded from the analysis because of a large amount of missing or falsified information.

attrition of this group was not nearly so great as that of the married whites. In part, these losses were the result of the greater difficulty in tracing women who marry, but they also might reflect the fact that women who married, especially whites, were reluctant to remain in the study. In their investigation of North Carolina unmarried mothers, Bowerman and his co-workers (1966) also experienced much greater difficulty in maintaining contact with white married women.

In one respect, these losses limit the applicability of this study. The original sample of pregnant adolescents was predominantly black, even at Time 1. Only 13% of the registrants under 18 in the prenatal clinics were white. At the completion of the study, the sample was even more homogeneous: only 9% of the women interviewed in the five-year follow-up were white. Although these women remained in the sample, they did not constitute a large enough proportion of the sample to permit a reliable comparative analysis of the careers of black and white adolescent mothers. The whites who remained in the sample no doubt were not representative of all white adolescent mothers or even of those who originally entered the prenatal clinics at Sinai. Nevertheless, for some of the purposes of the analysis we separated out the white respondents and treated them as a separate subgroup, although the reader should bear in mind the limitations of any findings based on racial comparisons.

If the white dropout rate was high, attrition among blacks, especially those who were married at Time 1, was exceedingly low. Indeed, the number of dropouts was so low that even if they were highly selective, they could not seriously affect any of the conclusions reported in subsequent chapters. For example, even if all the dropouts had married, were all high school graduates, or had all gone on welfare, inclusion of the missing respondents would change the results only insignificantly. A more critical question, then, becomes to what extent the adolescents in this study are representative of the larger population of black teenagers who become pregnant.

# THE SAMPLE

According to Margaret Bright (1966), a biostatistician at The Johns Hopkins University, in the 17 maternity clinics in Baltimore there were just over 3,000 births in 1964 to women 18 years or less, 69% of which births were firstborn children. Over two-thirds of these mothers were black and at the time of delivery were unmarried. The fact that most of the adolescents who registered at Sinai were black and unmarried was therefore to be expected. Bright's population was not wholly comparable to the pool of women who were eligible to register in the Sinai program because she included all women *18 or younger* who *gave birth* in 1964; whereas the participants in our study include only adolescents *pregnant for the first time* who were *under 18*. However, the two populations were close enough to warrant some conclusions about the representativeness of the Sinai sample.

Sinai's population included a somewhat higher proportion of unmarried blacks than might have been expected by chance, reflecting the influx of blacks into the area surrounding the hospital. Also, once the program began, referrals were made to Sinai from other social agencies in the city serving the lower-income segments of the population, which tended to be predominantly black.

Were we to consider *just the younger adolescents* in Bright's sample who were pregnant for the first time, there would be more reason to feel confident that the women who came to Sinai were not unlike their counterparts in the larger population of Baltimore. In the first place, their age range matched rather well the age distribution of the population reported on by Bright. Second, their marital status distribution also was similar to that of the women 16 and under in Bright's sample.

Since the young women who came to Sinai were requesting prenatal care, we can assume that this group excluded a certain fraction of the most severely disadvantaged adolescent mothers in the community. Women who do not register for prenatal care tend to be poorer and less educated than those who enter prenatal clinics; however, this bias cannot be too large since the majority of expectant mothers do receive prenatal care, and for many of the women in our sample the decision to seek the hospital's services was made by school or health authorities, not by themselves.

Data collected during the first interview with both the pregnant teenagers and their mothers provided a fuller profile of the characteristics of the families who participated in the study. This information showed that the sample consisted primarily of lower- and working-class individuals. Although the data on family income were not completely reliable since they were extracted from hospital records, they suggested that most of the families in the study were living near or below the poverty level. The median family yearly income was $3,000-4,000. Three-fourths of the families were managing to get by without welfare assistance, although at a mere subsistence level. Half of the families were headed by couples, two-fifths by women, and the remainder by a more distant relation. When a father was living in the house, he was generally employed in a low-skilled or menial job. Less than one-fifth of the men had skilled or white-collar jobs. In families in which the father was absent, the mother of the adolescent generally was employed but usually in an unskilled job. The education of the parents generally corresponded to their occupational status. Only one-fifth of the parents living in the home had completed high school, and over one-third had gone no further in their education than the eighth grade.

Early parenthood was a familiar problem to the families in the sample. Nearly half of the prospective grandmothers had had their first child before the age of 18, and at least one-fourth had borne a child out of wedlock. Furthermore, many of the pregnant adolescents had siblings who had become pregnant in their early teens. Accordingly, the households in which the young mothers resided at the time they became pregnant were large, with a mean of 5.1 children in residence. Over one-third of the households had six or more children living at home.

In some respects, our sample corresponded to the low-income or "poverty" population designated by the census bureau (U.S. Bureau of the Census, 1970b). Approximately the same proportion of our study families was headed by women and the household size was relatively similar as well. In income and education, our sample more closely resembled the general population of blacks residing in Baltimore. Apparently not all the young mothers came from the most disadvantaged segments of the black community; rather, they were drawn from a broader group that more or less corresponded, on a socioeconomic scale, to the bottom two-thirds of blacks living in the city of Baltimore. This conclusion also is suggested by a comparison of the family backgrounds of the young mothers and their former classmates (Table 2.2). Looking first at the socioeconomic position of the two populations, we can see that with the exception of the educational achievement of their parents, the two samples accorded rather well. A slightly lower proportion of the classmates' families was receiving public assistance when these women were children. Similarly, the families of the classmates were a bit more likely to have been intact when these women were growing up. Consistent but minor differences also were evident in the occupational status of the parents of the women in the two groups. However, in all cases the reported differences were minor, suggesting that, like the young mothers, the classmates came mostly from working- and lower-class homes.

The higher educational standing of the classmates' parents does not seem to have been translated into economic advantage. However, this educational difference might indicate that a higher proportion of the classmates' families was upwardly mobile in their aspirations, if not their performance. This difference, as we note in Chapter 3, might be an important factor in accounting for the greater incidence of unscheduled parenthood among the sample of young mothers.

The overall resemblance between the two groups seems to bear out the observation that the sample of young mothers was not a highly selective one,

Table 2.2. *Characteristics of the Sample of Adolescent Mothers and Classmates*

| Population Characteristics | Adolescent Mothers (323) | Classmates (221) |
|---|---|---|
| A. *Age at Time 4*[1] | | |
| Under 20 | 11% | 12% |
| 20 | 17 | 19 |
| 21 | 30 | 24 |
| 22 | 26 | 26 |
| 23+ | 15 | 19 |
| Mean Age | 21.2 | 21.1 |
| B. *Race* | | |
| Black | 91 | 87 |
| White | 9 | 13 |
| C. *Family Status among Unmarried Adolescents at Time 1* | | |
| Lived with Both Parents | 51 | 59 |
| Lived with Mother | 38 | 32 |
| Lived with Father | 3 | 2 |
| Lived with Neither Parent | 8 | 7 |
| D. *Education of Mother When Present in Home at Time 1*[2] | | |
| High School Graduate | 22 | 45 |
| Not High School Graduate | 78 | 55 |
| E. *Education of Father When Present in Home at Time 1*[2] | | |
| High School Graduate | 17 | 41 |
| Not High School Graduate | 83 | 59 |
| F. *Occupational Status of Parents*[2] | | |
| One or Both Skilled | 20 | 27 |
| Mother Working | 60 | 66 |
| Neither Parent Working | 20 | 7 |
| G. *Welfare Status during Childhood*[2] | | |
| No | 76 | 83 |
| Yes | 24 | 17 |
| H. *Marital Status at Time 1* | | |
| Single | 81 | 98 |
| Married | 19 | 2 |

[1] Five years after delivery.

[2] Information for adolescent parents was supplied at the first interview. The classmates reported the information at the second follow-up, three years after the adolescent mothers' delivery.

characteristic only of the area surrounding the hospital at which the study began and therefore not capable of bearing the weight of any general conclusions. Furthermore, this resemblance strengthens the contention that the classmates constituted an appropriate group to contrast to the young mothers we studied. If the two groups had been highly dissimilar, it would have been difficult to sort out the consequences of an unplanned pregnancy from the differences that divided the two groups at the outset of the study. Rather, it appears that before their first child was born, the young women who found their way into the study population could not have been easily differentiated from their peers who managed to avoid an early pregnancy. This fact will take on added significance as we examine the careers of the two groups.

In contrasting the social careers of the young mothers and their classmates, it is useful to know that premarital pregnancies—even during adolescence—occurred among many of the classmates as well. Nearly half (49%) of them acknowledged at Time 4 one or more pregnancies before marriage, and no doubt these self-reports undercounted the actual incidence of premarital conception. Of the 107 reported pregnancies, about half occurred during adolescence, and one in three happened before the classmates turned 18. Thus, comparisons between the classmates and young mothers probably slightly understate the impact of an early and unplanned pregnancy on the subsequent life course because some of the classmates shared this experience with the young mothers. In the analysis that follows, we subdivide the classmates by their premarital pregnancy experiences wherever this breakdown affects the reported findings.

Before setting out on the analysis, it is worth considering whether the women in our sample were members of a special cohort—the last of a generation likely to become pregnant unintentionally and for lack of an alternative compelled to carry their babies to term. Undeniably, during the decade since this study was launched, a marked improvement has taken place in the facilities available to teenagers for preventing unwanted pregnancies and births. Yet there is a good deal of evidence, some of it assembled quite recently, that family planning and abortion services are failing to have a significant impact on the incidence of teenage pregnancies. Although more teenagers now are using contraception than did so 10 years ago, the proportion who use it regularly is still quite low (Shal et al., 1975). Similarly, while the opportunity to obtain abortions has improved dramatically, a sizable number of babies are born to teenagers who might have elected to terminate their pregnancies if the process were more accessible and less frightening (Alan Guttmacher Institute, 1975). We shall return to this point again in the final chapter, but it is important to recognize at the outset that the forces producing unplanned parenthood have not abated appreciably. There is reason to believe that the women in our study are probably not very different from women who would be their current demographic counterparts. In any event, our subjects can hardly be considered the last of a disappearing species.

# 3. Becoming Pregnant

ALTHOUGH THIS BOOK focuses on the consequences of early parenthood, it is difficult to ignore the question of why certain women bear children in early adolescence. This chapter begins with a critique of theories of the etiology of unwed parenthood and proceeds to an empirical examination of the conditions that led to parenthood for the participants in our study. The data presented will take us to the point just after conception. In Chapter 4, we consider why some women marry following a premarital conception but others elect to become single parents.

## THEORIES OF UNWED PARENTHOOD

Unscheduled parenthood, particularly when it occurs out of wedlock, can be thought of as a social as well as a biological process. It follows a "natural history," a sequence of events beginning with the onset of sexual activity and concluding with the birth of a child.[1] At various points in this sequence, a potential recruit may accidentally or intentionally "drop out." She may, for example, experience infecundity, spontaneously abort during the course of pregnancy, or lose her child in delivery. Or, the sequence may be deliberately interrupted if she decides to use contraception, obtain an abortion, or marry before the child is born (Davis and Blake, 1956; Cutright, 1971a; Hartley, 1975).

To become an unwed mother, a woman must "successfully" negotiate the entire course. While this observation may appear to be obvious, it is far from evident in the research on unplanned parenthood. Most studies begin at the final

[1]The concept of a natural history was widely used in early descriptive studies of deviant behavior, particularly those in the Chicago tradition. The term implies that phenomena that come to be defined as social problems pass through a series of discernible stages that have a definite temporal order. One of the earliest discussions of the natural history concept appears in Fuller and Meyers, "The Natural History of a Social Problem" (1941). Only a few studies have treated parenthood as the outcome of a multistaged sequential process (see, for example, Davis and Blake, 1956; Pope, 1969; Cutright, 1971a; Rains, 1971; Zelnik and Kantner, 1974; Hartley, 1975).

37

stage of the process, more or less assuming that what came before is irrelevant. Treating illegitimacy in this ahistorical fashion distorts our understanding of why some women produce children out of wedlock but others do not. This omission becomes much more conspicuous when we examine theories that purport to explain the etiology of illegitimacy.

Characteristic of so many such theories is the unshakable conviction that an out-of-wedlock birth results from some special motivation which impels women to become unwed mothers.[2] For psychoanalytically oriented theorists, this proclivity is rooted in the unconscious. Having a child out of wedlock results from the women's acting out some hidden wish or deep-seated conflict (Young, 1954). Other psychological theories regard the underlying cause as more conscious and open, identifying the pregnancy as a means of attaining a needed love object or of gaining recognition when other channels to success or adult achievement are blocked (Vincent, 1961; Thomas, 1967). Sociologically oriented writers have rejected these explanations, contending instead that illegitimacy is a cultural phenomenon and that women who bear children before they marry are simply following accepted social practices within their group (Rainwater, 1966; Rodman, 1971).

Although these theories differ significantly in their particulars, they all rest on the assumption that the unwed mother becomes pregnant because she is motivated, consciously or unconsciously, to have a child outside of marriage. But all these explanations ignore the obvious fact that an illegitimate birth cannot occur unless (1) a single woman has sexual relations, (2) she conceives, (3) she brings the baby to term, and (4) she remains unmarried until delivery. For every woman who has an illegitimate child, there are numerous others who experience "close calls." Theories that disregard these "dropouts" can provide at best partial explanations; at their worst, they represent gross distortions. The situation is not unlike the one faced by a criminologist who bases his theories of etiology only on evidence collected from offenders who have been apprehended, adjudicated, and incarcerated (Biderman and Reiss, 1967). Undeniably, prisoners are a convenient population to study, but they are hardly a representative one.[3] By focusing exclusively on the final stage of unwed motherhood and disregarding the intermediate steps in the process, many theorists have embraced a purely

[2]Several writers on illegitimacy have brought out this assumption with varying degrees of criticism (see, for example, Vincent, 1961; Roberts, 1966; Pope, 1969; Rains, 1971). An especially powerful critique of the etiological naivete of many writers was presented by Jerome D. Paulker (1969:66) in a little-known article entitled "Girls Pregnant out of Wedlock." Paulker concluded:

> With respect to the causation of out-of-wedlock pregnancy, . . . it does seem that one explanation, or a very few, will not cover the entire group of women involved. It does seem, too, that a large share of the causation may be ascribed to chance, particularly among adolescent girls pregnant for the first time. The most parsimonious explanation would seem to be that out-of-wedlock babies are the result neither of the stork nor a desire for an out-of-wedlock child, but are rather the result of sexual intercourse.

[3]Students of other forms of deviant behavior have advanced similar criticisms of etiological theories based on captive populations (see, for example, Becker, 1963; Scheff, 1966).

mechanical viewpoint which holds that women who become unwed mothers necessarily possess an *advance commitment* to the status; that is, they are predisposed for either psychological or cultural reasons to want to have a child out of wedlock. Ignoring the close calls, these researchers magnify the differences between the population of women who become unwed mothers and their peers who for one reason or another manage to drop out of the process. The result is that they adopt a circular line of argument, assuming in effect that people do only what they want to do and that we can recognize what they want from what they have done. Irwin Deutscher (1973:283) has criticized this line of reasoning:

> The fact is that people sometimes do not do as they say and it is important to be attentive to such discrepancies. Although they may sometimes be more apparent than real, they are sometimes very real. Rather than attempting to explain such discrepancies away as "spurious," it is gratifying to recognize them for what they are and to begin to understand the processes that account for them. That is the function of science.

An alternative, but equally plausible, assumption is that most women who become unwed mothers do not set out to have a child out of wedlock. They do not engage in sexual activity for the purpose of becoming pregnant and are initially "recruited" into the ranks of unwed motherhood without possessing any advance commitment. What they do once pregnancy occurs is an interesting but separate question, which will be taken up later in this chapter. The point here is that commitment to parenthood need not always precede the fact. Such sentiment may develop after pregnancy, or it may never develop. In short, rather than being directed or drawn to it, most women "drift" into adolescent parenthood (cf. Matza, 1964).

The data collected from the adolescents in the Baltimore study afforded us an opportunity to examine the process leading up to unplanned pregnancy. Two questions in particular drew our attention. Did the adolescents who became pregnant have a special commitment or desire to bear a child out of wedlock? If not, why did they become pregnant while many of their peers did not? It is necessary to remind the reader that this study was not specifically designed to examine these questions; consequently, the analysis was frustrated at many points by limitations of the data. Nevertheless, some information could be gleaned from the interviews that served as a basis for the conclusions presented at the end of the chapter.

## THE ONSET OF SEXUAL RELATIONS

The process of recruitment into adolescent motherhood begins with sexual activity. Our data bearing on this question were fragmentary for there was little basis for differentiating the sexual careers of young mothers in our study. All were sexually active by their early or midteens.[4] Fortunately, a recent study of teenage women nicely supplemented our limited data, and we could draw also on the experiences of our sample of classmates, who had more varied patterns of sexual experience. Finally, retrospective accounts from the interviews conducted with the young mothers at Time 1 were a further source of information about the sexual careers of adolescent mothers.

In a study undertaken in 1971, just a year after the classmates were first interviewed, John Kantner and Melvin Zelnik surveyed the sexual experiences of a representative national sample of adolescent females (Zelnik and Kantner, 1972, 1974; Kantner and Zelnik, 1972, 1973). Nearly half the respondents reported that they had engaged in sexual relations by age 19. Black women were twice as likely as whites to be nonvirgins (81% versus 40%), and these racial differences did not disappear when a variety of statistical controls such as family income, education, and occupational status were introduced. Generally speaking, black adolescents were about three years "ahead" of their white counterparts in sexual experience. By age 16, about half of the black adolescents were non-virgins, a percentage not reached by the whites until age 19.[5] While lacking in the details that might help to account for the different sexual patterns, the Kantner and Zelnik study provided an important perspective on the question of recruitment to unwed parenthood. It showed that virtually all black adolescents and a high proportion of whites are candidates to become pregnant during adolescence. Half of the black adolescents were "at risk" by their midteens (also see Gebhard et al., 1958). The question, at least for most black women, is not whether they will have sexual relations before marriage but when or under what circumstances.

Data collected from the classmates of the young mothers in our study closely paralleled these findings. By age 20, 77% of the classmates reported that they were no longer virgins. The proportion for age 16 was 50%, almost the figure obtained in the national study. It would appear, then, that in their sexual practices the young mothers did not sharply diverge from their classmates or from the larger population of black adolescents. Insofar as any difference existed, it lay not in the fact that the young mothers engaged in sexual relations but in their willingness to do so at an earlier age than many of their peers.

Little is known about why certain women become sexually active at an early age while others defer relations until late adolescence. Undoubtedly this selective process is a complex one, depending on such factors as dating opportunities, social control, social expectations, personal inclinations, and physiological development (see, for example, Gebhard et al., 1958; Young, 1954; Reiss,

[4]In the context of this book, the term *sexually active* or *experienced* refers to coital activity.

[5]Had this study been extended to a population of unmarried women in their early twenties, the proportion of virgins undoubtedly would have been further reduced and possibly the whites—among those who remained unmarried—might have caught up to the blacks.

1967; Bell, 1966.) We were able to examine several components that entered into the decision by comparing the sexually active classmates with their peers who were still virgins. These comparisons yielded no dramatic differences; however, there was a general pattern of lower sexual activity among women who came from more highly educated families and who tended to be more educationally ambitious themselves. Three-fourths (74%) of the classmates with low educational goals and who came from families with little schooling were sexually active. By contrast, only 37% of their peers who planned to go beyond high school and whose parents were high school graduates were having sexual relations at Time 3. It could be that the latter group of teenagers was especially sensitive to the risks of sexual activity, fearing that an early pregnancy would jeopardize their educational goals. They may have deliberately deferred the onset of sexual activity, at least until graduation from high school. To what extent these self-imposed restraints were backed up by family regulations and restrictions could not be ascertained from the data at hand.

Although social activity is not synonymous with sexual activity, it provided the adolescent with the opportunity and, as we shall discover, often made it necessary for her to engage in sexual relations. Approximately one-fifth of the abstainers from sex compared to 6% of the nonvirgins did not date at all in early adolescence (though it is difficult to tell whether this lack of social life among the classmates was the result of personal preference, family mandate, or lack of opportunity).[6]

It seems safe to say, then, that there is a certain selectivity in the initial stage of recruitment. The women who became sexually active at a young age were somewhat less ambitious educationally and probably also less inclined to impose social limitations on themselves in order to realize their educational goals. By restricting social contact, certain adolescents, or perhaps their families acting in their behalf, are able to decrease the risk that a pregnancy may interrupt their education. It would be revealing to learn whether this pattern of minimal social activity is a deliberate strategy for reducing the prospects of premarital pregnancy or merely an unintended consequence of a particular family life-style or perhaps even a result of the adolescent's lower appeal in the social marketplace.

To what extent there are explicit norms about the initiation of sexual activity could not be answered from the fragmentary information collected from the classmates. It is unlikely that there are any clearly demarcated steps that provide a gradual entrance into sexuality. As we shall see, the absence of

---

[6]A tentative answer to this question was provided by an examination of the dating experiences of the young mothers, for whom we had more complete family information. Although early dating is associated with early pregnancy, there was no evidence that the adolescent mothers whose parents were strict about dating became sexually active at a later age. Indeed, there was a slight tendency for stricter regulation to be associated with the early onset of sexual activity, as Blake (1961) found in her study of premarital pregnancy in Jamaica.

normative boundaries for entering sexual relations complicates efforts to control the consequences of sexuality.

## SEXUAL ACTIVITY AND PREGNANCY

Frequent dating over a long period of time is eventually accompanied by sexual activity, and few adolescents are able to remain sexually active for long before pregnancy occurs. (We observed this pattern among the young mothers who were unusually socially active at an early age. At the time they conceived, nearly two-thirds of the adolescent mothers were going out at least several times a week.) Four out of five became pregnant within two years following the onset of intercourse, which generally occurred at age 15.[7] In addition to the likelihood that fecundity was low in this youthful population, a sporadic pattern of intercourse helped to reduce the probability of conception. Two-fifths of the young mothers indicated that they had intercourse as frequently as once a week, and less than one-fifth had relations several times a week or more.

Compared to the amount of social activity, the frequency of sexual relations seems remarkably low. No doubt, some disparity can be attributed to under-reporting. Some adolescents were reluctant to reveal that they were having intercourse on a regular basis. Even if we do not take the figures strictly, the self-reports suggest an unsteady pattern of sexuality. This finding in itself implies the lack of an advance commitment to becoming pregnant.[8]

It is difficult to understand this pattern of sexual behavior without delving further into the social meaning of sexuality for adolescents. Some writers have contended that youths, especially working- and lower-class blacks, treat sex casually and that this segment of the population diverges sharply from white middle-class adults in attitudes toward premarital sex. This generalization may be applicable to males; however, the existing evidence does not completely support the notion of a highly permissive standard among black females. Ira Reiss (1967), for example, found that while black females had more permissive sexual standards than whites, a majority of both adult and adolescent black women disapproved of premarital relations. Similar findings were reported by Rodman (1971); Rainwater (1970); and Bowerman and his collaborators (1966.)

The data collected from our study were consistent with these findings. In the first phase interviews a substantial proportion of the respondents in our study expressed restrictive views on premarital sex. Nearly half the mothers of

[7]This same pattern was evident among the classmates. They became sexually active several years later, but by age 20 and over, half of those who had been sexually active in their teens had experienced a premarital pregnancy. Zelnik and Kantner (1974) reported almost identical figures. Nearly half of the black adolescents who had intercourse during their teens became pregnant before age 20.

[8]The figures on sexual activity also correspond to the incidence reports collected by Zelnik and Kantner (1972). The respondents in their sample had a very low frequency of sexual activity, too.

the pregnant teenagers stated that they felt it was "very wrong" for a girl to have sexual relations before she married and another fourth said they felt it was "somewhat wrong." In general, the adults believed that their views were shared by their friends and acquaintances although they acknowledged that some people they knew might hold somewhat more permissive attitudes. When asked why they disapproved of premarital relations, the most frequent response was that it was "immoral"; however, one-fourth of the parents cited purely practical considerations. One parent, expressing both viewpoints, offered what was a fairly typical response:

> It's the possibilities of her becoming pregnant. It spoils her reputation. A lot of men really want pure women. I just don't like the idea. Ties them down too quick.

The adolescents' views on premarital sex closely resembled those of their parents. Nearly half of the teenagers stated that it was very important for a woman to wait until marriage to begin to have sex. Only one-third indicated that it did not matter at all whether or not one waited. Like their mothers, the adolescents frequently cited moral reasons for their views. Again, about one-fourth mentioned the risk of pregnancy as the primary reason for their disapproval of premarital sex.

Undeniably, there was an obvious discrepancy between the words and the deeds of the respondents. Many of the adults had had children out of wedlock, even more had experienced premarital pregnancies, and, without a doubt, most had engaged in premarital sex. In the case of the young mothers, their behavior was even more obviously out of line with their verbal standards. No doubt, some of the views expressed were merely "for the record." A number of them, especially when facing a middle-class interviewer in a hospital examination room, might have felt called upon to express a general commitment to social convention.[9]

However, to dismiss these attitudes as meaningless and inconsequential would probably be as much of a distortion as to take them at face value. Why the respondents should have misrepresented their views is not obvious, especially since they knew that the interviewer had some awareness of their sexual history. Furthermore, in other parts of the interview, participants volunteered responses that were not in line with conventional middle-class views. Therefore, it is difficult to escape the conclusion that many of the respondents—both the parents and the youths—were paying sincere allegiance to a sexual code to which they were unable to adhere. They had acquired one set of standards and had learned to live by another.[10] As we shall learn later, this ambivalence about their

[9]Irwin Deutscher (1973), in *What We Say/What We Do,* provides a penetrating discussion of the problem of collecting sensitive data using formal interviews.

[10]For an especially good depiction of the dual sexual codes, real and ideal, see Rodman (1963, 1971); Rains, (1971); and Ladner (1971). Ladner argues that the sexual standards of the larger society hold little relevance for black adolescent females, a thesis with which I do not completely agree. But her descriptive data provide some of the richest case material on the ambivalence that surrounds premarital sexual activity among adolescents.

sexual code made it especially difficult for these women to deal realistically with the consequences of their sexual behavior.

What compels some adolescent women to depart from their ideal standards? Part of the reason may be the long period they must wait before marriage is possible. Few of the adolescents in this population believed that they would or should marry before their early twenties. In the meantime, they were repeatedly provided with opportunities for sexual experience. Prior to becoming pregnant almost all of the young mothers were going out regularly—that is, at least once a week—usually with one man. While direct information on their boyfriends' views about premarital sex was not available, it is safe to assume that the men's views were considerably more permissive than those of the adolescent mothers.

A number of studies have shown that sexual experience occurs early among working- and lower-class men (Kinsey et al., 1948; Cannon and Long, 1971; Rainwater, 1966; Bell, 1966). This may be especially true for blacks although much of the available evidence has come from observational studies of small samples (H. Lewis, 1967; Bernard, 1966; Liebow, 1967; Broderick, 1965; Hannerz, 1969; Staples, 1971). In the interviews conducted with the fathers at the three-year follow-up, the pattern of considerable sexual experience at an early age was evident. By age 14, two-thirds of the males were sexually active, and they reported more frequent and more varied sexual patterns than the females.[11] According to Ira Reiss, attitudes of young black males toward sex are conspicuously more permissive than those of young white males, and Staples (1973:55) reported in his field study of black youth:

> In the male virility cult, status within the peer group is based on the number of women that one is able to have sexual relations with. Thus, the male who has a variety of premarital sexual experiences occupies a prestigious position within his peer grouping. Sexual conquest of women becomes strongly associated with the definition of masculinity. It is sex as a symbol of manhood that supposedly motivates the male's sexual interest as well as physical desire.

Among lower-class adolescent males, sex often has been portrayed as a contest with a clearly articulated set of rules and a definite scoring system (Whyte, 1949; Green, 1941; Hannerz, 1969). Points are given for endurance, versatility, and frequency. Within certain peer groups, special credit is accorded to the male for initiating sexually inexperienced females, and persuading a reluctant partner enhances the conquest. Consequently, many young women in their midteens face the problem of either negotiating some kind of sexual accommodation with their boyfriends or breaking off the relationship.[12] Not

---

[11] Half of the fathers, for example, indicated that before their partners became pregnant they were having relations with other women; whereas less than one-fifth of the young mothers reported that they had more than one sexual partner.

[12] Ladner provides an especially revealing discussion of this dilemma (1971:chs 5-6).

surprisingly, then, when the pregnant teenagers were asked why a female begins to have sexual relations, the most common response was inability successfully to resist pressure from the male.

> To be in with the crowd. The little black sheep that follows the rest of them. A lot of girls want to hang onto the boy they are dating and the only way is to give in.
>
> Some of them think they are in love and going to get married but they don't. Some just to get attention from the boy.
>
> They don't have no willpower. Even if they do have the willpower it seems like the boys can always turn your head.
>
> I guess because of the boy. He be just hinting around to it all the time.

Of course, it would be naive to believe the female is invariably the innocent and exploited victim of her boyfriend's dishonorable intentions. Clearly, as these comments illustrate, some of the young mothers began to have sexual relations willingly because of emotional involvement or curiosity or simply because they did not see any reason for waiting until marriage (see also Ladner, 1971).

Nonetheless, under different circumstances many women probably would wait at least until their late teens to begin having sexual relations. Only one-fourth of the adolescents thought that a female should begin to have relations before age 18; one-third said that she should be at least 18; and the remainder replied either that it depended on the circumstances (that is, on whether she had finished school, was ready to get married, or was in love) or that she should wait until after marriage.

In the interests of preserving the necessary social relationships, however, many adolescent females are prepared to "stretch their values," to borrow a useful term coined by Hyman Rodman (1963). When ideal standards are untenable they are replaced by more practicable codes of behavior. This process of conversion does not require abandoning the ideal norms, only suspending their observance until the time when they can be followed. Thus, we were not surprised to discover that many participants voiced allegiance to codes of morality while violating them.

Information as to how the adolescents managed this process was fragmentary, and pertinent material from our research was brief and only suggestive. Like the "techniques of neutralization" employed by delinquents who break laws to which they still generally subscribe (see Sykes and Matza, 1957), the young mothers invoked a number of justifications that permitted them to depart from their ideal norms. Some of these techniques served to counteract or nullify their feelings of guilt. Seeing themselves as persuaded or coerced by their boyfriends was obviously one such rationalization. Another was the notion that "everyone else is doing it." (Indeed, this observation is nearly correct, and it is a testimony to the tenacity of ideal norms that they can survive at all in the face of widespread violation.) Other rationalizations helped to offset the fear that negative consequences would result from sexual activity. Especially relevant for us was the belief shared by most participants in our study that they could avoid "getting caught." In order to preserve this belief, the adolescent had to conceal her sexual activity, thus maintaining the public fiction that she was still sexually innocent. The majority did not let on to their families or even to some of their friends that they were having sexual relations. And, although a high proportion (70%) confessed that they worried about becoming pregnant, most remarked repeatedly in the interviews, "I never thought it would happen to me." The belief that they would not get caught removed the fear that they could be exposed and thus subjected to social sanctions.

Although rationally this attitude seems quite incompatible with the fact that most of the teenagers had relatives and friends who had become pregnant, it is not so difficult to explain as it might appear at first. For every such friend or relative they knew, the young mothers could recall many more women who were having sex but not becoming pregnant. Furthermore, a large number of the women lacked adequate understanding of the possibility of becoming pregnant and were ignorant of the physical process involved. A number mentioned that they did not think it was possible to become pregnant "right away." Others thought that if they had sexual relations only "every once in a while" they would not become pregnant.[13] Finally, their behavior had a self-reinforcing quality. Because many were not yet fertile, as time went on they became increasingly convinced that they would not become pregnant. The longer they went without conceiving, the more likely they were to assume greater risks.

The adolescents were not alone in their efforts to preserve their virginal image. Their mothers frequently collaborated with them. Despite the fact that three-fourths of the parents said that most teenagers in their neighborhood were sexually active, the vast majority (77%) of mothers reported that they were "very surprised" when they learned that their daughter was pregnant. Fewer than one in four admitted that she had known that her daughter was having sexual relations prior to the pregnancy. As a check on whether the parents were misrecollecting previous observations, those with other adolescent daughters residing in the home were asked if those children were sexually active. Only 16% of the parents suspected, or made a statement to the effect, that their non-pregnant teenage daughters were currently having sexual relations. Extrapolating from the figures on the incidence of sexual relations among teenagers provided by Zelnik and Kantner (1973), we found the mothers' estimates so low as to suggest that the parent has a certain stake in remaining misinformed. By so doing, she is able to preserve the fiction that her daughter is "staying out of trouble." This, in turn, releases her from the responsibility of having to take

13The study of Zelnik and Kantner documented in depressing detail the woefully inadequate knowledge of the reproductive process possessed by adolescents. In the Zelnik-Kantner (1972) study, less than one-third of the respondents could correctly state the time of the month when the risk of pregnancy is greatest. It is a reasonable assumption that the young women in our sample would not have fared as well as the average adolescent in that national study.

some action to prevent a pregnancy from occuring. As we shall see, most of the mothers did not know what measures to take even if they were aware of their child's sexual activity. As a result, many preferred to keep themselves uninformed.

So long as sexuality is safeguarded from public view, it poses little danger to either mother or daughter. Consequently, each develops techniques for managing the clandestine act. Paradoxically, these techniques for concealment ultimately increase the risk of pregnancy. Had they been able to admit openly that their behavior might have this undesirable consequence, the adolescents might have been encouraged to take some sort of preventive measure. But it is important to recognize that from the point of view of the adolescent, using contraception may be extremely costly because it involves open acknowledgement of sexuality and thereby increases the threat of public exposure. Therefore, it was not surprising to find that prior to pregnancy, experience with birth control was quite restricted.

## BIRTH CONTROL KNOWLEDGE AND EXPERIENCE

Most of the adolescents had some limited knowledge of birth control. Almost all were aware that devices to prevent conception existed, only 6% were unable to identify any method of birth control, and most were able to mention at least two or three techniques. This information, usually acquired from casual conversations with relatives and friends or through the mass media, was, however, extremely superficial. The young women tended to be most aware of those forms of contraception to which they had least access and about which they had only limited practical knowledge (see also Rains, 1971; Kantner and Zelnik, 1973). Over 80% mentioned the pill as a "method of keeping you from having babies," but only two had ever used oral contraceptives. In both instances, the pills had been "borrowed" from their mothers.

Whatever practical knowledge and experience the adolescents had with birth control was confined largely to—in the vernacular of the respondents—"getting the boy to use something." Except for the pill, the condom was the most frequently identified method of contraception. Two-thirds mentioned prophylactics (rubbers and sheaths), and more than half of these respondents (37% of the total sample) had had some experience with condoms. As with the other methods, however, experience for the most part had been sporadic; only 15% of the women reported that condoms had been used more or less regularly when relations occurred.

There are many reasons for such irregular use, but by far the most common (mentioned by 54% of the users) was that the boyfriend was either unprepared or unwilling most of the time. The following comments were typical:

He just didn't feel like it that time.

He ran out of rubbers and didn't have no money to buy more.

He said that he couldn't enjoy it when he used them.

Of course, in retrospect some young mothers conceded that had they been more insistent their boyfriends might have been more compliant. Yet, as we observed earlier, the young mothers often seemed to hold out the hope that they would be among the lucky ones who avoided pregnancy. And, as mentioned before, risk taking increases over time when pregnancy does not occur.

Even those adolescents with some birth control experience shared the prevailing rationalizations discussed earlier for why they could or should not use birth control. Most believed that it was highly unlikely that they would become pregnant, and the great majority felt helpless to prevent a conception even when they worried about this possibility. In light of the meager preparation for sexual activity provided by their families, their expressions of passivity and denial are understandable.

## SOCIALIZATION TO SEXUALITY AND BIRTH CONTROL EXPERIENCE

Much has been written about the importance of parental sex education and the impact of the family in shaping children's sexual attitudes and practices (Bell, 1966; Broderick, 1966). Both as a source of information and as agents of control, parents are thought to influence the sexual patterns of their children. To reconstruct how and why birth control use is determined by family socialization, it is necessary to examine the specific instructions adolescents receive as well as the more general sexual standards to which they are exposed in the family.

Until quite recently, the sexual restraints found in the middle-class household were thought to be absent in the lower-class families. However, current evidence has shown otherwise: the lower-class family is, if anything, even more puritanical and prudish about sexual matters than families with higher incomes (Rainwater, 1965). Lower-class parents are reluctant to deal with sex not only because they fear that open discussion might stimulate sexual interest but also because they lack knowledge about sex and a vocabulary for discussing sexual functions. Despite these hindrances to sexual training, 59% of the mothers in our study had frequently attempted to talk to their daughters about sex, and 92% had had at least occasional discussions on the subject. Birth control, however, was not always the focus of such conversations. Indeed, it seems that most talks involved the mother's admonishing her daughter not "to get mixed up with boys" or to do anything that she would "be sorry for later."

Slightly more than 61% of the mothers and 45% of the daughters said that birth control had been explicitly discussed in the family.[14] Quite clearly, however, most of the instruction was casual and oblique at best. "If you're going to mess around, you better be sure that you get the boy to use something" or "Don't go unprotected" was the usual advice. Rarely were the adolescents told about effective contraceptive devices. No doubt this omission was partly a result of the fact that many of the mothers could not fully acknowledge that their daughters needed birth control instruction.

As mentioned earlier, most mothers preferred to believe that their daughters were not having sexual relations, enabling them to put off any discussion of this matter until the need arose. Even when the mothers did recognize the need for specific instruction, they could not offer much assistance. They were frequently poorly informed themselves, and at the time of the study in 1966, there was no place that a mother could send or take her teenage daughter for information. Thus, it is understandable that most mothers, if they provided instruction at all, were inclined to give only general advice and admonitions.

Although it was usually unspecific, this limited instruction nonetheless seemed to have had a definite impact. Women from families in which both the mother and the daughter reported discussing birth control were much more likely to use contraceptives or to have their partners do so. Within these families more than half of the adolescents (52%) had had some experience with birth control, compared to less than one-fourth (23%) from families in which no guidance was given (see Table A.1A). Moreover, the young mothers' reports revealed that the specific content of the training had a decided effect on whether or not birth control was practiced. If the mother counseled her daughter to use a specific method (typically, she urged her daughter to insist that the male use a condom), the adolescent was more likely to have had some birth control experience. However, when contraceptive instruction was extremely vague its effect on the adolescent's behavior was hardly greater than that of no instruction.

Apparently, then, the family can and does play a part in transmitting expectations about birth control use. In addition to imparting specific information, parents may promote contraceptive use for quite another reason. In raising the issue of contraception, the mother reveals an explicit awareness that her daughter is or may be having sexual relations. The adolescent, in turn, is allowed to acknowledge her own sexuality and hence may regard sex less as a spontaneous and uncontrollable act and more as an activity subject to planning and regulation.

[14]The lack of concordance between the reports of the mothers and their daughters probably stemmed from a number of reasons: faulty recollection, embarrassment on the part of the mother to admit that birth control instruction had not occurred or on the part of the daughter to admit that it had, or failure to agree upon what constituted birth control instruction.

If this interpretation is correct—and we must be cautious because of the selective nature of our sample—we would expect that women who reported that their mothers knew about their sexual activity would have been more likely to have used birth control. This prediction was confirmed. Birth control use was highest (58%) when the adolescent said her mother was aware of her sexual activity and this prior knowledge was confirmed by the mother in her own interview. (Interestingly, sexual activity was acknowledged by both mother and daughter in only 13% of the families in the sample. Typically, in over half of the families, both mother and daughter reported that the adolescent's sexual activity had been a secret.) Although discussions about birth control also were common in such households (see Table A.1B), the association between the mother's knowledge of her daughter's sexual relations and the latter's contraceptive use persisted whether or not discussion had occurred.

That the "sexual climate" of the household can affect an adolescent's contraceptive experience was even more apparent when the effects of the mother's sexual standards were examined directly. Women whose mothers strongly disapproved of premarital sexual relations were far less likely to have had experience with birth control than adolescents from more permissive families. Less than one-fifth of the former group had used contraceptives, as compared to nearly three-fifths of the women from more permissive families (Table A.1C). Again, this difference partly reflected the fact that birth control instruction was less likely to be given when the mother had stricter sexual standards. However, the mother's sexual norms, like her knowledge of her daughter's sexual activity, had a strong independent effect on the teenager's contraceptive experience, suggesting that daughters approach premarital sex differently when they know it is not condemned by their parents.

## COURTSHIP NEGOTIATIONS AND BIRTH CONTROL USE

Even when the mother accepted her daughter's sexual activity and encouraged her to practice birth control, use of contraceptives was still problematic. Usually, adolescents and their mothers expected the man to assume responsibility for "using protection." The mothers, to borrow a phrase used by Katz and Lazarsfeld (1955), experienced a "two-step removal of influence," for at best they could only urge their daughters to remind their boyfriends. While the young women were one step closer to the situation, they must successfully persuade their boyfriends of their interests. Within our sample, this process of negotiation invariably broke down. At least occasionally, and generally quite often, either the teenagers failed to insist on contraceptive use or their partners were unresponsive to their attempts at persuasion.

While only limited information was collected on the bargaining process, it was evident that the nature of the couple's relationship greatly influenced whether and how often birth control was used. The single most important factor was the extent of involvement between the adolescent and her sexual partner. Contraception was much more likely to be practiced by couples who had a stable romantic relationship.[15] Indeed, of those women who were still "going with" the fathers of their unborn babies at the time of the initial interview, nearly twice as many had attempted contraception as those whose relationships had broken off for one reason or another.

There are several reasons why the stability of a relationship might promote the use of birth control. First of all, the male may be more likely to purchase and carry condoms simply because he knows that intercourse is likely to occur. Second, in the context of a continuing relationship, he, like his girlfriend, may come to regard sex as less spontaneous and more under his control. Third, he may come to feel that should pregnancy occur he would be committed to assume responsibility for his offspring. Finally, the bargaining position of the female probably improves in a stable association. While a man may be able to ignore the request of a casual sexual partner that he use birth control, he is probably less likely to resist the urging of a woman with whom he is emotionally involved.

Conversely, in a temporary sexual encounter both partners are often unprepared for sexual relations. Consequently, the male is not so likely to be carrying a condom; the female is less likely to urge him to use contraceptives; and he is probably less inclined to honor such a request.

Indeed, judging from the young mothers' reports, we concluded that brief sexual encounters often were unexpected and undesired. Some of the young women, for example, reported that they had had relations only once or twice prior to pregnancy, often with men they hardly knew (see also Ladner, 1971; Rainwater, 1970). In such cases it made little difference whether or not the adolescent had received birth control instruction. Virtually none of these young women had ever used birth control. In contrast, we found that among the women who were still seeing the father of the child, a majority (69%) had used contraception if discussions of birth control had occurred in the home; when parental intervention was absent, only 22% had contraceptive experience prior to conceiving (see Table A.2).[16] Thus, to a great extent, the influence of the family depends upon the nature of the couple's relationship. If temporary, the family's influence is negligible for the adolescent herself has little power to persuade her sexual partner to take precautions. On the other hand, durable

15This finding is contrary to Liebow's (1967) observation that males are most likely to use contraceptives in casual relationships in which marriage is not contemplated.

16Other family factors—the mother's awareness of, and attitudes toward, her daughter's sexual activity—also appear to be affected by the amount of contact the female has had with the father of the child prior to becoming pregnant. However, these findings must be regarded as more tentative because of the limited number of cases in which reliable comparisons could be made.

relationships provide the teenager—and indirectly her mother—with a wider latitude to negotiate the use of birth control.

In view of their potential for intervention, why were the parents of the adolescent mothers unlikely to recommend birth control? We suspect that it was precisely because illicit sexual relations were so strongly condemned that mothers often refused to acknowledge the possibility that their daughters were sexually active. Consequently they may have been reluctant to urge their children to use contraceptives. The adolescent, in turn, tried to uphold her mother's unrealistic view of the situation. By concealing her sexual activity, she confirmed her mother's belief that instruction was unnecessary. The interplay ended abruptly when the teenager became pregnant. It was not hard to understand, then, why so many mothers were genuinely astonished to discover that their daughters had had sexual relations without their knowledge and why most adolescents were similarly distraught by having let their mothers down. Our findings suggested that premarital pregnancies do not stem from permissive attitudes among low-income blacks but may instead be the consequence of restrictive standards about premarital sexual activity (cf. Blake, 1961).

Even among the minority of families in which preparation for and acceptance of premarital sexuality were adequate, the instruction provided was not likely to prevent pregnancy. Adolescents were encouraged to look to their boyfriends for protection, and, as we have seen, males were likely to comply only when they had a strong stake in preventing a pregnancy. It is probably true that most men are not inclined to consider premarital pregnancy as costly and serious to the same extent as do the women they impregnate.[17]

## WHEN PREGNANCY OCCURS

From what we have seen thus far, there is reason to doubt that most adolescent mothers have an advance commitment to becoming pregnant. Indeed, it seems that many teenagers are prone to deny even the possibility that an unplanned pregnancy will occur. Yet, at the same time, both mother and daughter are prepared for this eventuality. Many of our respondents' had had direct experience with an out of wedlock pregnancy; virtually all of our subjects had friends, relatives, or neighbors who had had unplanned pregnancies.

The mothers' admonitions to their daughters "to be careful," "not to get into trouble," and "not to do anything they would later regret" communicated an apprehension, if not an outright expectation, that their daughters were risking pregnancy. This sort of interaction provided a script for the daughter's reaction

[17]Fragmentary data collected from the men retrospectively at Time 3 bore this out. More than half the men were happy when they learned their partners were pregnant. The sample of men was biased in this respect, however, as it included a disproportionate number of men who married the young mothers.

to finding out she was pregnant and was in effect a rehearsal of that scene. To some extent, a process of normative discounting had preceded the pregnancy. Before the rules were even violated, the groundwork was laid for moral redemption. As one respondent said, summing up her feelings when she learned that she was pregnant, "It was bound to happen sooner or later; it might as well be now."

### Initial Reactions to Becoming Pregnant

Despite this anticipatory socialization, pregnancies were greeted by most adolescents and their parents with astonishment. Three-fourths of the adults reported that they were very surprised to learn their daughters were pregnant. A large number of the adolescents related this same feeling of disbelief.

Shocked. I felt sort of funny. I couldn't believe I was going to have a baby.

Since these data on the initial reactions were collected retrospectively, usually a month or more after the discovery of the pregnancy, it is difficult to judge how much the recollections were affected by intervening events. Since most of the adolescents had by then become accustomed to the idea of being pregnant, our data are somewhat biased against the expression of negative sentiments. In view of this bias, it seems obvious that most of the young mothers had not counted on becoming pregnant, and the great majority were still shaken by the realization that they were about to become mothers. Once again their accounts offer little support for the position that adolescent mothers possess an advanced commitment to becoming pregnant.

Usually a feeling of despair accompanied the initial reaction of astonishment. Only one adolescent in five indicated that she had been happy about becoming pregnant (Bowerman and his collaborators [1966] reported similar findings on the adverse reaction to a first pregnancy among black teenagers.) And even these women qualified their responses by saying that they felt "kind of good" or "sort of happy" about getting pregnant. Another fifth of the sample reported mixed feelings about becoming pregnant or indicated that they had not been affected much one way or the other. As one respondent, typical of this group, remarked: "It's nothing to be ashamed of, but it's nothing to be proud of. [I felt] not too good, not too bad." Some of these women expressed a fatalistic resignation to their pregnancies, and many reacted by asserting that "everyone can make one mistake" (cf. Rains, 1971). A number of the adolescents with mixed reactions said that they looked forward to having a child, at the same time admitting that they were not really ready to be parents and that the child probably was going to interfere with their goals. Three-fifths of the expectant mothers stated their first reactions in unambivalently negative terms, and an even larger proportion (75%) said they wished they had not become pregnant. Many of these women, as the following quotations illustrate, explained that they were ashamed of being pregnant, did not want a child, and felt that their educational and occupational plans were jeopardized.

> I could have died. I couldn't believe it. I was shocked.
>
> I didn't know what to do, I was really worried about telling my mother. I just regretted it.
>
> I felt I didn't want the baby. I wanted to find some way to get rid of it. I felt it would mess up my whole life.

Other information from the first interview seems to lend credibility to the teenagers' retrospective accounts. Half of them could not bring themselves to tell their parents of the pregnancy for several months; in a quarter of the families, four or more months passed before the pregnancy was disclosed. More often than not, the adolescents never actually told their parents; the mothers learned about it through a third party or detected it on their own. Only 3% of the women said that their mothers were pleased, and half recalled that they were angry.

Two-thirds of the parents stated that they were very upset when they learned of their daughters' pregnancies, and their adverse reactions seemed to parallel closely the accounts offered by the adolescents. The parents frequently spoke of being "disappointed," "hurt," or "let down."

> It hurt my heart, that's all I can say. I really hurt pretty deep. I had so much confidence in her.

It is clear from the parents' comments that the pregnancies represented not only a violation of past trust but a harbinger of problems to come. As we shall see in greater detail in later chapters, parents were all too aware of the likely consequences of early parenthood. A number explicitly mentioned their expectations for the future in describing their initial reactions to the pregnancy:

> I didn't know whether I could have killed her or just died myself. . . . I could have killed him. Welfare tells me he will go to jail after the baby comes.
>
> I felt like knocking her head off. I felt terrible. She was doing so well in school.

## The Process of Accommodation

As we indicated, the response to the pregnancy is subject to considerable revision during the course of gestation. Adolescents and their families continually reevaluated their situation after conception depending on their particular circumstances. In nearly every instance, their responses became more positive as the pregnancy proceeded. One factor that caused many to shift their feelings was the realization of impending motherhood itself. Nearly all of the adolescents planned to keep the baby. Neither abortion nor adoption was seriously considered by many of the respondents (see Chapter 4). "You are going to have it," said one respondent, "so you might as well stick with it." There was a strong feeling among both the pregnant teenagers and their parents that a baby should not suffer for its mother's mistake. Only 6% of the prospective grandmothers felt that the child should be given up for adoption. This finding is completely consistent with results from other studies of premarital pregnancy among blacks (see Sauber and Rubinstein, 1965; Bowerman et al., 1966; Rains, 1971; Ladner, 1971), although we must keep in mind that the selective nature of our sample discourages generalization on this point.

Another reason for their increasingly positive feeling was that the initial penalties for early pregnancy were not quite so severe as the adolescents had anticipated. Their parents were angry and upset at first but eventually became more understanding and forgiving. At the time of the first interview, 70% of the parents indicated that they were already feeling less negative than they had been initially. As one put it,

> Each and every one of us make a mistake. She had a chance to rectify it. Not to do it again.

In cases in which the parents were more unrelenting, some of the adolescents learned to deal with the negative reactions of their families:

> My first thoughts were what my parents were going to do to me. Second thoughts were it's my life and not their life to live.

An initial source of great concern to the adolescents was the likelihood of being forced to leave school. However, some of the expectant mothers discovered that they could attend a special school for pregnant students, and others were informed that they would be allowed to return to classes after delivery. In fact, as we shall see in Chapter 7, their anxiety about the difficulty of remaining in school was well founded, but the immediate problems were not so overwhelming as they had feared.

Finally, many adolescents had been worried about the effect of the pregnancy on their relationship with the child's father. As it turned out, once again the complications were not so bad as they had imagined. Most continued to see the father, and many found him to be supportive and concerned about them (see Chapter 9).

> [I] still go with him, want to marry him in two or three years. Cause he says he wants to take care of his baby and wants to be with both of us.

Midway through pregnancy, when the first interview was conducted, most of the adolescents found their state of mind improved. Over half reported that they were happier than they had been when they discovered that they were going to have a child. But even in this later stage of pregnancy, the majority continued to characterize their feelings in qualified, if not negative, terms. Less than a third described themselves as "very happy," scarcely an indication that parenthood is preceded by a commitment. Furthermore, when we consider those among the sample who were "very happy" at Time 1, the postulate that adolescent mothers possess a special motivation to become pregnant seems even more untenable.

### Reactions to Pregnancy and Marital Status

Virtually the only women in the sample who were unambivalently positive about impending parenthood were the few (20%) who had married as of the first interview. A substantial majority (78%) of these women were "very happy" about becoming pregnant. By contrast, only a fifth of the single mothers expressed this sentiment. Responses to other questions in the Time 1 interview also pointed to the conclusion that the unwed adolescents were far less pleased about being pregnant. While 80% of the single mothers said that they sometimes wished they were not going to have a child, only 25% of the married women in the sample admitted to such feelings. When these separate items were combined into a single index of pregnancy reactions, we discovered that more than three times as many married as single women (51% versus 14%) classified their feelings as unambivalently positive.

In the interviews with the unmarried classmates at Time 3, a corresponding pattern occurred among women who had experienced an early pregnancy. About three-fifths of the classmates who were still single reported that they had neither wanted nor expected to become pregnant. Slightly less than one-third indicated that their first reaction to the pregnancy was positive. Again, there were striking differences in the responses of married and unmarried classmates to these questions. Single women were distinctly less happy about becoming pregnant and much less likely to report that prior to conception they wanted the child.

There was additional evidence that the marital situation of the young mother is a critical factor in shaping her response to an unplanned pregnancy. Among the single women, the closer an adolescent was to marriage, the happier she felt about becoming pregnant. Of the women with definite marriage plans at Time 1, 45% described themselves as "very happy" compared to just 10% of the adolescents who had stopped seeing the father of the child. Conversely, only 6% of young women who were close to marriage were overtly unhappy about the pregnancy compared to 46% of their peers who had stopped going out with the prospective father. It seems, then, that adolescents view pregnancy more favorably when it enhances, or at least does not diminish, their prospects of marriage. Marriage, as we shall see in the next chapter, offers a hope of repairing the damage done by an unscheduled birth, and the women who were in a position to rectify their situation reacted much more favorably to prospective motherhood. Yet even these women retained many misgivings about becoming parents. Again, our findings provide little support for the position that adolescent mothers are specially motivated to bear a child out of wedlock.[18]


## ATTITUDES TOWARD PREMARITAL PREGNANCY AMONG THE CLASSMATES

The evidence presented thus far has been based on retrospective reports—young mothers' recollections shortly after conception occurred of how they felt about becoming pregnant. As we noted earlier, these reports were subject to considerable redefinition. Some adolescents who before conception wanted to become pregnant may have later recognized that certain disadvantages would ensue and became less positive in retrospect. Perhaps more typically, the occurrence of a pregnancy may convince women to decide that they really wanted to have a child after all.

The classmate interviews conducted at Time 3 provided some information on how unmarried, sexually active women in their late teens feel before conception about the possibility of having a child. The sexually active classmates who had not conceived were asked to select the statement that best described the way they would feel if they were to become pregnant in the next few months. A majority of these classmates said they would be less than pleased. In general, the sentiments of the classmates corresponded to the retrospective reactions of adolescent mothers at the initial interview. In each case, about two-thirds indicated that they had not wished to become pregnant. However, the fact that nearly one-third of the sexually active single classmates said that they would be happy to have a child, even if few were actively hoping for one, should not be overlooked. Clearly, there were women within this population who were at least somewhat receptive to becoming pregnant and some who deliberately set out to have a child.

How much did the anticipated costs of a prenuptial conception enter into the projected reactions of the sexually active classmates? Their immediate marital plans did not greatly affect their feelings toward a pregnancy in the near future although these findings should not be weighed too heavily because of the small number of classmates who anticipated marrying in the months ahead. However, plans regarding education did influence their degree of receptivity to a premarital pregnancy. Women who were school dropouts or who had low educational goals had much more favorable attitudes toward becoming pregnant

[18]To the extent that the claim of a special motivation seems plausible, one might argue that certain adolescents deliberately become pregnant *in order* to marry. This possibility, as we shall see from evidence presented in Chapter 4 seems remote for most of the respondents in our study.

than those who planned to extend their schooling beyond high school or who were already in some postgraduate training. As we noted earlier, the sentiments of the latter were accompanied by more sexually circumspect behavior. Fewer of the women with higher educational ambitions were having sexual relations, and those who were sexually active typically had delayed the onset of relations until their late teens. Apparently these young women assessed the costs of pregnancy differently, a fact that both affected their attitudes about becoming pregnant and constrained their sexual behavior.

The information from the classmates, limited as it is, provides plausibility to our assumption that adolescent parenthood is almost always unplanned and usually undesired. Regardless of their feelings about becoming pregnant in the immediate future, few of the classmates at risk were using contraception on a regular basis (see Chapter 6). Although the interviews with the classmates were conducted in 1970, three years after the young mothers became pregnant, and the classmates accordingly were several years older than the young mothers had been at the time of the initial interviews, little had changed in the interim. Like the adolescent mothers, most classmates were leaving matters to chance; and many, no doubt, were soon to become premaritally pregnant.

## SUMMARY

The information presented in this chapter conflicts with the viewpoints implicit in many theories of illegitimacy. We have seen how it is possible for young black women to become pregnant at an early age without possessing any advance commitment to having a child in or out of wedlock.

The young black females in our study faced considerable pressure to engage in sexual relations once they began dating. While many adolescents had certain misgivings about permarital sex, the peer group provided a number of techniques for neutralizing the restrictive norms. Young women were tacitly encouraged by their parents to conceal their sexual status, thus removing controls that might otherwise be exercised by the family. For their part, the parents were quite willing to ignore the signs that their daughters were sexually active, probably because they felt helpless to intervene effectively. Consequently, birth control was left up to the male, and sustained contraceptive use on his part was relatively rare. Although pregnancy was generally unwelcome, most adolescents and their parents had been indirectly prepared to accommodate themselves to the event.

These findings reinforce our impression that early parenthood emerges from a complex social process rather than from a "special motivation." This perspective makes it easier to understand what otherwise appear to be contradictions between the behavior of, and ideals expressed by, adolescent mothers and their families. Looking at parenthood as a process helps to explain why adolescents claim that pregnancy is something that "just happens," even though they insist that they do not want to have a child. Similarly, we are able to reconcile their mothers' reports of being "shocked" to discover that their daughters were having sexual relations while acknowledging that most adolescent females in the neighborhood were sexually active. When looked at not as inconsistencies but as problems to be resolved, contradictions of this sort become more comprehensible to the outsider. In Chapters 4 and 5, which deal with marriage, we shall have occasion to observe additional contradictions in the life situation of the young mother.

# 4. The Decision to Marry

ALTHOUGH MANY ADOLESCENTS find pregnancy difficult to avoid because they are unable and unwilling to defer sexual activity and poorly prepared to use birth control effectively, unwed motherhood is not inevitable. Indeed, the outcome of most premarital pregnancies is not an illegitimate child (Gebhard et al., 1958; Cutright, 1971b; Zelnik and Kantner, 1974). A large number of teenage pregnancies—perhaps as many as one in every two—are terminated either spontaneously or deliberately before delivery (Sklar and Berkov, 1973). Our study afforded us no way to estimate the number of potential unwed mothers who "dropped out" by obtaining abortions. By the time they came to the hospital clinic, most of the adolescents had passed the point at which an abortion might have been performed. Thus, our sample excluded teenage women whose pregnancies ended shortly after conception.[1]

Another way of avoiding unwed motherhood *was* open to the young women in our study—they could marry before the child was born. In contrast to abortion, which was strongly disapproved of by most of the respondents, marriage offered an acceptable route of escape. Indeed, as we will show shortly, previous research indicates that in the past marriage has been the most popular solution to impending parenthood for the adolescent pregnant for the first time.

[1] Although it could not be specifically documented in this study, white adolescents may be more inclined to choose abortion (Zelnik and Kantner, 1974). Evidence suggests that, prior to 1968, induced abortion was relatively uncommon among blacks. When our study was initiated, it was still quite difficult to obtain a legal abortion. Furthermore, there is reason to believe that young black women hold, or at least at the time of the study held, rather negative attitudes toward abortion (Furstenberg, 1972). During the early years of the follow-up, very few blacks obtained abortions when second pregnancies occurred even though most of these conceptions were unplanned and unwanted and the mothers were advised that they could have an abortion at the hospital. Abortion was equally rare among the sexually active classmates; only 5% of those who had become pregnant indicated that they had obtained abortions. It is possible, of course, that these self-reports underestimated the true incidence of abortions, but even so it seems unlikely that induced abortion was a common way of avoiding unwed parenthood. Most of the mothers and their classmates expressed strong moral objections to abortion when asked their opinions at Time 3. In the Time 4 interview, there was evidence of a shift in attitudes toward abortion among both the young mothers and their classmates: by the time of the five-year follow-up, one in seven of the young mothers who had become pregnant again, and one in eight of the sexually active classmates, reported an abortion experience.

It hardly needs to be said that marriage drastically alters the career of an adolescent mother, affecting her future life chances. As we shall see in later chapters, early wedlock is at best a mixed blessing, resolving certain problems that develop as a result of a pregnancy but at the same time generating new ones. Regardless of how the marriage turns out, the decision to marry is a pivotal point in the life course of women who experience an unplanned pregnancy. Many of the negative consequences of unscheduled parenthood—dropping out of school, economic dependence, excessive family size, and childrearing problems— can be understood only when we take into account the marital histories of couples who wed in response to a premarital conception. Accordingly, in this chapter and the one that follows, we shall consider the impact of early pregnancy on the nuptial career of the young mother. In subsequent chapters, marital history will be related to a variety of other life events.

## PRIOR RESEARCH ON THE LINK BETWEEN PREMARITAL PREGNANCY AND MARRIAGE

Cutright (1971b), using data collected by Pratt (1965) and statistics assembled in the national natality survey 1964-66, concluded that close to half of all premarital pregnancies in the United States were legitimated by marriage before the child was born. Among teenage primiparae, the proportion of pregnancies legitimated by marriage after conception climbed to nearly three out of five, suggesting the special appeal, as well as the greater availability, of this alternative to younger women. Whites in particular were inclined to marry before delivery: 72% of those who conceived premaritally wed before their child was born as compared to 32% of black adolescents.

In their national survey on the sexual patterns of teenage females, Zelnik and Kantner (1974) provided a somewhat lower estimate. They found that 50% of whites and 8% of blacks who became premaritally pregnant married before delivery. However, their figures included all pregnancies, not only those that resulted in a birth. Since more than one-fourth of all conceptions in their sample ended in abortion, miscarriage, or fetal death, their estimates, when restricted to live births, are closer to Cutright's.

The pattern of precipitate marriages has received a good deal of attention in the sociological literature on the family because such unions are known to have a high probability of failure. Over the years there have been several studies on the subject of so-called forced marriage. Christensen (1953, 1960), in an early study of premarital sexual patterns, was able to calculate the proportion of pregnant brides by linking marriage and birth records in different localities. His data from a county in Indiana revealed that approximately one bride in four who was marrying for the first time was pregnant at the time of her wedding. A subsequent replication by Lowrie (1965), using data from Ohio, confirmed these figures. A survey conducted by the National Center for Health Statistics (1970) showed that in one out of every three first marriages, the bride was pregnant at the time of her wedding. In all these studies, teenagers accounted for the lion's share of the precipitate marriages. In fact, pregnancy almost invariably precedes marriage when the bride is under the age of 18, and it is a frequent antecedent of marriages that take place during late adolescence (Lowrie, 1965; Bartz and Nye, 1970).[2]

Although these data are readily available, they have been frequently overlooked in sociological discussions of marriage and family formation. For example, the effect of premarital pregnancy on marriage age has not been well documented by demographers although there is reason to suspect that fluctuations in the incidence of premarital pregnancy could have a sizable impact on the rate of early marriages (Carter and Glick, 1970). Similarly, sociologists have not considered the role that pregnancy plays in the decision-making process that precedes marriage. Many textbooks on the family mention the figures cited in the previous paragraphs but these statistics are rarely referred to in chapters on the courtship process. The sociological writings on the formation of the marital dyad tempt one to draw the conclusion that many family sociologists are as caught up in the romantic love complex as are the couples they study (Waller, 1938). Marital choice, so it is often said, is governed by romantic love, which in turn derives from a variety of underlying motives: the desire to maximize social position (status homophily); the search for psychological fulfillment (need complementarity); and the quest for social reinforcement (value consensus) (Kerckhoff and Davis, 1962; Moss et al., 1971). Useful as these social psychological theories may be in explaining why individuals are attracted to one another, they provide little help in identifying the specific process by which couples become committed to matrimony. It may turn out that career decisions, social pressure, or the imminence of parenthood are far more important than mutual attraction in ordering the marital career.[3]

Studies on early marriages—unions in which one or both of the partners are minors—have touched on the nuptial decision-making process especially as it relates to the occurrence of premarital pregnancy (Moss, 1964; Burchinal, 1965; Bartz and Nye, 1970). However, these studies have focused exclusively on the couples who ultimately married following a premarital pregnancy, ignoring those who chose not to wed when the woman was pregnant. Consequently, the elements that enter into the selection process have been left largely unexplored.

[2]Hetzel and Cappetta (1973) estimated that in 1968 approximately 60% of all births to teenage brides were conceived before wedlock. Zelnik and Kantner (1974) provided similar estimates from their national survey of teenage women. Only one-quarter of the babies among women in their sample were conceived after marriage—one-twentieth of the blacks and one-third of the whites.

[3]Arnold Green's (1941) classic work on courtship patterns in a Polish-American community a generation ago stands as one of the rare studies of how couples actually become committed to marriage (see also Waller, 1938). Green showed that the interplay of interests during courtship often results in a sexual bargain, the outcome of which may be a premarital pregnancy. In the face of little or no communication between the sexes, the pregnancy serves to resolve an ambiguous relationship by providing a rationale for marriage. Only a few writers have picked up on this theme (Ehrmann, 1964; Scanzoni, 1972).

A more inclusive strategy is to examine a population "at risk"—that is, a population of single pregnant women who must decide whether or not to marry.[4] This is precisely the situation in which most of the adolescents in our study found themselves at the time of the first interview.

While I have used such phrases as "decision-making," "choice," and "elect to" to describe the process that leads either to marriage or to unwed parenthood, it is important to recognize that these words convey a false sense, or at least an exaggerated notion, of free choice. Most of the young women in this study had relatively few options once pregnancy occurred and faced a series of constraints that narrowed their available choices. Becoming an unwed mother, as we shall see, often occurs because it is the most desirable of several undesirable alternatives.

## MARRIAGE PATTERNS AMONG THE ADOLESCENT MOTHERS

As a first step in our analysis, we inspected the nuptial patterns of the 323 individuals who were interviewed at the time of the five-year follow-up. Only 3% of the young mothers were married prior to conception, but a sizable proportion—nearly 20%—had wed before their first visit to the prenatal clinic. Others were making plans to marry when the first interview took place, and by delivery more than 25% were married. All but a few of these women married the father of the child. "Deferred," or postnatal, marriage was an even more common pattern. The rate of marriage was nearly as great in the two years following delivery as in the year preceding the birth of the child. Thereafter, the proportion of women marrying dropped off. In large measure the decline was a statistical artifact owing to the smaller pool of single women eligible for marriage after the first two years. When this factor was taken into account in the calculations, there still was a reduction in the rate of matrimony, especially after 18 months, though the differences were not quite so marked as before. At the five-year follow-up, more than one-third of the young mothers were single.

These figures were subject to a certain amount of error because one-fifth of the sample was lost to follow-up after five years. Also, the respondents interviewed at Time 4 were not contacted at exactly the same point in time from delivery, so that it is difficult to know whether the proportion who had married might change if there were strict comparability in this respect. Fortunately, both of these possible sources of error could be corrected for by using a life table

[4]Pope (1969) deserves credit for being one of the very few sociologists to follow this research design. Unfortunately, the data he collected with Bowerman in North Carolina were not well suited for an empirical examination of the decision-making process. For other researchers who have touched directly on this problem, see Whelan (1972) and Graves (1972), both of whom have conducted limited studies of the process of legitimating premarital conceptions.

procedure that estimates the probability of marriage occurring at standard intervals, measured in this case from the point of delivery. The marriage proportions (shown in Table A.3) do not differ greatly from the percentages cited earlier.

The decline in the incidence of marriage in the later years of the study raises the possibility that women who remain single may be either less receptive to, or less eligible for, marriage. There was a heavy concentration of marriages around the point of delivery, which accounts for most of the marriages that occurred within the five-year period of the study. Indeed, of those who married, more than one-third had done so by the time of delivery, half before the one-year follow-up, and three-fourths within two years after delivery. These statistics underscore how significant the pregnancy was in determining the timing of matrimony, strongly suggesting that were it not for this event most of the marriages would not have taken place when they did.

This conclusion seems warranted on other grounds as well. First, it was apparent that the marriage patterns of the adolescent mothers differed sharply from those of the general population. Over two-fifths of the young mothers were married by age 18. Using as a contrast group the population of 18- and 19-year-old blacks living in Baltimore city, we found that only one-fifth of women in this age category were married (U.S. Bureau of the Census, 1970a). The marriage patterns of the adolescent mothers and their classmates were even more discrepant. By age 18, only 21% of the classmates were married as compared to 41% of the young mothers. The difference was sharper still for marriages that occurred among women not yet 18 (30% versus 11%). Had the pregnancy not occurred, many fewer of the young mothers obviously would have married before the age of 18.[5]

It has been suggested that premarital pregnancy is a covert tactic for bringing about marriage when one (usually the male) or both partners are reluctant or hesitant to commit themselves (Green, 1941; Sklar and Berkov, 1974).[6] Unquestionably, pregnancy can be a means of resolving uncertainty in the courtship process, particularly among couples who are accustomed to relying on the pressure of external events to bring abut life changes. However, among the young adolescents in our sample, there was little evidence that pregnancy served this function. Most who married did so with obvious reluctance.

The adolescents were asked at the first interview the age they would like to be when they married and whether they expected to marry at the age they considered ideal. Only one in three felt very sanguine about the prospect of timing her marriage to correspond with her wishes for the future. And even these

[5]Overall, only 44 classmates (20% of the total group) had married without conceiving premaritally, despite the fact that nearly all of the women were in their twenties and considered themselves to be of marriageable age.

[6]There was, especially in some agricultural communities in Europe and America, a tradition of postponing marriage until after conception to ensure that the woman was fertile (Goode, 1963).

gloomy prognostications turned out to be, if anything, overoptimistic. Fewer than one in three of those who were wed by Time 4 had married at the age she considered to be most desirable. Both at the time they married and in retrospect, many women admitted that had it not been for the pregnancy they would not have married when they did, if at all. At the three-year follow-up, approximately two-thirds of those who had married claimed, in retrospect, that under normal circumstances they would have chosen to marry at a later age.

If most of the marriages that came about after conception were indeed "forced," how can we explain the fact that some women succumbed to the pressure to marry while others resisted? (The reader should note that whereas previously we posed the question of why premaritally pregnant women do not marry in order not to bear a child out of wedlock, we are now asking why some premaritally pregnant adolescents are more willing than others to risk marriage.)

In the sections that follow, we shall examine the nuptial patterns of the young mothers not only in the period preceding the birth of the child but through the five-year follow-up. Despite certain limitations in the data collected, particularly in the early stages of the study, the information available was complete enough to test several possible explanations of the pattern of marriage within the sample. Specifically, we will consider several general conditions that might have affected the decision to marry: (1) the readiness of the couple for marriage; (2) the extent to which matrimony was perceived to be consistent with other career plans; (3) the availability and eligibility of the father as a marriage partner; and (4) the normative pressure to marry in order to legitimate the child.

## READINESS FOR MARRIAGE

Age at pregnancy is of course a powerful determinant of nuptial patterns, especially in predicting whether an adolescent will marry before her child is born. Among the young mothers who were not yet 15 at the time of the first interview, only 1 in 10 married before delivery. By contrast, nearly one-third of the adolescents who were 17 and older at Time 1 married before the child was born. This difference by age was maintained throughout the first year, when almost half of the older teenagers married as compared to only one-seventh of the youngest. Thereafter the differential diminished, although even after five years there was still a considerable disparity between the two age categories. At Time 4, half of the youngest females, aged 19, were married; whereas almost three-fourths of their peers who were over 21 were wed (see also Sauber and Corrigan, 1970).

While age has a strong effect on the timing of matrimony, its ultimate impact on marriage rates is minimal. As the youngest females got older, they wed at about the same rate as females who were three years their senior. In other words, roughly half of each age cohort was married by age 18. Thus, it appears that a higher proportion of older girls were able to legitimate their children because they were more "ready" to marry when they happened to become pregnant. While this fact may seem obvious, it is often ignored in discussions of illegitimacy. Studies that compare illegitimacy rates among blacks and whites often have not taken into account the age of the mother at conception. One important reason why illegitimacy rates are so much higher among nonwhites is that on the average blacks conceive premaritally at a much earlier age than whites and consequently are in a poorer position to legitimate the pregnancy by marriage (Zelnik and Kantner, 1974). If there were no racial difference in age at conception, the ratio of black to white illegitimate births, instead of being seven to one, would drop by perhaps as much as half (Clague and Ventura, 1968).

Age affects nuptial patterns for a variety of reasons. The most conspicuous one is that early marriage is frowned upon in the United States. Recent investigations have revealed a high degree of agreement within the population on the best age for a woman to marry. Most women both expect and prefer to marry in their early twenties, and black women endorse a later marriage age than whites. Kuvelsky and Obordo (1972), comparing black and white adolescents living in the rural South, discovered that black females favored a marriage age about 18 months beyond that favored by whites. Three-fifths of the blacks in their sample wanted to be at least 23 before they married. Our data tended to corroborate these results. Nearly half of the young mothers hoped to be at least 22 before they wed. Only 3% thought it was desirable to marry before age 18. The ideal marriage age was almost identical among the classmates, suggesting that the views of the young mothers regarding the appropriate time for matrimony were not greatly influenced by pregnancy. Both in the population at large and in our sample of young mothers, the timing of black marriages was out of line with the stated aspirations of black females. While blacks favored a later marriage age than whites, they actually wed somewhat earlier (Carter and Glick, 1970), which suggests that circumstances such as premarital pregnancy compelled them to depart from their ideal standard. Here again we see an indication of the "value-stretch" pattern to which Rodman (1963) has referred.

The few women in our study who indicated that the best age for a woman to marry was under 19 were predictably more likely to marry younger. Two-fifths wed before their eighteenth birthday as compared to one-fifth of those whose ideal marriage age was 21 or older. The influence of marriage age norms on the timing of marriage was most evident among the older adolescents in the sample. The 17 year olds who did not favor a late marriage were much more likely to wed precipitately. However, standards about marriage age had little or no effect on the timing of marriage among adolescents who were under 16 when they became pregnant. These women were in no position to wed quickly even if they favored a relatively early marriage. At 14 or 15, they were still years away from the age at which they deemed marriage appropriate.[7]

When asked in the interview at Time 1 whether they would wed immediately if they met the "right person," only 17% of the adolescents under 16 replied positively. Virtually all the others stated that they lacked the maturity and experience to make a good marriage.

> I am too young to get married. If I waited until I was 24 or 25, I'd be able to accept the responsibility of marriage.

> I like to do different things, and with a husband you have responsibility— cook and cleaning. [You need] more of a dedication when you're married.

The adolescents in the study took the responsibilities of matrimony seriously, and most of the younger women recognized that they were unprepared to "settle down." Many felt that a young woman needed a period of independence and an opportunity to get some experience before marrying (Ladner, 1971; Stack, 1974).

The young mother who marries must not only be prepared to take on a number of additional responsibilities, she also must be willing to forego the advantages of remaining at home.[8] As they approached parenthood, most of the adolescents could count on receiving considerable help and guidance from their families. Although those who married would not be denied assistance, they could not expect to receive a comparable amount of aid. Marriage, therefore, had the considerable drawback of reducing the childrearing assistance a daughter might otherwise expect from her mother, imposing a double demand on the women who chose to marry. For most adolescents in their early or middle teens, the costs were simply too great. The view shared by most adolescents that they were too young to marry was strongly reinforced by their parents. Some of the mothers said that they would refuse to permit their daughters to marry before age 18. The majority thought that an early marriage merely to legitimate the child was a serious mistake.

> No use making it worse than it is now. I don't feel a girl has to get married because she is pregnant. If she marries somebody she loves and cares for, she has to be happy.

[7]Maryland law permits women 16 and over to marry without the consent of their parents in the event that the female is pregnant or has delivered a child. Girls under 14 are prohibited from marrying, and those under 16 must have parental consent and be pregnant before they are permitted to marry (Clark and Salsburg, 1974). Although these laws affected the status of the respondents, there was no indication that they had much bearing on the decisions of the adolescents or their families. Most of the young mothers seemed prepared to accede to their parents' wishes in the event that they opposed the marriage.

[8]In her study of kin relations in the lower-class black community, Carol Stack (1974) provides an excellent analysis of the way responsibilities are shared by the kin network of the unmarried mother.

More than a few of the mothers cited their own experiences as a reason for waiting. Many had married extremely young and were not eager to see their daughters repeat the same pattern.

> She isn't ready yet. My husband and I are separated and she might feel that is why she doesn't want to yet.

In alluding to their own marital histories, the parents who married young drew a lesson from their personal experience. Many felt that their future prospects had been irreparably damaged by an early marriage and were anxious to prevent their daughters from repeating the same mistake. These parents recalled that when they married they (and their spouses) were in no position to support a family. Had they waited to marry, they might have been better prepared to manage economically. Readiness for marriage refers, then, not merely to a stage of emotional commitment but implies as well the ability to establish and maintain a separate household.

## CAREER PLANS AND MARRIAGE PATTERNS

In attempting to answer the question of why certain adolescents marry more quickly and at a younger age than others, Bartz and Nye (1970) devised a framework for integrating the findings from previous studies. They concluded that the principal reason early marriages occur within the lower class is that the incentive to delay marriage for future career considerations is generally low in this group. Borrowing their somewhat . stilted and formalistic language (1970:265):

> The lower the social class, the more likely the positive discrepancy between satisfactions anticipated from marriage at an early age and satisfactions received from existing roles will be great.

Lower-class youth expect a lesser degree of material success. Consequently, they think they require less education and training for entrance into occupational roles. This, in turn, means that they move more rapidly into dating and intimate physical relationships. When pregnancy occurs, "marriage offers the least undesirable of several alternatives and [the pregnancy] is the direct motivation for a large proportion of marriages of very young couples" (Bartz and Nye, 1970:266).

This general explanation for youthful marriage can be directly applied to the special problem of why certain pregnant adolescents are more willing than others to marry. Some teenagers anticipate that the marriage will interfere with their career plans, whereas others have more modest or less clearly formed aspirations, with which marriage might conflict. In short, we expected to find that the young mothers who had higher career aims would be more reluctant to jeopardize their plans by an early marriage. Both qualitative and quantitative information from the interviews lent support to this prediction.

As will be explored in greater detail in Chapter 7, there was virtual unanimity among the participants in our study and their mothers on the goal of high school graduation, and many respondents aspired to more than a high school education. Similarly, both the adolescents and their parents were aware that if they were to marry, there might not be anyone available to care for their child while they attended school. Moreover, some felt that their husbands might be less than supportive if going to school meant economic hardship or personal discomfort for the family. Thus, a number explicitly stated their intention to defer marriage until they had completed school. The following quotations were more or less typical of the respondents who felt this way:

> I will finish school first. When I come out, I might [marry].
> First of all, I want to finish school and work for a few years.

Statements such as these led us to expect that the more committed a woman was to completing school, the less likely she was to marry, especially before or shortly after delivery. At the time of the first interview, we asked the pregnant adolescents about both their long-range educational plans and their determination to remain in school. Attitudinal items measuring commitment to schooling were combined into an index of education (see Chapter 7). The most ambitious students were by far the least likely to marry before delivery (10% versus 43% of the least ambitious), and a greater proportion were still single at the five-year follow-up (47% versus 23%). Similarly, women who married early were less able students and by their own accounts did not perform so well in the classroom. Two-fifths of the women who married before delivery characterized themselves as "poor" or "so-so" students. By comparison, only one-third of the young mothers who deferred marriage and one-fourth of those who never married described their academic abilities in such negative terms.

There is no mystery about why education is highly valued by most adolescents. They perceive schooling as the only certain route to obtaining a decent job and a measure of economic security. The great majority of adolescent mothers expected and wanted to work before marriage. Over four-fifths who were not yet married preferred to work for awhile before getting married, even if they already had met the "right person." When asked why, a number referred to the value of work for their personal development. A job would encourage them to become more independent, promote self-reliance, and help them to mature before they married. As one young mother told us:

> Until I finish school and work and be a settled person, I won't know what I really want.

Most of the women in our study, however, regarded the personal benefits of work as secondary. Unlike middle-class youth, the young mothers could not afford the luxury of evaluating a job in terms of its potential intrinsic satisfactions. Employment was valued principally for the economic benefits it provided. First of all, more than a few women pointed out that a steady job would ultimately improve their marital prospects. Adolescents who planned to marry the father of the child viewed working as a chance to accumulate some savings to relieve the economic strain on their future husbands. They looked forward to providing a kind of dowry to start their marriage off on a proper footing:

> Cause then I could save up money and buy our furniture. When we get married, [we would] not have many bills.

Those not intending to marry the father saw work as a way of finding the "right kind of man."

> I really want to have a decent job first so I could meet a decent man. Once you get a little class, you have a chance.

Whether they planned to marry the father of the child or not, most young mothers thought of work as more than a form of protective insurance or something to fall back on in the event that marriage did not work out. To them, having a good job meant not having to choose between being economically reliant on a male or being dependent on public assistance. They regarded marriage as an option but not a necessity. Being able to make it on their own did not necessarily imply that they did not expect help from the father, his family, or most of all from their own kin. But they expected and wanted to contribute to their own economic support (see Chapter 8).

Although similar sentiments are common among adolescents in the middle class, the determination to be self-supporting was such a pervasive and recurrent subject in the first interview that we conclude that most young mothers, while wanting to marry, really did not expect their marriages to work out. Approximately half of those who said that they intended to work before marriage either implied or flatly stated that they were not sure their husbands would be able to support them after marriage. The following quotations were fairly typical of this group:

> You know you might find the right boy but you need some security you could fall back on. It is good to have your own things.
>
> So I can get some type of experience. Then after I'm married and my husband should leave me, I'd have some experience to do something.
>
> Because I want to be able to work to have my own income and can support myself. So if my husband doesn't do right, I'll walk out or put him out.

What holds many teenagers back from marriage is not just that they are young, have not yet completed high school, or lack working experience (although each of these conditions may provide some cause for delay). Rather, it is the meaning these circumstances take on in light of the male's situation that makes marriage so ominous. Therefore, an adolescent who marries immediately faces a double dilemma. First, there is the strong possibility that her husband will be unable to support her and their children. A second peril she faces is that if the marriage does not work out, in all likelihood she will not be able to support herself. By deferring marriage, she minimizes both of these risks. Additional time gives her an opportunity to consider whether her boyfriend is the "right person" and also to improve her own prospects of economic independence.

It was not surprising, then, to discover that the marriage rate began to rise sharply as the young mothers reached their late teens. By this time, they had had a chance to complete their education and to gain some working experience. More important, the fathers were beginning to find steady employment. Although our data on the males at the time conception occurred were fragmentary, they were sufficient to suggest that the economic situation of the males was an important determinant in the decision to wed and in the timing of marriage.

## THE ECONOMICS OF MARRIAGE

In a technical sense, virtually all of the fathers were eligible for marriage, that is, only a few had fathered a child adulterously, and over 90% were still seeing the expectant mother (generally on a regular basis) when the first interview was held. Fewer than 1% of the pregnant adolescents reported that they did not know who the father was or where he was at Time 1.[9] In fact, two-thirds of the single teenagers indicated at Time 1 that there was at least a good chance that they would eventually marry the father of the child. Even a year after delivery, half of those women who were still single reaffirmed their intention to marry the child's father.

These projected marriages took place among nearly half of the young mothers who were unmarried at the time of conception.[10] Indeed, of all the marriages that occurred during the study period (amounting to two-thirds of the sample), 70% involved the parental couple. This pattern was most marked during the early years of the study. Predictably, a high proportion (94%) of the

[9]Pope (1967) provided similar findings from the data he and Bowerman collected on unwed parenthood in North Carolina. Ninety-five percent of the black fathers were eligible to marry. Pope's findings also showed that black couples were particularly likely to have long-standing relationships prior to pregnancy: "Although none of the Negro-white differences are pronounced, the Negro more often than the white alleged father was integrated into the unwed mother's social life" (1967:565).

[10]This is a much higher figure than that reported in most previous studies of black women who experienced a premarital pregnancy (Bowerman et al., 1966; Cutright, 1971c; Whelan, 1972; Graves, 1972). The difference is that most previous studies did not follow up women for sufficiently long periods to determine their marriage patterns. In their five-year longitudinal study, Sauber and Corrigan (1970) presented figures close to the results obtained in this study. The black women in their sample were particularly likely after delivery to have married the father of the child. Though they did not give a precise figure, it would appear that at least one-third of the younger black women in their sample followed this pattern.

adolescents who wed before delivery married the father of the child. But for the following year, the figure was almost as great—81% of the marriages involved the parental couple. Thereafter, the proportion of women who married the father steadily declined, but it was not for another two years that it became more common for the young mother to marry someone other than her child's father. By the fifth year, marriage of the parental couple was extremely rare. Only two such couples married after that point.

Why did some young mothers marry the father of the child while others did not? Of course, in certain instances, one or the other partner was unwilling to marry. Approximately one-third of the adolescents at Time 1 indicated that they did not plan to wed the father, and undoubtedly some of the males—not necessarily the partners of the same third—felt similarly disinclined to marry. Indirect and anecdotal data gave us reason to suspect that the personal inclinations of the young mothers were shaped by a keen perception of external realities. Specifically, most of the participants in our study wanted to marry the father of the child *if* and *when* they thought he would be capable of supporting a family (cf. Pope, 1969). Although direct evidence on the attitudes of the male was lacking, his willingness to marry the mother perhaps depended on similar economic considerations (Liebow, 1967; Schulz, 1969; Staples, 1971).

In assessing the father's eligibility, the adolescent mother obviously must have taken his age to be a critical indication of his immediate economic prospects. Three-fifths of the couples were two or fewer years apart in age, and only one couple in four had an age difference of more than four years. Thus, most of the males were quite young when the pregnancy occurred. The father's age, in fact, was a slightly better predictor of whether marriage occurred before the child was born than was the mother's age. In cases in which the male was 20 or over, 36% of the couples married before delivery as compared to only 6% when the father was not yet 18.

When considered in combination, the age of both parents had a powerful impact on the pattern of early marriage. When both parents were very young— the father not yet 18, the adolescent mother under 16—only 4% married before delivery. By contrast, 42% of the oldest parents (the male over 20, the female at least 17) were married before delivery. Again, the father's age apparently carried far more weight than the mother's in the decision to marry rapidly (Table A.4).

Among the younger couples particularly, the pattern of delayed marriage or "technical illegitimacy" was quite common. Many couples were unwilling to rush into marriage when one or the other parent was very young. As one adolescent mother explained her situation:

> He wants to get married now but I am afraid so that we will wait until after the baby comes.

And, many couples did defer marriage until after high school graduation or until the father had a steady job and a predictable source of income.

While it may be true, as Bartz and Nye (1970) stated in their study of youthful marriages, that lower-class men are prepared to enter the labor force at a younger age than middle-class youth, it is nonetheless the case that teenagers, particularly those under 18, have a difficult time locating a job that pays enough to support a family. In our sample, only 46% of the males under 18 for whom employment information was available were working full-time when the pregnancy occurred compared to 83% of the men 21 and older.

Marriage was much more likely to occur during the prenatal period if the father held a full-time job. Among the men working full-time 34% married before delivery; the rate of prenatal marriage among the unemployed males was only 4%. Although our information on the employment history of the males was very sketchy, it appeared that the couple was especially likely to marry if the male had been working for a year or more prior to the pregnancy. Unfortunately, we had no information on the earning capacity of the fathers. However, we suspect that income data may prove to be the best predictor of whether or not a wedding takes place shortly after pregnancy.

The effect of employment status on marriage predictability was most pronounced among the older couples. If the couple was young—both father and mother not yet 18—marriage was not likely to occur regardless of whether the male was working or not. Obviously, in such cases, other considerations—maturity, educational goals, and the amount of money provided by the job—entered into the decision to delay marriage. However, among older couples the employment status of the male was an especially important determinant of the timing of marriage. In those cases in which the father was 21 or older,[11] 43% of the young mothers married before delivery when the male was working full-time as compared to only 11% when he was unemployed.

As the father grew older and his employment prospects improved, more of the couples married. This helps to explain why a large number of marriages occurred in the two years following delivery. By this time, a higher proportion of the males were in their late teens or early twenties and many had located a job; the young mothers often had completed their schooling and a number were employed. As we shall see in later chapters, when both parents were working it often was possible to produce a large enough income to establish a viable family unit.

If marriage did not occur in the first two years following the child's birth or shortly thereafter, the relationship between the young mother and the father usually deteriorated. At the three-year follow-up, a number of women who were still single realized that marriage with the child's father was becoming increasingly improbable. The proportion of parental couples still dating had dwindled to 25%. Less than one-fifth thought that there was still a good chance that they would marry the father of the child. Even those who thought that marriage might occur were beginning to have their doubts:

[11] We used father's age only because there was not a sufficient number of cases to take into account the mother's age as well.

> I am waiting for him to say OK. He is still in school and claims he will marry me after he finishes. But I want to get married now . . . it will be seven years this June.

The younger woman was in the most vulnerable position vis-à-vis the father of her child. Only 31% of those 15 or under at conception ultimately married the father of the child compared to 53% of the 17 year olds. Since the younger adolescents were several years away from marriage, they had to endure a rather lengthy period in which the relationship with the child's father was unregulated by any clear set of expectations. Problems—perhaps the same ones that would have occurred had they married—often arose during this time, and many came to realize that the relationship was not going to survive.

The boyfriends of the younger women more often were school dropouts and were less likely to find steady jobs than the other fathers. While some of them went on to complete school and get jobs after the child was born, most did not. When the adolescent mothers were asked in the third interview why they had not married, a common explanation was that the father of the child had been unable to support them.

> He and I definitely broke up. He doesn't have enough education. Marriage with him wouldn't work out.

> Because really I found out if he keeps going the way he is now, there will be no future in marriage for us. He is very unsettled in jobs.

Breaking up with the father of the child by no means ended a young mother's chances of marriage. Indeed, most of the women who broke off with the child's father soon began going out with someone else. By the five-year follow-up, more than one-third who had not married the father of their child had married another man. However, women who do not marry the father are at least somewhat disadvantaged in the marriage market. A substantial proportion of the young mothers acknowledged in the Time 4 interview that a woman's chances of ever getting married (to someone other than her child's father) are jeopardized if she has an out-of-wedlock child. And, as we shall see in subsequent chapters, the women who do wed other males experience more problems in their marriages.

## SOCIAL PRESSURE TO MARRY

Age, career plans, and evaluation of the father's earning prospects were sometimes outweighed by an even more pressing consideration. A certain number of the adolescents in our study felt acutely embarrassed by their pregnancies and considered themselves to be morally compromised as long as they remained single. The rational concerns of future security were far less significant than the immediate danger of what they regarded as a "spoiled identity" (see Goffman, 1963). In contrast to their peers, whose adverse reactions to becoming pregnant were based more on practical considerations, these women could less easily afford to defer marriage until after delivery.

The moral response to premarital pregnancy has received a good deal of attention in previous discussions of unwed parenthood. Harold Christensen (1953 and 1960) demonstrated that the timing of marriage preceded by a pregnancy is strongly related to the general climate of acceptance of premarital sex within a culture. Bowerman and his colleagues (1966:124) offered a similar explanation to account for differences in the rates of marriage in North Carolina between black and white couples who had experienced a premarital pregnancy. Taking note of the fact that white couples more often married before delivery, the researchers concluded that there was "more pressure on white men and women to avoid the stigma of illegitimate birth, from both self-imposed pressures and external social pressures."[12] But this argument is sometimes applied too glibly to explain racial differences in rates of illegitimacy. From the evidence that blacks are substantially more permissive in their sexual attitudes and have higher rates of illegitimacy, some writers have concluded that out-of-wedlock pregnancies are treated with great casualness and that little or no pressure exists in the black ghetto to confine childbearing to marital unions.[13] This particular conclusion seems to be an unwarranted extension of Christensen's original hypothesis. The argument that normative climate affects timing of marriage is certainly plausible, although the evidence that Christensen and Bowerman and his collaborators offered was based exclusively on macrosociological patterns. Specifically, they have shown that marital patterns after conception are related to general sexual standards within a society or subculture but they have not established that within those aggregates the individuals who are most permissive tend to delay marriage longest. A more conclusive test of this hypothesis requires that the relationship hold for individuals as well as for aggregates. The Baltimore data provide a chance to test this assumption.

Several indicators were available from the first interviews with the adolescent and her mother to gauge the acceptability of premarital sex within the family. It might be expected that prior occurrence of illegitimacy in the family would lessen the pressure to marry rapidly (Graves, 1972). After all, mothers could not display too much moral outrage if they themselves or other close relatives had previously given birth to a child out of wedlock. As one parent put it, "Everybody is entitled to one mistake. I did it myself." Although their reports indicated that the teenagers' mothers were not less upset about the pregnancy in families in which an illegitimacy had already occurred, there may

[12] See also Pope's (1969) extension of this argument and the preliminary study by Graves (1972).

[13] Consider, for example, the following quotation from an early study by Lee Rainwater: "For girls in the Negro slum, pregnancy before marriage is expected in much the same way that parents expect their children to catch mumps or chicken pox. If they are lucky it will not happen, but if it happens people are not too surprised and everyone knows what to do about it" (1966:186).

be fewer moral recriminations in these families once the pregnancy is discovered. Therefore, consistent with our expectation, we did find that rapid marriage occurred less often in families in which there was a history of illegitimacy. It seemed not to matter whether the out-of-wedlock birth had occurred to the pregnant adolescent's mother or to someone else in the family (an aunt, a sibling, or a cousin); a smaller proportion of adolescents whose families had had such an experience married before delivery (13% versus 34%).

However, a history of illegitimacy in the family had almost no effect on the young mother's ultimate decision to marry within the study period. About three-fifths of the women married within the five-year period regardless of any prior experience with illegitimacy. This finding is important because it suggests that there is little or no tendency toward a permanent pattern of illegitimacy. Instead, it seems that women who do experience less family pressure to marry immediately can more easily allow other considerations to enter into the decision of when to wed.

It is not necessary to rely exclusively on an indirect measure of the climate of permissiveness within the family. Both the adolescents who were still single at the Time 1 interview and their mothers were asked about attitudes toward premarital sexual relations. Among both mothers and daughters, restrictive attitudes were associated with a pattern of precipitate marriage. This finding showed up despite the fact that the adolescents from what were undoubtedly the most restrictive families were not included because they had already married before the first interview took place and hence were not asked about their premarital sexual attitudes. The relationship between restrictive attitudes toward premarital sex and hasty marriage was more pronounced among the parents, suggesting that the presence or absence of family pressure may be a decisive factor in the adolescent's decision to marry. When mother's and daughter's standards were examined simultaneously, their effect in combination was especially noteworthy. Only 4% of the daughters who had highly permissive standards themselves and whose parents shared their tolerant views married in the period between the first interview and delivery. By contrast, 17% of the most restrictive group wed during this time (Table A.5). Had we been able to take into account the women already married by Time 1, no doubt the contrast would have been even more striking.

Unlike patterns of illegitimacy, sexual standards in the family had a persistent effect on the marriage rates. Women with permissive standards had lower rates of marriage over the five-year period of the study. At the very least, this finding indicated that these young mothers were indifferent about the timing of marriage; a more extreme interpretation was that they were permanently estranged from marriage. The former explanation seems the more likely since the great majority of those women whose sexual standards were most permissive expressed at both Time 1 and Time 4 an intention to marry. Evidently they were prepared to wait to marry until their circumstances improved or were unwilling to be hurried into marriage merely because they had had a child out of wedlock.

Although paucity of whites in our sample makes generalizations hazardous, the white adolescents followed a predictable pattern. Far fewer reported a history of illegitimacy in their families, and almost without exception the mothers held restrictive standards. Accordingly, we expected and did in fact find that most of the whites married before delivery. Whereas only 16% of the blacks had precipitate marriages, over 70% of the whites married before delivery. Thus, it would appear that Bowerman and his collaborators were (1966) correct in assuming that one reason for the higher rate of illegitimacy among blacks is that the external pressure to marry following a premarital conception is lower than is generally the case for whites.

This sharp racial difference raises the question of whether the findings regarding social pressure and marriage patterns apply to both blacks and whites. It is not possible to test this proposition adequately for whites because so few in our sample appeared to have overtly permissive standards. However, removing the whites from the sample did not significantly change the relationships reported. When only blacks were considered, we still found that precipitate marriages occurred more often among respondents whose families had less experience with illegitimacy and whose standards about premarital sex were more restrictive. Controlling for standards regarding the acceptability of premarital sex reduced the differences between blacks and whites in the proportion who married before the child was born, but a substantial disparity between the two racial groupings still remained.

Some of this residual difference might be due to other unmeasured social pressures such as differences in peer group reactions to premarital pregnancy. Much of the difference that remained undoubtedly could be explained by the social and economic factors discussed earlier in this chapter. Whites in the sample tended to be older and more often were dating an older male. Furthermore in general it has been found that whites who become pregnant are less ambitious in their educational goals and more willing to abandon future plans if they can marry. Finally, whites have more reason to feel sanguine if they do marry: white males have better prospects of finding work and achieving some measure of economic security in the future since they are not confronted with the barriers of discrimination that black males face.

## SUMMARY

The large racial differences in marriage patterns seem to result from the aggregate effect of four factors that were identified in this chapter as determining the likelihood that the premarital conception would be legitimized prior to the birth of the child: (1) younger women in the sample rarely married before delivery; (2) marriage generally occurred when the couple was old enough to have realized their minimal educational goals or was willing to sacrifice these goals in order to marry; (3) generally, marriage did not occur unless the male had a job and until the female could gain some employment experience; and (4) women under strong pressure to marry so as to avoid social embarrassment were generally more willing to forego the advantages of deferring marriage.

We came to the conclusion that most of the women in this study, and in particular blacks, were unusually sensitive to the hazards of marriage, no doubt through familiarity with the experiences of family and friends. Many deemed it essential to defer marriage in order to become economically self-reliant since they foresaw a likelihood that they would be called upon to share or perhaps assume the full responsibility of providing for their families. These findings contradict the views of certain commentators who have suggested that the high rate of illegitimacy among lower-income black women is related to their present-orientation and their inability to anticipate the future (Banfield, 1970). We found little evidence that these traits explain the occurrence of unwed parent-hood among the young women in our study. To the contrary, there is some reason to believe that a certain amount of illegitimacy occurs precisely *because* black women are so conscious of their future. Knowing that marriage is prob-lematic at best they wait to wed, hoping that their chances of establishing a successful marital relationship will improve in time. In this regard, what Eliot Liebow (1967:64-65) learned about the men on Tally's Corner is true for many of the women in our study as well:

> But from the inside looking out, what appears as a "present-time" orienta-tion to the outside observer is, to the man experiencing it, as much a future orientation as that of his middle-class counterpart. The difference between the two men lies not so much in their different orientations to time as in their different orientations to future time or, more specifically, to their different futures.

# 5. Conjugal Careers

DESPITE THEIR RESOLUTION to move into marriage cautiously, most young mothers found it difficult to resist matrimony for very long. After a year or two of protracted courtship negotiations, many women simply decided that it was time to "give it a try." Some had begun to realize that their situations were not going to improve materially by delaying any longer. If their boyfriends offered them little security now, it was not certain how much more could be provided in the future, or whether their prospects would be enhanced if they elected to break off the relationship. One young mother, in describing her decision to marry, summed up this sense of resignation:

> My husband he said we love each other, we have [the child], we will get married anyway, [so] it might as well be now, and I loved him.

Carol Stack (1974:108) has observed that wedlock is a wager that most low-income blacks make despite the near certainty that they cannot win. As she so aptly put it:

> The emptiness and hopelessness of the job experience for the black men and women, the control over meager (AFDC) resources by women, and the security of the kin network militate against successful marriage. . . . Women and men nonetheless begin buoyant new relationships with one another and fall in love, as all races and classes do. But they must wager their relationships against the insurmountable forces of poverty and racism.

Most of the young mothers in our study fully recognized the problems in store for them. Still, they held out the hope that they might somehow be exceptions. Although, as we shall soon see, their chances for success were miniscule, it is not so surprising that they were willing to assume the risks, given their problematic and often deteriorating economic situations.

This chapter discusses the process of disenchantment that occurs in the early years of marriage. The question we shall consider is to what extent marital instability can be traced to the occurrence of the unscheduled conception. For the women in our study and for other women like them, it might be said that marital dissolution is overdetermined. There are so many hazards associated with

81

matrimony that most women escape some perils only to confront others. To appreciate the special circumstances of the adolescent mother, it makes sense to begin with a brief review of research on prenuptial pregnancy and its impact on marriage. This survey of the literature in turn will serve as an introduction to the analysis of the marital career of the adolescent mother.

## RESEARCH ON PREMARITAL PREGNANCY AND MARITAL INSTABILITY

Beginning with Harold Christensen's (1953, 1960, 1963) pioneering examination of how the timing of the first birth affects the stability of subsequent marriage, a series of studies have shown consistently that premarital pregnancy greatly increases the probability of eventual marital dissolution (Monahan, 1960; Lowrie, 1965). By linking records of marriages, births, and divorces, Christensen was able to show that couples who had experienced a premarital conception were more than twice as likely to divorce within the first five years of marriage. In a more recent longitudinal study of marital dissolution, Coombs and Zumeta (1970) also discovered a strong association between premarital pregnancy and marital breakup. Of the women who had conceived premaritally 41% were no longer living with their husbands five years later compared to 18% of those who had not conceived prior to marriage. Several other studies focusing on the effects of illegitimate births on marital stability also reported a high incidence of dissolution.[1]

Although existing studies have been able to connect premarital pregnancy and marital instability, researchers have not as yet explained why these two phenomena are linked. A number of explanations have been advanced as to why pregnancy before marriage might adversely affect the prospects for a stable union. Our discussion will focus on four explanations that will be examined empirically later in the chapter.

1. Some investigators have assumed that one reason for the association is that individuals who conceive premaritally are distinctive in their personalities and/or their cultural values (Vincent, 1961; Paulker, 1969). The same set of personal or cultural factors that may predispose certain women to become premaritally pregnant is also thought to reduce their chances of achieving a stable marriage. In other words, marriages preceded by a pregnancy do not survive because the individuals entering such relationships are less capable of, or committed to, creating a successful union (Chilman, 1966).

2. It has been hypothesized that a premarital pregnancy may cut short the process of preparing for married life. Christensen (1960:38) speculated that

[1]Sarrel (1967), in a small retrospective study of black adolescents who became pregnant before wedlock, reported that within a five-year period, three-fourths of the marriages were no longer intact. Sauber and Corrigan (1970) carried out a larger study with a more diverse sample that traced the marital careers of unwed mothers in New York City. At the six-year follow-up, half of those who had married during the study period no longer lived with their husbands.

marriages of pregnant women often occur "without adequate preparation, or in the absence of love, or in the face of ill-matched personalities." Couples who marry precipitately may not be ready to settle down, may have reservations about the suitability of their mates, and may be unwilling or unable to assume the responsibilities of married life (Havighurst, 1961). Compounding their own uncertainties are the frequently voiced doubts of their families. If they do not encounter outright opposition, the husband and wife often lack the kinship support generally provided at the time of marriage (Winch and Greer, 1964) and may lose the assistance that would be provided by kin if they remained single (Stack, 1974).

3. The third explanation considers the economic costs resulting from a premature marriage. Such a marriage often begins without the benefit of accumulated savings, and since the partners typically are young, the problems of making an adequate livelihood are severe. Not only is the male restricted in his occupational opportunities, but the female often is unable to contribute to the family income because of child care responsibilities. Moreover, the couple faces the added expenses of raising a child, which from the outset places an extra burden on the wage earners (Schorr, 1965; Coombs et al., 1970). It might also be expected that early marriage would restrict the occupational mobility of both parents since they often must begin working before completing educational or vocational training which might have improved their job prospects (Rapaport, 1964). Furthermore, their ability to change jobs is limited by the greater family responsibilities they must meet in the early years of marriage.

4. Finally, another potential source of strain in conjugal relations is the accelerated family building that frequently accompanies a marriage preceded by a pregnancy. It has been suggested that the abrupt introduction of a child into the family hinders the growth of conjugal solidarity (Pohlman, 1969). The child can become an object of jealousy and competition if husband and wife are not confident of their relationship. Attention and energy inevitably are withdrawn from the marriage and invested in the child, and this sometimes results in resentment and hostility. Marital relations may be complicated further by a rapid succession of additional pregnancies. The husband in particular may begin to feel trapped by the accumulating economic and emotional responsibilities. The wife may resent the heavy burden of child care and have little energy to invest in her marriage.

Clearly, none of these problems—personal instability, lack of preparation for marriage, insufficiency of economic resources, or pressures from rapid family building—is peculiar to those who enter matrimony as a result of pregnancy. All have been identified as common problems in blue-collar marriages (Komarovsky, 1964; Chilman, 1966) and probably hold true for many middle-class marriages as well. It is obvious, however, that premarital pregnancy, particularly at an early age, aggravates each of these problems and thus compounds the already considerable probability of marital difficulties. Without empirical investigation, however, it is difficult to say whether any or all of these reasons are responsible for the association between premarital pregnancy and conjugal instability. The following analysis is an attempt to resolve this question.

## MARITAL EXPECTATIONS

The women in our study did not need to consult the research literature to realize that the prognosis for a happy married life was poor. As we have already said, most entered marriage with limited hopes and considerable doubts. Unfortunately, their hopes usually remained unrealized and their doubts were confirmed.

The young mothers' conceptions of what constitutes a successful marriage were remarkably modest. Their idea of the basis for a good marriage could be summed up in a single word that was voiced over and over again in the interviews—"security." For some this word simply meant a steady source of economic support, but for most it suggested something more: someone they could count on to share the responsibilities of establishing a household and the obligations of raising a family.

> I think I was luckier than a lot of 'em was. Well, he was a good provider, he valued his marriage. If he said he was goin' to do somethin' he did it.

The preoccupation with security does not imply that the participants in the study placed a low value on emotional compatibility or companionship. However, most lower-class women simply cannot take it for granted, as do women in the middle class, that they will be adequately provided for economically after they marry. Therefore, the feature of marriage that they value most is the one they regard as the most problematic. Emotional gratification is a luxury that many of the young mothers did not dare to demand or expect.

Although the young mothers' aspirations for marriage were limited to begin with, after pregnancy they become scaled down even further. At the time of the first interview, more than half were certain that their marriage prospects would not be adversely affected by the pregnancy. Fewer than one in four were so sanguine by the time of the last follow-up. The erosion of confidence occurred among the women who married as well as among those who remained single throughout the study. Significantly, their experiences did not substantially undermine their belief in the desirability of marriage. Less than one-fourth thought that most women would be better off if they never got married. Apparently, while the odds for a successful marriage were not perceived to be favorable, most women in our study felt that it is nonetheless worth the risk (cf. Ladner, 1971).

## PATTERNS OF CONJUGAL INSTABILITY

How did the forecasts of marital success jibe with the actual experiences of the women who married during the course of the study? Since marriage occurred at different points in the period from 1960 to 1972, the proportion of marriages that was still intact at Time 4 was not a very useful figure for it did not take into account the fact that risk of marital dissolution varies with the length of exposure to marriage. Therefore, a comparison of the proportion of unstable marriages among the adolescent mothers with that of their classmates would be misleading since the latter on the average married two to three years later and thus had less opportunity to separate during the study period. By performing a life-table analysis we adjusted for these limitations by calculating the probability of separation at standard intervals from the point at which the marriage took place.

Table 5.1 shows the "mortality" of marriages among the sample of the young mothers and their classmates. The low expectations of marital success expressed by the adolescents were amply justified by their own later experiences. Marriages that took place during the study had less than an even chance of surviving beyond the first few years. Using probability figures, we found that about one-fifth of the marriages broke up in one year and nearly one-third were dissolved within two years. By four years, fewer than half of the couples were still together. The rate of separation slowed down thereafter, though the numbers on which the estimates were based are so small that the figures become less reliable. Assuming their validity, we learn that three out of five of the marriages will break up within six years.

By any standard, these rates are incredibly high. Carter and Glick (1970, ch. 8) reported that in a population of white women married for at least 10 years by 1960, about 13% of the marriages had dissolved; the figure for nonwhites, 28%, was high but still less than half the rate for adolescent mothers in our sample. Although these data were based on the marital experiences of a different cohort, it is still interesting to note that nonwhite women do not begin to approach the rate of marital instability experienced by the young mothers in our study even after 25 years of marriage.

Table 5.1. *Cumulative Probability of Separation by Timing of Marriage among Adolescent Mothers and Classmates*

| Months from Marriage Date | Adolescent Mothers (231) | Classmates (94) | Classmates Who Were Premaritally Pregnant[1] (40) | Classmates Who Were Not Premaritally Pregnant[1] (40) |
|---|---|---|---|---|
| 12 | .20 | .09 | .13 | .08 |
| 24 | .32 | .17 | .23 | .16 |
| 36 | .44 | .25 | .30 | .24 |
| 48 | .51 | .30 | * | * |
| 60 | .56 | * | * | * |
| 72 | .60 | * | * | * |

*Probability not reported when base is under 10.

[1]Determined only for women interviewed at Time 4 (excludes women who were interviewed at Time 3 but not Time 4).

The classmates provide another basis for comparison. Although the rate of marital breakup among these peers was not low, it was still only half as great as the rate for the adolescent mothers during the first 3.5 years of marriage. Beyond that point, the classmate cases dropped off to the point at which comparisons become unreliable, but the pattern of differences continued. By two years after marrying, the mothers had already experienced a higher proportion of marital dissolution than the classmates after four years of marriage. When the cases of the classmates who married after conception were separated out, the differences were even more striking. Among the women who had not conceived premaritally, the probability of the marriage breaking up within the two years was less than half that calculated for the adolescent mothers (Table 5.1). The figures for these women were similar to those cited earlier on black women in the general population. Finally, the extent of marital instability among the classmates who married after becoming pregnant was noticeably higher, though it still was lower than the rate for the young mothers. Apparently, the mothers were especially disadvantaged in marriage because their pregnancies occurred earlier in adolescence than those of the classmates, raising the possibility—which we shall consider later—that marrying young itself reduces the chances of conjugal stability.

It is interesting to consider whether the young mothers were able to improve their chances of marital success by delaying matrimony. In the previous chapter, we learned that many women believed that they would lessen the probability of failure if they waited to wed. The results of our analysis suggest otherwise: the strategy of deferred marriage, if anything, boomerangs. Marriages that occurred before the child was born had the best probability of survival.

This finding does not take into account the fact that women who marry prenatally almost invariably wed the father of their child. Since nuptial stability, as we shall see later, is greater when the parents of the child marry, we had to examine separately the patterns of cohesion for women who married the child's father and for those who did not. This control did not change the overall results. Young mothers who married before delivery had by far the best chance of remaining married even when compared to those women who wed the child's father postnatally (Table A.6).

## SOURCES OF INSTABILITY

In the introductory section, we briefly reviewed four ways of explaining why couples that experience a premarital pregnancy have a high rate of marital instability. We shall now see how well each explanation accounts for the high rate of separation among the young mothers who married during the course of the study.

## Individual Predisposition

The first interpretation holds that women who become pregnant before they wed have greater difficulty staying married because personal or cultural attributes that make people prone to prenuptial pregnancy may also make them prone to marital instability. In other words, females who become pregnant during adolescence may be predisposed by culture or character to fail in marriage (Cavan, 1964).

With the data at hand, it is difficult to rule out this interpretation completely. Nevertheless, it appears highly implausible to us. Many of the young mothers in our sample were from broken families and therefore presumably more prone to divorce and separation. Two recent studies (Heiss, 1972; Duncan and Duncan, 1969) failed to find an intergenerational correlation of marital instability, though findings reported by Pope and Mueller (1976) suggest that the matter is not yet settled. Our data revealed no tendency for marital instability to be contagious. Young mothers from broken families were not more likely to separate during the study than those from intact families. The possibility that a history of illegitimacy in the family may have created a predisposition to marital instability, by weakening the commitment to marriage, also was examined. The probability of separation was almost the same for young mothers who did and for those who did not have a family history of illegitimacy. Finally, several indicators of the socioeconomic status of their families were found to be unrelated to durability of marriage, which suggests that women from especially impoverished backgrounds are not less able to assume the responsibilities of marriage. Thus, it would seem that the high probability of conjugal dissolution among the young mothers who married cannot be explained by the fact that many grew up in families that were structurally variant or economically disadvantaged.

If the predisposition for marital instability were transmitted culturally, then we would have found that women whose marriages break up hold distinctive standards and expectations regarding matrimony. At the five-year follow-up, the separated women did indeed express slightly less confidence in the desirability of marriage, but this sentiment seemed to be a consequence rather than a cause of marital unhappiness. Women in marriages that broke up were no less likely to have voiced confidence in the institution of marriage at the time of the first interview; they were equally inclined to state their desires and intentions to marry at Time 1. Thus, the tendency on the part of some women in our study to discount their prospects of success before they ever wed apparently had little influence on the outcome of their marriages. Moreover, in the final interview, there was no difference between the married and separated women in their opinions about the sources of marital strain, definitions of the proper division of labor within the family, or the decision-making authority of husband and wife (Furstenberg, 1975). Even after the dissolution of their marriages, the separated women voiced attitudes about matrimony similar to those of their married counterparts.

Examination of results obtained from the classmates on the same set of questions further confirms the conclusion that the separated women did not hold a "deviant" set of sentiments about marriage. The classmates' responses to the various attitudinal measures mentioned above closely resembled the positions taken by both the separated and the married young mothers. There were no sizable differences between the subgroups. It seems implausible, then, that the higher level of marital instability is a consequence of a distinctive cultural code transmitted by the family during childhood.

## Preparation for Marriage

### Age at Marriage

Previous studies have shown that age at marriage is a powerful determinant of the stability of the union (Burchinal, 1965; Lowrie, 1965; Bumpass and Sweet, 1972). As we learned in the previous chapter, the mothers were aware of the disadvantages of marrying at a young age. Most felt that a woman should be at least 20 before she married, and although the question was not posed, we could safely assume that they thought males should marry even later. Few of the couples timed their marriages to conform to these ideals, but some managed to defer marriage longer than others. Consequently, we had an opportunity to see whether age at marriage was related to stability during the study period.

Contrary to expectation, age at marriage was not consistently related to nuptial stability. The unions of mothers who married before age 17 were slightly less stable, but the differences were not statistically significant. The association between age at marriage and conjugal stability actually was curvilinear; the oldest age group (women 18 and over) achieved the least success in marriage. Introducing the marriage age of the males did not help, and even when the age at marriage of both partners was examined simultaneously, no consistent patterns appeared.

In part, these findings are another reflection of the result reported earlier that deferred marriages have a lower probability of survival than do precipitate unions. Since couples who postpone marriage are likely to be older when they wed, the effects of age at marriage may not be visible. However, holding constant the timing of the marriage and the status of the husband does not increase the significance of age. It would seem, then, that age at marriage is not related to marital success, at least during the early years of wedlock.

This unexpected finding perhaps resulted from the characteristics of the women in this sample. If a great number of couples had waited until their early twenties to marry, perhaps the contrast by age would have yielded different results. Yet, there is reason to doubt this possibility. Couples in the sample who waited several years before marrying were not more, but less, successful in maintaining their marriages. Moreover, data from census records indicate that marriage age for nonwhites does not have the same impact on stability as it does for whites: while for white females marital stability is consistently lower for women who marry before the age of 18, this is not the case for nonwhites. Regardless of their age at marriage, nonwhite females have about the same chance of experiencing a divorce (Carter and Glick, 1970).

One reason for this difference may be that among blacks, younger couples tend to marry only when their economic prospects are reasonably bright or at least when they are probably no worse off financially than their older peers. Hence the correlation between age at marriage and outcome might have been obscured within our sample. It would appear that age, at least among the participants in this study, is not a very reliable indicator of how adequately prepared couples are to assume the responsibilities of setting up a household. Consequently, we found it necessary to consider other more direct signs of readiness for marriage such as family support and courtship experience.

### Family Support

A few investigators have suggested that early marriage is perilous in part because such unions are not accorded legitimacy and supported by kin (Winch and Greer, 1964; Burchinal, 1965). The information collected on kin support for the marriages in our study is extremely sketchy. In the first interview, a number of adolescents mentioned that their parents were unenthusiastic about the prospect of their marrying or had expressed doubts about their boyfriend's character. Their comments seemed to fit Stack's (1974) observation that marriage may be resented by parents because it pulls their child out of an intimate and mutually supportive domestic network. Nevertheless, no relationship existed between the reported attitudes of the mothers of the adolescents toward marriage and the success of subsequent conjugal careers. Furthermore, none of a large number of items used in the first interview to measure parent-child relations and family supportiveness was associated with conjugal stability. Couples living with their in-laws at the outset of marriage had about the same probability of staying together as those living in separate households. Admittedly, this analysis constitutes a rather limited test of the hypothesis that kin disapproval undermines marital cohesion, but our preliminary findings suggest that lack of familial support does not appear to be a conspicuous reason for the high rate of marital dissolution in this population.

### Courtship Experience

The prenuptial relationship of marriage partners has been a widely accepted indication of the couple's prospects of marital success. Textbooks on marriage and the family sometimes stress courtship as an important stage in preparation for marriage (Winch, 1971; Moss et al., 1971). The courtship period is a filtering process as well as an opportunity for the couple to explore and to negotiate future patterns of marital interaction. Ambivalence and uncertainty, while not completely laid to rest, usually are lessened by sustained contact before marriage. Indeed, previous studies have demonstrated that brief courtships are generally associated with higher conjugal instability (Locke, 1951; Burchinal, 1960).

A premarital pregnancy generally cuts short this period of what Willard Waller (1938:268) referred to as a "mutual exposure to the possibilities of involvement." In Chapter 4, we showed that most of the young mothers who married before or shortly after delivery would not have done so had they not been pregnant. We expected two consequences to follow. First, since the normal process of socialization to marriage was interrupted, we thought that postmarital adjustment would be that much more difficult. In precipitate marriages, couples have but meager knowledge of one another and unclear marital expectations. Second, the pressure to marry may be followed by resentment in the early years of wedlock. Not having had time to resolve ambivalences, the couple's doubts about the wisdom of the marriage may quickly surface. This is evident in the retrospective comments of the young mothers on why they married when they did:

> Well, I was pregnant. He said he loved me and I thought I loved him. I figured it looks bad when you have children and don't marry.

> Just a foolish love, young love, childish love. Neither one of us were ready.

Several findings suggest that certain couples were indeed psychologically unprepared for marriage and therefore experienced marital problems. An index was developed to measure the couple's relationship prior to marriage. Items included the amount of time the partners had known one another before marriage, how frequently they had been dating, and whether the mother had been seeing other men in addition to her future husband. Low interaction prior to marriage clearly was associated with marital failure. The rate of separation was about half as high for women who had had frequent and intensive contact with their future husband for at least a year before marriage (Table A.7).

Another indication that the premarital relationship affects marital cohesion came from an analysis of patterns of sexual activity before marriage. Women who reported having had sexual relations with more than one partner during the period just prior to becoming pregnant were far less likely to achieve stable unions than women who had had exclusive sexual relationships. A woman in this category was perhaps less committed to the man she eventually married and hence more likely to encounter subsequent marital problems (Table A.8).

These findings fit into a larger configuration of results having to do with the strength of the prenuptial bond. Earlier it was reported that women who wed the father of their first child achieved more stable unions. Now it is possible to explain why. These spouses generally had a much stronger premarital tie than couples in which the husband was not the child's father. We have designated these relationships as *developed* because almost without exception the marital partners had been involved in a long-standing and exclusive alliance. By contrast, some women entered into *extemporaneous* unions with other men based on relationships formed hastily after their child was born. Some of these relationships commenced shortly after the young mother broke up with her child's father. The extemporaneous relationship is similar in some respects to the "rebound relationship" experienced by young divorcees (Hunt, 1966).

Having a child takes on a very different meaning in these two types of unions. Among couples with a developed relationship, the child reinforces the conjugal bond, serving as a common interest and focus of attention and as such constitutes a constraint against marital dissolution. The effect of the child can be just the opposite within the extemporaneous union, in which he or she serves as a divisive force, an ever present reminder that the origins of the relationship are recent and not exclusive. In a certain sense these marital dyads are in fact triads, consisting of husband, wife, and father of the child.[2]

Although the history of a relationship has a definite impact on its outcome, it is not sufficient to account for the high rate of marital instability within the sample of young mothers. Three out of four women who wed during the study married the father of the child. In any case, brief courtship was more the exception than the rule. Most relationships had all the features of a developed courtship—they were long-standing, exclusive, and intimate. Thus, we could not assume that most couples were totally unprepared emotionally for marriage.

There is another reason to doubt that courtship relations can entirely explain the high rate of conjugal instability. When the courtship histories of the classmates were examined, we found that they closely resembled those of the young mothers. Since the classmates experienced much greater marital stability, it does not seem likely that the courtship pattern alone accounts for differences between the two samples.

### Economic Resources and Marital Stability

Although researchers disagree about why it is so, almost all existing studies show that economic resources are strongly linked to marital stability (Scanzoni, 1970; Cutright, 1971c; Furstenberg, 1974b). Economic resources matter even more for blacks than for whites. Not only do black males face limited employment opportunities, restricted occupational mobility, and unfair compensation rates, but they sometimes must face the fact that their wives are more employable than they are. Black women often take jobs that their husbands, and society at large, deem unacceptable. The willingness of black women to work at menial jobs that are poorly paid, dirty, and irregular creates a double problem in the

[2]This finding helps to explain why age was not related strongly to marital success. Those younger couples who married were especially likely to have relationships that were developed rather than extemporaneous.

family. On the one hand, the husband feels that his role as provider is being undercut; his wife, at the same time, is likely to resent his unwillingness to support the family (Rainwater, 1970).

There is every reason to suspect that this situation was common within our sample. Most married men possessed none of the qualities that might have overcome the considerable obstacles black men face in finding decent jobs. The husbands tended to be young, inexperienced, and unskilled. Predictably, economic difficulties were high on the list of reasons offered by the mothers as to why their marriages did not work out. More than one out of every four women explicitly attributed the failure of her marriage to her husband's inability to support his family. A close reading of other responses coded as "personal incompatibility" revealed that many women were inclined to redefine lack of economic success as a shortcoming in the husband's personality.

The impact of economic insufficiency on marriage could be examined directly by considering the relationship between a male's earning capacity and the chance that his marriage would survive. As a rough measure of their earning potential, two status categories were established for the husbands. Men were classified as lower-status if they had not completed high school and held an unskilled job. High school graduates and/or skilled workers were classified as higher status. Although these groupings might be crude, this index turned out to be the single best predictor of marital stability. Among the lower-status males, the probability of separation within two years of the wedding date was .45, while it was only .19 for the men who were classified as higher status. The relative difference between the two groups was maintained throughout the study period. Although the estimates became less reliable after three years, there was a difference of about .30 at years four and five.

This finding strongly suggests that the most important link in the chain between an unplanned pregnancy and later marital failure is the weak economic position of the male who fathers a child out of wedlock or marries a single mother. Most of these men have a low earning potential before they ever wed. An ill-timed marriage may further limit their prospects for economic advancement by compelling them to terminate school and enter the labor force under less than favorable circumstances. Consequently, the fathers of unscheduled children are hard pressed to find stable and well-paying jobs.[3]

How much would the fathers in our study have profited if they had been able to postpone the pregnancy and the ensuing marriage is not easily answered by the data at hand, but at least one study of white couples has shown that early unplanned parenthood has an adverse effect on a man's earning capacity over an extended period (Freedman and Coombs, 1970). The effect of a premarital

[3]Most of the fathers interviewed at Time 3 were unemployed (17%) or working at unskilled factory or service jobs (60%). Less than half were making more than $3 an hour, and some of these males reported that they were not regularly employed. Considering that the men we interviewed were on the whole better off than the total sample of fathers, it was evident that even three years after delivery of the first child, many fathers were not in a strong position to support a family.

pregnancy may be even more severe for black men, who have less flexibility to recover from a financial drain at the outset of marriage.

One way of putting this speculation to the test is to examine the economic status of the men who married the classmates, comparing them to the spouses of the young mothers. There was a noticeable difference in status level between the two groups of men, especially after we separated out the couples who married after a premarital pregnancy. Half the husbands of the young mothers were in the higher socioeconomic category as compared to three-fifths of the spouses of the premaritally pregnant classmates and 85% of the husbands of those class-mates who married before becoming pregnant. Furthermore, it should be noted that the findings probably understate the differences between the samples because we excluded cases in which information was lacking on the husband. Since those husbands whose whereabouts were unknown to the young mothers were primarily lower status, the disparity would have been much greater if the missing mates had been included.

Many of the young mothers shared responsibility for supporting their family, and therefore it is important to consider the impact of their status on the stability of the marriage. Again using the same socioeconomic index to measure the earning capacity of females, we discovered that marriages of higher-status women also tended to be more stable. However, much of this association was accounted for by the fact that individuals of higher status tended to marry one another. A simultaneous examination of the status of the husband and wife revealed that marital cohesion was more strongly related to the economic success of the male than to that of the female, although their economic well-being as a whole contributed to conjugal stability (Furstenberg, 1975).

In a previous paper, I have shown that men who hold lower-status jobs, or what some economists refer to as "secondary positions," command less marital loyalty primarily because they offer less long-term financial security. Not only is the current economic contribution of the secondary worker unacceptably low, but his prospects for improvement are poor, if not nonexistent (Gordon, 1972). Conspicuously absent in the case of the lower-class male is an economic career, a progressive sequence of positions in the direction of higher earnings and greater job security. In his own eyes and in the eyes of his spouse, the lower-class male is a poor investment. Probably for this reason, a high rate of marital instability occurs among men holding secondary jobs.

Although the study provides only a brief time span in which to trace patterns of social mobility, there is more than a strong hint that material stability is tied to economic advancement. The small group of males who improved their economic status during the course of the study had a noticeably higher rate of marital stability than men whose status declined or remained low during the period between the early and later follow-ups (65% versus 40%).

Thus, the success of a marriage depends on a complex matrix that shifts with the economic fortunes of both partners. Stress on the marriage fluctuates in response to both the accumulation and the distribution of economic resources.

Clearly, other factors as well enter into the decision to remain together. As we noted earlier, most young mothers reported that personal incompatibility was the major reason their marriages broke up. However, personal differences are necessarily evaluated with less tolerance when economic resources are low. There is simply less reason to maintain a problematic relationship when the female is not dependent on the male for support. For this reason, unions in which the woman's earning capacity is greater than her husband's have low rates of survival.

Under certain circumstances, men may assume other family functions and thus compensate for low earning capacity. Although the proposition could not be tested with the data at hand, there is reason to believe from other studies that lower-class families have a limited capacity to reallocate family responsibilities. Traditional notions of "man's work" and "woman's work" are likely to present barriers to innovation in the marital division of labor. Although women often share in the responsibility for supporting the family, lower-class men are frequently reluctant to assume domestic and child care responsibilities (Komarovsky, 1964; Bott, 1971). Moreover, if studies from the Depression serve as any guide, men are especially unwilling to do so when they are not performing in their primary role as provider (Cavan, 1959).

### Accelerated Family Building

Apart from the impact that an unplanned pregnancy has on the earning prospects of the male, it also increases the economic strain on the family in other ways. Although there is not complete agreement in the literature, a number of studies have reported that frequent childbearing is related to marital instability (Rainwater, 1960; Pohlman, 1969; Coombs et al., 1970; Hurley and Palonen, 1967). It is not surprising that this should be so. Accelerated family building means that greater economic resources will be required to support the family. At the same time, the contribution that the wife can make is restricted severely if she is pregnant frequently and must remain at home to care for young children. The male alone must increase the family's income. To the extent that this pressure is a divisive factor in marriage, the timing of the first birth as well as of subsequent pregnancies may be a further cause of marital dissolution.

The relatively brief span of our study precludes a definitive answer to the question of how marital stability is affected by patterns of family building over the long term. Knowing that relatively few women had more than two children by Time 4, we first examined the relationship between total number of pregnancies and conjugal cohesion in order to maximize the number of highly fertile women. This analysis produced no consistent evidence that frequent conceptions early in marriage have an adverse effect on the rate of stability. The incidence of dissolution did not rise even among women with three or more conceptions in the five years. Multigravidous women actually were more likely to remain married than primigravidas, perhaps because marital difficulties might have dissuaded some couples from having additional children (Sweet, 1974). Whatever the reason, very low fertility did not forecast marital success within this population. When we examined patterns of childbearing rather than pregnancy, the same general pattern appeared. Two-child families had the best record of marital success, though differences by parity were miniscule and probably the result of chance variations.

The possibility that spacing of births may be more critical for marital harmony than the number of pregnancies was also considered. From interview data collected at Time 2, we knew that virtually none of the young mothers wanted to become pregnant again for at least two years. Marital strain, therefore, should have been greater when subsequent conceptions occurred during this period. Again, the evidence for the hypothesis is equivocal at best. The marital stability of women who had another pregnancy within 18 months was contrasted with that of women who deferred additional childbearing. This comparison revealed no differences, suggesting that child spacing is not an important determinant of conjugal stability, at least in the short term.

Several reasons might explain why our data failed to show a connection between high fertility and marital instability. First, only a small proportion of women showed extremely high fertility within the duration of the study. Only 28 married women had borne three or more children by the five-year follow-up. Second, mothers with several children were just as likely to be married to higher-status husbands as were women with one or two offspring. Possibly, at least at that point in the couple's marriage, the number of children was more a response to, than a determinant of, economic status. In other words, the five-year follow-up was perhaps too soon to assess the extent to which children created an economic strain on the family because most couples had not had sufficient time to build large families and many of the larger families were better off economically.

Also, the presence of children temporarily may have a cohesive effect on the marriage. If the husband has participated actively in the decision to have children, he may be more reluctant to abandon his family. Similarly, a wife with more children in the early years of marriage is more dependent on her husband and hence less willing to see the marriage break up, even if it is not going well (cf. Figley, 1973; Cohen and Sweet, 1974).

Finally, the presumed negative association between high fertility and marital instability is confounded in another respect. Couples whose marriages are going well may desire additional children, and obviously couples who stay together have a better chance of producing children. Consequently, it is difficult to test the effect of accelerated family building on marital instability, especially in the short run. In order for such a relationship to show up, the negative effect of additional children on marriage would have to be both potent and rapid, which did not seem to be the case in this study.

## SUMMARY

As other studies have shown, our data reveal that couples who married after a pregnancy experience a high rate of marital instability. Approximately three out of five couples separated within five years of their wedding date. This chapter examined four possible explanations for the high rate of marital failure. Two of the hypotheses are supported by the results; two were not.

There was no confirmation of the premise that marital breakdown is the product of a distinctive set of cultural standards held by females who become pregnant premaritally. Individuals who experience conjugal dissolution are no less committed to matrimony at the outset, or predisposed to instability because of family background, or prone to adopt divergent values during marriage. Also refuted was the expectation that rapid family building in the early years of marriage increases the probability of conjugal instability. The number and timing of subsequent births were unrelated to marital breakup during the five-year period of the study. While these two unsupported hypotheses could not be ruled out completely because of limitations of the data, our results at least call into question their general usefulness in explaining the link between premarital pregnancy and marital instability among women like those in our sample.

Our findings provide much more support for the causative argument that premarital pregnancy disrupts the courtship process and cuts short a necessary stage in preparation for marriage. Unions are unlikely to survive unless the couple had a long-standing and exclusive relationship prior to the pregnancy. The marriages that have the best chance of lasting occurred among parental couples who married soon after conception.

The hypothesis most strongly upheld by the data is the economic one. Regardless of the couple's initial stake in the relationship, marriages frequently founder because the man who marries a premaritally pregnant woman is unable to support a family. An ill-timed marriage may serve to erode further the black male's already tenuous position in the labor market. Even in instances in which the scheduling of matrimony is ideal, many black couples begin married life at a disadvantage as a result of racial and economic discrimination. When pregnancy forces a revision of the nuptial schedule, the marriage is seriously jeopardized from the start.

## A POSTSCRIPT ON THE AFTERMATH OF
## MARITAL EXPERIENCE

Since our study spanned only five years in the lives of the young mothers, it is impossible to estimate how many women will be permanently disinclined to marry as a result of their first unsuccessful attempt. However, if our data provide any indication, the proportion may be substantial.

Few of the women whose marriages had ended became divorced. Only one-fifth of the women whose marriages were no longer intact at Time 4 were divorced. Of course, in some instances the interview occurred only a short time after the couple had separated, so that there had not been time to complete the divorce proceedings. However, over half of the young mothers had been separated for two or more years, providing ample time for a formal termination of the marriage. While the proportion of divorces did increase over time, most women remained technically married even after four or more years of separation. Furthermore, the majority of these women showed no inclination to divorce although they no longer considered their marriages to be binding.[4]

There are several reasons for the low incidence of divorce among the sample. The legal procedure can be costly, time-consuming, and emotionally demanding. Since alimony or support payments are not likely to increase as a result of legal proceedings, many women in the sample saw no financial incentive for obtaining a divorce. Finally, unless marriage is contemplated, there is no need to obtain a divorce. Few of the young women had current plans to marry again.

One of the consistent findings of research on divorce is that an unsuccessful marriage does not diminish enthusiasm for the institution of marriage (Goode, 1956; Jacobson, 1959). The data from our study do not fit this generalization. Most of the formerly married young mothers were highly skeptical of their chances for a successful marriage. When asked if a woman is better off if she never marries, nearly half of the separated women answered affirmatively, more than twice the proportion of still married and never married mothers who gave the same reply. Only 10% of the separated women thought that most marriages work out, and over half thought that very few succeed.

Of course, these negative sentiments toward marriage may change over time as the separated women become involved in new relationships. However, there was no visible trend in that direction. Most, in fact, were engaged in new relationships but their views about marriage did not seem to be greatly modified as a result. Moreover, attitudes toward marriage did not appear to become more positive over time. Women who had been separated for three or more years were just as likely to express negative views about marriage as were women whose marriages had broken up recently.

Apart from their attitudes, separated and divorced women like those in our study face certain objective barriers to remarrying (Carter and Glick, 1970). To say that their position in the marriage market is unfavorable is something of an understatement. Most of the adolescent mothers had at least two children by the time their marriages broke up, which presents a formidable challenge to the earning power of potential mates. To add to her difficulties, the young mother usually has limited economic assets to contribute to a new marriage. As we shall

---

[4]According to Maryland law (Clark and Salsburg, 1974), women separated from their husbands for three or more years are eligible to receive a no fault divorce. Nevertheless young mothers often did not take advantage of this option. Apparently, many were willing to remain in a state of conjugal limbo.

see in Chapter 8, the separated woman can find only low-wage employment because of her lack of education and work experience. With several children, she also faces severe obstacles to finding a job that pays enough to make it profitable for her to work. Consequently, the young mother is usually not in a position to share the responsibilities of supporting a "ready-made" family. Respondents in our study often acknowledged that men are reluctant to support children who are not their own. Two-fifths of the separated women admitted that this factor lessened their chance of successful remarriage. Therefore, even when remarriage is openly desired, the previously married woman is at a disadvantage in the marriage market.

Ironically, most young mothers who managed to avoid single parenthood by marrying either before or shortly after delivery ended up as single parents several years later. And many of these women no doubt will never remarry. Therefore, it might be said that once an unplanned pregnancy occurs in adolescence, it hardly matters whether or not the young mother marries. In time, she may be almost as likely to bear the major, if not the sole, responsibility for supporting her child.

# 6. Further Childbearing

A RECURRENT THEME in discussions of early parenthood is the imminent risk of repeat pregnancy (Sarrel, 1967; Osofsky, 1968; Menken, 1972; W. Miller, 1973). The term *risk* is used advisedly, for some teenagers, as we shall see, welcome a second child soon after the first even when the initial pregnancy was unplanned and unwanted. Nevertheless, evidence to be presented in later chapters points to the conclusion that the second child often represents a major setback to the future plans of the young mother, damaging especially her prospects of economic self-sufficiency. A major aim of service programs for teenage parents has been to prevent teenagers from "fall[ing] into a pattern of repeat pregnancies both in and out of wedlock," as one government official characterized the sequence of childbearing during adolescence.

Although not a great deal is known about the history of pregnancies among teenage parents, existing evidence seems to support the prevailing belief that a pregnancy in early adolescence does indeed signal the beginning of a rapid succession of unwanted births. One of the earliest studies of fertility of young mothers was conducted by Philip Sarrel (1967). Using hospital records, he traced the fertility of 100 teenage parents over a five-year period. Ninety-five percent of the young mothers became pregnant again at some point during the five-year period, and the 100 women in his sample produced a total of 340 babies. While more recent studies drawing upon larger and more carefully selected samples have not reported results quite as dramatic as Sarrel's, they do confirm his conclusion that the rate of second pregnancies among adolescent parents is quite high. Marion Howard's (1968) evaluation of a special education program in Washington revealed that nearly half the participants became pregnant within three years of the birth of their first child. Similar findings were reported by Sauber and Corrigan (1970) in their six-year follow-up of a population of unwed mothers. Eighty percent of the women who were teenagers when their first child was born became pregnant again within the period of the study, and half the young mothers had at least two additional children six years later. More recent data from evaluations of family planning programs also have pointed to a high rate of repeat teenage pregnancy in the early years following the first birth (Siegel et al.,

1971; Jorgensen, 1973; Dickens et al., 1973; Klerman and Jekel, 1973). Although estimates vary depending on the experiences of the women following the first birth, most published studies show that at least one-half of teenage mothers experience a second pregnancy within 36 months of delivery (Ricketts, 1973).

But these figures tell us very little about why second pregnancies occur. It is very difficult to estimate how many of these second children may be planned or wanted because the populations invariably combine women of differing marital status, contain no information on family size aspirations, and usually do not present precise data on the interval between the first birth and the second conception. Moreover, the absence of comparative data from other populations of fecund women makes it hazardous to draw any conclusions regarding the vulnerability of young primiparae to repeat pregnancy. Although the figures for second pregnancies appear to be quite high, can we assume that the pace of childbearing is more rapid for women who have a child during adolescence than it would be if they had delayed the first pregnancy?

Explanations of why adolescent mothers often become pregnant again shortly after the birth of the first child have been based largely on speculation. Not surprisingly, the commentaries are reminiscent of the disputes over the etiology of unplanned parenthood (see Chapter 3). One school of writers argues that the high parity of teenage parents is consonant with their cultural aspirations and life-styles. (O. Lewis, 1968). Many women, it is said, especially in the lower classes, regard large families as a source of prestige and an accomplishment. Although they may not time the second pregnancy exactly to their liking, they become pregnant again primarily because they want additional children. Sharply diverging from this position are the researchers who contend that childbearing patterns reflect not parental aspirations but the availability of resources for controlling unwanted pregnancies. These authors assert that more family planning services would sharply reduce repeat pregnancies (Jaffe and Polgar, 1968).

Drawing on the experiences of the young mothers in our study, we shall examine in this chapter each of these positions. Our starting point will be the number of children they claimed to want. These attitudinal data will provide a baseline against which their actual childbearing experiences can be compared. As has been done in previous chapters, the histories of the young mothers and their classmates will be contrasted in order to determine whether early pregnancy increases the rate of family building and the number of offspring produced. Next, we shall take up the question of when and why subsequent pregnancies occur. Can we show that certain life events after pregnancy shape the course of fertility in the early years of adulthood? More concretely, how do these events directly affect the efforts of young mothers to regulate or restrict their childbearing? This final area of analysis should help us reach a judgment about the validity of the differing explanations of adolescent fertility.

# FAMILY SIZE ASPIRATIONS AND EXPECTATIONS

As will be recalled from the data presented in Chapter 3, nearly all of the first pregnancies were unplanned, and most were unwanted at the time conception occurred. Having had one unplanned pregnancy conceivably might sensitize the young mother to the possibility of another. On the other hand, one could also argue that after the first pregnancy, the perceived costs of additional births would decline. If the first pregnancy resulted in a change of life course, no special reorientation would be required for a second child. Consequently, we wanted to know how the family size aspirations of the young mothers were affected by the birth of the first child, especially when these aspirations were contrasted with those of the classmates.

Only a few studies have been conducted on the family size intentions of adolescents (Westoff and Potvin, 1966; Gustavus and Nam, 1970). The results have consistently shown that family size preferences are acquired early in life and tend to be fairly stable over time. Susan Gustavus (1973) carried out a panel study of the family planning intentions of high school youth. Originally the black adolescents in her sample stated a desire to have smaller families than did the whites; however, the pattern appeared to have been reversed by the follow-up interview. Nevertheless, over four out of five children of both racial groups in Gustavus's sample desired between two and four children, and three-fourths of high school seniors studied planned to have either two or three children (cf. Bell, 1965; Kuvelsky and Obordo, 1972).

The data from our study seemed to bear out Gustavus's findings. The adolescent mothers were asked at three points in time how many children they would like to have. Contrary to the pattern Gustavus discovered for white adolescents but consistent with her findings for blacks, the young mothers in our study slightly increased their ideal family size over time from 2.6 at Time 1 to 2.8 children at Time 4. Despite this inflation, the young mothers still expressed a desire for somewhat smaller families than did their counterparts in the Gustavus's study (2.8 versus 3.1).

The mothers' family size aspirations were almost identical to those expressed by the classmates. The young mothers were slightly less likely to favor a very small family, but the difference between the two groups was not statistically significant (2.8 versus 2.7). Evidently the experience of early childbearing did not measurably affect desired family size, and any variations in fertility between the two groups could not be attributed to differences in family size preferences.

While the family size considered ideal among the young mothers rose slightly during the study, the number of children expected steadily declined over time (from 3.0 to 2.6). Again, the projections of the young mothers were fairly close to those of the classmates (2.6 versus 2.4). What was more significant was that both samples expected to have fewer children than they actually desired. Approximately one-third of each group indicated they would like a larger family than they thought they eventually would have.

The mothers were questioned in an earlier interview regarding the reasons for this discrepancy. Of the various explanations offered, money was one of the most important. When confronted with the choice of more children or economic dependency, many women revised their family size plans. As one young mother told us:

> Because a lot of children come into the world mothers can't afford 'em; fathers don't want 'em. You're just stuck with a kid that you gotta raise. Burden on you—burden on your family—child's a holdback.

Unmarried mothers frequently express doubts as to whether they will marry (or remarry) in the future, and the prospect of remaining single appears to diminish their enthusiasm for having a large number of children. The responsibilities of parenthood also take their toll. In our study, women struggling to care for their offspring recognized that they would not have the energy to raise additional children, particularly if they had to contribute to the economic support of their families. While they fancied the idea of additional children, they recognized that it would be foolhardy to have a large family.

## TIMING THE SECOND PREGNANCY

Ultimate family size goals may be of little consequence in determining immediate behavior. After all, nearly all of the young mothers planned to have additional children. If they were indifferent to spacing their children, a large number might still have welcomed another pregnancy soon after their first child was born.

Evidence from the second interview contradicted this supposition. One year after delivery, the entire sample was asked when they planned to have their next child: only 6% said they hoped to become pregnant again "soon." Asked to estimate how long it would be before they had a second child, 80% of the women predicted that it would be at least two years hence (or when their first child would be about three years old), and almost half preferred to wait three more years before having another child. The remainder could not say exactly when they wanted their second child because their decision was contingent upon educational or marital plans, but nearly all women in this group were quite certain that they did not want to become pregnant again for at least a few years.

At Time 3, the 363 young mothers described how they would feel "if they were to become pregnant in the next few months." Only 7% of the total said they were hoping to have another child at the present time, and another 17% replied that although they were not planning to have a child they would be happy if they were to become pregnant. Had the young mothers been successful in implementing their childbearing aims, the rate of second pregnancies during the study, particularly in its early years, would have been extremely low.

## FERTILITY AMONG THE YOUNG MOTHERS

In fact, the gap between family size intention and experience was considerable. A year after the birth of the first child, almost 80% of the sample hoped to wait at least two more years before becoming pregnant again. Less than half of them managed to realize this goal. Not only did many women experience timing failures in the birth of their second child, but by Time 4 some women had already reached or exceeded the number of children they wanted although they were still in their early twenties. Asked at Time 4 when they would like to have their next child, more than one-fourth of young mothers declared "never."

Taking into account that our figures might have underestimated somewhat the conceptions that actually occurred during the study, we present in Tables 6.1A, 6.1B, and 6.1C data on the number of reported conceptions, the outcome of these pregnancies, and the parity of the young mothers at the five-year follow-up.[1] One-third of the sample had become pregnant again at least twice since the first child was born. (Within this subgroup, a substantial proportion—more than 10% of the entire sample—had at least three additional conceptions.) Slightly more than a third of the respondents had one further pregnancy during the study period, and the remaining third had not conceived again. As some indication of the unacceptability of the repeat conceptions, the rate of abortion rose sharply with increased parity, though most of the reported pregnancies came to term.[2]

Table 6.2 presents a life table of the cumulative probability of becoming pregnant a second and a third time. This table depicts rather nicely the tempo of

---

[1] At each interview a fertility history was taken, and during the final follow-up a complete record was made of the outcome of each pregnancy. No doubt some pregnancies went unreported because a miscarriage occurred shortly after conception and the young mother was unaware that she had become pregnant again or was reluctant to recount pregnancies that terminated abruptly. Information from different interviews was used to cross-check reported pregnancies, and we were able to correct for a certain amount of misreporting in the later interviews.

[2] The proportion of women who lost their first child was extremely low because by the time of the first interview the participants in the study had already passed through the earliest stage of pregnancy. It was interesting to observe the change in abortion practices that occurred with the rise in parity. At the outset of their childbearing careers, few of the young mothers were willing to consider abortion. Their views on this issue were almost uniformly negative, as stated during the Time 3 interview. Although most of the mothers continued to hold negative sentiments at Time 4, a larger number became reconciled to this strategy of family size control if all else failed. Elsewhere I have examined the influence of childbearing on abortion attitudes and practices (see Furstenberg, 1972).

Table 6.1A. *Outcome of First Four Pregnancies among Adolescent Mothers and Classmates at Time 4*

| | Sample | | Currently Pregnant | Miscarriage | Abortion | Child Deceased | Living Children |
|---|---|---|---|---|---|---|---|
| First | Adolescent Mothers | (321) | – | 2 | 1 | 3 | 94 |
| Pregnancy | Classmates | (140) | 6 | 9 | 4 | 2 | 78 |
| Second | Adolescent Mothers | (219) | 3 | 12 | 4 | 3 | 79 |
| Pregnancy | Classmates | (54) | 7 | 11 | 11 | 6 | 65 |
| Third | Adolescent Mothers | (96) | 6 | 17 | 19 | 3 | 55 |
| Pregnancy | Classmates | (16) | 13 | 38 | 19 | – | 31 |
| Fourth | Adolescent Mothers | (33) | 21 | 6 | 18 | 9 | 46 |
| Pregnancy | Classmates | | – | – | – | – | – |

Table 6.1B. *Number of Pregnancies by Marital Status at Time 4*

| | Adolescent Mothers | | | | Classmates | | | |
|---|---|---|---|---|---|---|---|---|
| Number of Pregnancies | Total (323) | Single (120) | Married (106) | Other (97) | Total (211) | Single (128) | Married (67) | Other (16) |
| 0 | – | – | – | – | 36 | 46 | 21 | 19 |
| 1 | 33 | 51 | 21 | 23 | 39 | 41 | 39 | 25 |
| 2 | 38 | 30 | 49 | 34 | 19 | 12 | 27 | 31 |
| 3 | 20 | 14 | 18 | 29 | 3 | – | 8 | 13 |
| 4+ | 10 | 5 | 12 | 14 | 3 | 1 | 6 | 13 |
| Mean Number | 2.11 | 1.75 | 2.25 | 2.39 | 1.00 | .66 | 1.59 | 1.89 |

Table 6.1C. *Number of Children by Marital Status at Time 4*

| | Adolescent Mothers | | | | Classmates | | | |
|---|---|---|---|---|---|---|---|---|
| Number of Children | Total | Single | Married | Other | Total | Single | Married | Other |
| 0 | 2 | 3 | 1 | 1 | 47 | 58 | 32 | 19 |
| 1 | 43 | 63 | 34 | 32 | 41 | 36 | 46 | 50 |
| 2 | 41 | 22 | 53 | 51 | 11 | 6 | 19 | 25 |
| 3+ | 13 | 12 | 12 | 16 | 2 | 1 | 3 | 6 |
| Mean Number | 1.66 | 1.33 | 1.76 | 1.86 | .69 | .48 | .97 | 1.17 |

Table 6.2. *Cumulative Probability of Subsequent Pregnancies by Marital Status at Time 4*

| | Second Pregnancy | | |
|---|---|---|---|
| Months of Exposure | Total (319) | Ever Married (199) | Never Married (120) |
| 12 | .23 | .29 | .15 |
| 24 | .43 | .52 | .28 |
| 36 | .55 | .66 | .38 |
| 48 | .62 | .73 | .44 |
| 60 | .66 | .76 | .51 |
| | Third Pregnancy | | |
| | Total (205) | Ever Married (150) | Never Married (55) |
| 12 | .27 | .26 | .32 |
| 24 | .39 | .41 | .35 |
| 36 | .47 | .52 | .47 |
| 48 | .56 | .60 | * |

*Denotes base under 10.

family building according to marital status at Time 4. Among the women ever married, more than one-fourth became pregnant within the first year after delivery, and one-half conceived for the second time within 24 months after delivery. Nearly all of these women were running well ahead of their desired family size schedules. While the single women proceeded less rapidly in family building, they, too, deviated from the timetables they set for themselves in the early interviews. Very few of the single women at Time 1 or 2 expressed a desire to have another child before marrying, yet the majority became pregnant again out of wedlock.

The timing of the third pregnancy is an even more sensitive barometer of the ability of the young mothers to follow their childbearing schedules. As Table 6.2 shows, the tempo of childbearing actually picked up slightly in the first year after the birth of the second child.[3] Nearly one woman in four became pregnant again within 12 months of the birth of the second child. The rate slowed down slightly in successive years. Nevertheless, by three years, half of the women with two children had become pregnant a third time. Third conceptions followed a different pattern, depending on the marital status of the young mothers. After two pregnancies, single women were *more* likely to experience a rapid third conception than women who were married, although the probability of a third pregnancy for the married group eventually surpassed that for the single mothers.

Since pregnancies are especially likely to be unplanned in the first year or two after the second child is born, evidently there is a small subgroup of single women who have little or no ability to regulate their fertility to conform to their desires. While married multiparae may be slightly more adept at preventing unwanted third pregnancies, it should be noted that their record is not much better. More than two married women in five (who had two offspring) become pregnant a third time within 24 months of the birth of their second child.

The skeptical reader may wish to question whether these subsequent conceptions in fact were unwanted. Although it is easy to document that most were unplanned at the time of conception, it is still possible that the second pregnancies were regarded positively. Obviously, feelings about pregnancy are not unambivalent. There are degrees of desirability that are subject to considerable fluctuation depending on current circumstances as well as long-range family size plans. The most persuasive evidence is the postconception reaction since we know from the data collected during the first pregnancy that there is a tendency to redefine a pregnancy in more favorable terms once it has occurred. Thus, retrospective reports actually provide an exaggerated estimate of desirability.

One woman in five who had become pregnant again by Time 3 reported that she had been hoping for a second child, and an equally large proportion stated that although the pregnancy was unplanned, they were nonetheless happy about

[3] The interval for women who miscarried or aborted during their second pregnancy begins at the month in which their second pregnancy was terminated.

it. Half of the young mothers stated that they had not wanted to become pregnant again. (As might be expected, the third pregnancy elicited an even more negative reaction. According to the mothers, only 10% of those with three pregnancies had been planning to become pregnant a third time.) As we expected from the findings presented in Chapter 3, reactions to pregnancy were highly related to both current and probable future marital status. Women married or soon to be married were far more positive about the second pregnancy. But even a sizable minority of the women who married during the study (42%) expressed strong reservations about subsequent pregnancies, and their sentiments were quite stable over time. In the most recent follow-up, respondents were asked to recall how they felt about their last pregnancy. The results closely replicated the accounts provided in the previous interview. Two-thirds of the single mothers and two-fifths of those who had married expressed negative feelings about becoming pregnant a second time. (An even higher proportion— 83% of the single women and 58% of those married—had an adverse reaction to their third pregnancy.)

The frequency, and evaluation of childbearing point to the conclusion that most of the young mothers in our sample were not able to regulate their fertility to conform to their plans or desires. As mentioned earlier, a great deal of attention has been focused on the childbearing career of the adolescent mother to support the view that she is especially likely to experience repeated unwanted pregnancies. But is she in fact more vulnerable to unwanted pregnancies than her peers who do not make a premature entrance into parenthood? We sought to answer this question by comparing the childbearing patterns of the classmates with those of the young mothers. Presumably, the classmates should have had fewer unplanned and unwanted pregnancies.

## FERTILITY AMONG THE CLASSMATES

When the classmates were first interviewed at Time 3, nearly two-thirds had never been pregnant and almost all who had become pregnant had done so in the preceding 24 months. By Time 4, slightly over half of the single classmates and four-fifths of those who were married had conceived at least once. Although the incidence of childbearing among the classmates was increasing, they were well behind the adolescent mothers in number of pregnancies and showed no signs of catching up. At this time, two-thirds of the young mothers had had at least two pregnancies, and nearly one-third had had three or more. By contrast, only one-fourth of the classmates had become pregnant more than once, and only 6% had conceived three or more times. This disparity diminished slightly when marital status was held constant, but it still remained quite marked. Among the women never married, the young mothers on the average had 1.09 more pregnancies; the difference among the marrieds was 0.66.[4]

While the discrepancy in family size between the young mothers and their classmates was substantial, especially in view of the similarities in their backgrounds, our data did not show that early parenthood inevitably increases the tempo of childbearing. This conclusion was evident from a life table we constructed for the classmates that expressed the probability of their becoming pregnant in the preceding five years—the length of time the young mothers were exposed to the risk of pregnancy after the first child was born. Because pregnancy history may be recollected inaccurately, the life table comparison should be read as only a rough approximation of the probability of conception. Taking this into account, we found the similarities between the two samples in rate of pregnancy impressive. Childbearing proceeded at almost the same pace for both groups. Among the women never married, approximately half became pregnant in the 60-month period, and the figures for each 12-month stretch were remarkably similar. The same was true for the women who married, except that their rates were a great deal higher. At five years, three out of four of both mothers and classmates had become pregnant.

It must be recalled that the comparison being drawn is between the rate of *second* pregnancies among the young mothers and the rate of *first* pregnancies among the classmates. It could be argued that the young mothers might have been expected to produce fewer children during this period because they could have experienced postpartum sterility; they could have had greater access to family planning services; they could have been more aware of the risk of becoming pregnant; and they could have been more motivated to avoid conceiving. While these possibilities should not be overlooked, it is also important to recognize that the classmates were bearing about the same number of children despite the facts that a large number were not sexually active during the observation period and that fewer were married for any length of time during the period of the comparison. Consequently, we might have expected that the classmates would have produced fewer children than the adolescent mothers during the five years of our study.

A more precise comparison was made by considering the rate of repeat pregnancy among the classmates who had one child. Was the rate of second pregnancy slower among the classmates who first became pregnant an average of two or three years later than the young mothers? Among the married classmates, the timing of the second pregnancy was found to be quite similar to that among

[4]The classmates generally had a more favorable reaction to their first and second pregnancies than did the young mothers, although the differences were not sizable. The classmates also expressed dissatisfaction with the timing of their first conception and were only slightly more content with the timing of the second pregnancy (Furstenberg, 1975). Given equal fecundity, the classmates were somewhat more inclined to resort to abortion, although this tendency perhaps reflected the increased availability of abortions. The classmates' sentiments about abortion were almost identical to those of the adolescent mothers. Exactly the same proportion—57%—felt certain that they would never decide to have an abortion.

the young mothers. However, the single classmates were decidedly less likely to experience a repeat pregnancy in the three-year period following the birth of their first child. The rate of second pregnancy at 36 months after delivery was only half as high for the single classmates as for the young mothers who did not marry. Apparently, the single classmates were better able to avoid a second pregnancy than were the single mothers. Is this difference the result of differences in maturity, motivation, skill, or access to contraceptives? A consideration of the specific factors linked to the occurrence of a repeat pregnancy will shed light on this question.

## MARRIAGE AND CHILDBEARING PATTERNS

As is obvious from the data already presented, explaining fertility in our sample involves an understanding of the transition to marriage. Although it may appear self-evident that married women will become pregnant more often than women who remain single, the explanation for this regularity is not quite so obvious as it might at first appear. Almost all the young mothers who were single were also sexually active and were consequently exposed to the risk of becoming pregnant. And, as has already been reported, most of the married women were eager to defer a second conception, and relatively few desired a third child. Moreover, married women, like their single counterparts, typically intended to work after the birth of their first child, and many expressed the belief that they could not afford to have a second child immediately. Had the married women been successful in planning their families, fertility in our sample might not have been as differentiated by marital status as it turned out to be.

If exposure to the risk of pregnancy and different family size plans were the only factors at work, we might have expected to find that the timing of marriage is strongly related to the number of pregnancies and the likelihood of a hasty second conception. But this was not the case. Women who married prior to delivery were only slightly more likely to conceive again in the year following the birth of their first child than those who deferred marriage. Thereafter, they were somewhat *less* likely to become pregnant a second time than were the women who married postpartum. Moreover, the mothers who married before the birth of their first child on an average had slightly lower fertility by Time 4 than those who had deferred marriage.

This anomalous finding could be explained if women who married prenatally separated from their husbands earlier and consequently had a shorter period of exposure to marriage than those who wed after delivery. Yet learned from the findings presented in Chapter 5 that the marriages contracted prenatally were actually somewhat more durable. Nevertheless, correlating the number of pregnancies with the total time spent in marriage revealed that there was no association between fertility and length of time married: women with longer marriages were not more likely to become pregnant sooner or more often than women who were married only for a brief time. Consistent with this conclusion was the fact that the young mothers who were separated at Time 4 had pregnancy histories fairly similar to those of the women who were married at that time. While we did not conclude that this uniformity would necessarily persist, it would appear that fertility is not strictly a function of the timing or the duration of marriage.

This discovery prompted a consideration of prenuptial childbearing among women who had wed during the follow-up period. Single women who married following delivery were almost as likely to experience a second conception (while still single) as women who were married before delivery, and they were nearly twice as likely to become pregnant a second time as were the mothers who never married during the study (Furstenberg et al., 1972). In other words, fertility among this group of women anticipated their change in marital status.

This finding raised an intriguing possibility. The women who deferred marriage geared their childbearing to their prospective rather than their current marital status, thus conforming in advance to the behavior of their future reference group. There was some empirical support for this interpretation. The women who married postpartum expressed childbearing intentions at Time 2 that were in between the plans of the women who never wed and those of the women who were already married. One reason why women who defer marriage may be more willing to become pregnant again is that the second pregnancy frequently provides an entry into marriage, especially if they are no longer seeing the father of their first child. In our study, women who married another man were far more likely to experience a rapid repeat pregnancy than women who wed the father of their first child.

In Chapter 4, the possibility was raised that a second pregnancy may provide a means of demonstrating the viability of a new relationship. Given their reluctance to support the child of another man, some males may insist on a pregnancy before a new relationship can progress to marriage. The second pregnancy may solidify the relationships of women who eventually marry the father of their first child as well, smoothing the transition to marriage for couples whose plans are initially up in the air. To conclude that the second pregnancy causes the ensuing union, however, ignores the delicate process of negotiation that frequently precedes the marital decision. It is probably more correct to say that the second pregnancy helps to bring about an event that might otherwise not occur:

> The reason why I got married is because we were in love and we wanted to be together and we wanted to raise our family together. This is what we wanted to do and nobody could stop us.

However, second pregnancies do not invariably lead to marriage, as was evident from the facts that half of the single women became pregnant again without marrying and that a number of women who had already made the transition to marriage before delivery also rapidly reconceived. Consequently, we looked to other circumstances to account for fertility among the young mothers in our sample.

## THE RELATIONSHIP BETWEEN FAMILY SIZE ASPIRATIONS AND SUBSEQUENT PREGNANCIES

Although it already has been shown that a relatively small proportion of the second pregnancies and even fewer of those that followed were planned, the perceived costs of additional children were obviously not the same for all the young mothers. As was suggested by earlier findings, married women clearly have less to lose by becoming pregnant again. Even within marital subgroups, there was considerable variation in family size desires, intentions, and expectations. The findings cited earlier indicated that women who married before or shortly after their first child was born often welcomed a second child even though they had not planned to become pregnant again. It might be expected that these preferences would have some impact on childbearing, assuming that the women who wanted larger families would be less concerned about the timing of a second child and less motivated to avoid a rapid repeat pregnancy.

There are certain difficulties in testing the influence of family size goals on childbearing patterns. Attitudes about desired family size are subject to a certain amount of variation over time. Thus, we asked: at what point (if ever) do family size plans begin to constrain behavior? Some writers have maintained that stable family size preferences are established rather early in life (Duncan et al., 1965; Gustavus, 1975). Though not necessarily insisting that these patterns are transmitted directly from parent to child, they nonetheless assume that family size preferences develop in response to economic conditions in the family, sibling and peer experiences, or sexual role conceptions. Westoff and Potvin (1966:496), for example, have asserted that "a normative family range of family size . . . is internalized by the girl during the period of late adolescence (say, 8 to 13) in much the same way as a child learns other values and styles of interaction." There has been relatively little empirical evidence to affirm or disconfirm the effect of early socialization on adult childbearing behavior.

A number of items measuring the economic status of the young mother's family of origin and her mother's family-size attitudes and childbearing behavior were found to be unrelated to the adolescent's history of pregnancies after the birth of her first child. The size of the adolescent mother's family of origin was related slightly to the number of pregnancies she experienced during the study (tau$_c$ = .148). This finding is consistent with the view that an orientation toward acceptable family size is acquired early in life. However, most other data from the grandmother's interview did not point to this conclusion. The grandmother's notion of desired family size were unrelated to her daughter's history of pregnancies. Moreover, the parent's family size goals were unrelated to her daughter's family size aspirations and expectations, lending no support to the theory that family size goals are directly passed on from one generation to the next.

The question of how much impact family size goals have on actual childbearing experience was pursued more directly by examining the relationship between family size preferences and expectations expressed by the mothers at Times 1 and 2 and actual fertility in our sample throughout the study. The results pointed to the inescapable conclusion that the relationship between goals and behavior is very slight. Preferences and expectations regarding family size expressed during pregnancy were not related to whether or not a second pregnancy occurred, the timing of a repeat pregnancy, or to the total number of pregnancies that took place in the five years after the first child was born.[5]

Since many single women were not in a position to realize their long-term aims, perhaps it was unwise to include them with women who married during the study. Although general family size aspirations were not related to current marital status, their impact on childbearing should have been more apparent for married women since they were freer to implement their plans. In fact, however, separating the two groups turned out to make little difference. Married women were not significantly more likely to adhere to their family size goals than were the women who remained single.

In considering the interplay between family size desires and childbearing, it is important to examine the effect of the first pregnancy on subsequent patterns of childbearing. Women who reacted negatively to the first conception might have been inclined to practice birth control or to terminate any subsequent pregnancy that did occur. Eventually, this may turn out to be the case, but in the early years of family building, no effect from the initial pregnancy could be detected. Women whose reaction to their first pregnancy was negative were not more likely to defer the second conception or to restrict their childbearing than those mothers who were happy about the first pregnancy. Apparently, the response to the initial conception was based on a specific evaluation of how well it fit into their immediate life plans and did not color the young mothers' feelings about subsequent childbearing.

Our results appear to indicate that family size goals expressed by the young mothers in the early interviews had little bearing on their patterns of family building. Before reaching that conclusion, however, we must examine the relationship between their pregnancy histories and their statements of immediate birth plans at the one-year follow-up. Married women were distinctly more likely

---

[5]It was interesting to discover that the degree of confidence expressed by the young mother in her own ability to realize her family size goals, measured by the concordance between preferences and expectations, also was unrelated to her pregnancy history. Women who expected to have more children than they desired at Time 1 were not more likely to experience a greater number of pregnancies over the next five years than women who felt they would be able to control the number of children they bore. This finding does not support the notion that unplanned fertility is primarily the result of a fatalistic orientation.

to be planning a pregnancy in the next two years (25% versus 8%). Differences were equally visible over the longer range. Half of the married women said that they would like to become pregnant in the next four years as compared to a fourth of the single mothers. How well did these plans work out? In fact, women who intended to wait a longer time became pregnant less quickly and experienced somewhat fewer pregnancies during the study than those who wished to become pregnant sooner. In neither marital subgroup, however, were child spacing intentions highly correlated with actual childbearing patterns although they were a slightly better predictor of future behavior than were general family size goals.

Since they were based primarily on the mother's current situation, child spacing intentions were more likely to take into account the immediate costs of having another child. This is why single and married women differed so sharply over the desirability of a pregnancy in the near future. Thus, women engaged in career preparations at Time 2 were less receptive to the idea of having another child in the next few years. Indeed, one of the principal reasons that married women or women about to be married were more prepared to contemplate a second child was that their commitment to educational and occupational advancement was not so high as that of the women who remained single.

## EDUCATIONAL COMMITMENT AND CHILDBEARING PATTERNS

As we shall consider in more detail in Chapter 7, women with strong commitments to a career generally opt to remain in school, putting off marriage at least for a time. Predictably, the women in our study most highly committed to education were also less likely to hope for a second child within the few years following the first. Their childbearing was generally in line with their desires: a much greater proportion of highly ambitious women were able to avoid a rapid repeat pregnancy. This pattern held true for both single and ever-married women (Table A.9). Single mothers—women remaining unmarried throughout the study—who at Time 1 expressed low ambition for more schooling were more than three times as likely (.39 versus .12) to become pregnant again within two years of delivery as their peers who had high educational ambitions during pregnancy. (The measure of ambition will be discussed in Chapter 7.) Married women who had a strong commitment to remaining in school were just as likely eventually to become pregnant again as were women who had little interest in education; however, there was a noticeable difference in the timing of the second conception. Almost half the married women with low ambition became pregnant again within 12 months, while fewer than a fourth of those women with high ambition conceived again so soon. Educational ambition was related also to the total number of pregnancies, but the association was much weaker, particularly among ever-married women, indicating that there is a tendency for women who defer childbearing in order to complete their schooling to catch up with their peers who become pregnant again right away.

The interpretation that a highly valued educational career is a deterrent to an early second pregnancy was supported by additional data on the relationship between school attendance and fertility. Women who returned to school immediately following the delivery of their first child were much less likely to experience a second conception in the 12-month period after the birth of their first child (Table A.10). Fertility patterns continued to diverge in subsequent years. Even after four years, the women who returned to school had lower rates of second pregnancy. Since the dropouts disproportionately tended to marry, it was necessary to reexamine the relationship of educational achievement and childbearing patterns for each marital subgroup separately. Although the relationship was less striking for the women who married, the pattern of a lower rate of second pregnancies for women who returned to school held true regardless of marital status.

The total number of pregnancies was also much higher for women who never went back to school. Two-fifths of the women who quit school after their first child was born had at least two more pregnancies, while only one-fourth of the women who returned to school had an equally high rate of reconception. These patterns did not disappear when marital status was held constant, although again the difference occurred mainly among the women who never married.[6]

Obviously, the relationship between educational achievement and fertility patterns is a reciprocal one, and in the next chapter we shall explore the complex causal nexus between childbearing and educational achievement. Women may defer childbearing in order to attain their educational goals, but they may also discontinue their education when they fail to prevent an unwanted pregnancy. In testing the hypothesis that commitment to education strengthens the young mother's resolve not to become pregnant again, we emphasized the importance of educational goals in shaping childbearing careers; however, we could just as easily have argued that by limiting fertility, the young mother is able to remain in school and to realize her educational ambition. Accordingly, we found (even holding educational ambition constant) that women remain in school (at least until graduation) if they are able to defer further childbearing. Whichever way we interpret the direction of causality, it is clear that school attendance represents an alternative to rapid family building.

[6]Half of the unmarried dropouts had at least two more conceptions during the study as compared to only 11% of those women who returned to school. Among married women, the proportion of women who had two additional pregnancies was about the same among those who returned to school (35%) and those who did not (37%). Despite these negligible differences, the married women who remained in school still did not completely catch up to their peers who dropped out since a significantly smaller proportion had three or more children (19% versus 10%) by the fourth interview, indicating that the second conceptions were more recent and probably more often desired.

# WORK EXPERIENCE AND CHILDBEARING PATTERNS

Harriet Presser (1971) has drawn a similar conclusion about the impact of unscheduled childbearing upon subsequent work patterns, proposing that early and unplanned pregnancies lock women out of rewarding occupational positions just as they restrict access to schooling. In turn, the woman's limited chances of social mobility encourage additional pregnancies. Presser (1971:354) specifically has suggested that the prevalence of early pregnancy, combined with limited job options, may help to explain the high rate of unwanted pregnancies among black women:

> When nonfamilial role options to be shared with motherhood, and possibly wifehood, are limited to a few low-status choices, subsequent fertility— wanted or unwanted, legitimate or illegitimate—may be easier to accept.

If Presser is correct in her assumption that women excluded from attractive nonfamilial roles will have less reason to limit childbearing, we might anticipate that family building will proceed most rapidly among young mothers who have the lowest investment in work roles. Contrary to this expectation, however, we found that expressions of interest in employment stated in the first two interviews were completely unrelated to patterns of childbearing during the study. Women who indicated in the Time 1 and 2 interviews a greater desire to work were not more likely to restrict their fertility during the follow-up period. Similarly, expressions of satisfaction with the domestic role had no bearing on subsequent childbearing in our sample. Young mothers who stated at the one-year follow-up that they liked staying at home and caring for their child were not more likely to become pregnant a second time in following years or to have a larger number of children by the end of the study. Perhaps these findings attested only to the low salience of the attitudinal items from the early interviews, but measures of labor force participation were only slightly more discriminating.

Women who worked continually obviously exhibited lower fertility; however, at any given point in the study, working women were not conspicuously more successful in controlling their fertility in the following time segment than women who were not holding jobs. In other words, mothers who did not become pregnant again were able to work, but jobholders were nearly as likely to become pregnant in the future as were women who were not working. At both Time 2 and Time 3, working women had much smaller families. However, when their *subsequent* childbearing pattern was examined, we found that they had almost the same probability of becoming pregnant as women who were not employed. Since students are less likely to be in the labor force, it is possible that they accounted for these unexpected findings. But even when we removed students from the sample, we found that the working women were not less likely than the nonworking women to become pregnant again during the study.

To a certain extent this comparison was loaded because many of the nonworking women were currently pregnant or had just delivered. Consequently, it might have been expected that they would have had a lower chance of experiencing yet another pregnancy when compared to the working women, who for the most part were primiparous. To correct for this bias the effect of work experience on subsequent childbearing was examined only among women who had not become pregnant a second time. While working women were slightly more likely not to become pregnant again, the differences were very modest. This held true even for the single women, who were undoubtedly not looking forward to a second child.

Presser (1971) also raised the possibility that jobholding may not be sufficiently rewarding to motivate working mothers to prevent a second pregnancy. If this is true, we might have expected to find different patterns of childbearing among the women with the best jobs. In fact primiparae who were working at stable, well-paid, and personally rewarding jobs at Time 3 were just as likely to desire another child in the near future (even controlling for parity) and equally likely to become pregnant in the interim between Time 3 and 4 as were women holding low-status jobs. Again, this finding suggests that women who might be classified as "careerists" display no greater inclination to regulate their childbearing than do women who are less attached to their jobs (cf. Presser, 1975).

## ECONOMIC STATUS AND CHILDBEARING PATTERNS

One of the most hotly debated issues in the social policy literature is the impact of public assistance on fertility. A popular argument voiced by opponents of welfare programs is that public assistance encourages childbearing out of wedlock because it provides a means of supporting additional children for unmarried women (Moynihan, 1968). The "broodsow myth," as Placek and Hendershot (1974) so aptly labeled it, received no confirmation from our data. Although women with larger families were much more likely to receive public assistance, the welfare mother was not significantly more likely to become pregnant again *after* she went on relief than the young mother who was not receiving public assistance. Among the single mothers, 42% of those on welfare at Time 3 became pregnant again by Time 4 as compared to 38% of the women who were not on relief. Among the ever-married women, the difference was somewhat larger, 50% versus 38%, but was still relatively trivial. The similarity in fertility of the welfare and the non-welfare groups suggested that there is no reason to single out the welfare mother as incapable of regulating her childbearing. She does about as well or as poorly as her peers who are not on welfare. (For a further discussion of these findings, see Chapter 8.)

In a more general sense as well, the data from this study did not support the proposition that the pace of childbearing will reflect the economic costs and benefits of additional children. Childbearing patterns were independent of the economic situation of the young mother's family of origin, her own economic situation, and, when married, her husband's earnings. It would appear, then, that while certain women are relatively more successful in regulating their child-bearing than others, most young mothers are little able to coordinate their childbearing aims with their current economic situation or future career plans.

The remainder of this chapter discusses this apparent contradiction, center-ing on the problems that the young mothers in our study encountered in using contraception.


## BIRTH CONTROL EXPERIENCE AMONG THE YOUNG MOTHERS

In Chapter 3 we learned that prior to their first pregnancy, most of the young mothers had only the most superficial knowledge of contraceptive techniques. During the prenatal period, almost all the respondents (94%) stated that they had received some information about family planning from the hospital. Three-fifths of the sample had been assigned (on a random basis) to a special Adolescent Family Clinic which, during pregnancy, offered regular group meetings devoted in part to contraceptive instruction and equipped the young mothers with methods of birth control after delivery. The other two-fifths of the sample attended the regular prenatal clinic, where most of them received family plan-ning information on an individual basis from staff members.

Regardless of the young mother's prenatal experience, a substantial shift in knowledge and sentiments about contraception took place between the gestation period and the one-year follow-up. A year after delivery, participants in both programs were much more likely to endorse birth control, especially the use of contraceptive pills; they had fewer reservations about the effectiveness of contra-ception; and they were much more confident about the safety of birth control pills (Table A.11). The fact that the patterns of change were almost identical in the two groups indicated that the attitudinal change had as much to do with general experience acquired during pregnancy as with selective participation in either prenatal program.

Initial use of birth control was high in both groups, although only 80% of those who attended the regular clinic practiced contraception during the year after their first child was born as opposed to 92% of those who participated in the AFC. One-third of the nonusers explained that they had not practiced contraception because they were not sexually active; one-fifth stated an aversion to birth control; and the remainder offered a variety of other reasons for nonuse.

Only two (4%) of the nonusers reported that their abstention resulted from their desire to become pregnant again. Participants in the AFC were much more likely not to be using contraception because of sexual inactivity than because of aversion or indifference. (One-half provided this reason as compared to 16% of the women attending the regular clinic.)

Using a life table procedure, we calculated the rate of continuation for the total number of young mothers who used contraception, broken down according to their program experience during pregnancy. The results made it clear why the rate of second pregnancy was so high among the young mothers. Among those who began to practice contraception after the birth of their first child, more than one-third had abandoned birth control after one year; nearly two-thirds, by two years. Thereafter the rate of decline dropped off. However, by the five-year follow-up, only about one woman in five had used contraception continually during the entire study. If those women who never used birth control were included, the figure dropped still lower (Table 6.3).

A perceptible and persistent difference occurred in the patterns of contraceptive use among the AFC and the regular clinic participants. After one year, there were 10% more users among the AFC participants than among the regular clinic attenders. This modest disparity remained fairly constant for the next two years although the relative difference increased because of the sharp rates of discontinuation. In the fourth year the dropoff for attenders of the regular clinic was steeper, and the relative difference between the two groups widened somewhat. In fact, the proportion of continuers was twice as high among the former AFC participants. It should be pointed out that these differences were calculated on a shrinking base and might not be highly reliable. One way of establishing their import was to compare the rates of second pregnancies among the two populations. The results were convincing. Among the women who attended the special program, 39% did not become pregnant a second time as compared to 25% of the regular clinic participants. In view of the fact that the two groups

Table 6.3. *Cumulative Probability of Birth Control Continuation among Adolescent Mothers by Program Experience*

| | Users Only | | | | Total[1] | |
| Month | Total (331) | AFC (208) | Control (123) | Total[2] (380) | AFC (227) | Control (153) |
|---|---|---|---|---|---|---|
| 12 | .64 | .66 | .62 | .56 | .60 | .49 |
| 24 | .38 | .40 | .36 | .33 | .36 | .29 |
| 36 | .29 | .31 | .27 | .25 | .28 | .22 |
| 48 | .24 | .26 | .19 | .20 | .24 | .15 |
| 60 | .22 | .26 | .15 | .19 | .24 | .12 |

[1] Includes non-users.

[2] Includes six cases of women who were assigned to the AFC but attended the regular clinic (GOC).

were identical in every other respect at Time 1, a difference of this magnitude over five years is considerable.[7]

Although in the aggregate, differences in contraceptive practice clearly resulted from exposure to the program, the special benefits of birth control information and training were attenuated over time. Regardless of their prenatal experiences, the majority of women in *both* groups discontinued contraception and became pregnant again, typically without planning or wanting another child. It should be noted that by comparing the results of the AFC to those of the regular program, we were applying a rather stringent standard to assess the success of the special clinic. After all, the regular program also offered contraception to women who requested it and even made some effort to promote its use. In fact, then, we were comparing the results of two different family planning settings, only one of which was deliberately designed to serve an adolescent population and which was embedded in a more comprehensive program of services.[8]

Although it may be unfair to judge the results of the Adolescent Family Clinic against the baseline of the regular clinic, the fact remains that both programs met with limited success. The question of why the results of these efforts were so modest, while specific to this study, has a much broader import. In recent years, a large number of programs similar to the one begun in Baltimore have been initiated throughout the country. While relatively few careful evaluations have been conducted, in all cases for which follow-up results are available, the results consistently show that family planning programs for pregnant adolescents have relatively low long-term rates of success (Klerman and Jekel, 1973; Ricketts, 1973). Most participants discontinue contraceptive use after a short period. Typically, at least one woman in three terminates birth control within a year. Although most studies do not extend beyond 18 months, the rates of termination for the few longer studies show a steep decline in practice after the first year, as happened in the Baltimore sample. Clearly, the experiences of the young mothers in our study were not atypical.

[7]The program had a greater impact on women never married than on women who wed. Sixty percent of the single women who attended the AFC did not become pregnant again as compared to 40% of the single participants in the regular program. By contrast, the special program had only a modest effect on the mothers who married—26% did not reconceive versus 17% of the regular clinic attenders. Significantly, the AFC had its greatest impact in reducing second pregnancies. The overall difference in the rate of third pregnancies was minimal (27% of the AFC participants became pregnant a third time as compared to 32% of the control group).

[8]While the AFC participants did report slightly more contact with the hospital staff prior to delivery and in the early months postpartum, the clinic experience of the two groups did not differ greatly. Regular clinic attenders were just as likely to be familiar with their physicians and received as many prenatal examinations as AFC mothers, though the latter group had more extensive relations with the nursing and social service staffs both prior to and after delivery. Perhaps, then, it is not so very surprising that the two populations did not diverge greatly in their patterns of contraceptive use and rates of repeat pregnancy.

# MARITAL EXPERIENCE AND
# CONTRACEPTIVE USE

Earlier, it was established that respondents who married and those who remained single perceived the costs of a second pregnancy differently. Accordingly, we might expect that women who had married by the time their first child was born would have been especially likely to adopt a casual attitude toward contraceptive practice. Risk taking, carelessness, and low tolerance for difficulty in use should have been higher among the women who married early. As anticipated, contraceptive practice was found to differ sharply depending on the marital histories of the young mothers. Overall, women who wed were much less likely to use birth control at any given point in the study. The trend was established immediately. Six months after delivery, more than one-fifth of the ever-married women who began using birth control stopped; one-tenth of the single women did likewise. The gap widened by the end of the first year. Close to half of the women who married during the study stopped using contraception, while more than three-fourths of the single women were still using birth control at Time 2. Therefore, the rate of continuation was about twice as high for the women who remained single (Table A.12). It is little wonder that the rates of pregnancy diverged so sharply in the two populations.

The effectiveness of contraceptive practice was almost perfectly correlated with the incidence of pregnancy. Regardless of marital status, about four out of five women who had never used contraception became pregnant within the first six months after delivery. Married women, as might be expected, conceived more rapidly than single mothers, though the overall rate of repeat pregnancy was about the same for the two groups if contraceptive practice was held constant. This suggests that the somewhat lower rate of intercourse among the single women offers little protection against pregnancy. At best, a lower rate of sexual activity serves only to delay reconception for a brief period. The primary reason that single women are less likely to experience a repeat pregnancy is that they practice contraception more faithfully.

The findings on contraceptive use among the married women parallel the results reported earlier on the impact of marriage timing on pregnancy patterns. To begin with, contraceptive use among late marriers who did not wed the child's father was conspicuously low. During the first year after delivery, while they were still single, this group of young mothers performed similarly to women who eventually married. But by the end of the second year, as they came closer to marriage, nearly all of these women stopped using birth control. At 24 months, fewer than one in five was still using contraception, half the rate of the women who married the father of the child and one-third the rate of the women who remained single throughout the study. It would seem that most of these women abandoned contraception as they entered a new sexual partnership.

How much difference did contraceptive instruction make in the practice of birth control among the various marital subgroups? It can be argued that married women will be more responsive to family planning efforts since they are most likely to engage in regular sexual relations. On the other hand, single mothers have more to lose from another pregnancy and consequently may be more affected by contraceptive instruction. In fact, the AFC program had relatively little impact on women who married whereas single women who graduated from the AFC were almost twice as likely to practice contraception than their single counterparts in the regular program. It seems plausible that the AFC program had greater impact because those women who were most sensitive to the costs of an additional child were better able to profit from the extensive instruction and reinforcement provided by the AFC staff. The more detrimental the effects of a second pregnancy to the young mother, the greater and the more tangible are the benefits of a special contraceptive program (cf. Reiss et al., 1974).

## EDUCATIONAL COMMITMENT AND CONTRACEPTIVE EXPERIENCE

If this interpretation is correct, we might also have anticipated that women with high educational goals would be more likely to practice contraception, particularly those who were exposed to the comprehensive family planning program. The data confirmed this expectation. The more ambitious women in both clinic programs were more likely to adopt some method of contraception following delivery and to practice it more faithfully thereafter than women with low ambition. Similarly, women who returned to school were more likely to use birth control and to practice it more conscientiously. As expected, the success of the AFC program was to some extent contingent upon the young mother's educational goals and performance. The program was less successful in increasing the probability of continuation of contraception among women with low ambition and among those who did not return to school after their first child was born than among those most interested in educational advancement. Although the number of cases became extremely small, the findings seem to apply to both single and married women, suggesting that a lesser educational commitment may have accounted in part for the lower rate of success that the AFC had with women who married.

We have shown that women who had most reason to want to prevent a second pregnancy were more likely to use contraception effectively, particularly when given intensive training. However, even those who had a great deal to lose by a second pregnancy—the single women who returned to school or went to work and explicitly expressed a desire not to become pregnant again—discontinued contraceptive use at a substantial rate. Three years after delivery, more than half of these young mothers had stopped using birth control. When even the most motivated women do not use contraception on a long-term basis, it becomes critical to ask what makes contraceptive practice so difficult to sustain.

## REASONS FOR TERMINATION OF BIRTH CONTROL

At each follow-up, the young mothers who had stopped using contraception were asked why they had abandoned birth control. Regardless of the time at follow-up, it was rare for a young mother to indicate that she had done so in order to become pregnant, although the proportion of such women increased slightly over time. Just as uncommon was explicit expression of a casual or indifferent attitude toward the prospect of pregnancy. Even when combined, these two categories never constituted more than one-fifth of the sample. Again, this result seems to confirm our earlier observation that few women were deliberately attempting to become pregnant again during the follow-up years.

A small proportion of the young mothers stated that they did not need to use birth control at that time because they engaged in little or no sexual activity. A few stated that personal reservations about contraception had convinced them to discontinue use. Most of these women objected to birth control on religious or moral grounds. But by far the most common explanation for terminating use was that specific problems had arisen with the method of contraception they were using. In some instances women mentioned physical problems that they had encountered from the outset—a heavy menstrual flow, nausea, pain, or weight gain—but more often they referred to the fear of negative side effects—sterility, cancer, or thrombosis. From their comments it is obvious that many had become frightened by reports in the mass media about the hazards of oral contraceptives or intrauterine devices. These fears were particularly prevalent in the follow-up interviews conducted during or shortly after the 1970 Senate hearings on the possible health hazards associated with oral contraceptives (cf. Ross, 1970). However, throughout the study apprehensions were voiced, fueled by television and magazine reports on the dangerous side effects of particular methods of birth control.[9] This theme was evident from the responses of the young mothers in the follow-up interviews:

[9]Such complaints were most common from women who had used the IUD, although they also were very frequent from women formerly on the pill. The greater incidence of medical difficulties associated with the IUD may be a major reason that our data did not correspond to the findings of previous studies based on adult populations that showed that rates of continuation were higher among women who used intrauterine devices than among those using oral contraceptives (Ricketts, 1974). The AFC staff generally encouraged adolescents to use oral methods, which seemed to be consistent with most adolescents' inclinations. A high proportion of the young mothers expressed reservations about contraceptive devices that were "put inside them."

> I didn't need them. My mother kept hearing on TV about people dying from the pill.

> I've heard it was harmful. I had a prescription but I never got it filled.

Several characteristic patterns of phasing out of contraceptive use were evident in the women's comments. A small minority of the young mothers made a deliberate decision not to use birth control either because they wanted to become pregnant or because they found contraception objectionable and were willing to accept the consequences of nonuse:

> I wasn't too sure of it. It was new and I was afraid of it.

> I became engaged and don't mind if I have another child.

Most women, however, did not decide to terminate but merely interrupted practice. In some instances, this process occurred abruptly when they began to experience physical symptoms or side effects that they associated with birth control. In light of the adverse publicity surrounding contraception, these symptoms were viewed with alarm and often convinced the women to suspend use until they could obtain medical advice. Frequently, however, there was a lengthy delay between the time the problems arose and the clinic appointment. Often the young mother, fearful of physicians or deterred by the formal setting of the hospital, put off contacting the clinic. Despite her resolution to "be careful" in the interim, she became pregnant within a short time. Here is a typical comment from a young mother who stopped using oral contraception:

> I lost them. I wanted to use it. I thought only the doctor who gave it to me first could give it to me again. And I haven't seen him since then. He wasn't there when I went up.

Other young mothers discontinued use more gradually. Finding it difficult to follow the regimen of pill taking, they began to take chances. Not becoming pregnant immediately after they had skipped a few pills served to reinforce this strategy and to increase their willingness to assume greater risks. In time, some stopped using the pill altogether. Sooner or later their luck ran out and they became pregnant. This gradual abandonment of contraceptive use was especially common among the mothers who were married and could "afford" to take chances. As one respondent explained:

> I forgot for a month and nothing happened so I didn't take them in January. And in February I didn't come on [menstruate].

A third mode of phasing out birth control was especially familiar to single and separated women who were not having sexual relations on a regular basis. Women who went for several weeks without having intercourse were less willing to put up with the regimen and side effects of pill use. Once they stopped taking the pill, they were disinclined to resume use and elected to take their chances with either a nonprescription method or no method of birth control at all. From comments gathered in the interviews, it seemed that pill use was particularly problematic for women who were engaging in sexual relations only episodically. One unmarried mother reported why she was no longer using contraception:

> Because I haven't been going steady and the friends I go with are just casual friends.

Neither the AFC nor the regular clinic was well equipped to deal with the specific problems the young mothers encountered in using birth control. The services of both programs were provided primarily in the prenatal period and in the early months of postpartum. The assumption was that if the young mothers were sufficiently acquainted with contraceptive techniques and received adequate instruction on how to use the pill or the IUD, they would be fully prepared to practice birth control indefinitely. In the event that problems arose, the young mother could seek advice and assistance from the hospital. Clearly, this "inoculation approach" did not work out very well.

Significantly, there was little or no relationship between how involved the young mother had been in the hospital program prior to delivery and her success in using birth control during the study. Women who had received a large number of prenatal examinations, frequent contact with the nursing and social work staffs, and regular participation in the group meetings were not less likely to abandon contraception after the first year. Little or no attendance at group meetings was associated with lower success in practicing contraception during the first year after delivery. However, this relationship seemed to result specifically from the fact that women who did not attend group meetings were less likely to have had contact with the hospital immediately after delivery (Ricketts, 1973).

Postpartum contact with the hospital was decidedly linked to contraceptive continuation. Women who received consultation about birth control during the first year after delivery were less likely to terminate. In particular, discussions with the staff about how the birth control method was working out were especially critical for continued use. The fact that the AFC participants were more likely to receive consultation appears to be the main reason that they had a better rate of success than the participants in the regular clinic. After they began using contraception, seventy percent of the women who attended the AFC stated that they had discussed with a staff member how birth control was working out as compared to 38% of the control group. The number of discussions was related directly to the rate of continuation. Regular clinic participants who had taken part in an equal number of postpartum discussions as AFC participants had the same rate of continuation, suggesting that follow-up discussions were primarily responsible for the greater success of the AFC program.

Follow-up discussions had several functions. They provided an opportunity for the young mother to bring up problems she was having in using birth control, giving her a chance to allay anxieties about physical reactions to the method of contraception. Women who reported at Time 2 that such discussions had taken place during the previous year were more likely to express the opinion that their knowledge about birth control was sufficient and were less likely to voice doubts about the safety or desirability of using birth control. Thus the follow-up discussions served both to increase knowledge about contraceptive methods and to reduce the negative sentiments that often surfaced when difficulties in using contraception arose. The follow-up discussions also reinforced the resolve to use birth control, countering the inclination to take risks. The clinic physicians frequently took the opportunity during the discussions to remind the young mother that she might get pregnant again if she did not use contraception. Many of the mothers needed this reinforcement in order to put up with the initial discomfort or inconvenience of using birth control methods. Discussions with the hospital staff also may have helped to mobilize support from family and friends and to sustain commitment to birth control practice in the event that such support was lacking.

Not all of the AFC participants received the benefit of follow-up discussions during the period immediately after delivery. Nearly one-third of the women who attended the special program reported that they had had no further consultation with the hospital staff after beginning to practice contraception, and another one-fifth had had only one follow-up session after the six-week postpartum checkup. Only one-third of the AFC graduates had received as many as three consultations in the year after delivery. Although the regular clinic attenders were given even less attention after delivery, the two groups were perhaps more similar than different in the amount (or lack) of attention they received after they began using contraception.

After the first year, follow-up was even less frequent. While the participants in the AFC were invited to seek assistance from the clinic whenever they encountered problems, it was up to the mothers to take the initiative in making contact. Few did, and those who continued to visit the clinic were a highly selective group consisting mainly of the single women who had remained in school. Consequently, this group had the highest rate of contraceptive continuation and accounted for much of the difference between the two programs.

Considering the minimal contact offered by both hospital programs, it is not surprising that a substantial minority of women continued to have reservations about birth control after their first pregnancy or confessed to being not fully informed. The women who expressed doubts about contraception at the one-year follow-up were much more likely to discontinue use than young mothers who were firm in their opinion about the desirability of birth control. Similarly, we discovered that support for birth control use from the family, friends, and sexual partners of the young mothers greatly enhanced the probability of long-term contraceptive use. Women who were favorably disposed toward contraception and who received strong social support tended to do well whether or not they participated in the AFC (Ricketts, 1973). To the extent that it had an effect, the follow-up was an important supplementary source of knowledge, tension management, and support for contraceptive practitioners. Regrettably, however, the AFC failed to provide an adequate substitute for the informal supportive network that was often lacking in the crucial period following the birth of the first child.

In view of the importance of follow-up, why did the program not make a greater effort to maintain contact with former participants? In the first place, the problem of maintaining commitment to birth control use was not foreseen by the individuals who designed the program. It was taken for granted that if the young mother wanted to prevent a subsequent pregnancy and was given contraceptive instruction, she would use birth control effectively until she was prepared to have another child. Her ability to use contraception was greatly overestimated, and the staff did not foresee the problems that arise when birth control is practiced by the inexperienced and wary. Finally, the program was designed to provide services in the prenatal and early postpartum periods and it was not sufficient flexibile to extend services beyond the first year.


## SUMMARY


At the outset of this chapter, we briefly alluded to several alternative explanations for the high rate of repeat pregnancies among adolescent mothers. Our findings provided some basis for choosing among these various views. The "culture of poverty" explanation that additional pregnancies are welcomed, if not desired, that the birth of the first child relaxes childbearing restrictions, and that adolescent mothers will be unreceptive to birth control was contradicted by many of our findings. At the same time, we found little support for the contention of some family planning advocates that the mere accessibility of contraceptive information and devices will eliminate unwanted pregnancies.

While neither of these views is wholly correct, both contain elements of truth. The adaptation to the first child lessens the perceived costs of additional births for certain women, making them less conscientious about using contraception than they might otherwise be. On the whole, however, the experience of the pregnancy increases their support for birth control.[10] Most women respond to an unplanned pregnancy by becoming more, not less, willing to control their childbearing. When subsequent pregnancies occurred, the young mothers in our study typically responded by improving contraceptive practice. Exposure to contraceptive instruction obviously does increase compliance, as the higher success of the AFC program demonstrated. Yet, given the difficulty of using particular contraceptive techniques, the anxiety regarding the safety of certain

---

[10]Significantly, a greater proportion of the young mothers practiced birth control at both the three- and five-year follow-ups than did sexually active classmates. Among the single women, for example, 86% of the mothers were using contraception at Time 4 as compared to 75% of the unmarried classmates. Comparable differences occurred among the married and separated respondents.

methods, and the lingering sexual prohibitions that make it difficult for a woman to speak openly about problems in practicing birth control, it is not surprising that women frequently abandon contraception even when they prefer not to have more babies.

In our sample, those who had most to lose by becoming pregnant again showed the greatest ability to persist in their contraceptive efforts in the face of these obstacles. Eventually, however, many of these highly motivated women also succumbed. Thus, even programs designed for the highly committed contraceptive user will fail if a sustained effort is not made to deal with the difficulties and apprehensions that inevitably arise. If programs are to have more than modest success, they must make it easy for women to accept and to use their services. In Chapter 11, we shall return to this point.

# 7. Early Parenthood and Schooling

AT THE TIME 1 INTERVIEW, the young mothers were asked to recall how they felt upon discovering that they were pregnant; a number replied that they first thought about the difficulty they would have remaining in school. More than half acknowledged that having a child would reduce the chance of attaining their educational objectives and might even prevent them from completing high school. Even in the early months of pregnancy, some women had already felt compelled to leave school, and many more eventually succumbed to the pressure to drop out.

Both in professional circles and in the popular press, the term *dropout* has become synonymous with failure. Over the years results from educational research have created the impression that dropping out of high school is a costly mistake. However, several studies have indicated that the evidence that economic prospects are significantly improved by completion of high school is ambiguous (Bachman et al., 1971). Jencks and his collaborators (1972) have raised serious questions about the effect of educational training on social mobility. Nevertheless, even if certain effects of schooling are more apparent than real, the fact that many people believe them to be true endows them with a kind of social reality. Most young mothers who drop out of school are convinced that they will be economically and socially disadvantaged as a result, although they may not in fact suffer any such handicaps.

A young mother's fear that pregnancy will adversely affect her chance of completing high school appears to be well founded. A number of investigations have shown that prenuptial pregnancy and early marriage frequently result in permanent withdrawal from high school. While estimates vary widely, somewhere between one-half and two-thirds of all female dropouts cite pregnancy and/or marriage as the principal reason for leaving school (Stine et al., 1964; Coombs and Cooley, 1968). At the same time, however, it is important to recognize that there has been no careful longitudinal study verifying these estimates or describing the process by which pregnancy leads to dropping out.

127

# BARRIERS TO EDUCATION OF THE
# SCHOOL-AGE MOTHER

Although the evidence on the association between pregnancy and dropping out is incomplete, educators and governmental officials have begun to take notice of the growing number of school-age mothers. In 1972, S. P. Marland, then U.S. commissioner of education, issued a statement calling for a comprehensive program for school-age parents and announced that his department was taking charge of a governmental effort to develop and promote a "successful services integration model" to meet the problems of school-age parents (*Sharing*, March 1972). Commissioner Marland declared:

> Every girl in the United States has a right to and a need for the education that will help her prepare herself for a career, for family life, and for citizenship. To be married or pregnant is not sufficient cause to deprive her of an education and the opportunity to become a contributing member of society.

The sincere pronouncement that every pregnant adolescent has a right to continue her education has not as yet led to the creation of facilities and supportive services to ensure that right (Children's Defense Fund, 1974). Opportunities for school-age parents vary enormously throughout the country. In some localities, teenagers are pressured to leave school as soon as it is known that they are pregnant, and no alternative education is provided. In other areas, special services are offered to the teenager who becomes pregnant, and she is encouraged to continue her education at home or in separate facilities for pregnant adolescents. Finally, an increasing number of school districts are permitting the expectant mother to attend regular classes.[1]

While some educators justify their exclusion of pregnant teenagers on the ground that only special educational programs can meet the particular needs of expectant mothers, relatively few programs of this nature exist. In 1967, there were 35 such programs throughout the country. By 1972, as a result of governmental efforts, the number had climbed to about 225, but these programs were serving roughly only one out of five (40,000 out of 210,000) pregnant

---

[1]A number of legal actions have been undertaken to clarify the educational rights of the pregnant teenager. The judicial response thus far generally has affirmed her right to educational instruction. In a few instances, however, the courts have sustained the action of local school boards in removing pregnant teenagers from the classroom (Nolte, 1973). While the courts generally have upheld the view of most educators that a pregnant student should not be deprived of educational opportunities, decisions in this area have only begun to undo traditional exclusionary practices of school boards. A 1960 survey of educators in Ohio (Noland and Sherry, 1969) revealed that the majority favored allowing a pregnant student to remain in class as long as her condition was not apparent to others. In 1966, a national inventory of educational practices revealed that only 39% of the school districts permitted unmarried pregnant teenagers to attend regular classes (Atkyns, 1968). During the period following delivery, the availability of special services is even more scarce.

teenagers (Howard, 1972).[2] More effective delivery of services is hampered by limited information and considerable misinformation about the educational situation of the school-age parent. Besides a few scattered articles on the demographic characteristics of school-age parents and several evaluations of comprehensive programs for this group, most research on the topic has yielded only well-intentioned pronouncements on the inadequacies of efforts thus far (Ravacon and Dempsey, 1972).

While it is widely accepted that a link exists between pregnancy and withdrawal from school, this connection is not at all obvious or agreed upon by educational authorities. In fact, an analysis of the literature reveals three quite independent explanations for the association that suggest radically different policies and programs for the school-age parent.

The first explanation posits that among less committed and less competent students, pregnancy serves as an excuse for withdrawing from school. Pregnancy in this view does not "cause" dropping out, it merely provides a convenient rationale for leaving school. Low educational ambition and abilities thus explain both why teenagers become pregnant and why they drop out. As Bowerman and his colleagues (1966: 325) remarked:

> Pregnancy is often not the cause of school dropout but rather a concomitant or something that is allowed to happen because there is no desire and no concrete plan to continue in school. It is as true to say that increased motivation for an education will reduce premarital pregnancies and subsequent school dropouts as it is to say that better morals among our youth will reduce school dropouts.

There is slim evidence to support or discredit what might be referred to as the *status-failure hypothesis*. Several studies have suggested that adolescents who become pregnant early are not conspicuously able students (Havighurst, 1961; Keeve, 1965), but other research has suggested that when female dropouts are carefully matched against their peers on demographic characteristics, academic differences are not marked (Coombs and Cooley, 1968; Paulker, 1969).

A second explanation of the link between pregnancy and discontinuation of schooling can be labeled the *status-conflict hypothesis.* Inevitably, parenthood prematurely forces a young adolescent into adult roles. Serious strains arise when a young woman simultaneously attempts to meet the demands of student, parent, and wife (Howard, 1968; Osofsky, 1968; Klerman and Jekel, 1973). While some adolescents with unusual skill, determination, and energy manage to

2There are no official estimates, but Shirley A. Nelson, director of the Consortium on Early Childbearing and Childrearing, estimated that by the beginning of 1975, there may be 350 programs, reaching one pregnant student in three. The situation has improved in the past decade but many school-age mothers still face barriers if they wish to continue the education in their regular classroom, and special programs (during and especially after pregnancy) are unavailable to the majority of adolescent parents (Children's Defense Fund, 1974).

handle these conflicting demands, most find them irreconcilable. Generally, students who give priority to marriage and childrearing will withdraw their commitment to education unless extraordinary support is provided by family and school. In contrast to the status-failure explanation, the status-conflict view assumes that low commitment to education is a consequence, rather than a cause, of an unplanned pregnancy.

A third way of accounting for the high rate of dropping out among pregnant adolescents emphasizes the part played by school policies and educational institutions. As we noted earlier, the traditional posture of educators toward pregnant students has been extremely unsympathetic. If the pregnant teenager is not officially barred by restrictive regulations from attending school, often she is unofficially discouraged from continuing her education by administrators, guidance counselors, and teachers (Atkyns, 1968; Howard, 1968; Children's Defense Fund, 1974). Although school officials are generally less hostile to such students once they have had the child, those who are unmarried still encounter considerable informal disapproval. In any event, once they leave school, returning is difficult (Hoeft, 1968). Time lost in school cannot easily be made up, and the student is generally put back a year. Moreover, young mothers—both those who marry and those who do not—may feel out of touch with their fellow students and regard themselves as different even when they manage to maintain class standing. Finally, individuals unaccustomed to performing in school may find this role difficult to take up again, particularly if they return to a different setting and receive little support from their teachers and peers. Thus, it is not unreasonable to conclude that a certain amount of dropping out may be explained by what we will term *status disruption*.

As we have stated before, these three explanations are not necessarily distinct, and they need not apply to all cases to be valid. None of these hypotheses has been subjected to rigorous empirical examination; they all are based only on informed speculation and a small number of descriptive studies. The data collected in our Baltimore study provided us with an opportunity to determine whether any or all of these explanations are useful in accounting for the educational careers of pregnant adolescents.

# PREGNANCY AND EDUCATIONAL ACHIEVEMENT

Some disagreement exists among educational researchers as to which indicator to employ when measuring withdrawal from high school. The measure used most often and the one that is easiest to understand is merely noncompletion of high school (Bachman et al., 1971). The major limitation of this measure is that it fails to account for any of the particulars of the process of dropping out—that is, the timing or sequence of educational discontinuation. Consequently, the indicator we used in our study was somewhat more complicated.

Following delivery, some adolescents returned to school while others did not. Of those who did not, a small number had already graduated from high school before their child was born and therefore we classified them as non-dropouts. Among those who resumed their schooling, some had completed high school by the five-year follow-up, some had not yet graduated but were in school, and still others had dropped out in the interim between delivery and the final interview. Most high school graduates were no longer attending school, but a small number had entered a postgraduate college, or a paraprofessional training program. The typology we developed arranged these six contingencies in ascending order from dropouts who never returned to school to postgraduates who were still in school at Time 4 (see Table 7.1).

The impression that emerged from examining this array was that no single pattern predominated. The sample was split almost evenly between women who dropped out and those who graduated from high school. Before terminating, nearly half of the dropouts had made some attempt to complete their schooling, and 16% of the nongraduates were enrolled in school at Time 4. Fifteen percent of the graduates had completed high school before the birth of their first child, but the remaining 85% had returned to school postpartum to obtain their diplomas. Nearly 10% of the entire sample were in a postgraduate program at the time of the last follow-up.

In the abstract, it is difficult to assess the educational achievement of the young mothers. However, even as they stand, these findings cast some doubt on certain widely held beliefs about the educational careers of adolescent mothers. First, it is obvious that pregnancy was not being used as a convenient excuse to drop out of school, as some writers have suggested; most adolescents (three-quarters of the sample) resumed school after delivery. It was equally apparent that teenage parenthood per se is not an insurmountable barrier to educational

Table 7.1. *Educational Achievement of Adolescent Mothers and Classmates*

| Education | Young Mothers | Classmates with Premarital Pregnancy | Classmates without Premarital Pregnancy |
|---|---|---|---|
| *Less Than High School* | 51% | 18% | 11% |
| Never Returned | 23 | | |
| Returned, No Longer in School | 20 | 14 | 9 |
| Returned, Still in School | 8 | 4 | 2 |
| *High School Graduate* | 49 | 82 | 89 |
| Never Returned | 7 | | |
| Returned, No Longer in School | 33 | 65 | 62 |
| Returned, Still in School | 9 | 17 | 27 |
| | (323) | (113) | (107) |

achievement, as some observers have maintained; half of the sample completed high school, others were close to graduating at Time 4, and a small minority had gone past high school.

Yet, against the young mothers' own educational goals, their achievements did not measure up quite so well. At the time of their pregnancy, all but 10 adolescents reported that they hoped to complete high school, and nearly half looked forward to some type of higher education. While many conceded that in all likelihood these aspirations would not be realized, most (84%) still expected to complete high school, and over one-fourth anticipated finishing some higher education. Evidently, then, a large number of the young mothers failed to reach their expected goals. And it is probable that the aims they voiced at the first interview were downgraded to some degree as a result of pregnancy.

A useful strategy for measuring the impact of the pregnancy on schooling is to compare the educational careers of the young mothers with those of their former classmates. Eighty-six percent of the classmates had completed high school by the time of the five-year follow-up, and 19% of those who had not graduated were still in school. More than one-fourth of the classmates had obtained some amount of higher education, in most instances one or more years of college. Perhaps it was merely coincidence, but after five years the classmates had achieved almost exactly the level of education that the young mothers in the initial interview had stated that they expected to reach by that time.

The figures cited in the preceding paragraph actually understated the differences between the two groups, for the classmates included a minority of women who, like the young mothers, became premaritally pregnant before completing their schooling. When this subgroup was removed from the sample, the percentage who completed high school rose slightly (to 89%), and the proportion who attended college climbed to more than one-third. Even the classmates who became premaritally pregnant attained significantly higher levels of educational achievement than the mothers, which indicates, not surprisingly, that there is a considerable relative advantage in delaying a premarital pregnancy.[3]

Comparison of the educational careers of the young mothers and the classmates indicated that the impact of pregnancy on educational achievement was substantial, even if it was not quite so severe as the literature implies. On the average, the adolescent mothers had approximately two fewer years of schooling than the classmates. This finding brings us back to the question raised at the beginning of this chapter: How and why does pregnancy affect educational achievement?

[3]The nulliparous classmates had achieved a slightly higher level of education than the national standard, equalling the achievement of white females and exceeding the attainment of black females of similar ages. The mothers, by contrast, had significantly lower levels of educational achievement than their age and race counterparts (U.S. Bureau of the Census, 1972b).

# STATUS FAILURE AND DROPPING OUT

As noted, the most widely accepted but least documented explanation for the link between pregnancy and withdrawal from school holds that adolescents who become pregnant lack the background, ambition, and competence to achieve in school. Parenthood offers a socially acceptable alternative role to the untalented student. We attempted to test the validity of the status-failure hypothesis first by determining whether in the aggregate the adolescent mothers ranked low according to the criteria that forecast academic success and then by examining whether those young mothers who did drop out were less motivated to continue their education and possessed fewer skills to sustain them in school than those who completed high school.

## Socioeconomic Status and Dropping Out

Most young mothers were from either working- or a lower-class background, a fact that led us to expect a relatively low level of academic achievement within the sample (Duncan et al., 1972). Yet, at the outset of the study, the socioeconomic standing of the adolescents was very similar to that of the classmates, suggesting that socioeconomic background alone cannot be responsible for the high rate of dropping out among adolescent mothers. If this were true, there would be an equally high proportion of nongraduates among the classmates.

Within the sample of adolescent mothers, a number of comparisons were made to determine whether the women from economically disadvantaged families were more likely to drop out of school following pregnancy (see Table A.13). While the results tended to support the expectation of higher educational achievement among women whose families were relatively better off, the differences were not large or completely consistent. There was a moderately strong relationship between family income and educational achievement; however, the relationship between the parents' education and work status and the daughter's educational level was not sizable. Apparently, either the variations in parental status were not large enough to have much effect on the educational careers of the mothers or other factors outweighed this one.

Such noneconomic indicators of family position as composition of the family and prior history of illegitimacy were examined as well. The findings showed that adolescents from families headed by women were no more likely to terminate their education than those from households headed by couples. Dropping out was somewhat higher among adolescents who had some history of illegitimacy in the family, but again the differences were quite modest across the various categories.

## Ambition and Dropping Out

While previous studies show that family background has an independent effect on educational achievement, it has been found that the influence of social class origin is largely mediated through intervening experiences in the family, peer group, and neighborhood. A vast amount of research has described social class differences in socialization for schooling (Rosen et al., 1969; Jencks et al., 1972; Duncan et al., 1972). Children from middle-class backgrounds are trained from an early age to *feel* competent and *be* competent in school (Clausen, 1968; Deutsch et al., 1968; Kerckhoff, 1972). Even before they enter school, they are actively encouraged to develop academic ambition and scholastic skills, and by the time they enter the first grade they are well equipped to outperform their peers from less advantaged backgrounds. The training and support they receive at home are reinforced in school. Teachers appreciate and respond to a child who is enthusiastic and confident, and consequently the ambitious and competent student is likely to find school more rewarding and the classroom situation more congenial (Toby, 1957). Thus, initial disparities are likely to widen during the course of a child's educational career.

This familiar scenario might lead us to anticipate that prior to becoming pregnant many of the adolescents in our study would have held a rather dim view of schooling. At the first interview, the expectant mothers were asked a series of questions designed to determine their educational plans following delivery. Contrary to expectation, their answers revealed that a great majority were not indifferent students. Almost all (90%) reported that they intended to continue their schooling at least until they completed high school. Over one-half, although in the midst of their pregnancy, were currently attending school, and two-thirds of those who had dropped out said that they planned to resume their education after delivery. When asked to compare their educational prospects with that of their peers, four-fifths said they expected to go as far as, if not further than, their friends in school.

Obviously, these answers were highly subjective and reflected considerable fantasy; nevertheless, they did not reveal a distaste for schooling. Since we lacked similar information from the classmates at Time 1, it was not possible to draw any conclusions about the level of aspirations of the young mothers relative to their immediate peers. Nevertheless, on the basis of information collected in other studies, the goals of the mothers did not seem appreciably out of line with the educational aims of other youth (Gottlieb, 1964; Coleman et al., 1966; Rosenberg and Simmons, 1971).

Although the general level of aspiration was higher than might have been expected, there was considerable variation in the adolescents' responses to each of the questions posed. Consequently, four separate items—educational goals, educational expectations, desire to return to school, and educational goals compared to those of friends—were combined into a single index of educational ambition. Women at the low end of the continuum expressed lower goals (intending to go no further than high school) and were also less committed to remaining in school at Time 1, while those who were high in ambition invariably intended to go beyond high school and were strongly attached to school.

Ambition turned out to be a powerful predictor of educational attainment (Table A.14). Over half of the mothers with low ambition (those in the lowest quartile) never returned to school after delivery, and almost another third subsequently dropped out before completing high school. Only 8% had managed to graduate by the five-year follow-up. The top quartile (those with high ambition) revealed an almost diametrically opposite pattern. Only 3% never went back to school after delivery, and another 11% subsequently terminated their education. Eighty-five percent of the mothers with high ambition had completed high school by the final interview, and one-quarter were then enrolled in institutions of higher education. In short, ambition strongly predicted educational attainment.

### Academic Competence and Dropping Out

The effect of school performance on educational achievement also was examined, although this part of the analysis was hindered by the lack of an objective measure of the students' ability.[4] As a makeshift measure of academic competence, we calculated whether the respondents were in the expected grade level according to their age at the beginning of the study. One-fourth were one grade or more below the expected level. A significantly greater proportion of the less able students dropped out of school either before or shortly after their child was born (64% versus 36%). This relationship persisted even when the level of ambition was held constant. There was an even stronger relationship between perceived competence and educational achievement: adolescents who claimed that they were among the more able and interested students were more than twice as likely to graduate as those who reported that they did not do well in school. Again, controlling for ambition did not eliminate the relationship between perceived competence and school performance after delivery. Although not nearly as strong a determinant as ambition, prior academic performance does help to explain the educational careers of the adolescent mothers.

### Family Influence on Educational Achievement

What has been variously labelled "family support" and "family pressure" also consistently showed up as an important determinant of academic achievement (Simpson, 1962; E. Cohen, 1965; Sewell and Shah, 1968). Considering the

[4]Efforts to assemble school records were not successful. In the early stages of the study, a letter was sent to various schools that young mothers had attended. Less than 20% supplied records, and the information in many of these records was undecipherable.

rather tenuous social and economic situation of the adolescent mother, we might expect that support from her family would be a particularly critical factor in determining whether or not she remained in school. Parents may either help to define pregnancy as a legitimate excuse to leave school or back up an adolescent's decision to continue her education by encouragement and assistance.

Our initial interview contained several measures of the family's attitudes toward continued schooling. Most of the parents (71%) replied that they would be "very disappointed" if their daughters were not able to return to school as soon as the child was born. Only one parent in the entire sample responded that she would be satisfied if her child did not finish high school, and more than half of the parents hoped that their daughters would go beyond the twelfth grade. Finally, nearly three-fourths believed that it was "very likely" that their pregnant daughters would resume their schooling after delivery.

It was possible to demonstrate that the parents' views actually had a considerable influence on their children's behavior. We did so by examining the intrafamily correlations of educational attitudes and behavior. An index, constructed from several of the items obtained in the interview with the prospective grandmother (see the preceding paragraph), was employed to measure the parent's expectations about her pregnant daughter's education.[5] The signs of maternal influence on the educational careers of the mothers were unmistakable. Over two-thirds of the women whose mothers had very low expectations for them dropped out before completing high school as compared to less than one-fifth of those whose mothers had very high expectations. Part of this relationship was due to the association between mothers' and daughters' educational standards, but even when the daughters' ambition was held constant, the influence of the parents' expectations on the daughters' educational achievement persisted.

Indirect evidence suggested that the attitudes of peers affected the mothers' decision to continue in school after the birth of their child. Adolescents were asked how many of their friends they thought would complete high school. About two-thirds of those who replied that "less than half" of their friends would finish high school dropped out themselves, compared to one-third of those who reported that most of their friends would graduate. Again, the relationship between perceived peer achievement and educational patterns continued to show up even when the level of ambition was held constant.

### Conclusions on Status-Failure Hypothesis

The preceding analysis reached what may at first have seemed contradictory conclusions. Clearly, our evidence consistently showed that the

---

[5]There was a moderately strong association between the educational standards of the mothers and the goals of their daughters, confirming what has been reported in previous studies: parents are a major influence on their children's educational standards (Furstenberg, 1971c).

mothers as a group were not conspicuously incompetent or disaffected students. Three out of four were at the grade level appropriate to their age. The great majority reported that they enjoyed school, did moderately well, and wanted to return to school after delivery. These aspirations were not idle statements or pronouncements issued largely for the benefit of the interviewer, as was demonstrated by the fact that most of the adolescents did in fact return to school after their child was born and half of them managed to remain in school until graduation. At the same time, the analysis provided clear support for the position that status failure is one reason that many adolescent mothers do not complete high school. Ambition, academic performance, and family expectations all were highly predictive of whether the young mother remained in school until graduation.

What appear to be conflicting results can be reconciled: not all or even most of the adolescents who become pregnant are predisposed or predestined to drop out of school. Most of those who did drop out, however, were marginal students before becoming pregnant, and probably some of them would have left school even if they had managed to avoid early parenthood. For these individuals, motherhood provides a compelling rationale for withdrawing from school. Perhaps as many as half of the women who left school could be classified as disaffected students. But what of the remainder? Nearly half of the dropouts were at least moderately able students and were unequivocally committed to obtaining a high school diploma. To understand the behavior of these women, we considered the other explanations for the link between pregnancy and dropping out.

## STATUS CONFLICT AND DROPPING OUT

It has been noted frequently that the passage to both marriage and parenthood is usually difficult in our society (Waller, 1938; LeMasters, 1957; Rossi, 1968). These events often are marked by a high degree of uncertainty, and the individual may assume these new roles ill equipped to handle the responsibilities they bring. Regardless of whether the tensions accompanying marriage and parenthood have been generally exaggerated, as certain critics have contended (Dyer, 1963; Hobbs, 1968), they probably exist for the adolescent. Particularly when early marriage and early parenthood occur simultaneously, the teenage mother is likely to experience a sudden dislocation. Managing this rapid transition is difficult enough in itself, but when the problems the adolescent mother faces in remaining in school are added to it, the strain can become unbearable.

Inevitably, the adolescent mother is forced to make certain choices, and, depending on her priorities, she generally elects to downplay one or the other status (Goode, 1960; Burr, 1972). We have already seen that some women choose to defer marriage until they complete their schooling; others, in order to remain in school, turn over some, if not most, of the childcare responsibilities to a parent or sibling. But many, as we shall now discover, decide that they cannot continue their education.

### School or Marriage?

Even though they were generally older, and hence closer to completing high school, the young mothers who married during pregnancy had the highest rate of dropping out (50%), followed closely by those who married within the first year after delivery. Withdrawal from school was somewhat lower among the young women who waited several years before marrying (46%) and lowest of all among mothers who remained single throughout the study (33%). It would seem, then, that marriage does interrupt an adolescent's educational career.

Controlling for educational ambition, however, forced us to revise this conclusion to some extent. Since the women who married early tended to be those most lacking in academic ambition, we could not distinguish between the effects of low ambition and marriage on educational achievement without looking at both factors simultaneously. Table 7.2 presents the relationship between marriage and school completion, holding educational ambition constant. It is clear from our data that marriage per se does not interrupt schooling; rather, in conjunction with low ambition, matrimony tends to curtail the educational career of the adolescent mother. This finding followed from an earlier conclusion that marriage provides a socially acceptable alternative to school continuation for women with low commitment to education. It is now possible to elaborate on that conclusion in light of what has been said about the teenagers' difficulties in handling simultaneously the roles of student, newlywed,

Table 7.2. *Educational Achievement of Adolescent Mothers by Marital Status at Time 4 and Ambition*

| Education | Low Ambition | | Medium Ambition | | High Ambition | |
|---|---|---|---|---|---|---|
| | Single | Ever Married | Single | Ever Married | Single | Ever Married |
| *Less than High School* | | | | | | |
| Never Returned | 26% | 65% | 19% | 18% | 3% | 3% |
| Returned, No Longer in School | 58 | 17 | 12 | 24 | 9 | 14 |
| Returned, Still in School | — | 12 | 15 | 9 | 3 | — |
| *High School Graduate* | | | | | | |
| Never Returned | — | — | 3 | 13 | 6 | 14 |
| Returned, No Longer in School | 11 | 6 | 48 | 31 | 41 | 54 |
| Returned, Still in School | 5 | — | 3 | 6 | 38 | 16 |
| | (19) | (52) | (67) | (114) | (34) | (37) |

and mother. Unless an adolescent is strongly committed to completing high school, she is very likely to drop out when she marries; however, if her commitment is high, she often manages to perform both roles at once at least for a time.[6]

Interestingly, we also learn from Table 7.2 that most single mothers with low and medium ambition managed to remain in school despite a relatively weak commitment. Apparently, having less reason than their married peers to drop out, unmarried mothers usually returned to school after delivery, and nearly half of this group had completed high school by Time 4. Undoubtedly, some of these women became more committed to school after they resumed their education, while others may have been encouraged by family, friends, and school personnel to complete high school.

Married women face a different kind of social pressure, one propelling them away from, rather than toward, additional schooling. No longer living with their families, they are deprived of the psychological as well as practical support that their parents may provide. In some cases they must also overcome their husband's reservations. Although not all males espoused a traditional view of the female role, some obviously felt that education was not a legitimate reason for turning over child care to someone else.

My husband took me out. He wanted the baby to get to know her mother.

The interviews did not contain questions on the males' attitudes toward schooling; however, it was possible to draw inferences by comparing the educational careers of married women whose husbands had completed high school with those of the women who married high school dropouts. This comparison revealed that women who married high school graduates were at a distinct advantage. Almost three-fifths completed high school themselves as compared to one-third of those who married nongraduates. It would appear that the better educated males were more likely to endorse (or less inclined to block) their wives' attempts to further their education after they married, while the less educated males may have been more reluctant to see their wives obtain more schooling than they had been able to achieve.[7] Also, the former were in a stronger economic position and perhaps could more easily support their families during the time their wives attended school. The luxury of additional schooling may not have been possible for young mothers on the economic margin.

[6]About half of the married high school graduates wed after they completed high school, while the other half completed high school after marriage. Strong ambition was especially characteristic of this latter group.

[7]Of course, this finding may also be explained by the tendency of better-educated women to marry men of equal or superior educational status. However, the finding held true for women who married before completing high school as well as for those who married after graduation. In any case, some of the latter group might not have finished school prior to marriage had they not received encouragement from their future husbands.

### The Complications of Child Care

Marriage not only brings new responsibilities and obligations; it also complicates and adds to the burdens of parenthood. The women who remained unmarried could more often count on child care assistance from their mothers or other relatives living in the household. Some married women received such help from their families, but the help they got was usually less substantial or predictable.[8] Few lived with their families, making child care assistance more difficult to deliver. Moreover, the grandparents were sometimes reluctant to intrude once their daughters had married. Finally, the young women themselves were probably less likely to seek help from their parents and more inclined to rely on their husbands for assistance in childrearing. As a result, the single women who chose to remain in school were at quite an advantage.

The adolescents themselves reported that the responsibilities of parenthood were the major reason that they withdrew from school. One-third of the young mothers listed this reason as the main factor adversely affecting their ability to continue their education. As one respondent explained when asked why she did not expect to go as far in school as she would have liked:

> Wouldn't have anyone to watch the baby. Wouldn't be able to afford to care for it.

This explanation fits with a finding reported earlier that family income is related to withdrawal from school. Few of the young mothers were in a position to pay someone to watch their child on a regular basis. A calculation was made to determine how many of the mothers had a family member available who could assume this responsibility. Using information on family structure that was provided in the first interview, we developed a very rough measure of the availability of child care assistance. This measure was based on whether the young mothers resided with adults who were not working. It turned out that less than one-third of the young mothers were living in households in which they could count on another adult to share child care duties during the day. Almost none of the married women and only about half of the single mothers were living with a relative who did not have a regular job.[9]

Interestingly, in discussing their options, the young mothers cited the practical obstacles of arranging for child care less often than their reservations about leaving their child. However, a number told us that they were unwilling to forego the gratification of caring for a newborn or to turn over the responsibilities of child care even to another family member. In the words of one respondent, "I wanted him to have good care, and I felt only I could do that." Another young mother confessed that if she left her child with someone else, "he would know her better than me." Even when someone else was available to

[8]Stack (1974) makes this point, and findings presented in Chapters 8 and 9 provide corroboration.

[9]The presence of such a person was related to the mothers' return to school although the association was quite weak. Unfortunately, it was difficult to tell from the data collected at Time 1 whether a nonworking adult in the household was willing or able to assume child care responsibilities. In many instances we must assume that the nonworking adult was looking for work and was not available for child care.

stay with the child, some of the adolescents felt that they could not handle two careers at once. Confronted with the choice, those who had been marginal students almost invariably elected to become full-time mothers. Typically, these students engaged in a self-induced process of "cooling out," in which their commitment to formal education was drastically revised as soon as they became involved in parenthood. Many mothers re-entered school after delivery but found it difficult to maintain an interest in their studies. One out of every three women who returned to school dropped out within a year. One of these young mothers summed up her feelings: "I couldn't get interested in school after the baby came. I had too much to do."

### The Effects of Additional Pregnancies

If first pregnancy disrupts the educational career of a young mother, additional childbearing generally brings it to an abrupt halt. Both the number and the timing of subsequent pregnancies of the mothers were strongly related to educational achievement. Only one-third of the young mothers who did not become pregnant again during the course of the study failed to complete high school. With each successive pregnancy, the proportion of dropouts rose, and among these women who had three or more subsequent pregnancies, more than 85% had left school before obtaining a high school diploma. While it was difficult to separate the effects of the number of additional births from the effects of the timing of additional births, we found, predictably, that additional births that occurred early in our study had a more deleterious impact on the educational career of the young mother. When one pregnancy followed quickly after another, the mother almost invariably dropped out (see Table A.15).

Naturally, there was a degree of self-selection involved as to which of the mothers experienced a rapid repeat pregnancy. Married women, of course, were more likely to conceive again, and fertility among this group is another reason that the married women were less persistent students. Single women were not so likely to experience additional pregnancies, but when they did, they were almost as likely as their married peers to drop out of school.

As we noted in Chapter 6, educational ambition is an important element in determining which adolescent mothers become pregnant a second time. Repeat pregnancies are far more prevalent among women with lower educational ambition, but even discounting the effect of educational commitment, we found that the birth of a second child seriously damaged a woman's prospects of continuing her education. The reasons that subsequent pregnancies upset educational plans hardly require much elaboration. If the problems of managing a dual career are difficult with one child, they are virtually insurmountable with two or three young children. In most instances, multiparae managed to complete high school only if their schooling was concluded before the birth of the second child. A

young mother who became pregnant a second time explained why she had left
school:

> The children. After I had M_____ I didn't get a chance to reregister and then
> R_____ came along.

## STATUS DISRUPTION AND DROPPING OUT

Additional pregnancies led to dropping out for another reason as well.
Often the young mother interrupted her schooling around the time of delivery—just before or after her child was born. Even a temporary departure
from school increased the probability that her educational career would be
terminated permanently. This pattern is part of the more general process of
status disruption.

A major reason that individuals continue to perform roles is that they are
sustained in their activities by a series of routines that make their performance
predictable (Blumer, 1962; Goffman, 1959; Hughes, 1971). These routines are
maintained when others support and reenforce patterns of social interaction. It
might be said that, once established, a kind of inertia inheres in the performance
of social roles that makes it difficult for individuals to move with ease from one
position to the next. However, a break in the accustomed routine may release
the individual from binding expectations, at the same time exposing him or her
to alternative roles that may become equally captivating.

Research on problems associated with status disruption—illness, divorce,
unemployment—has repeatedly taken note of the strain involved in reclaiming a
former status (Parsons and Fox, 1952; Davis, 1963; Waller, 1930; Goode, 1956;
Bakke, 1940; Liebow, 1967). Part of this strain derives from motivational
elements—interruption opens the former occupant to feelings of uncertainty as
to whether he or she is willing to resume responsibilities. A crisis in motivation
may arise then merely because role relations are suspended. A lengthy
pause in these routines may cause an individual to reconsider whether or not he
or she is capable of continuing to perform a certain role, a thought that might
not so readily occur to one who is absorbed in the activities of that role.

The return to school after pregnancy is a case in point. Interruption of
schooling puts the adolescent mother out of phase with her peers. In order to
reenter school she often is required to drop back a year, which both defines her
as a failure and removes her from her former friends and classmates. Even if she
returns to her former class, she has grown unfamiliar with school routines. This
unfamiliarity may breed doubts as to whether she is capable of resuming her
former status—particularly if her scholastic abilities were modest to begin with.
Finally, she may find herself pulled in the direction of home, for reasons that
were mentioned in the previous section, or pushed in the direction of the labor

market, because of either economic necessity or impatience to begin gainful activity. As one mother told us:

> I found a good job and I didn't want to quit to go back to school because a good job without an education is hard to get.

For all these reasons, we might anticipate that a break in schooling during pregnancy would significantly diminish an adolescent's chances of completing high school. There was indeed a strong relationship between interruption of schooling during pregnancy and dropping out. The earlier in the pregnancy the interruption occurred, the less likely the young mother was to resume schooling and to graduate following delivery. Obviously, this relationship was somewhat contaminated by the fact that those who withdrew quickly from school were a self-selected segment of the sample. Predictably, married women and those with low ambitions were much more likely to leave school soon after becoming pregnant. However, holding these factors constant did not eliminate the relationship between interruption of schooling during pregnancy and eventual permanent withdrawal, suggesting that educational continuity in its own right is an important determinant of educational achievement (Tables A.16A, A.16B).

This finding suggests that pregnant teenagers should be encouraged to remain in school. Continuity in school significantly influences whether or not a young mother will drop out after her child is born. A number of educators have extended the argument behind this policy, contending that the prospective mother will do better in a special program for pregnant students because such a program will ease her adjustment to parenthood and also eliminate the problems remaining in her regular school may create. Presumably, schools for pregnant students minimize the possibilities of status disruption following childbirth both by ensuring that the student remain in school during the prenatal period and by preparing the young mother to handle the problems of adjusting to school after delivery.

The data from our Baltimore study provided an opportunity to test the value of this approach. Three-fifths of the mothers who remained in school during pregnancy attended the Edgar Allan Poe School, a special facility for pregnant students, while the others continued in their regular schools. While the two populations were not necessarily comparable, the contrast between them was nonetheless illuminating.[10] Overall, the patterns of educational achievement were very similar. Approximately one-fourth of each group dropped out after delivery. The students who attended regular classes during the prenatal period were somewhat less likely to return to school after delivery than the Poe students. However, although Poe students did have a better record of graduating from high school, the difference (70% versus 59%) was not sizable. The students

10The Poe School was not in existence during the first year of the study and many of the women who remained in school could not avail themselves of this alternative. However some of the mothers who delivered during the summer months were able to avoid dropping out by concealing their condition.

who had attended regular classes were actually more likely still to be in school at the time of the five-year follow-up, but again the disparity between the groups was not large (32% versus 19%).

Of course, it is possible that initial dissimilarities between the two groups might have obscured differences that otherwise might have appeared. If, for example, the regular students were more ambitious or competent, then the comparison would be unfair. In fact, the data showed that the Poe students were if anything slightly more capable and motivated when the interview was conducted at Time 1. By holding ambition constant, it was possible to be more specific about the effects of the special program. Among the students with a strong commitment to education, it made little difference whether they attended regular classes or the special school. Students with lower ambition, however, were somewhat more likely to complete high school if they enrolled in the special program. Possibly, the Poe program was geared to help the marginal student, and thus the more competent students may not have benefited as much from the special curriculum. Although the more ambitious students were not significantly handicapped by attending the Poe School, their experience did not enhance their future educational performance.

Our findings raised some question as to whether special educational programs are the most appropriate way of assisting the pregnant student. The aid the Poe School supplied even to marginal students was modest at best. It may be that segregated programs do not in fact reduce the problem of educational disruption, that removing students from regular classes may actually make their subsequent return to school more difficult. The special attention provided to these students during pregnancy could complicate their readjustment to a regular school *if* they are offered little support and encouragement upon their return. Despite the skills and strengths acquired in the special program, the reentering student may be unprepared to function in the indifferent and often unsympathetic environment of the regular school. The most promising solution—and one being given more consideration of late—may be to provide special services within the regular school. Alternatively, as we shall discuss in the final chapter, special schooling might be extended beyond the prenatal period.

## SUMMARY

Several conditions conspire to make it difficult for a young mother to remain in school. In our study, a sizable minority of adolescents were marginal students before they became pregnant. Such women find it especially difficult to cope with the conflicting demands of school and parenthood after the child is born. If they marry or experience a second pregnancy, their chances of completing high school are negligible. Even without these further complications, the marginal student may find it difficult to handle academic tasks when her child is quite young. And if she drops out of school during the neonatal period, she faces a number of obstacles to resuming her education. Some are practical, such as the problem of arranging for adequate child care. Of equal importance are the psychological problems of readjusting to the student role after a lengthy absence.

School authorities have been slow in responding to the special needs of school-age parents. Traditionally, these mothers have been treated like pariahs, and even today they are barred from regular educational programs in many states. Special programs for the school-age parent may offer high-quality services during pregnancy, but they rarely extend into the period beyond delivery. It appears that educators have grudgingly agreed to assist the adolescent in handling the "crisis" of parenthood but refuse to assume responsibility for the more routine but enduring problems that arise during the time of childrearing. In short, services are least available when they are most needed.

It is a remarkable testimony to the strength of their educational commitment that half of the young mothers in our sample managed to complete high school despite the minimal assistance provided by educational programs. It is likely that the proportion of graduates would have been significantly higher if more support had been provided these women. The only reasonable conclusion is that inflexibility in the school system is at least as important a cause of educational failure as is the lack of ability or motivation on the part of the student.

# 8. The Economic Career of the Adolescent Mother

ILLEGITIMACY RECEIVES PUBLIC OPPROBRIUM not only because it violates sexual codes and rules about family formation but also because out-of-wedlock childbearing offends certain economic interests. In the mass media, the unwed mother is generally portrayed as a willing and chronic recipient of public assistance. A large proportion of the public fervently believes that many women deliberately have children before marriage in order to qualify for AFDC and that once they become economically dependent they intentionally produce more babies so as to increase their welfare grants (Ryan, 1971; Placek and Hendershot, 1974).

Presumably, family formation is socially regulated in order to guarantee that the means of providing for the newborn exist before he or she does. When parenthood occurs precipitately, couples are forced to improvise an economic arrangement that often is less satisfactory than the one that might have evolved if the onset of childbearing had been deferred. The stereotype of the unwed mother as a welfare dependent serves to remind the public of the costs of a disorderly family career. Whether or not this stereotype is accurate is a separate issue, one that will be explored in this chapter.

Certainly, the popular association of out-of-wedlock pregnancy with economic destitution is not completely without basis in fact. Findings from various studies lend plausibility to this conclusion. Consider, for example, the following widely publicized facts:[1]

A large disparity exists between the incomes of one- and two-parent families. Single parents are much more likely to be living below the poverty line.

Families headed by a female are far more likely to rely on public assistance for either part or all of their income.

[1] These findings are scattered throughout a number of demographic and sociological reports (see, for example, Martz, 1963; Podell, 1967; Rein, 1972; Weissberg, 1970; U.S. Bureau of the Census, 1972a).

Most families that seek public assistance are headed by a female either because the mother is unmarried or because she has been deserted by her husband.

Families headed by a female are more likely to receive public assistance for extended periods of time.

A disproportionate number of children on public assistance are born out of wedlock or premaritally conceived.

Families on public assistance with out-of-wedlock children are more likely to remain on welfare.

Each of these findings implies that premarital pregnancy may bolster economic dependency; yet none sufficiently demonstrates this proposition. To verify this assertion one must do more than show that a high number of women who are economically dependent have a history of premarital pregnancy for it remains unclear how many women with *similar* childbearing careers manage to remain economically independent or how many with entirely *different* histories ultimately end up on welfare.

Studies that have followed an entire population of mothers who experienced premarital conceptions provide a more refined procedure for evaluating the economic costs of unplanned parenthood. Unfortunately, previous research of this type is both scarce and inconclusive (Trussell, 1975). Bowerman and his colleagues (1966), in their study of unwed mothers in North Carolina, discovered that little change in labor force participation occurred as a result of unplanned pregnancy. They were unable to learn whether or not the occurrence of out-of-wedlock births led to a decline in economic status. Diverse patterns were evident in their data, with some women improving their positions but others experiencing a deterioration. This same finding appeared in a study conducted by Sauber and Corrigan (1970), in which a group of unwed mothers in New York was followed for six years after the birth of their first child. As was true of the unwed mothers in North Carolina, no single pattern of economic adjustment predominated. Few of the women did well, but half managed to remain self-sufficient throughout the study. Employment did not drop off over time; however, an increasingly large proportion of the sample had resorted to public assistance at each successive follow-up.

These two studies challenged a popular misconception about welfare populations: having a child out of wedlock is no certain predictor of economic dependency. Yet, both studies lacked a control group of women who did not become pregnant premaritally, making it impossible to ascertain just how much the economic status of the unwed mothers was affected by prenuptial conception. Only two studies have made use of a comparative design, and their results are contradictory.

Phillips Cutright (1973) examined a national sample of women under the age of 60 who had borne one or more children. Dividing the sample into those who had experienced a premarital pregnancy and those who had not, he found no sizable differences in either income or employment among whites or non-whites as long as those women who had become pregnant premaritally had married following pregnancy. Cutright found unwed mothers to be significantly worse off economically. He (1973: 594) concluded:

> In both white and non-white populations the long-run effects of timing of the first birth among ever-married women seemed small. . . . Most premaritally pregnant mothers act in ways that tend to overcome an initial disadvantage for themselves and their children.

Paradoxically, Lolagene Coombs and a series of collaborators (1970), using data from two studies of married white women, discovered that couples whose first child was conceived prior to marriage remained economically disadvantaged (in both earnings and accumulated savings) for an extended period of years. Even when numerous controls were introduced, the economic costs resulting from the timing of the first birth persisted, although they were attenuated somewhat over time.

It is entirely possible that methodological variations in the design, samples, and measures used in these two studies caused their divergent conclusions. However, even without attempting to reconcile their differing results, we can see that in one respect the two studies are in basic agreement: under certain circumstances, *some* couples are able to overcome the economic disadvantages created by an unscheduled pregnancy. Neither study, however, explained how the process of recovery is achieved, and alluded to, but did not identify, the critical conditions that determine whether or not the economic consequences of a premarital pregnancy will be temporary or persistent.

Which events influence the economic well-being of the young mother and why are the subjects of this chapter. Our analysis begins with the familiar but still unanswered question of the degree to which an early pregnancy economically handicaps the young mother. In order to make this assessment, we compared the economic situations of the mothers and the classmates. Subsequently, the discussion turns to a matter that has received less careful consideration in previous studies: how certain career contingencies affect the economic status of the young mother.

## PATTERNS OF ECONOMIC SUPPORT AMONG THE YOUNG MOTHERS

One difficulty in reconciling the findings from previous research on the economic consequences of unplanned parenthood is that no two studies use the same measure of economic well-being. Total family income, personal income, position vis-à-vis the poverty level, accumulated savings, participation in the labor force, type of job, and receipt of public assistance are only a few of the indicators of economic status that have been employed. It is not possible to evaluate these measures in detail here. Yet, we will present a general description of the various sources from which the young mothers reported receiving income and financial assistance. To ensure that the outcome of our analysis was not affected by the arbitrary choice of an inappropriate measure of economic well-being, we developed a subset of measures based on these data to use in our analysis.

## SOURCES OF SUPPORT

At Time 4 in order to assess their financial status, we showed participants an inventory of potential sources of income and asked how much money they had received during the past year. While there may have been some problems in recall and occasional reluctance to report earnings from extralegal sources, the list provided a reasonably full accounting of the economic position of the respondents.[2] Since three-fifths of the respondents received income from more than one category on the list, it was difficult to construct a simple typology that neatly classified the income sources for all of the mothers. However, the pattern of financial support was less varied than it seemed at first. Most of the respondents reported at least two sources of income, but only 5 of the 323 young mothers relied on more than three sources of income, and only 14% had more than two. Of the 10 sources on the list, only five were mentioned by more than 10% of the sample. In order of prevalence, they were income from personal earnings, public assistance, income from husband's earnings, assistance from the father of their first child and financial assistance from their families. Only the first three of these sources were mentioned by more than one-quarter of the young mothers.

When we considered the relative contribution from each of the possible sources, it became evident that there were only a few ways of coping with the problem of support. To demonstrate this, we computed for each respondent the proportion of total income provided by each of the five major sources. Again,

[2]The interviewers were instructed to probe extensively to check possible sources of income not immediately volunteered. A cross-check using records from the welfare department revealed that 90% of the women then on welfare reported that fact in the interview. The income data undoubtedly understated the contribution made by other family members living in the household. Young mothers still living as dependents often were ignorant of the various sources of income of the other adults residing in the household. The income data also did not take into account forms of economic assistance that do not involve exchange of money such as room and board and child care, as well as other services provided by family, friends, and charitable or government agencies.

the modal pattern of support was personal earnings from employment. One fourth of the respondents obtained most, if not all, of their income from working (Table A.17). Welfare barely edged out income from spouse as the second most common method of support. Although two-fifths of the respondents were receiving some type of welfare, less than one-fifth relied on public assistance exclusively or even primarily as a means of livelihood. Almost the same proportion of young mothers relied on the husband's income as the principal source of support. This figure would have been even higher if not for the fact that so many of the married respondents were themselves employed. About 14% of the families were supported by the earnings of both partners, with neither spouse accounting for as much as four-fifths of the total family income. These four types of support—self-support, welfare, husband's income, and economic partnership in marriage—encompassed all but about 4% of the women, who were supported by their families, by the father of their first child, or by some other method such as survivor's insurance or social security.

These results do not completely square with popular beliefs about the economic consequences of premarital pregnancy although they are consistent with the conclusions of the studies discussed earlier. In the first place, public assistance constituted only a small proportion of the total economic resources available to the young mothers and was not the most common means of family support. In fact, welfare payments made up less than one-fifth of the total income received by the young mothers in the year preceding the final interview. It is also noteworthy that relatively few of the women looked to their parents for financial support. Only a handful were totally dependent, and less than 5% received as much as one-fifth of their total income from their parents. Of course, their families contributed other forms of help such as child care, room and board, and gifts, but complete economic dependency on their family was extremely rare. The predominant pattern was self-support or economic partnership with a spouse. Half the respondents were currently employed. About two-thirds of these women carried the major burden of supporting the family while the rest either collaborated economically with their husbands or received supplemental income from other sources. In total, three out of five young mothers either were self-supporting or were nonworking women married to wage-earning males.

## ECONOMIC LEVEL

For the entire sample, excluding the small number of women who did not supply income data, the median level of family income was just over $5,400. The income distribution approximated a normal distribution, with slightly more than one-third making under $3,000 and slightly less than one-third earning as much as $7,000. Using the yardsticks devised by the census bureau, we found the young mothers to be in a clearly economically precarious position. Nearly half were living below the 1972 poverty level of $4,275 for a nonfarm family of four.

As might be anticipated, total family income varied sharply depending on both the number and the type of revenue sources. The median income of women forced to rely on one source was only 71% of the income of those who had more than one method of support ($4,100 versus $5,800). But even more noticeable was the relationship between income level and principal mode of support. Women who relied primarily on welfare for support were significantly poorer (excluding, of course, supplementary benefits), than those who received most of their income from other sources. In particular, women receiving income from their husbands were better off economically: married women had more than twice as much income as their nonmarried peers ($8,500 versus $3,100). In part this was because frequently both husband and wife worked. Even when they did not, the total income of married women remained higher owing to the fact that employed males earn more than females. The median income of husbands was more than one-third higher than the income of the young mothers who were employed ($6,700 versus $5,000). Accordingly, women are almost invariably better off economically if they are living with a man who is employed. It is important to note that the benefits conferred by marriage last only as long as the marriage itself. Separated women are slightly worse off than single women largely because, as will be shown later, the formerly married are less employable than those women never married.

## ECONOMIC POSITION OF THE CLASSMATES

Although the young mothers did not fully live up to the negative stereotype discussed earlier, obviously most were not making out very well. But can we attribute the low economic position of women like our respondents to the occurrence of an unplanned pregnancy in adolescence? To the extent that the classmates were like the young mothers, except for the pregnancy, they represented the best baseline against which to measure the economic costs of early parenthood.

Looking first at their means of livelihood, we found that the classmates reported an almost identical number of income sources. There were, however, noticeable differences in the predominant sources of income. Classmates were more likely to be working (63% versus 48%) and were more often completely self-supporting if they work. Nearly two-fifths of the classmates were living almost completely on their own incomes as compared to one-fourth of the mothers. This difference was reflected in the proportion of each sample who relied on welfare for part or all of their income at Time 4. Only 15% of the classmates were receiving welfare payments, and just 5% depended completely on public assistance. This figure was just one-third as great as the proportion of mothers who obtained all of their income from welfare.

The dissimilarity between the groups became even more visible when we subdivided the classmates according to whether or not they had experienced a premarital pregnancy. While one-third of the young mothers were receiving at least one-fifth of their income from welfare, only 4% of the classmates who had not conceived premaritally relied on public assistance. Moreover, a much higher proportion of the classmates who did not have a prenuptial conception contributed substantially to their own support (70% versus 45%) through employment. In respect to both welfare and employment, the premaritally pregnant classmates fell in between those of their peers who did not become pregnant before marriage and the young mothers.

Despite this distinctively different pattern of income sources, the disparity between the total family income reported by the young mothers and that of the two subgroups of classmates was still surprisingly small. The median family income of the young mothers was $5,100 as compared to $5,200 for the classmates who had conceived out of wedlock and $5,400 for the other group of classmates. This similarity, however, was created in part by the fact that a somewhat higher proportion of the mothers were married at the time we collected this data. Holding marital status constant altered the picture somewhat. Among both the single and the married subjects, the adolescent mothers were less well off than their classmates who did not become premaritally pregnant, although the magnitude of the difference was still not as large as might have been anticipated (Table 8.1A).

Looking at total income minimized the real differences in economic status since the mothers had a larger number of dependents than did their classmates. To correct for this bias, we recomputed income on a per capita basis (Table 8.1B). Between the young mothers and the classmates who also had conceived before marriage, there was little or no difference. However, a more significant disparity appeared between these two groups and the population of classmates who had avoided premarital pregnancy. At Time 4, these women had a much higher per capita income. As a total group, their median per capita income was at least two-thirds greater than the figure for the young mothers and the premaritally pregnant classmates.[3] The difference remained sizable when marital status was held constant.

In addition to the objective data on economic standing collected in interviews, certain subjective evaluations of the respondents' life situation were recorded by the interviewer at Time 4. In particular, an evaluation was made of the quality of the neighborhood, the condition of housing and furnishings, and

[3]Per capita income was based on the total family income divided by *all* family members residing in the household. Since the mothers were more likely to be living in expanded families—the differences in per capita income were perhaps somewhat exaggerated because sources of income provided by other family members were not always fully enumerated. However, even when the family type was held constant, the per capita income of classmates remained at least one-third higher than that of the adolescent mothers.

Table 8.1A. *Median Family Income of Adolescent Mothers and Classmates*

| | Adolescent Mother | | | Classmates With Premarital Pregnancy | Without Premarital Pregnancy |
|---|---|---|---|---|---|
| Marital Status | *All* | | *All* | | |
| Total | $5,200 | | $5,300 | $5,200 | $5,400 |
| Single | | 3,400 | 4,200 | 3,700 | 4,400 |
| Married | | 8,500 | 8,600 | 8,200 | 9,500 |
| Separated | | 3,000 | 4,900 | 4,900 | – |

Table 8.1B. *Median per Capita Income of Adolescent Mothers and Classmates by Marital and Fertility Status*

| | Adolescent Mother | | | Classmates With Premarital Pregnancy | Without Premarital Pregnancy |
|---|---|---|---|---|---|
| Marital Status | *All* | | *All* | | |
| Total | $600 | | $750 | $570 | $1,000 |
| Single | | 400 | 500 | 500 | 670 |
| Married | | 1,000 | 1,300 | 1,400 | 1,250 |
| Separated | | 500 | 600 | – | – |

the appearance of the respondents as a means of identifying the social class of the young mothers and the classmates. Obviously, these criteria are not independent of income although they provided us with a fuller portrait of the economic position of the respondents. Classmates who did not become pregnant premaritally received consistently higher ratings on these items than the young mothers; the scores of the premaritally pregnant classmates fell in the middle but were somewhat closer to those of the young mothers. A higher proportion of the classmates was judged to be middle class (45% versus 28%), and the young mothers were much more likely to be regarded as "poverty class" (34% versus 8%). Again, the differences were much more marked among the women who were not married at Time 4.

There was a final indication that the economic position of the classmates who had not conceived premaritally was noticeably different from that of the young mothers and the other group of classmates. When asked how much money a week they needed to be really comfortable, these women provided a median figure of $195, 69% higher than the estimate of $135 provided by the young mothers and the classmates who had become pregnant premaritally. When asked the least amount they could get by on the responses were not quite so disparate but again a pattern of differing expectations was revealed. It was clear that the classmates who did not become pregnant premaritally had come to expect and require a higher standard of living.

Regardless of the economic indicator used, a premarital pregnancy exacts a considerable economic cost from women and their families. The economic position of the young mothers was considerably below that of their classmates who had avoided an unscheduled pregnancy. Interestingly, the timing of the pregnancy had only a slight effect on economic status. Classmates who became pregnant premaritally in their late teens and early twenties were hardly better off than the young mothers and in some instances actually did less well in the five years following delivery.

To some extent, these findings reported were dependent upon the marital status of the young mothers. Three-fifths of the young mothers who were not married at Time 4 were living below the poverty level as compared to only 8% of the mothers who were living in stable unions. Of course, we should keep in mind that economic well-being affects the survival of marriages, which may have accounted for the large disparity between the marital subgroups. It also seemed that the classmates who did become pregnant premaritally enjoyed a higher per capita income partly because a greater proportion of these women married and a smaller proportion separated or divorced. These conditions were especially associated with relative affluence or poverty, respectively. To the extent, then, that premarital pregnancy is linked to marital stability, it also becomes a determinant of economic well-being. Although in our sample the young mothers in stable unions did not reach financial parity with their classmates who did not become pregnant premaritally, they came much closer to this group in economic status than to those women who remained single or whose marriages dissolved.

The differences in income between the young mothers and the classmates or between marital subgroups within the two samples could be traced almost wholly to variations in the sources of income and in particular to the proportion of women in each group who were employed at Time 4.[4] To explain the divergent economic position of the two samples, we need to discover why it is that some women are able to work and others are forced to seek welfare.

## WELFARE EXPERIENCE OF THE ADOLESCENT MOTHERS

The young mothers divided rather evenly into two categories: those who worked and those on welfare. At first glance it would appear that the young mothers separated neatly into subgroups, each on a different economic track. This conclusion, however, is highly suspect on the basis of previous research on work and welfare careers among the poor. Studies that have sought to draw a rigid boundary between individuals who work and those on welfare have found the

[4]Although the classmates who did not become pregnant before marriage tended to marry somewhat higher-status males, differences in earnings between their spouses and the husbands of the married mothers were trivial. This is not quite so paradoxical as it might first appear. If marriages survive in part because of economic factors, then we might have expected that over time few differences would remain among the women who were married since marriages with lower-status men are more likely to break up. Similarly, we found that there was little difference in earnings or occupational standing between those young mothers and their classmates who were working. As we shall see, the young mothers who found jobs tended to be similar to the classmates who were employed.

distinctiveness of the two populations difficult to justify empirically. Within low-status populations, there is considerable shifting between the status of worker and that of welfare recipient (Klausner, 1972; Kriesberg, 1970; Goodwin, 1972; Rein, 1972). A large number of unskilled workers have had some experience with being on welfare and, conversely, most welfare recipients have been employed in the not so distant past and probably will work again some time in the future. Indeed, a not inconsiderable number of individuals on welfare are simultaneously employed.

The welfare career patterns of the young mothers display much of the instability and change shown in past studies. Almost two-thirds were on welfare at some time during our study. At the last follow-up, two-fifths of the women were receiving relief, so that 36% of the women who had had welfare experience were no longer on the rolls.

Similarly, many of the young mothers on welfare at Time 4 had worked in the past. Almost one-third had been employed at Time 3, and 16% were still working at Time 4, although their earnings were not sufficient to make them fully self-supporting. Moreover, most of the women who were on welfare at the five-year follow-up were not long-term recipients. Slightly more than one-half of this group had been on welfare for more than 12 months, and only one-third had been on welfare for 30 months (roughly half of the period since delivery of their first child). While a majority of the mothers had been on welfare sometime during the course of the study, only a small minority could be classified as chronic recipients, even using a very liberal definition.

The high turnover in the welfare population might lead us to suspect that people who go on relief do not possess a different world view from that of people who work. Much previous research has examined the background experiences or special attitudes of individuals who go on welfare (Greenleigh Associates, 1960; Jeffers, 1967; Rein, 1972; Sheppard and Striner, 1968; Kriesberg, 1970). Some of these studies have looked into the idea that women are predisposed to become welfare recipients by a cultural system that condones public assistance. By and large, however, investigators have had little success in proving that welfare clients are a self-selected population who embrace a set of attitudes, values, and beliefs different from those of the public at large (Weissberg, 1970; Moles, 1969). For example, several studies have been conducted on the attitudes of welfare recipients toward work and welfare (Goodwin, 1972). Although these studies are looked upon with some suspicion by critics and given little credence by the public at large, the results are so uniform that they cannot be discounted. Virtually all researchers have found that the great majority of welfare recipients would like to find employment. Individuals on public assistance agree with the general view that it is degrading to be on relief (Horan and Austin, 1974). No study has found that a substantial proportion of welfare clients views welfare as a desirable way of life.

Our study is no exception. Almost all the young mothers vehemently rejected the notion that welfare is an acceptable alternative to work. Here, for example, are a few typical responses to the question of whether "there is much point to working when you can make about as much by going on welfare."

> Because it's nothing like your own. I love having my own money and also I like the idea of being independent and also feel as though you shouldn't take advantage of the welfare. It's for the needy not the greedy.
>
> Welfare is once a month and I want to get off as quick as I can. You spend most of it and spend the rest of the month waiting for the next check.
>
> I get more by working and there is somewhat of a humiliation with welfare. I like to be independent.

Only 2% of our respondents replied that if given the choice between a job that paid $80 a week and the chance to receive $60 on welfare, they would prefer welfare. When the interviewer then asked how they would feel if the amount they could receive from welfare were equal to what they could earn, few respondents changed their opinions. Only 8% said that they would select welfare. Clearly, these attitudes could not necessarily be used to predict the decision the respondents would make if actually given such an option, but they did indicate the choice the women would ideally make.[5]

### Intergenerational Patterns of Welfare Experience

A debate has taken place in the literature on public assistance over the question of whether welfare status is transmitted and maintained over generations (Kriesberg, 1970; Weissberg, 1970; Banfield, 1974). The little evidence to date suggests that children of welfare clients are somewhat more likely to be on relief themselves as adults; however, the intergenerational correlation is very low. Most people who receive public assistance did not grow up in relief families, and most people who were on welfare as children do not remain on welfare in adulthood. Moreover, even a strong correlation would not necessarily signify that welfare status is directly passed on from one generation to another as a result of socialization. Children from welfare families might have a greater

---

[5]There were two main types of objection to welfare. Almost two-thirds of the respondents cited moral objections of one kind or another to going on relief. A number mentioned that going on welfare was a sign of faulty character, inability to make it alone, or laziness. About an equal proportion of the young mothers had very different reservations about welfare. They mentioned the practical disadvantages, the bureaucratic regulations, the humiliating examinations, the inconvenience, and most of all the difficulty in trying to adjust their expenditures to the monthly payments. This second group, predictably, spoke more from the insider's point of view. Most of these women had been or were then on welfare and were in a better position to appreciate the everyday difficulties of trying to subsist on public assistance. In any event, their own use of welfare made it difficult to make moral pronouncements condemning the use of public assistance.

probability of receiving relief when they grow up merely because they have fewer economic resources when they reach adulthood.

Although our sample was not broadly representative, we did collect evidence on intergenerational patterns of welfare experience. Using data from welfare records and the interviews at Time 1, we examined the question of whether the young mothers had been exposed to special influences during childhood that might have made them more receptive to welfare support as adults.

Clearly, the probability of being on welfare as adults was greater for the young mothers who received public assistance when they were growing up. These women were almost twice as likely to be receiving public assistance at the five-year follow-up then were those without childhood welfare experiences (60% versus 36%). At the same time, we could find no evidence that women who had received welfare during the study were more likely to come from families that were structurally variant at the outset of the study or that subscribed to a markedly different code of values. Young mothers who came from single-parent households or families in which one or more members had had a pregnancy out of wedlock were not significantly more likely to become welfare recipients after delivery or to be on relief at Time 4. Furthermore, the values of our respondents' parents regarding work, education, sex, or marriage were consistently found to be unrelated to whether or not the adolescents received public assistance following delivery.

More to the point, the young mothers' own attitudes about work, their sexual standards, educational ambitions, marriage intentions, and family size aspirations revealed no consistent pattern of differences linked to welfare status after their child was born. To test whether welfare recipients tended to be more resigned to low achievement or more pessimistic about their prospects for the future, we developed an index of fatalism based on the discrepancies between aspirations and expectations of realizing certain goals. This measure was unrelated to subsequent welfare status. In sum, these findings did not provide any evidence that either cultural values regarding life goals or commitments or a sense of futility about the future predisposed the young mothers to seek welfare.

## Structural Determinants of Welfare Experience

Our results point to a structural rather than a cultural explanation for the intergenerational persistence of welfare. Women from impoverished backgrounds, of course, have more difficulty supporting a family, especially when they remain single. But their low economic status is not the only reason that they are more likely to receive welfare as adults. The young mothers who grew up on AFDC were already known to the welfare department and were able to qualify for additional assistance with a minimum of difficulty after they became pregnant. In some instances, the procedure was even initiated by a welfare worker, and the assistance was granted more or less automatically. When they set up their own households or no longer qualified as dependent minors, these women were able to maintain their eligibility for welfare without having to redefine their status. Thus, the transition to welfare was a natural one. Although these women did not necessarily endorse the welfare system, their previous knowledge about, and contacts with, the welfare department increased the likelihood that they would receive public assistance as adults.

Except for the young mothers' economic status prior to becoming pregnant, no other fact emerged from the data collected at Time 1 that proved useful in predicting who would go on welfare after delivery. By contrast, a number of events following pregnancy were linked strongly to the adolescents' welfare status during the study. The marital career was the most powerful determinant of patterns of receiving public assistance. Married women—especially those who had wed before or soon after the birth of their first child—had a relatively low rate of welfare experience, and very few were on relief at Time 4. A substantial proportion of these women had received assistance at some point during the study, but almost all remained on welfare for only a very brief period. By contrast, a high proportion of the women never married were on relief at the most recent follow-up, and relatively few had stopped receiving welfare during the study. The segment most prone to welfare experience, however, was not the single mothers but the women who had been married briefly but were separated. Nearly four-fifths of these women were receiving welfare at Time 4 as compared to one-half of the single women and less than 10% of the women then married (Table A.18).

A major reason that previously wed women are particularly likely to be on welfare is that many have more than one child. When we controlled for parity, there was little difference in the welfare patterns of the women who had never married and those whose marriages had broken up during the course of the study. Among both groups, there was a striking difference between the women with one child and those with two or more children. Four-fifths of the unmarried multiparous women were on welfare at Time 4, and many of them were long-term recipients. Less than one-half as many of the unmarried primiparae were on relief; a high proportion had been able to exit from welfare after their first child was born (Table A.19). At the other extreme from the unmarried multiparae were the married women with only one child. None of these women was receiving public assistance at Time 4, and only one-fifth had been on relief at some point since their first child was born. A high proportion of the former group of recipients who were married had two or more children and had wed after delivery. Presumably, many of these young mothers were able (or perhaps compelled) to terminate their public assistance only when they entered marriage. Thus, by considering both marital status and parity, we could account for most of the variation in welfare patterns.

### Work and Welfare

Marriage and childbearing are linked with going on welfare because they ultimately affect a woman's prospects for employment. For married women to some extent, and for single women to a much greater degree, going on or off welfare is very much a function of position in the labor market. This can be seen from the data presented in Table 8.2, in which we have classified the young mothers according to work status at Time 4. Nearly one-fifth of the unemployed married mothers and almost all the unemployed (never-married and separated women) were on welfare at the five-year follow-up. Conversely, the women who had been steadily employed during the two years preceding the final interview, none of the married women and only a tiny fraction of the single mothers were receiving public assistance. One-quarter of the recent entrants into the labor market were still receiving welfare payments, presumably to supplement their limited incomes.

The data reported in Table 8.2 also reveal that past work experience was not a shield against economic dependency when employment terminated. At Time 4, the women who had been working at previous points in the study were just as likely to be on relief if they did not then hold jobs as were women who had no past employment record. Again, this finding points to the conclusion that going on welfare is a specific response to unemployment, not a reflection of unwillingness to seek work. Genevieve Carter (1968: 1) summed up the employment potential of AFDC mothers very well:

> The AFDC mothers . . . are an interacting part of a larger population-at-risk. The game of musical chairs played by new cases, previous cases that return, and cases that close for a while or for good reflects the interaction of the

Table 8.2. *Welfare Status of Adolescent Mothers by Work History According to Marital Status at Time 4*

| Work History | Percentage on Welfare at Time 4 | | | |
| --- | --- | --- | --- | --- |
| | Total | Single | Married | Other |
| Never Worked | 65 | 89 | 17 | 92 |
| | (114) | (36) | (41) | (37) |
| Not Employed Since Time 2 | 75 | * | * | * |
| | (16) | | | |
| Not Employed Since Time 3 | 55 | 87 | 20 | 64 |
| | (42) | (15) | (15) | (12) |
| Employed at Time 4 But Not at Time 3 | 26 | 27 | 4 | 53 |
| | (66) | (26) | (23) | (17) |
| Employed at Times 3 and 4 | 5 | 3 | 0 | 14 |
| | (79) | (34) | (24) | (21) |

*Percentage not calculated when base is under 10.

welfare system with the unstable employment conditions of the irregular, dead-end job economy available to them.

It is not motivation but jobs that are lacking. The vast majority of young mothers on assistance expressed an unequivocal desire to work if given the opportunity: 79% indicated that they would take a job immediately if offered one. Moreover, these women were exceedingly realistic about the kind of job they could expect to find. Three-fourths indicated that they would be content to find an "unskilled" job, and very few expected to be hired for a job for which they were not then qualified. Asked how much they would need to make it worthwhile to work, half the women replied that they could get along on less than $85 a week take-home pay. In view of the actual employment situations of the working mothers, these answers were not unrealistic. Over one-third of the working mothers held white-collar or skilled jobs, and their median salary when employment began was $80-85 a week. The nonworking mothers did not overvalue their worth in the marketplace (cf. Shea, 1973).

Even though they were willing to take routine and low-paying jobs, a large number of the nonemployed mothers could not find work. Nearly one-third stated that the only reason they were not working was that they had been unable to find a job. Unemployment statistics corroborated this report. Studies conducted in 1970 revealed that at least one-third of inner city black women in their early twenties were unable to find jobs (Twentieth Century Fund, 1971).

Many of the welfare mothers indicated that they lacked information on job opportunities. Only about one-fourth had consulted employment counseling agencies or had requested work from potential employers. There is thus a definite need for employment counseling. However, in view of the scarcity of adequately paying jobs for black women, it is unlikely that information would have had a significant effect in increasing the rate of employment among the participants in our study. To quote Genevieve Carter (1968: 2) again:

> [The AFDC mother] has no choices in deciding on a most favorable job among the opportunities available nor in deciding what source of economic help she should turn to if there is no job.

Already facing a tight job market, the young mother finds her employment options narrowed further by the problem of arranging for child care. This was typically the case for the women on welfare. Almost two-thirds stated that lack of child care facilities was the reason that they were unable to work. One mother explained:

> I had two babysitters but I found the last babysitter was not good, so I thought my children needed me; that's all. . . . When you go to apply for jobs I've found that they really don't like to hire young mothers because of babysitting problems.

Some skeptics have questioned this explanation, pointing to those working mothers who do make adequate child care arrangements. They argue that the welfare mother is more reluctant than mothers who are not on relief to turn over her children to a caretaker. In fact, however, there was little evidence of such reluctance among the welfare mothers in our sample. All the respondents were given a list of child care arrangements that might be made in the event that suitable employment could be found. Welfare mothers were no more likely than working mothers to exercise selectivity in designating which arrangements they would regard as acceptable. When combined into a single index, the welfare mothers had a slightly higher average score, indicating that they were less, not more, discriminating in the child care arrangements that they would be willing to use.

Welfare mothers generally had larger families and younger children. As will be shown later, both of these factors decreased their ability to make use of child care options since it was difficult to arrange care for several young children outside the home. Moreover, welfare mothers were less likely than working women to report that a relative in the home or nearby would be available if a job opened up. Nearly one-fifth said that they would have no way of caring for their children if offered a job, and over one-half of the rest said they would have to look to a friend, babysitter, or institution to provide child care. It is significant that most of the working mothers in our sample were able to call upon relatives to care for their children. Less than one-fourth had to resort to babysitters or day-care facilities. Most respondents stated a preference for entrusting their children to relatives not only because they were familiar and reliable caretakers but also because alternative day-care arrangements were costly. It would seem, then, that a supportive kinship network is one of the critical factors in determining whether a woman is able to work or is forced to rely on welfare.

The evidence presented thus far is in line with the conclusions of previous investigators who have contended that most women seek relief not out of choice but out of necessity. Few of the young mothers in our study displayed any allegiance to the welfare system, and the vast majority insisted that they would gladly work if they could make suitable child care arrangements and could find a job that would pay enough to support themselves and their children. To a great extent, our results suggest that a certain amount of luck is involved in whether women are able to avoid going on welfare: some young mothers happen to find a job and can make suitable arragements for the care of their children. Yet, it is also clear that more than chance is involved: certain women have a distinct advantage over their peers in competing for the small number of available jobs. The remaining part of this chapter discusses in greater detail who is most likely to succeed in the competition for work.

## WORK PATTERNS AMONG THE YOUNG MOTHERS

Over the course of the study, the proportion of young mothers in the labor force steadily increased. At the time of the first interview, only 5% of the adolescents were employed, and in most instances they held either part-time or irregular jobs. By a year after delivery, one in four held a regular job. The proportion of workers increased to more than one-third by the three-year follow-up, and at the last interview just under one-half of the young mothers were holding jobs, almost all (89%) of them full-time.

The pattern of full-time employment was not so much a result of preference as of the fact that part-time jobs were extremely scarce and generally paid too little to offset the costs of going to work. Two-thirds of the young mothers declared that if money were no object, they would have liked to work part-time.[6] In reality, of course, money always was an issue.

As mentioned before, there was considerable job turnover within the sample. Almost one-half of the mothers employed at the most recent interview had not been working at Time 3; only one-fourth had been employed for two or more years, (approximately the time between the second and the final follow-ups). This situation was partly a consequence of the growth over the course of the study of the proportion of women working, but it also was a reflection of the fact that a large number of the women had difficulty retaining jobs. In order to take these shifts into account when we considered who goes to work, we constructed a typology of attachment to the labor force. At one extreme were the women who had never worked; at the other were the stable jobholders, women who had worked continually for at least two years; in between were the women who had recently departed from, or entered, the work force.

### Interest in Work

To explain the pattern of employment in our sample we had to answer two separate questions: (1) who wants to work and (2) who is able to find a job. In our previous discussion we touched on the question of who wants to work. Using the strict measure of desire for work utilized in government surveys— whether or not an individual has actively sought employment—we found that slightly more than one-fourth of the nonworking young mothers would be officially classified as "unemployed." Not long before the final interview these women contacted potential employers or employment agencies about job openings. Women who had not taken such action, regardless of their desire to work, were not counted as members of the labor force although there was every indication that a substantial number of these women also wanted to work (Furstenberg and Thrall, 1975). When asked at Time 4 why they were not working, only 14 out of 172 jobless women indicated that they did not wish to be employed. Most others, as mentioned earlier, cited the difficulty of arranging for child care as the only reason that they were not looking for a job. In response to the question of whether they would want to take a job immediately or would prefer to wait a while before going to work, approximately four out of five of the nonworkers said that they wanted a job right away. After eliminating

[6]Regarding the desire to work, it bears reporting that only 7% of the mothers indicated that they would choose not to work if they had enough money to be "very comfortable."

the women who expressed no interest in working and those who were not prepared to take a job immediately, we determined that about three-fourths of the women who were not employed at Time 4 were available for work.[7]

Attitudes toward employment within this sample were not a major determinant of labor force participation. This conclusion was buttressed by several findings. Work patterns could not be explained by attitudes and values acquired from the family early in life about the desirability of work. As was the case with welfare participation, none of the measures of family experience was related to work patterns. Women who grew up in families headed by females were no less likely to achieve stable work patterns than those who came from households headed by couples. Similarly, the economic status of the mother's family of origin was unrelated to her employment experience. Finally, a variety of indicators of commitment to the work ethic that were included in the Time 1 interview were not associated with employment experience at later points in the study. In short, early family experience or work attitude did not appear to have any significant bearing on the pattern of employment.

One exception must be noted. There was a strong relationship between the measure of educational ambition developed from the Time 1 data and subsequent work experience. Women with high ambition were twice as likely to be employed at Time 4 (66% versus 32%) and also to have appreciably more stable work patterns than the young mothers with low ambition. Since ambition is largely independent of the measures of work interest and commitment to the work ethic, its link to work patterns probably derives from another reason. Ambitious women were better prepared to compete for jobs since more of them had completed high school.

### Employability

Facing an abundant labor pool, employers are forced to develop some procedures for screening job applicants. Selection criteria not only increase the efficiency of the recruitment process for the employer but also justify and rationalize hiring practices. Although objective standards are defined by employers as necessary and nondiscriminatory, it has been shown that they are often arbitrary and exclusive (Berg, 1971). Relatively few jobs that the young mothers held required great skill or experience. Yet the poorly educated, younger, and inexperienced women faced severe problems in finding even menial work.

Less than one-half of the women who had not completed high school had been employed sometime in the five years of the study, and only one-third were

[7]This figure was much higher than the estimate provided in Labor Department surveys, which are a conservative measure for gauging the level of unemployment (Furstenberg and Thrall, 1975).

working at the last follow-up. By contrast, four-fifths of the high school graduates had had some work experience during the study, and three-fifths were working at Time 4. Particularly striking was the effect of education on work stability. Only 15% of the nongraduates had been employed for the previous two years as compared to 38% of those women who completed high school.

It might be argued that it is not education as such that affects employment patterns but rather the fact that the more stable and ambitious adolescents are better equipped both to persevere in school and to find work. In this interpretation, personality traits, not educational credentials, would appear to be the key to success in finding and keeping a job. Although this line of reasoning is plausible, it does not coincide with other results. The absence of a relationship among family background, work attitudes, and employment patterns casts some doubt on this view. Moreover, we found that the relationship of ambition to work patterns was relatively weak when educational attainment was held constant. While it did not completely disappear, the association was barely evident for the nongraduates and was considerably attenuated for the graduates. Educational status is definitely a stronger determinant of work patterns than ambition (Furstenberg, 1975: 413).

While employers may argue that educational achievement is a legitimate criterion to use in hiring, it is less easy to make a case for age requirements. With one exception, all the women in the sample at Time 4 were at least 18, yet their age continued to exercise an important influence on their work status. With each advancing year there was a steady increase in the proportion employed. Less than one-fourth of the 18-year-old women were working as compared to three-fifths of the women aged 23 or older. Clearly, women had to wait in line for work, and to a great extent their position in the queue was determined by age. Given the limited supply of jobs, age is one of the factors that is used to ration employment.

### Availability for Work

Job continuity could be explained not only by the greater employability of some women but also by their greater availability for work. As we have noted at earlier points, child care obligations kept many women from participating in the labor force—not so much because children reduce the mother's interest in employment as because it is simply more difficult for women to work when they have young children. The problems faced by working mothers are well documented (Kreps, 1971; Sweet, 1973). In the first place, women with children must schedule activities more carefully to avoid conflict between work and family roles. Consequently, the working mother often needs more organizational capacity and stamina than the woman who devotes all her time and energy to child care. Second, the employed mother with young children requires some assistance from others to coordinate her work and family obligations. As we discovered earlier, many young mothers simply could not count on regular help from a relative or the facilities of an institution to care for their children while they were at work. Finally, unless relatives or subsidized day-care facilities are available, the job must be lucrative enough to cover the costs of child care. As one respondent, commenting on her employment status, told us:

> I can't find a job. If I find a job I have to find one that will pay enough for me to find a babysitter.

All of the young mothers, except for a few whose children had died or been given up for adoption, had at least one child. Therefore, it was difficult to measure the precise effect of children on labor force participation among the sample of adolescent parents. However, it obviously was considerable. Of the six women who had no children living with them, five were working at Time 4.[8] Over three-fourths of the childless classmates were employed, and most of the rest were either in school or looking for work.

Another way we demonstrated the effect of children on labor force participation was to contrast the working patterns of the primiparae with those of the young mothers who had borne additional children during the study. Two-thirds of the women who had not had additional children were employed at Time 4 as compared to less than one-third of the women with two or more children (Table 8.3). It is interesting to observe that after the second child, additional children have only a slight effect on work patterns. Apparently, one more child is already too many. It is also significant that the rate of employment of the young mothers with one child was only slightly lower than that of childless classmates who worked (67% versus 76%).

As suggested earlier, stability of employment is especially affected by family size. At Time 4, 43% of the young mothers who had not had an additional child had been employed steadily for the past two years as compared to only about 10% of the multiparous women. Indeed, over half of the young mothers with at least two children never worked during the five years of the study. Controlling for marital status did not change these findings. What we learn is that marital

Table 8.3. *Work Status by Marital Status and Parity of Adolescent Mothers and Classmates*

| Number of Children | Percent of Young Mothers Employed | | | | Percent of Classmates Employed | | | |
|---|---|---|---|---|---|---|---|---|
| | *Total* | *Single* | *Married* | *Other* | *Total* | *Single* | *Married* | *Other* |
| None | * | * | * | * | 76 | 72 | 89 | * |
| | | | | | (102) | (77) | (21) | |
| One | 67 | 65 | 71 | 69 | 53 | 37 | 46 | 60 |
| | (140) | (76) | (35) | (29) | (89) | (46) | (33) | (10) |
| Two or More | 29 | 23 | 33 | 30 | 43 | * | 44 | * |
| | (177) | (40) | (70) | (67) | (30) | | (16) | |

*Percentage not calculated when base is under 10.

[8]As will be shown in Chapter 9, some women in addition to these six were not residing with their children. Most of these mothers found it necessary to place their children with relatives or friends so that they could take jobs.

status was largely irrelevant to work patterns when childbearing was held constant. Almost the same proportion of married women worked as single and separated women at each level of parity, particularly when we took into account the fact that the single mothers were slightly younger and more likely to be still attending school than the ever-married women.

By introducing the factor of parity, it also was possible to eliminate virtually all the difference between the rates of employment of the mothers and the classmates. In some subgroups, the young mothers actually had higher rates of employment; in others, more classmates were gainfully employed. Overall, family size largely accounted for the employment patterns of the young women in the study. Alluding to our earlier findings on economic position, it is important to note that when family size was held constant, differences in income and welfare experience between the young mothers and the classmates all but disappeared.

Larger family size, of course, further complicates the already difficult problem of arranging for child care. Typically, additional children also raise the costs of daytime supervision. Since within this sample the youngest in a multichild family was typically under four and generally under two, the mothers of larger families had to contend with the problem of arranging for the care of an infant or toddler as well as a preschooler. Our findings suggested that the presence of a young child presented a further barrier to employment. Two-thirds of the women were working if they had no child younger than four. By contrast, only 20% of the mothers were employed when their youngest was not yet two. Both in single- and multichild families, the presence of a young child reduces the chance that a woman will be employed. Still, the data presented in Table 8.3 suggest that having an additional child regardless of his or her age may deter employment.

Women with larger families require higher wages to make it worthwhile to take a job. With each additional child the need for income rises, particularly if child care costs are not subsidized.[9] This poses a particular dilemma for the young mothers on welfare. Since welfare benefits increase with each child, many women in our study found it impossible to locate a job that provided significantly more income than public assistance. Especially if they lacked education and experience, as was the case with most of the young mothers with large families, the prospect of finding a job that matched welfare payments was extremely poor. Many women with large families thus became trapped in the welfare system even though they were more than willing to work. Lack of skills and experience limited their prospects of finding employment; child care responsibilities restricted their ability to enter the work force should a job turn up; and

[9] It is interesting to observe that unemployed women with more than one child said that they were willing to work for less money than those with a single child—perhaps because they were accustomed to a lower standard of living or were aware that they could supplement their incomes through other sources if they found a job. Whatever the reason, even the women with larger families continued to hope that they would be able to find work.

low monetary incentives made it problematic as to whether they would be able to afford to work.

## SUMMARY

A pregnancy in early adolescence adversely affects the economic position of the young mother. At Time 4 a lower proportion of young mothers were employed and a much higher percentage were receiving public assistance compared to the classmates. Like previous studies, our research suggests that the decision of whether to work or to go on welfare cannot be explained by differences in normative standards. Virtually all the young mothers preferred to work, and welfare was almost universally regarded as an inferior alternative to employment. However, following the first pregnancy, certain factors influenced the young mother's chances of remaining economically independent.

One such factor is marriage. Whatever the economic disadvantages caused by the timing of the first birth, they are relatively trivial when weighed against the costs of being a single parent. Under the best of circumstances, single parenthood in our society is a difficult proposition. Our economy is reasonably well suited to the two-parent family in which husband and wife share the responsibilities of child care and earning a livelihood. While this arrangement is not without costs, it has definite advantages over the single-parent family, in which the parent, usually the mother, must shoulder both work and family responsibilities alone. The single parent with young children is virtually barred from labor force participation unless she can arrange for child care.

Regardless of her marital status, the young mother also is severely restricted in her employment prospects on a number of other counts. She enters a labor market in which good jobs are scarce and employers can afford to be selective. Limited education disqualifies her; age and inexperience count against her; and she is discriminated against on the basis of sex and race as well. It goes without saying that the job she can find is usually undesirable. The real question is not whether she can get a good job but whether she can find a job that pays enough to cover the expenses of working. In part, this decision will depend upon the availability of family and community resources that make it feasible or profitable to work. The married woman must consider whether her contribution can add significantly to the family income, while the unmarried parent must balance the advantages of getting a job against the benefits of going on welfare.

Child care problems are even more severe for women with large families. In our sample, the single most powerful determinant of whether a woman worked or went on welfare was family size. Almost 80% of the unmarried women with two or more children were receiving welfare. By contrast, the single-child families were usually self-sufficient, especially when the lone child was at least four years old at the last interview. While few of the primiparae were well off by middle-class standards, they were not much worse than their classmates in similar marital circumstances who had not experienced an early pregnancy. Thus, while avoiding a second pregnancy offered no guarantee of economic success, at least it provided some protection against almost certain economic disaster.

# 9. The Management of Motherhood

EVEN UNDER THE MOST propitious circumstances, many women in our society find it difficult to negotiate the passage into parenthood. So common are the problems of adjustment following the first birth that some writers have characterized the onset of parenthood as a crisis (LeMasters, 1957; Dyer, 1963; Hobbs, 1965). Rather than view this period as a crisis, Alice Rossi (1968) has suggested that it may be more fruitful to regard the early years following the birth of the first child as a transition point in the life cycle of the family. She contends that the onset of parenthood typically raises a series of problems for both the marital dyad and the parents as individuals. Discussions of the transition to parenthood that have followed Rossi's lead, however, have tended to focus on the situation of the mature woman who enters parenthood after several years of marriage (Hobbs, 1968; Hill and Aldous, 1969; Lopata, 1971). Much less has been written about the predicament of the adolescent parent (LaBarre and LaBarre, 1969).

In her original statement of the problem, Rossi observed that the transition to parenthood is likely to be far more stressful when the change in status is unforeseen and unwanted, and she pointed out that younger females find becoming a mother more problematic than mature women. Extending Rossi's analysis to the case of the adolescent mother, we might expect that her entry into parenthood would be especially complex (cf. Hill and Aldous, 1969).

The feelings of uncertainty and unreadiness expressed by relatively mature women are probably far stronger in the female who becomes pregnant in her early or middle teens. If maternal responsibilities are regarded with some ambivalence by women who have enjoyed the carefree early years of marriage, one can imagine that the adolescent who becomes pregnant has even more reason to resent the constraints of parenthood. Having just broken loose from the restrictions imposed on her by her family, she often feels unprepared and ill equipped to meet the obligations of raising a child, especially if the pregnancy

171

occurred unintentionally (Pohlman, 1969). The adult female may feel isolated and alienated if her husband refuses to assume a fair share of the duties of child care, but her sense of abandonment is hardly commensurate with that felt by the adolescent mother, who frequently must shoulder the full responsibility of supporting and rearing her child.

Perhaps because early parenthood is beset with so many difficulties, it is more or less taken for granted that many young mothers do not possess the same commitment to parenthood as women who become mothers later on in life. And it generally is believed that adolescent mothers, regardless of their commitment, are less capable performers of the parental role. A recent review (Jenstrom and Williams, 1975) of problems of infant care conveys this widespread assumption:

> Young mothers and fathers often feel ambivalent toward their children. Certainly, the responsibilities and restrictions of early childrearing place heavy burdens on adolescents. The infant concretely represents these added responsibilities. If a young mother feels torn between her own developmental needs and desires and those of her infant, conflicts and guilt feelings can result. . . .
>
> Most mothers feel some insecurity about their ability to care for their child. These feelings may be compounded in adolescent mothers who, like many young people, may lack self-confidence. Problems that led to or derive from the pregnancy may cause these feelings to be even more pronounced.

Although these observations may indeed be correct, they are supported only by impressions and fragmentary clinical accounts. The few studies that have collected systematic information on the consequences of early parenthood have focused on the period immediately following delivery and have not examined how motherhood is managed over the long term. These accounts therefore have tended to exaggerate the ambivalence and stress felt by the adolescent mother and have failed to consider the adaptive responses that emerge in time.

This chapter examines the process of adaptation to parenthood of the adolescent mothers, particularly their adjustment in the later years of the study. Our discussion begins with a fundamental but as yet unsettled issue: to what extent are adolescent parents actively involved in rearing their children? The limited literature on this subject creates the impression that the teenage mother, whether because of unwillingness or inability, frequently turns over child care responsibilities to someone else (Rains, 1971; Jenstrom and Williams, 1975). Without first establishing the part played by adolescent mothers in rearing their children, it makes little sense to attempt an evaluation of their commitment or competence as parents.

Accordingly, we first sought to determine the adolescents' caretaking responsibilities; this determination put us in a better position to consider the issue of how well or how poorly the young mothers in our study managed the maternal role. But in making this assessment, we still faced certain problems. We could not so easily resort to the strategy of comparing the young mothers with classmates. Few of the classmates had children close enough in age to the young mothers' children to yield pertinent comparative data on maternal adaptation.[1] Since there was no suitable baseline against which to contrast the parental experience of the young mothers, our analysis necessarily centered more on sources of variation within the sample.

We examined the impact on maternal adaptation of three conditions commonly associated with early parenthood. First, we considered the effect of limited preparation for motherhood by comparing the experience of the younger and more reluctant mothers with that of their peers who were older and more receptive to becoming pregnant. Next, we studied the relationship between child care arrangements and maternal adjustment, contrasting the attitudes of full-time mothers with those of women who shared child care responsibilities with relatives or close friends. Finally, we tried to relate the management of motherhood with certain events and contingencies that followed delivery. The most important of these, the role that the father played in childrearing, will be explored in the final section of this chapter. In short, the prevailing belief that early parenthood negatively affects maternal performance was tested by examining the link between adjustment to the maternal role and intervening conditions such as poor preparation for parenthood and limited parental involvement.

## MATERNAL INVOLVEMENT IN CHILD CARE

One of the presumed consequences of early parenthood is a high degree of instability in the mother-child relationship. As we have mentioned, it is believed that many adolescent mothers, particularly those whose pregnancies were unwanted, turn over the care of their child to a family member, and it has even been suspected that the pattern of teenage pregnancy is sometimes tacitly supported by the adolescent's mother, who is reluctant to give up her maternal role (Schulz, 1969; Stack, 1974). Some researchers also have alluded to the possibility that conflict arising over the care and supervision of the child may disturb the child's relations with his or her mother (Rainwater, 1970). The data from our study provided an opportunity to examine these observations in a more systematic fashion.

From the three follow-up interviews and information from hospital records, we constructed a fairly complete history of mother-child separations. Formal separations were relatively rare, and in only a few cases were they permanent. At Time 4, just four of the parents (1% of the sample) had elected to give up their children for adoption.[2] In addition to these cases, approximately 10% of the children were known to have lived apart from their mothers at one or more

[1] Most of the classmates with older children (37), like the young mothers, had their children in early adolescence, and these births usually occurred out of wedlock as well.

[2] This figure slightly underestimated the true proportion of adoptions because white families, who were more often lost in the follow-up, had a slightly higher rate of adoptions. Hospital records indicated that about 3% of the original sample's children were put up for adoption or placed in foster homes. At Time 4, 16 (5%) of the children who had remained with their mothers were no longer living. Most of the mortality occurred during the first year; only 1% of the children died after the first 12 months.

points during the study. At Time 4, the point at which our information was most complete, 21 children (6.8% of the 307 who were still alive) were not residing with their mothers. However, in half of these cases the mothers spent at least part of the week living with their children despite the fact that they maintained a separate residence.

Most of these separations occurred because the mother could not arrange for child care in hours of employment or because of illness. In a few instances, the mother had left the child with a relative in order to take up residence with a man. From the responses provided at Time 4, we concluded that most of the mothers who did not reside with their children said that they expected to re-establish a common household in the near future. These projections seemed to be supported by data collected during prior interviews: the majority of women who had not been living with their children at previous points in the study were reunited at the most recent interview. Of 13 children who were known to be separated from their mothers at either Time 2. or 3, 8 were living with the mothers by the five-year follow-up.

Although few of the young mothers relinquished their maternal role completely, a large number reported that another individual shared the responsibilities with them of caring for the child. Indeed, when asked at Time 4 who spent *most* of the time caring for their oldest child, slightly less than half of the mothers replied that they alone were the principal caretakers; two out of five listed another person; and the remainder indicated that they divided the child care duties more or less equally with someone else. Among those women who reported that they were not the sole caretaker, most shared child care with a relative living in the household or neighborhood and a lesser number (16%) with a neighbor or close friend. In only 18 families was a child care facility listed as the usual daytime custodian.

The proportion of young mothers who claimed to have primary responsibility for raising their children steadily diminished during the course of the study. One year after delivery, three out of four reported that they were the main caretaker. This figure dropped to three out of five two years later and to less than half at the last interview. Moreover, as the child grew older, supervision occurred outside the home more often. More than half of the children not being cared for primarily by their mothers at Time 4 did not remain at home during the day.

### Determinants of Maternal Involvement

What are the circumstances under which a mother turns over child care responsibilities to a relative or friend? One might interpret this pattern as an informal adoption procedure whereby a surrogate actually assumes the role that would normally be performed by the mother. If this is the case, we might have expected to find that the caretaking pattern would be related to the willingness and capacity of the adolescent to enter motherhood as well as to her marital status after delivery. Neither of these suppositions was supported by the data. The women who were 15 or under at the time they became pregnant were just as likely as their older peers to list themselves as full-time caretakers at the five-year follow-up. The mother's reaction either before or after delivery to becoming pregnant had no bearing on whether or not she assumed the role of full-time caretaker of her child. Finally and most important of all, the women who remained single were only slightly more likely to share their maternal duties with another person than were those who married: 40% of the single mothers were full-time caretakers as compared to 51% of those who were married at Time 4. Moreover, the timing or the stability of marriage was not strongly related to the pattern of caretaking that we found at by Time 4.

Even considering the extreme cases—those in which the child was not living with his or her mother—it was still not possible to find support for the hypothesis that women who separate from their children do so because of reluctance to assume the maternal role. A slightly higher proportion of the youngest women in the sample (those under 16 when they became pregnant) were not residing with their children, but the difference by age was trivial. Women who had reacted negatively at Time 1 to becoming pregnant were just as likely to be living with their children as those who had been positive initially. As many parent-child separations occurred among women who married before delivery as among those who married subsequently or not at all. Finally, mother-child separations occurred no more frequently among women who did not marry the father of the child than among those who did. In sum, there is little reason to conclude from our study that separations were engineered by the mothers who rejected or were unable to live up to the maternal role.

A single factor accounted almost completely for the pattern of caretaking that was established at Time 4. Only 5 % of the women who were working reported that they were the principal caretaker, while nearly all (82%) of the nonworking mothers said that they took care of their children most of the time. The longer a woman had worked, the more likely she was to turn over child care responsibilities to someone else, particularly to a person who resided outside the home. Residential separations, as we mentioned in Chapter 8, occurred most frequently among women who had recently entered the labor market, suggesting that job circumstances or the difficulty in arranging for daytime child care compelled the mother to board the child with a relative or friend. One woman living apart from her child explained how that arrangement occurred:

> Mostly because of the way I have to work. It's very hard to find someone that can take care of them 'till the late hours of the night.

### Amount of Mother-Child Interaction

Further evidence that the caretaking pattern is primarily a response to economic pressure rather than an indication of role abandonment was supplied by the young mothers at the Time 4 interview. The respondents were asked how many hours a week they spent "doing things together" with their oldest child. As might have been expected, the time indicated varied directly with the caretaking pattern. However, with the exception of those mothers not living with their children, most women who were not the principal caretaker managed to spend a good deal of time with their children. Although the amount of total interaction was only estimated, our data indicated that the full-time mothers spent an average of 10 hours a week more with their oldest child than did the mothers who shared child care with someone else. Other studies of working women have likewise reported that they are generally able to budget nearly as much time for domestic duties as are nonworking women (Rossi, 1972). One reason why this difference between the two groups was so small was that the working mothers in our sample had fewer children and therefore probably could devote more time to their firstborn.[3]

Despite their efforts to compensate for time spent away from their children, the mothers who were not full-time caretakers were inclined to feel that they spent too little time with them. In the final interview, the majority of working mothers indicated that if money were not an issue they would prefer to work fewer hours so that they could spend more time with their children. This sentiment also was evident when the women in the study were asked if they spent the "right amount of time" with their children. Only 20% of the full-time caretakers expressed the opinion that they spent too little time, but nearly one-half of the mothers who shared childrearing duties with someone else and over three-fourths of the mothers who were not living with their children held this view. Once again, our findings appear in conflict with the interpretation that adolescent mothers *prefer* to entrust their maternal responsibilities to another person.

## MEASURING THE ADAPTATION TO PARENTHOOD

A description of the physical relationship between the mother and her child may contribute to an understanding of family life-styles but it is at best a dubious indicator of the quality of mother-child relations (Maccoby, 1961). This observation applies especially in the case of teenage mothers because their participation in the socialization process often depends on factors outside their control—their educational status, employability, marital situation, and the availability of child care assistance. At least in our study, the full-time mothers were not necessarily more committed to taking an active part in childrearing.

[3]Working mothers reported that they spent somewhat less time watching TV with their children, but they were no less likely to read to the children or take them to the playground on a regular basis. It appeared that mothers who were not full-time caretakers made a special effort to spend recreational time with their children.

This being the case, it is important to consider measures that more directly address the question raised earlier: how well does the adolescent mother manage her maternal role? What constitutes successful accommodation to parenthood, however, is a subject of much disagreement among childrearing authorities. Different theorists are inclined to look at different indicators of adjustment and to interpret the same indicator in very different ways (Glidewell, 1961; Clausen, 1968). We included in the final interview a variety of measures to evaluate the adaptation of the mother to parenthood by the five-year follow-up. The information collected can be classified into three general areas:

1. *Maternal Interest.* At Time 4, respondents were asked to rate the degree of interest they had in parenthood on a scale from zero to 100. This measure had both the virtue and the defect of being explicitly subjective.[4] Several slightly more objective indicators of maternal interest were also collected from the respondents: mothers were requested to supply the names of their children's friends and were asked what, if any, books and articles about raising children they had read recently. Finally, if they had children enrolled in school, they were asked if they ever attended parent-teacher meetings. In addition to these self-reports on maternal interest, the fieldworkers who visited the home were instructed to record their observations on the quality of the mother-child relationship.[5] One area in which they registered their impressions was the degree of interest the mother showed in her child.

2. *Maternal Performance.* At Time 4 the mothers were asked to evaluate their style of parenting on six dimensions: warmth, communicativeness, patience, demandingness, confidence, and control. These items were analyzed separately and also combined into a general index measuring the mother's self-rated ability. Data were also collected from the mothers on childrearing techniques they employed. Following the procedures used by Sears, Maccoby, and Levin (1957), we asked the mothers to describe their methods of sanctioning the child, styles of interaction, and problem-solving strategies. In the analysis that we then performed, these items were treated separately for the most part since it proved difficult to develop reliable indices of childrearing techniques. In addition, interviewer assessments were made during the home visit regarding the mother's competence and skills in relating to her child.

3. *Maternal Success.* The mother was asked to score her child on eight dimensions: cooperativeness, outgoingness, cleanliness, smartness, politeness, interest in learning, happiness, and obedience. Again, in the

[4]Rossi (1968), in her discussion of the transition to parenthood, noted the absence of studies on parental satisfaction and contended that it would be useful to record the parents' assessments at different points in the life cycle.

[5]The evaluations of each interviewer were coded separately by an editor. When different assessments were apparent, the editor was instructed to assign a separate code that indicated that the observations were unreliable.

analysis, the items were treated separately first and then combined into a general index of maternal acceptance. Mothers also were given a list of eight behavioral disorders common among preschool children and asked how often they experienced these difficulties with their oldest child.[6] An index was constructed to measure the frequency of these behavior problems.

These measures should be regarded with some caution. Intercorrelations among separate items and between indices in the three areas were modest at best. The specific evaluations of the mothers and the fieldworkers were related only weakly, raising questions about the validity of the various measures.[7] Undoubtedly, the measures provide a more accurate reading of the mother's definition of the situation than of her actual performance as a parent, but as such they are useful for assessing the mother's adaptation to parenthood. The indicators were probably less reliable in measuring the young woman's actual maternal skill and competence, and this limitation should be kept in mind by the reader.

### Preparation for Parenthood and Maternal Adjustment

During the past century, professionals have had a growing influence on defining acceptable practices of childrearing (Winch, 1971). The weakening of ties with extended kin, the general value placed on specialized knowledge, and the pace of social change all have contributed to this trend. As parents have become more responsive to the advice of experts, it would appear that confidence in their own judgment and abilities has declined. At the very least, parents seem to be more sensitive to potential deficiencies in their qualifications.

As noted earlier, most experts concur that teenage parents are especially likely to experience problems in childrearing (Jenstrom and Williams, 1975). And we had every reason to believe that many of the young mothers shared these misgivings at the time they became pregnant. In the first interview a large number stated that they felt acutely ill prepared and unready to care for a child. One respondent described her initial reaction to her pregnancy:

[6]Unless the problem came up at least once a week, it was not regarded as serious. The index counted the number of serious problems that the mother reported. The problems included getting into fights with other children, trouble getting to sleep at night, keeping to oneself all the time, refusing to eat at mealtimes, taking other people's things, bed wetting, inability to control temper, talking back to grownups, not wanting to play with other children, and not telling the truth.

[7]Correlations between the fieldworkers' evaluations of the mothers and their self-evaluations were not statistically significant. Separate items in the mother's self-evaluation were moderately related (gamma's ranged from 0.37 to 0.46), suggesting that the mother tended toward a consonant view in her general self-rating. In light of the limited observations of the interviewers, we could not estimate the validity of the mother's self-assessment.

Babies were born to women who wanted them and could take care of them—not for girls like me.

In many instances, their doubts subsided during the course of pregnancy as they became more accustomed to their situation. At Time 2, only 15% of the young mothers were distinctly negative about becoming parents, and approximately 50% expressed very positive feelings. Nevertheless, even several years later, at the three-year follow-up, nearly three-fourths of the sample agreed with the statement "I had a child before I was ready to become a mother." To what extent was their initial uneasiness confirmed and reinforced by their experiences as parents?

## Age and Maternal Adaptation

As we might have expected, the youngest women in the sample—the mothers who were 15 and under at the time of pregnancy—felt least prepared to become parents: 64% were openly negative about becoming pregnant as compared to 45% of the women who were aged 17 at conception. If age figures prominently in the process of adjustment to parenthood, the youngest women in our sample should have been more disaffected; they should have expressed less confidence in their abilities as parents; and they should have encountered more problems with their children. Of course, we were comparing mothers within a relatively narrow age range; the oldest parents in our sample were only 17 at Time 1. And yet, if immaturity seriously impairs the parenting process, we might have expected differences to show up among the women 17 and older, the 16 year olds, and the adolescents who were 15 or under during pregnancy.

However, there was no indication from either the subjective or the objective measures that women who entered parenthood earlier were any less committed to the maternal role. They were just as likely to be familiar with their child's friends, to have read literature on childrearing, and to have visited their child's school. The youngest mothers were just as enthusiastic about parenthood, scoring themselves equally high in interest and receiving equally positive ratings on this criterion from the interviewers. At the five-year follow-up, the youngest mothers were slightly (though not significantly) more likely to say that there were things that they would have liked to change about the way they had brought up their children thus far. But their self-ratings of maternal performance were no lower than those of the other two age groups.

The interviewers were asked to evaluate the mother's sense of confidence in dealing with her child during the home visit. While small variations appeared in these assessments, the youngest women received higher scores than women who had been 16 at the time of pregnancy, and their evaluations were only slightly lower than those of the oldest group.

No sizable differences could be detected among the various age groups as regarding the behavior of the child and his or her relationship to the mother. Contrary to expectation, the children of the youngest mothers did not experience a greater number of behavioral problems. The number of reported problems was about identical in the three age groups. The youngest mothers were somewhat more critical of their children when asked to evaluate various specific positive and negative traits. Yet the variations were so small that they did not reach statistical significance. Again, the interviewers' ratings tended to confirm the mothers' reports. No differences were detected that could be attributed to the age of the mother.

As indicated, these subjective ratings perhaps inadequately measured maternal performance. However, it is important to note that other information collected from the mother on her treatment of the child also showed no distinctive patterns in terms of the mother's age at the time of the first interview. An assessment of sanctioning techniques, rule making, and the amount of interaction between parent and child revealed no tendency among the youngest mothers to adopt different strategies for dealing with their children.

Singly these findings do not carry much weight but collectively they seem not to support the common sense notion that the earlier the entry into parenthood, the more difficult the adjustment to motherhood will be. Of course, if the age range within the sample had been greater, the predicted differences might have appeared.

Although the classmates with preschool children (three years old or over) were not the ideal comparison group for the reasons we have mentioned, most of them entered parenthood just a year or two later than the adolescent mothers. Consequently, the classmates provided another way of testing the effect on maternal adaptation of age at parenthood. Despite the fact that the classmates generally became parents in their late teens, their self-evaluations and their evaluations of their children were remarkably similar to those provided by the young mothers. This finding again suggested that early age per se is not critical in determining adjustment to motherhood.

One reason for this unexpected finding is that early entry into parenthood may not have the same impact on childrearing among black women as it does among whites. As we have seen, most of the young mothers in our study could count on assistance from their relatives, and this important resource perhaps offset the disadvantages of their youthfulness or the negative feelings they might have had at the time they became parents. At Time 4, more than three out of four of the nonmarried mothers were living in a household with at least one other adult, and of the remainder, some undoubtedly had relatives living nearby. Of those women who remained near their families, many actually received more support and guidance during the early years of parenthood than those who married and moved out of the neighborhood.

Although they may have felt economically and emotionally unprepared for parenthood, most of the young mothers were not unaccustomed to child care responsibilities. The majority of them had gained considerable experience caring for siblings and nieces and nephews. The lower-class adolescent mother in fact may be far more practiced in child care than the middle-class female who becomes a parent in her early twenties. The latter is probably more likely to have grown up in a small and closely spaced family and to have acquired most of her experience in child care from babysitting occasionally.

### Reaction to Pregnancy and Maternal Adjustment

Chronological age may have less to do with the process of adaptation to parenthood than the young mother's initial reaction to pregnancy and her subsequent feelings about becoming a parent. Psychologists have long contended that the transition to parenthood is more problematic for mothers who react negatively to becoming pregnant (Shereshefsky and Yarrow, 1974). The longer these negative feelings persist, the more likely it is that they will affect the way the mother evaluates and performs her role. If this premise is correct, then women who continued to be negative about motherhood either late in pregnancy or after delivery should have had the most severe difficulty in adjusting to the maternal role and perhaps also should have still found it difficult to accept their children at the five-year follow-up. Consequently, their children might be expected to display a greater number of behavioral problems at age five.

Looking first at the relationship between the initial reaction to pregnancy (as measured at Time 1 by the index of happiness about becoming pregnant) and subsequent adjustment to parenthood, we could find no evidence that the early response was linked to the way the young mothers evaluated or performed their role five years later. None of the subsequent measures of adjustment was associated significantly with their pre-delivery feelings about pregnancy. Maternal interest, self-evaluation, interviewer assessments, the index of the mother's acceptance of her child, and her reports of her child's behavioral problems all were unrelated to her initial response to pregnancy.

There was some indication that mothers who expressed overt unhappiness about parenthood in the first year after delivery continued to experience greater adjustment problems over the long term. A greater number of these women experienced low interest in their children (47% versus 13% of the "very happy" mothers), and slight differences in the objective measures of interest also appeared in the predicted direction. The more rejecting parents also had lower self-ratings on the index of maternal performance than their peers. When asked to evaluate their skills as parents, a much higher proportion (40% versus 22%) had an average score below 60 on a scale from zero to 100.

Perhaps parents become more reluctant to admit to feelings of rejection as their child grows older. Thus, observational measures of rejection may be more discriminating than self-ratings. However, the interviewers' reports did not reveal large differences in observed patterns of parent-child interaction among the mothers who did and those who did not previously express reservations about becoming parents. On only one item was there a noticeable variation in the predicted direction: the "rejecting" parents were more likely to be evaluated as lacking confidence in dealing with their children than the women who were happier about becoming parents at the one-year follow-up. One-half of the latter group were rated as highly confident as compared to less than one-third of the women who had more negative feelings about being parents.

The mothers with more negative feelings at Time 2 also seemed to have a less favorable view of the personal qualities of their offspring than did the mothers who were more positive about their maternal roles at the one-year follow-up. More than one-half of the former assigned relatively low ratings to their children compared to one-third of the young mothers who were positive about parenthood in the early postpartum period. Similarly, almost one-half of the rejecting parents said that their children had two or more persistent problems compared to about one-third of the most accepting parents.

Although our findings are consistent with both commonsense observations and theories of personality development that assume that parental rejection causes developmental difficulties in children, two qualifications should be noted. Relatively few of the young mothers could be classified by any standard as rejecting parents. Although most of the adolescents had negative reactions to becoming pregnant, all but a small proportion (15%) were rather content with motherhood after the child was born. Moreover, even many of those parents who did express feelings of dissatisfaction at the one-year follow-up adjusted rather well to parenthood. According to both their own evaluations and the judgments of the interviewers, a majority felt at least reasonably competent as parents and were experiencing few serious difficulties with their children. Although the risk of encountering problems in childrearing was greater among the rejecting mothers, many of the women who had expressed negative feelings earlier in the study were adapting successfully to parenthood.

### Maternal Involvement and Adaptation

It should come as no surprise that many of the young mothers who voiced serious reservations about parenthood early in the study eventually adjusted successfully to the maternal role. Some derived unexpected pleasure from raising children and over the course of the study became increasingly committed and capable parents. Parental experience itself may provide reassurance and rewards, enhancing the parent's sense of confidence and competence. If this is the case, the full-time parent would have adapted more readily to her role, displaying more satisfaction with childrearing activities, than the parent who had to share her duties with a caretaker.

Although there is an extensive literature on the impact of maternal involvement on child development, few studies have been conducted on the issue of how the amount of mother-child interaction affects the parent's role performance or the way she views her role. A modest amount of research has been done on the effect on maternal behavior of employment outside the home (Clausen, 1965). Professional opinion on this subject is sharply divided, and the viewpoint of experts may be as much a reflection of ideology as a response to evidence (Rossi, 1964; Skard, 1965). The few studies that have examined how maternal attitudes and performance are affected by employment fail to find any general pattern that applies to all working or all nonworking mothers (Nye and Hoffman, 1963). Observers most familiar with this area of research suggest that the effects of a separation of mother and child because of employment depend on the conditions surrounding the employment and the caretaking arrangements provided when the mother is absent (Goode, 1964b).

Our results also point in this direction. Looking first at the mother's expression of interest in childrearing, we found no relationship between her degree of involvement in child care and her assessment of interest as a parent. Our more objective measures of interest—knowledge of the child's friends, familiarity with books and articles on childrearing, and participation in the child's school—were unrelated to caretaking patterns. Not only did the working mothers show as much interest in their children as did the full-time mothers, but women who spent less time with their children were just as likely to rate themselves high on the index of maternal performance. If anything, these mothers were slightly less critical of their abilities as parents. They perceived themselves as somewhat more confident and competent in the maternal role than did the full-time parents (cf. Rossi, 1964). Though the trend was neither strong nor statistically significant, higher maternal self-ratings occurred among women living apart from their children. Perhaps these parents felt more defensive and hence were simply more unwilling to admit their shortcomings.

Parental reports about their child's behavior also showed no discernible effects related to the caretaking pattern. Mothers who shared child care responsibilities were neither more nor less likely to report behavioral problems with their children. When asked to evaluate qualities in their children, full-time mothers actually turned out to be slightly, though not significantly, more critical than mothers who shared parental responsibilities with someone else. Perhaps women who spend more time with their children have a greater opportunity to detect negative traits, or they may simply be less patient or indulgent when their children misbehave.

The independent assessments of the interviewers provided little reason to question the parents' self-reports in this area. In evaluating maternal interest and competence, the interviewers detected no difference between full-time and part-time mothers. In general, their ratings indicated that the quality of the relationship did not vary according to the pattern of caretaking within the family.[8]

[8]One interesting difference did emerge. Interviewers were somewhat more inclined to report that the mothers who were solely responsible for rearing their children treated their children less independently than the mothers who spent more time outside the home. Although the variations were not large, they are consistent with the results of previous studies on the

Even when we examined the extreme cases in which mothers were living apart from their children, this conclusion remained unchanged. Maternal interest, self-evaluation, reported socialization practices, assessments of child behavior, and interviewer evaluations revealed little difference between the mother-child dyads living apart and those living together. Perhaps the lack of difference was attributable to the fact that many of these separations were short term and involuntary. Moreover, when separations occurred, the child usually was placed with relatives, which probably lessened the emotional impact of the mother's absence.

In focusing on the costs of lower maternal involvement, investigators have tended to neglect the advantages gained by reduced parent-child contact. Mothers who receive assistance in child care may have more enthusiasm for maternal duties than those who are full-time caretakers. Moreover, collaborative child care is just as likely to increase as to diminish the mother's confidence regarding her ability to handle her child. Thus, young mothers who are not able to assume full child care responsibilities fare quite well, especially if they are fortunate enough to share their duties with an experienced relative, as was usually the case among the women in this study.

On the basis of our tentative results it would be unreasonable to claim that adolescent mothers adjust to parenthood as easily as do women who become pregnant when they are more mature. Our findings do, however, challenge the assumption that early and unplanned parenthood usually leads to childrearing problems. At least from the mother's perspective, we find little supporting evidence for this hypothesis.

## Socioeconomic Status and Maternal Performance

In earlier chapters, we showed that women who become pregnant at an early age are less likely to succeed educationally and economically. Previous studies have shown that both of these factors are related strongly to patterns of childrearing (Sears, Maccoby, and Levin, 1957; Kohn, 1969; Elkin and Handel, 1972). Although there is some disagreement as to why such differences occur, a good deal of evidence points to the conclusion that less educated and economically disadvantaged parents encounter many more problems in raising their children. In a comprehensive review of the literature that bears on the general relationship between poverty and family behavior, Catherine Chilman (1966) assembled from a wide variety of studies findings that suggest that lower-class

---

socialization practices of working and nonworking mothers (Nye and Hoffman, 1963): employed women show a greater tendency to grant autonomy to their children than women who remain at home full-time, and children are likely to develop independence from their parents at an earlier age when their mothers work.

parents are less confident, accepting, and rewarding in their treatment of their children.[9]

If this view is correct, unplanned parenthood may indirectly intensify socialization difficulties merely because it creates economic hardship for the young parent. In examining this supposition, we are confronted again with the problem of homogeneity of the sample. However, there is sufficient variation in the economic status of the young mothers to make a restricted test of this hypothesis. If the mothers who were more economically disadvantaged experienced greater problems in relating to their children than did their peers, we might conclude that economic deprivation is an important link between unplanned pregnancy and maternal adjustment.

We used both welfare experience and total family income at Time 4 as indicators of the economic position of the young mothers. Neither measure turned out to be related consistently to the mother's adaptation to her role. Lower-income mothers and mothers on welfare were as likely to rate themselves high in maternal interest as higher-income mothers. An equal proportion of low-income mothers had read material on childrearing, had visited their child's school, and were knowledgeable about their child's playmates.

The measure of maternal self-acceptance also was unrelated to economic status. Welfare and lower-income mothers were no more critical of their own performance and no more inclined to feel they needed to improve it. The observations of the interviewers in the home did not identify any consistent patterns in the way that mothers within the various income categories treated their children. Welfare mothers were just as likely to receive high scores on confidence, warmth, and communicativeness as women who were not on public assistance. Similarly, total family income was unrelated to the interviewers' ratings of the mother's behavior toward her child.

Mothers in the lower-income groups were somewhat more critical of their children than those with higher incomes. One-third of the women on welfare assigned low ratings to their children as compared to one-fifth of the non-welfare mothers. Whether these assessments were based on objective differences is, however, questionable. The children of the welfare mothers did not experience a greater number of persistent problems than other children in the study, suggesting that welfare mothers simply may have higher (and perhaps unrealistic) expectations for their youngsters. Since welfare mothers spent more hours with their children during the day, it is possible that they, like other full-time mothers, simply had less tolerance for their children's misbehavior.

[9]Chilman, it should be said, was more careful and cautious in interpreting the data than many other researchers who have drawn similar conclusions about the childrearing patterns of the lower classes (Lipset, 1960; Bettleheim, 1969; Banfield, 1974). These researchers are so strongly convinced that lower-class women are ineffective parents that they overlook evidence that contradicts this premise and overemphasize the findings that confirm it. A number of recent studies have raised some doubt as to whether the childrearing patterns among the various classes are as different as they have sometimes been portrayed (see, for example, Kriesberg, 1970; Erlanger, 1974).

There was no evidence that mothers on relief treated their children more punitively or restrictively. They were not more likely to impose stricter regulations or to punish their children when family rules were violated. In almost all respects, the very low-income mothers said they adhered to the same child-rearing ideology and practices as the other women in the sample (cf. Moles, 1965).

When comparisons were made among educational rather than income groupings, the outcome was much the same. Self-ratings on parental interest were nearly identical: about the same proportion of dropouts and graduates scored high on both the subjective and objective measures of maternal interest. No consistent differences appeared in the index measuring maternal self-evaluation, and about one-fifth of each group indicated that they were dissatisfied with the way they performed as parents. Again, the reports of the interviewers revealed little difference in the way parents with more and less education treated their children during the interview.

There was, however, some indication that the more educated parents experienced fewer problems with their children. High school graduates were somewhat more likely to evaluate their children's performance favorably, and a slightly lower proportion of high school graduates (35% versus 43%) reported that their children had two or more problems of a persistent nature. Consistent with previous findings, this comparison showed that the more educated parents stressed obedience less, had fewer rules for their children, and tended to employ noncorporal techniques to control their children's behavior. High school graduates also placed greater emphasis on explaining regulations to their children and gaining compliance by discussion and persuasion (cf. Kohn, 1969). While these differences followed a regular pattern, they were of a minor magnitude.

On the whole, our results do not confirm the expectation that severe economic disadvantage disturbs the adaptation to parenthood. Of course, the economic range within the sample is perhaps too small to uncover differences, or possibly the measures of adjustment used in this analysis are not sufficiently sensitive to detect problems in adjustment. Assuming, however, that the results are not an artifact of these methodological limitations, there is another way of interpreting these findings: among the economically disadvantaged, motherhood is one of the few sources of satisfaction in an otherwise bleak and unrewarding existence. In contrast to marriage and work, parenthood, particularly during the early years, provided a more constant source of gratification for the women in our study. Not surprisingly, then, even the most impoverished women in the sample expressed a strong commitment to the maternal role.

## PATERNAL INVOLVEMENT AND ITS CONSEQUENCES

As we reported in earlier chapters, relations between the parents deteriorated steadily during the course of the study. At the one-year follow-up, nearly one-fifth of the mothers had lost touch with the father of their child, and this proportion increased to about one-fourth at the three-year follow-up. By two years later, when the child was approximately five, 37% of the fathers had not been in contact with the family during the past year. Some of these absent fathers were dead (5%), some were in jail (8%), and some had moved away (29%); yet most of them (58%) still lived in Baltimore but had terminated relations with the family.[10]

While the proportion of the fathers who defected steadily rose over the years, the majority of males (63%) maintained relations with their children at the five-year follow-up. At Time 4, 21% of the fathers were living with their children. Typically, children in these families had resided with both parents during most, if not all, of their early childhood, but even in one-third of these "stable" relationships, the father and child had been residentially separated for two or more years.[11] Another fifth of the fathers maintained what David Schultz (1969) has referred to as a "supportive biological father" relationship; that is, they saw their children on a regular basis (at least once a week) but did not reside with them. Supportive fathers, as we shall see, often are in transition either to or from marriage and enjoy many of the privileges and responsibilities of residential fathers. The remaining 21% of the fathers had an episodic relationship with their child: the father visited the child on an irregular basis. Usually these relationships were in the process of ending and contact between father and child had declined steadily over the years of the study; ritual ties were maintained despite the fact that visits occurred only occasionally.

### Marital Status and Paternal Involvement

We thought that the most intense, intimate relations between father and child would occur when the male was married to the young mother and living in the home. Slightly less than two-thirds of the residential fathers spent time playing with their children every day, while most of the others interacted with their children at least several times a week.[12]

The participation in childrearing of the father who was not living in the home depended largely on the state of relations between the couple. Predictably, father-child contact was generally higher when the father had been formerly

[10]These figures were based on the 303 families interviewed at Time 4 in which children were still alive and had not been adopted.

[11]Generally these children had seen their fathers on a regular basis even though these fathers lived elsewhere.

[12]When asked to describe the relationship between their husband and their child, the great majority of the married young mothers (82%) stated that the time the two spent together was very enjoyable to both. If the women had any criticism, it was that they thought the father did not spend enough time with his child.

married to the mother. More than one-third of the estranged husbands continued to have regular contact with their child, while one-third broke off relations completely. In part, this pattern could be attributed to the emotional bond that developed during the years that the father and child lived together. The longer the time the male spent in the home, the higher was the rate of father-child interaction (Kendall's tau C=.30). In addition to fostering an emotional commitment to the parent-child relationship, marriage establishes a father's claim to visiting rights. The women in our sample apparently were either less inclined or less able to deny the father the right to see his child once he had legitimated his paternity and he, in turn, was more, disposed to exercise that right if marriage had occurred.

When neither parent had been married, the father-child relationship was shaped by a somewhat different set of factors. A relatively high proportion of the couples who had never married continued to enjoy cordial relations. Thirty percent of the unmarried males living outside the home visited regularly. In instances in which interaction was frequent, some couples continued to be emotionally committed to one another and still contemplated the possibility of marriage. Although not sharing the same household, they behaved in many ways very much like a residential family. In most cases, however, the child was the principal basis of the relationship.

The situation was quite different when the young mother married a man who was not the father of the child. In these families, none of the children saw his or her biological father on a regular basis, and only 7% had even occasional contact. Even when relations were not ruptured before the mother's marriage occurred, they almost invariably became strained afterward. Continued relations between the child's biological parents not only increased the risk of rivalry between the child's father and stepfather but also threatened the husband's loyalty and obligation to his stepchild. Thus, young mothers who married another man sometimes acted as gatekeepers, restricting contact between the father and the child. As one woman in this situation explained to the interviewer:

> He doesn't know him. After I put him out I would never let him see him and he never bothered to come around.

Although data were not collected directly from the fathers in these families, they, too, may have had reasons for not wanting to see their children. In some instances, their initial unwillingness to assume financial responsibilities had created a breach in their relationship with the mother, and some of these men may have been only too glad to be relieved of their parental obligations. Others may have reluctantly reached the conclusion that their participation was unwelcome after the mother's marriage occurred. Whether as a gesture of resignation or of resentment, eventually they severed relations.

The effect of the father's marriage to another woman was similar though less pronounced. Only 3% of the fathers who married someone else maintained regular contact with their children, but 43% made occasional visits. So long as the mother herself did not marry, she usually welcomed the father's interest and made no attempt to restrict his visits. He, in turn, often continued to feel some obligation to provide support for the child, although his assistance sometimes assumed a token form.

An important way in which the nonresidential fathers demonstrated a commitment to their children and established their right of access was through the provision of financial assistance. Men who had regular contact with their children were much more likely to contribute to the children's support than those who only had occasional contact. Three out of five fathers who saw their children at least once a week also made regular support payments as compared to one-third of those who had more unstable patterns of interaction. This association held true for the formerly residential fathers as well as for the fathers who had never married. Significantly, almost as many of the latter category helped to support the child (though to a lesser extent) at the five-year follow-up on the former (Table A.20).[13]

The young mothers who were not living with the child's father were asked who made the important decisions regarding the child. Only 2% answered that the father had the most authority; another 10% replied that they acted in concert with the child's father when important decisions had to be made. Answers to a similar question about the residential fathers revealed that 6% of the fathers had preeminent authority and 78% participated equally in important childrearing decisions. With few exceptions, the nonresidential fathers who were accorded decision-making authority were those who contributed to the support of the child and visited the home regularly. More often than not they were ex-husbands, but single fathers who assumed financial responsibility had as much influence in childrearing decisions as the men who had formerly been living in the home. Former husbands lost their parental rights when they stopped contributing to the child's support; single fathers maintained their parental rights by providing financial assistance.

---

[13]We might anticipate that without some form of economic exchange, relations between the parents, as well as between the father and child, would have been more strained, and indeed they were. If the father did not contribute to his child's support, the mother was more likely to characterize relations between the father and child in less positive terms (97% of the noncontributors were rated negatively compared to 29% of the regular contributors). Apparently, men who come closer to fulfilling the traditional role of provider enhance their standing within the family (cf. Liebow, 1967). Possibly, relations with their children were more intimate and gratifying because the males sensed that their appearance in the home was more appreciated when they helped to support the child. Undoubtedly, the young mothers held them in higher esteem when they contributed regularly, and this opinion may have been conveyed to the child. Men who had occasional relations with their children and who did not provide regular support payments tended to rely on gift giving as a way of relieving the potential strain and of acknowledging their paternal role obligations. Rituals such as shopping trips, visits to the toy store, or small cash contributions before departure were used to symbolize the father's interest in the child.

### Contact with the Father and Maternal
### Role Performance

In Chapter 10 we shall consider directly the effect the father's participation in the family had on the social development of the unplanned child. As a preliminary step in that analysis, we considered whether the mother's role performance, as she defined and evaluated it, was influenced by the amount of paternal involvement in the socialization process. Although studies of families headed by women make frequent mention of the heavy burden placed on the single mother, there is a dearth of specific information on this critical problem. The impression one gets from discussions of families headed by women is that the absence of the father negatively affects the mother's socialization attitudes and practices (Glasser and Navarre, 1965; Herzog and Sudia, 1970; Ross and Sawhill, 1975).

A popular theme in the literature on single parenthood is that the father's absence is resented by the mother, who takes out her feelings of hostility on the child. Consequently, the female family head often is portrayed as critical, lacking in warmth, and punitive toward her children (Kriesberg, 1970). This attitude, it is said, fosters feelings of contrariness and rebellion in the child and often sets the stage for parent-child conflict (A. Cohen, 1955).

Other researchers have described socialization patterns in the female-headed family quite differently; still they stress the pathological nature of the mother-child relationship. It is sometimes reported that the absence of the father leads the mother to rely completely on her children for emotional gratification. As a consequence, the lone female, fearful of the consequences of denying her children's wishes, adopts an extremely indulgent or permissive style of parenting (Radin and Kamii, 1965; Biller, 1970). The child accordingly becomes extremely dependent, which may be a source of disciplinary problems or behavioral disorders.

That such contradictory theories coexist in the literature is perhaps a sign of an underlying bias against families headed by women. Much research on this phenomenon, as some critics have recently pointed out, has sought to demonstrate the deleterious effects of paternal absence, and a diligent search has been made for indications of pathology in the socialization process (Herzog and Sudia, 1970). Little attention has been paid to the possibility that families might adapt successfully to the absence of the father (Ross and Sawhill, 1975).

### The Consequences of Paternal
### Participation

By-and-large, our data provided little support for the contention that the absence of the father from the home adversely influences the mother's adaptation to parenthood. Neither marriage pattern nor paternal involvement was related to either maternal commitment or performance as reported in the Time 4 interview. Substantiating the mother's subjective impressions, interviewers' ratings of maternal behavior did not uncover differences among the various types of family situations. Maternal warmth, confidence, and the general quality of maternal relations were no higher when the father lived with, or interacted regularly with, his child.

There was a slight association between paternal participation and the number of behavioral problems the mother reported for her child. Less than one-third of the children living in unbroken families experienced two or more chronic problems. A similar proportion of children with two or more chronic problems was found in families with which the father did not reside but toward which he assumed a supportive role. In father-absent families, 43% of the children had two or more problems, and almost half of the children had two or more problems in families in which the father had only occasional contact with his child. Consistent with this result was the somewhat lower evaluation that mothers made of their children's performance in families from which the father was absent or with which he had an irregular pattern of interaction. The differences between the full-time and nonresidential supportive fathers were minimal, but the findings did indicate that the mothers perceived that their children were experiencing greater difficulties in families from which the father was completely—or in effect—absent. In the next chapter, we shall see whether the data collected directly from the children bore out these reports.

There was no evidence to support the hypothesis that mothers are especially punitive when the father is not in the home. Measures of maternal childrearing patterns designed to tap the degree of restrictiveness and rejection revealed no consistent variations among the family types. Moreover, the interviewers also failed to observe differences that might have indicated a greater degree of maternal control in father-absent households. At the same time, the families headed by women showed no signs of fostering dependency in the children. Both in their reported beliefs and in practice, mothers who assumed sole responsibility for childrearing were no less likely to endorse or promote independent behavior in their children. Again, the assessments of the interviewers did not give us any reason to question the mothers' self-ratings.

While the typology of paternal participation is a reasonable measure of the father's role in the family at Time 4, it has obvious limitations. One in particular is its failure to take into account family arrangements that might have been in effect before the final interview. Conceivably, the father's participation in the family earlier in the study had a more marked effect on the mother's adjustment than his involvement at the five-year follow-up. This possibility was investigated by comparing the adaptation of women who had separated from the child's father with that of mothers who were residing with the father at Time 4. There was no indication from either the mothers' reports or the evaluations supplied by the interviewers that the absence of the father from the home seriously complicated the relationship between mother and child. Separated women displayed no less interest in their children and did not hold a lower opinion of themselves as parents. From the mothers' reports, we concluded that the departure of the father did not appear to create adjustment problems for the child. Women who had separated from the father during the study were no more likely to report that their child was having problems and were just as likely to evaluate their child's adjustment favorably as women who were residing with the father.

Similarly, the delayed entrance of the father into the home appeared to have little impact on the mother-child relationship. Again, both the reports of the mothers and the observations of the interviewers produced no evidence that maternal performance was affected markedly by deferral of marriage. In no instance was maternal adjustment related to the timing of marriage. Most significant of all, we found that women who remained unmarried throughout the study gave no indication of being less interested, confident, or competent in their childrearing.

Possibly, the absence of the father did not have the adverse effect so often predicted in the socialization literature because his place frequently was occupied by another man. However, replacement of the father did not seem to be a mitigating condition. In fact, those women who married someone else appeared to encounter slightly more difficulty in managing motherhood. Compared to those who married the father of the child, the young mothers who married other men were somewhat more inclined to express doubts about their ability as parents; they reported more behavioral problems; and they were slightly more critical of their children (Furstenberg, 1975).

Severing relations with the father seems to complicate the young mother's adaptation to parenthood. Possibly, problems arise that are similar in nature to those we observed in the chapter on conjugal stability. Although no longer on the scene, the absent father may continue to occupy a symbolic position in the family, disrupting relations between the spouses themselves or between the stepfather and child. Although our data provided only limited evidence on this topic, it would appear that tensions and rivalries are more likely to emerge when the young mother marries another man.

## SUMMARY AND CONCLUSION

The findings presented in this chapter do not support many widely accepted characterizations of the adolescent mother's adjustment to parenthood. Despite their initially unfavorable reaction to pregnancy and their feeling then that they were not ready to become parents, most of the young mothers in our sample apparently made a successful adjustment to motherhood. The overwhelming majority (92%) stated that they enjoyed the time they spent with their children.

Similarly, most of the young mothers defined themselves positively when asked to rate the way they behaved as parents, and less than one-fifth felt very strongly that they would like to change the way they were as parents. Similarly, most expressed feelings of satisfaction with their children's performance.

This rosy picture may not reflect the reality of family life. Many parents may simply be unable to admit to their feelings of dissatisfaction or to recognize their own faults and their children's problems. Self-reports are not the best ⟵ indicator of parental adjustment. Although the limited supplementary data collected by the interviewers was hardly a sufficient corrective, it did not undermine the parents' views. Indeed, it tended to be corroborative.

Throughout the chapter we mentioned that the homogeneity of the sample possibly obscured differences that otherwise might have been more evident if comparable data had been collected from mothers who had planned their entry into parenthood. The absence of differences between the mothers' and the classmates' childrearing reports did not support this expectation; however, the classmates with older children were perhaps not sufficiently different from the sample of young mothers to provide a stringent test.

Our results showed little variation in maternal adjustment and childrearing practices according to age at onset of parenthood, feelings about the pregnancy, socioeconomic status, and degree of maternal involvement. Perhaps the measures we used were not sensitive to subtle differences. Conceivably, more distinctive patterns will emerge in time. However, it is also possible that the significance of these factors has been overrated somewhat and that the capacity of the young · parent to respond adaptively to the challenge of parenthood has been underrated.

Ironically, a partial reason that the young mothers managed as well as they did with so little assistance from the child's father may be the generally high rate of family dissolution among lower-income blacks. While the broken family is hardly the preferred pattern, it is not an uncommon one, and women are prepared to raise their children with little or no help from the father. Childrearing assistance from relatives and friends also helps to offset the low involvement of the father. Moreover, since little is expected of him, even the minimal assistance provided by a nonresidential father is welcomed and appreciated. As some indication of this, over three-fourths of the mothers reported that the nonresidential father enjoyed a positive relationship with his child, a figure nearly as great as that for the residential father. In the eyes of the mother and probably the child as well, the nonresidential father comes to be accepted for what he can offer rather than denigrated for what he cannot.

# 10. Unplanned Children

EXISTING INFORMATION on the consequences of early parenthood is almost exclusively about the impact pregnancy has on the young mother. Although it is widely assumed that unplanned parenthood may damage the life chances of the child as well, little systematic evidence can be found to support this assumption. Some information exists on the medical hazards of early childbearing for the child, but almost no data are available on the psychological and social risks (Menken, 1972; Nortman, 1974).

The findings presented in Chapter 9 create the impression that most women in our study adjusted rather well to parenthood and enjoyed generally successful relations with their children. However, these results were based primarily on the reports of the young mothers themselves and must be regarded with some skepticism. At best, these self-evaluations provided a measure of the mother's perception of her competence as a parent and were perhaps unrelated to her actual skill as a socializer. Indeed, many women may feel comfortable and capable in the maternal role but in fact perform that role rather poorly.

In this chapter we shall look more directly at the adjustment of the child. A short interview designed to assess cognitive development and social maturity was administered to the study children who were 42 months or older at the five-year follow-up. Comparable data were collected from the classmates' children who were old enough to be tested at the time of the last interview, as well as from several other samples of preschool children who differed in race and socioeconomic background from the children of the young mothers. These data make it possible to reach some general conclusions about the cognitive skills and interpersonal development of the study children in comparison to those of the other populations.

Our analysis had two aims. First, we looked for evidence indicating that the children of the adolescent parents experienced cognitive, social, and psychological disadvantages traceable to the timing and circumstances of birth. Second, we wanted to identify the specific conditions that produced cognitive or social impairment. For both theoretical and practical reasons, we recognized that

195

evidence of developmental impairment would not be helpful in drawing conclusions about the effects of early childbearing unless we understood why such disadvantage occurs.

The question we are exploring in this chapter can be viewed as a special instance of a broader issue. To what degree can the perpetuation of social inequality be explained by early socialization within the family? In the sociological literature on stratification, there is an ongoing debate on the significance of the transmission of social disadvantage during early childhood (Riessman, 1962; Chilman, 1966; Leacock, 1971). A number of writers have contended that because of either structural weakness in family organization or distinctive styles of childrearing, certain children are ill prepared to take advantage of existing opportunities for social mobility (Sheppard and Striner, 1968; Glazer and Creedon, 1969; S. Miller, 1969). In opposition to this position, other researchers have argued that differences in family structure are of little consequence and that training in early childhood is not a primary determinant of subsequent mobility patterns (Rainwater and Yancey, 1967; Rossi and Blum, 1969; Leacock, 1971).

The families in our study constitute an especially strategic group in which to examine the transmission of social disadvantage in childhood. If social impairment is a by-product of unstable or unrewarding conditions in the family during the first years of life, the children in our study should have fared poorly on developmental tests as compared to the control groups. Moreover, we should have found distinct variations within the sample of study children according to their early experiences: children who experienced less familial disruption and economic deprivation during childhood should have scored better than their less fortunate counterparts.

In Chapter 9 we examined several consequences of early parenthood that we thought might be related to problems in maternal role performance: (1) the degree of preparation for parenthood, (2) the amount and type of parental involvement, and (3) economic and educational achievement. None of these factors was related strongly to the mother's evaluation of her childrearing abilities or her assessment of her offspring's adjustment. However, it was still possible that these conditions would be more closely related to measures of development obtained directly from the child.

## MEASURES OF CHILD DEVELOPMENT

At the outset, we should say that we do not have unqualified confidence in the measures used in the study to assess the development of the children. Formidable problems exist in devising suitable tests for evaluating the cognitive and social development of preschool children. Available tests have been criticized soundly, and the literature on measurement is replete with sensible cautions about the conceptual and methodological hazards of applying nonclinical measures to very young children (Yarrow et al., 1968).

Although we were not unaware of this problem, the absence of information on the impact early parenthood has on child development led us to undertake this analysis. The measures used admittedly were imperfect, providing at best only a crude answer to the question of whether early parenthood creates developmental problems for the child. The conclusions we reached of course, are no sounder than the tests we used. Consequently, in this section we shall discuss the measures and their limitations.

### Cognitive Performance

There are a number of measures designed to evaluate the cognitive performance of children. However, few of these are applicable to children under the age of six, especially those who come from economically impoverished backgrounds or certain ethnic subgroups of the population. Specifically, measures that require a high degree of verbal skills put the lower-class black child at a considerable disadvantage, and many critics have found fault with the implicit biases in measures that rely on knowledge of a social world in which the child is not a participant.

Recognizing the limitations of available measures for this population, a team of investigators conducting research on the Head Start Program devised a test specifically to gauge the effects of social disadvantage on the cognitive performance of children three to six (Preschool Inventory, 1970). As the following passage from the test manual indicates, the Preschool Inventory (PSI) is designed principally to measure preparation for school among children with limited educational experience:

> The Preschool Inventory is a brief assessment and screening procedure designed for individual use with children in the age range of three to six years. It was developed to give a measure of achievement in areas regarded as necessary for success in school. The Inventory is by no means culture-free; in fact, one aim in its development was to provide educators with an instrument that would permit them to highlight the degree of disadvantage which a child from a deprived background has at the time of entering school so that any observed deficits might be reduced or eliminated.

We used a somewhat shorter form of the original inventory; it contained 64 items measuring the child's basic knowledge about numbers, concepts, vocabulary, and elementary visual and motor skills. The PSI took about 15 or 20 minutes to administer. Most children had no difficulty with the format of the test.[1]

---

[1] Out of the 303 study children we interviewed, 27 were unable to complete the PSI because of severe physical or psychological handicaps, and another 12 made only a minimal effort in responding to the questions. The scores of these children were judged by the interviewers not to reflect their cognitive knowledge, and therefore these results were not included in the analysis discussed in this chapter.

### Interpersonal Development

No comparable tests could be located that measure social maturity among preschool children. A review of developmental literature turned up no suitable, widely accepted standardized instrument for assessing the interpersonal skills of children below the age of six.[2] It is not difficult to understand why there is a paucity of suitable measures. In the first place, it is difficult enough to agree upon the relevant dimensions of social maturity (Baldwin, 1960; Glidewell, 1961). Even if one is successful in mapping out these dimensions, it is question- able whether they can be captured in nonclinical tests that can be administered readily to large populations of very young children (L. Yarrow, 1960; M. Yarrow, 1960). As one developmental researcher (Zivin, 1973) concluded after surveying the available tests purporting to measure self-esteem among children, "the cognitive demands of these instruments on the preschool child remain preposterous."

Rather than ignore this area, however, we created a test of interpersonal development suitable for the study population. Using techniques developed in early studies of the formation of racial self-image and attitudes (Horowitz and Horowitz, 1938; Clark and Clark, 1939; Porter, 1971), a doll-play game was constructed in which the child was asked to help the interviewer make up a TV story about "a child . . . exactly like you." The respondent was given a set of small dolls and encouraged to act out the story with the interviewer. One of the dolls represented him or her; another, his or her friend; and a third, his or her mother. In a series of predetermined hypothetical situations, the child was asked to make certain choices that involved picking one of the figures for the story. To encourage the children to project their own feelings into the story, we instructed them to give their own name to one of the dolls and refer to the friend doll by the name of a friend.

The doll-play story was divided into two parts that had parallel themes. One story was about a child at home; in the other, the scene changed to a classroom. Similar events occurred in each story so that it was possible to get responses on at least two items for each dimension. In all, the game took only 15 or 20 minutes and usually received enthusiastic cooperation from the young respon- dents.

Although most of the children appeared to enjoy the doll game, the task of responding to the structured inquiries proved to be too difficult for some. Consequently, 23 of the 303 children interviewed were entirely excluded from this part of the analysis because in the judgment of the interviewer the child did not understand the point of the game or generally was responding in what appeared to be a random or incoherent fashion.[3]

---

[2] I received valuable consultation in this endeavor from Dr. Joy Osofsky of Temple University and Dr. Judith Porter of Bryn Mawr.

[3] Occasionally, children had problems responding to particular questions in the interview even though most of their answers were intelligible. In such instances, we made no effort to

The children's interview contained questions on four discrete dimensions of social development. Each of these areas have been mentioned frequently as influencing the child's prospects for success outside the family and particularly in school (Riessman, 1962; Chilman, 1966; Elder, 1968; Clausen, 1968; Heise, 1972). A brief synopsis is given here:

1. *Ability to Defer Gratification.* The children in the story were given two situations in which they were asked if they would prefer to receive a small present right away or a larger gift some time later. At the end of the interview, the respondents were actually given the choice of accepting a small amount of candy then or a larger supply later. Responses to the hypothetical and real situations were combined into an index.

Example:

Then (his/her) friend goes home and [CHILD] is playing by (himself/herself). Mommy comes in and she has two candy bars. She says, "[CHILD], you can have either this one [SHOW PICTURE OF LITTLE BAR] right now or this one [SHOW PICTURE OF BIGGER ONE] later, before bedtime. Which one does [CHILD] choose, this one [POINT TO LITTLE BAR] *now* or this one [POINT TO BIG BAR] *later, before bed?*"

2. *Efficacy.* This dimension was intended to evaluate the child's willingness to intervene in his own behalf if the situation called for it. This index might also be considered a measure of activism versus passivity. Two circumstances were created in which the child in the story was going to be punished wrongly by an adult. The child was asked if he would take any steps to rectify the situation or whether he would simply accept the punishment.

Example:

They come home from the store, and [CHILD] plays while mommy talks to her friend. After awhile, mommy looks at the table and sees that the milk has spilled. She thinks that maybe [CHILD] was the one who spilled the milk but [CHILD] *really didn't do it.* She comes over and says she's going to hit [CHILD]. What does [CHILD] do? [LET CHILD RESPOND SPONTANEOUSLY]

3. *Trust.* In each of the two instances in which the child was about to be punished, he was asked if an adult would believe him if he explained that he had not committed the offense. Children who indicated that adults would accept their explanation were scored as more trusting than those who said that they would not be believed.

---

reconstruct or salvage their responses. Instead, they were removed from the portion of the analysis that involved that index. This procedure substantially reduced the number of cases on two of the indices, excluding a number of the younger and less advanced children. Nevertheless, it seemed wise to adopt a conservative policy in coding and analyzing the data.

Example:

[CHILD] decides to tell (his/her) mommy that (he/she) really didn't spill the milk. When (he/she) tells her, what does mommy say?

4. *Self-esteem.* The child was asked to select between his alter ego and friend as to which would perform more adequately in three different situations. Children who responded that they would perform more capably were scored as higher in self-esteem.

Example:

Then someone knocks at the door. It's [CHILD'S] friend _____ again and (he/she) wants to play. [CHILD] and (his/her) friend are playing in the house for a while, but they're not having very much fun because one of them feels angry and not very nice. Which one feels angry and is not very nice? [SHOW DOLLS, CHILD AND FRIEND]

Each measure was represented by at least two items in the doll-play story, and two of the dimensions—deferred gratification and self-esteem—were comprised of three items. Although the items constituting each index were related positively, the intercorrelations were weak. (Except for the index of deferred gratification, the gammas were below 0.30, indicating a low level of reliability.) The poor reliability of the measures suggested that it was wise to treat the findings on interpersonal development (presented later in this chapter) as both preliminary and tentative.


## CONTRAST POPULATIONS


From earlier interviews we knew that about 40 of the classmates had children who would be approximately four years old in 1972. Although, as was pointed out in previous chapters, the classmate mothers of preschool children shared many characteristics with the adolescent mothers, the conditions under which they became parents differed in several important respects. The classmate mothers were nearly two years older than the adolescent mothers, on the average, when their first child was born. Although most were still in their teens at that time, 59% were over 18. Because of this difference, a slightly higher proportion of the classmate children was living with both parents (29% versus 22%), and the educational status of their mothers was considerably higher (77% graduated from high school versus 50% of the adolescent mothers). Thus, the backgrounds of the classmate and study children were sufficiently different to provide a basis for comparison.

Interviews were completed with 36 classmate children who were at least 42 months old at the last follow-up. These children were only slightly younger (about three months on the average) than the study children (see Table 10.1). About the same percentage had attended or were attending some educational program as were the children of the young mothers: three-fifths of the study children and two-thirds of the classmate children had had some school experience when the Time 4 interview was conducted.

To supplement the information collected from the children of the young mothers and the classmates, we interviewed 194 children attending preschool programs in the City of Baltimore. Our original intention was to collect comparable data from a racially mixed sample of middle-class children from two-parent families in order to provide a baseline against which the test performances of the offspring of the classmates and adolescent mothers could be compared. Arrangements were made with eight preschool programs to send forms to the parents requesting permission for their child to participate in the study.[4] On the permission form, the parents were also asked to provide information on their marital situation and educational backgrounds. As it turned out, many of the parents were not from the middle class as defined by educational background.[5] Nevertheless, we decided to interview all the children whose parents agreed to cooperate in the study, thus increasing the range of contrast.

Table 10.1 presents the background information on the 194 preschool subjects divided into three subgroups—a sample of middle-class whites, middle-

Table 10.1. *Age Distribution, Sex, and School Experience of Study Children and Contrast Samples*

| Sample Profile | Study Children (270) | Classmates' Children (34) | White Working-Class (78) | Black Middle-Class (50) | White Middle-Class (64) |
|---|---|---|---|---|---|
| *Median Age in Months* | 57 | 56 | 57 | 58 | 55 |
| *Sex* | | | | | |
| Male | 47% | 58% | 49% | 56% | 70% |
| Female | 53 | 42 | 51 | 44 | 30 |
| *School Status* | | | | | |
| In School | 39 | 41 | 100 | 100 | 100 |
| Not in School | 61 | 59 | — | — | — |
| *Marital Status of Parents* | | | | | |
| Married | 32 | 35 | 94 | 98 | 97 |
| Other | 68 | 65 | 6 | 2 | 3 |

[4]We contacted schools known to serve middle-class families, but no effort was made systematically to select preschool programs in the Baltimore area. Because contact with the children occurred in the classroom, the interview schedule was modified slightly to reduce the overall length. However, the procedure followed in collecting the supplementary data was similar in other respects to the one followed in interviewing the study and classmate children. With few exceptions, the interviewing was carried out by the same team of interviewers. The preschool sample had less difficulty with the interview than the study children, and a higher proportion completed all parts of the test.

[5]White children were considered to be middle class if either or both parents had *completed* college. Relatively few black families met this criterion, and we classified them as middle class if either or both parents had *attended* college. Consequently, many of the whites were from upper middle-class families, while more of the blacks were from lower middle-class backgrounds.

class blacks, and working-class whites. Virtually all of the children from the three supplementary samples resided in households headed by couples. By contrast, the majority of the study and classmates children were living in families headed by women. The median age of the children varied only slightly among the three groups and closely matched that of the offspring of the young mothers and of the classmates. Some differences in sexual composition appeared: the middle-class sample contained an overrepresentation of males, for reasons not known. Table 10.1 also reminds us that the educational experiences of the five groups of children were significantly different, a fact we considered in comparing them on our measures.

## SAMPLE COMPARISONS OF COGNITIVE PERFORMANCE

We began our analysis with an examination of the cognitive performances of the different groupings of children. Table 10.2 presents the median percentile scores of the five different samples of children on the Preschool Inventory. The scores are expressed in percentile standings (based on national norms) that were standardized for the child's age. This removed the possibility of variations due to differences in age composition of the five samples.

In certain respects, the results of our analysis followed a predictable course; in other regards, they were somewhat surprising. Sizable differences occurred between the children of the young mothers and the samples drawn from the preschool programs. Performance on the PSI was much higher among the contrast samples than among the study children, and the disparity was most conspicuous according to race, with the white children doing somewhat better. The children of the classmates also performed well below the preschool groups, scoring only slightly higher than the study children.

At the same time, the median scores of the children of both the young mothers and the classmates were above the fiftieth percentile, indicating better than average preschool readiness for this group compared to the population of

Table 10.2. *Cognitive Performance of Study Children and Contrast Samples*[1]

| Educational Status | Study Children | Classmates' Children | White Working-Class | Black Middle-Class | White Middle-Class |
|---|---|---|---|---|---|
| Total | 67 | 72 | 99 | 91 | 99 |
| | (250) | (32) | (70) | (50) | (65) |
| In School | 82 | 80 | | | |
| | (99) | (14) | | | |
| Not in School | 59 | 66 | | | |
| | (151) | (18) | | | |

[1]Cells contain median percentile scores.

Head Start children on whom the test was standardized. In part, this unexpected result perhaps was traceable to the fact that the majority of children in these two samples had had some preschool experience, and the test may be better suited to populations with no such exposure. However, even when we considered only those children who had never attended school, the scores were somewhat above the norm. Thus, when compared to a broader sample of low-income children—the population on which the PSI norms were based—the study children did not rank too badly. Nor was their performance on the PSI far below that of the children of the classmates, whose backgrounds were somewhat more favorable.[6]

While the study children were perhaps no less equipped for school than other economically disadvantaged children, it was clear that they were far less ready than black and white middle-class children as well as white children from working-class backgrounds. A portion of the difference was not directly attributable to family background as such: all the children in the three contrast samples were enrolled in preschool programs. Conceivably, this educational advantage explained why these preschool samples achieved higher scores on the PSI. One way of correcting for the effect of this difference was to exclude the study children who had had no educational experience. This procedure reduced the initial disparity by approximately one-half, but a sizable difference remained (Table 10.2). How much of this residual difference could be attributed to conditions associated with early parenthood will become clearer in the following discussion of sources of variation among the study children.

## EARLY PARENTHOOD AND COGNITIVE PERFORMANCE

Looking at the aggregate comparisons, we could not say for certain whether or to what extent early parenthood was the source of the disparity between the groupings. To establish the existence of a link between early parenthood and poor cognitive development in children, it is critical to pinpoint the conditions that result from an unplanned pregnancy that may have a deleterious effect on the intellectual development of children during their preschool years. In this section, we consider several alternative ways of linking the two phenomena, examining how much support our data provided for each of these explanations.

### Preparation for Parenthood

Among the various reasons mentioned in Chapter 9 as to why young mothers may find it particularly difficult to be parents is the unplanned and

[6]Even when we included the children whose performance on the PSI was judged by the interviewers as not reflecting their true abilities, more than half of the study children performed above the fiftieth percentile.

abrupt transition to a new role that they must make. In the preceding chapter, we were unable to discover any lasting traces of their initially negative reaction to parenthood when we examined the mothers' adjustment to parenthood five years later. It was pointed out that the residual effect of the hasty transition might have been too elusive or too well masked to be registered in the self-report data that were the basis of our analysis. The information collected from the children provided another opportunity to explore the hypothesis that the unanticipated transition to parenthood disturbs the child's socialization.

We might expect that the more difficult the transition to parenthood, the less skilled the parent would be in her early dealings with the child. For reasons mentioned earlier, entry into parenthood was probably most difficult for the mothers who were very young (under 16) when they became pregnant. Not only did they *feel* less ready to become mothers but they generally were less equipped to perform the tasks of rearing a child as a result of their youth, inexperience, and lack of education. Previous studies have uncovered medical risks as well as social complications associated with early childbearing (Nortman, 1974). Did the adolescent mothers' lack of readiness for parenthood interfere with their parental performance? If so, the children of the youngest mothers should have been most impaired in their cognitive development.

The data did not bear out this expectation. The achievement of the study children was unrelated to mother's age during pregnancy. The children whose mothers were not yet 16 at the time of the first interview did as well as the offspring of women who were 16 and older during pregnancy. This finding was especially surprising in view of the fact that the youngest mothers were somewhat less likely to complete school, marry, or achieve economic self-sufficiency.

While the mother's age during pregnancy was not related to the cognitive development of the child, the mother's initial attitude toward parenthood was related to how well her child did on the Preschool Inventory at Time 4. The test performance of the child was significantly higher when the mothers had been more positive about becoming pregnant. Almost three-fifths of the subgroup whose parents had been very happy about becoming pregnant scored in the top quartile as compared to slightly more than one-third of the children whose mothers were very unhappy at the time of the first interview. This difference seemed to be related less to the direct effect of the mother's attitude than to the circumstances that shaped her initial feeling about becoming pregnant. Mothers who were happier about becoming pregnant were more likely to marry the father of the child and, as we shall soon see, this event had an important impact on the child's cognitive performance.

Curiously, the mother's reaction to the child after birth was related only weakly to his or her PSI score at the five-year follow-up. Only in families in which the mother was extremely negative toward the child after birth did we find any indication of diminished cognitive performance. Otherwise, the mother's response to the child at the one-year follow-up was unrelated to his or her subsequent performance.[7]


## Parental Contact and Cognitive Performance

Except for the measure of maternal attitude toward the child at Time 2, we had no other indicator of the quality of the mother's relationship with her child during infancy. In the absence of more specific data, it was useful to search the marital history of the young mother for clues about the early involvement of the parents. We could safely assume that when marriage took place before delivery, the child was more likely to receive attention from both parents.


### Marriage Patterns and Paternal Contact

The relationship between the cognitive performance of the child and the marital history of his or her parents is complex. It first appeared that the cognitive scores were higher if the parents had married before delivery. Children whose parents married prior to delivery did somewhat better than those whose parents married later or not at all. However, the effects on the child of the timing of marriage were confounded with the effects produced by the choice of husband. Women who married prenatally were much more likely to marry the father of the child than those who deferred marriage. When both these marriage factors were considered simultaneously, it was evident that whom the mother married was more important than when she married. If the mother married the child's father, the child was more likely to perform in the top quartile than if she married another man. Indeed, the children of women who married a man other than the child's father performed no better than those whose mothers remained single during their early childhood (Table A.21).

Why do children whose biological parents marry do better? One might suspect it is because these parents are older and more economically secure. However, we have already shown that the age of the mother was unrelated to the child's success on the PSI. The economic status of the couple, as we shall see, was an important correlate of the child's cognitive performance; however, the status of the stepfathers was, if anything, somewhat higher than the status of the biological fathers who married the mothers. Consequently, economic factors alone also could not account for the variation in test scores.

On the basis of a variety of indicators, our results suggest that the critical factor in cognitive performance is the continuity of the relationship between the

[7]Only under certain conditions did the mother's early response to the pregnancy remain a critical factor in the child's development. The impact of the mother's first response was more noticeable for women who remained single throughout the study. Women who married may have had more reason to revise their feelings.

father and the child. We found that regardless of economic status the absence of the father from the home had a detrimental effect on the PSI score of the child. Children whose parents married early and remained married throughout the study performed at a higher level than children in other family situations. Indeed, their performance on the PSI approached that of the comparison groups of preschool children.

### Maternal Involvement

If children benefit from contact with their fathers, does maternal involvement similarly enhance their cognitive development? Our results indicated otherwise. There was a negative relationship between the extent of maternal participation in child care and the child's test score: children did not perform as well when their mothers assumed full responsibility for their care, and they performed best when they were cared for outside the home. This finding was partially spurious because the children cared for outside the home were likely to be older and hence to have received some preschool education. However, even when these conditions were held constant, the children of the full-time mothers did not do quite so well on the cognitive tests as the children of mothers who shared childrearing with another adult.

In Chapter 9, we discovered that mothers who turned over child care responsibilities to another person did not do so from any lack of interest in the maternal role. This pattern occurred when the mothers went to work or, in a few instances, when they were completing their education. Such women usually made a concerted effort to spend time with their children while they *were* at home. Although they were engaged in child care for fewer total hours than the full-time mothers, they were at least as likely to engage in recreational activity with their children. Consequently, when the mothers shared child care with someone else, their children probably received as much, if not more, contact with adults.

When collaborative patterns of child care are established, children usually have more overall contact with adults. Of course, this supplementary contact may be primarily custodial and therefore of little benefit. However, it is probably more often the case that the person who assumes responsibility for the child is at least as attentive and involved as the full-time mother. Typically, the person who cares for the child of an adolescent parent is a close relative, usually a grandparent with considerable child care experience. Because this caretaker is likely to have a strong stake in the child's welfare, she probably enriches rather than restricts the child's learning opportunities.

In some respects the pattern of collaborative child care has some of the same consequences as marriage, ensuring that the child has contact with at least two adult figures. Although this arrangement may increase the likelihood that the child will experience some conflicting expectations, it undoubtedly provides a more challenging and stimulating social environment than that provided by a single socializer (cf. Coser, 1964). Not surprisingly, we discovered that the advantages of collaborative child care were much more evident for the children of single or separated mothers than for the offspring of the married mothers. When a second parent is absent from the home, it is more critical for the mother to have the assistance of another adult in raising the child.

We can now better understand why the mother's age at delivery was not related to her child's cognitive performance. Although our reasoning that younger mothers would be less capable parents may be correct, we did not take into account the fact that younger mothers generally received child care assistance from other family members. This adaptive pattern helped to prevent the harmful effects that might have resulted had the young mother been forced to assume complete and sole responsibility for the child.

## Socioeconomic Status and Cognitive Performance

The children of the full-time mothers suffered another disadvantage that contributed to their poorer performance on the PSI. Their parents were generally less well educated, less likely to be working, and more impoverished. Each of these factors was related to the child's score on the PSI although the variations by socioeconomic position were somewhat more marked for unmarried than for married women. The children of the unmarried mothers who had completed high school and had held a steady job did nearly as well as the children of the married women, even those who had wed the father of the child. However, the children of the unmarried women who had never worked scored considerably lower than any other group. Only 13% of these children scored in the top quartile of the PSI as compared to half of the offspring of single parents who were employed at Time 4.

The mother's economic impoverishment at the time of delivery had less impact on the child's cognitive performance than her economic career after childbirth. The effects of economic disadvantage did not persist when the mother's socioeconomic position improved over time. At the five-year follow-up, the offspring of the young mothers who had been (but no longer were) on welfare did nearly as well as those whose parents had no welfare experience. Similarly, children whose mothers began working at Time 4 did nearly as well as those whose mothers were employed at both Times 3 and 4.

This outcome might be attributable largely to the characteristics of the women who were able to improve their economic situation during the course of the study. Young mothers who advanced economically over the five years of the study typically had higher educational ambitions, were more successful in school, and were able to restrict their family size. Each of these factors was related independently to the child's cognitive performance. As we learned in Chapter 9, mothers who were working at Time 4 had higher educational goals for their children and took a more active part in their children's education.

Consequently, children of working parents were more likely to have been enrolled in a preschool program. In sum, the working mothers—the women who most often shared child care with another adult—were the most successful and upwardly mobile segment of the sample. Therefore, it was understandable that their children should perform at a higher level on the tests of cognitive skills.

Earlier we discovered that the cognitive level of the study children was considerably lower than that of the comparison groups and slightly below that of the classmate children. It now should be clearer why we obtained these results. The study children were socially handicapped in two significant respects. First, they were less likely to have had steady contact and attention from a male than were the other children. This interaction appeared to be important for the development of cognitive skills. Second, the educational and economic levels of the adolescent parents were much lower than those of the comparison groups. Low socioeconomic status is linked to both attitudes and actions that have important consequences for a child's cognitive development. The children of lower-status mothers are less likely to receive educational training during the preschool years, and less educated and occupationally successful women appear to be less effective in developing cognitive skills in their children.

The problems of low-income single mothers are compounded when they are the sole agents of socialization for their children. The effect of their status on the child is mitigated when childrearing responsibilities are shared with another adult. In sum, certain by-products of unplanned parenthood—paternal absence, lower education, and economic deprivation—are clearly associated with low cognitive achievement on the part of the child. Will the evidence on social development reveal a similar pattern of disadvantage?

## SAMPLE COMPARISONS OF INTERPERSONAL DEVELOPMENT

A set of comparisons was made among the five samples on each of the development indices derived from the doll-play test (deferral of gratification, efficacy, trust, and self-esteem). The results, in contrast to the findings on cognitive performance, showed no sizable or consistent patterns of difference among the various groupings of children. It was, in fact, striking how closely the scores of the study children resembled those of the other samples. With few exceptions, the average range between the extremes on all four indices was about 10%. More important, no sample consistently performed better or worse than the others on the four measures. Overall, our data did not indicate that the study children were psychologically disadvantaged as a result of the circumstances of their birth or their early family experience. On none of the measures was there a marked difference between the study children and the other children and in no instance were their scores much lower than those of the other groups (for specific results, see Furstenberg, 1975: 422).

Several factors might explain these findings. The first was mentioned when the measures were introduced earlier in this chapter. Because of their low reliability, the measures of social adjustment were perhaps too weak to reveal variations among the different samples. Assuming, however, that the findings were accurate, it is still possible that the negative impact of unplanned parenthood on the child's adjustment had not yet emerged. Possibly this effect will show up more clearly after the child enters elementary school. We found no indication, however, of greater divergence in the adjustment of the older children or of those children enrolled in school at the five-year follow-up.

We wondered whether the negative effects of early parenthood on the child's social adjustment are confined to a limited group of children. Conceivably, these social and psychological costs show up only under special circumstances. In the remainder of this chapter, this possibility is explored.

# EARLY PARENTHOOD AND SOCIAL ADJUSTMENT

Do social and psychological differences emerge between subgroups of study children which can be traced to the situation of the young mother when she became pregnant and to her marital and economic experiences during the follow-up period?

## Preparation for Parenthood

Both objective and subjective criteria pointed to the conclusion that the women in the sample who were under the age of 15 at the time they became pregnant were least ready to become parents. If a difficult transition to parenthood produces long-term complications in the relationship between mother and child, then the children of these mothers should have been doing least well at the five-year follow-up.

The evidence did not support this expectation. No association appeared between the mother's age at the first interview and her child's ability to defer gratification, his or her sense of trust, or his or her self-esteem. On only one of the indices of social adjustment—efficacy—did a difference in the predicted direction occur, and it was modest.

The young mother's pre-delivery feelings about her pregnancy and her reaction to her child at the one-year follow-up provided a more direct way of assessing her psychological adjustment to parenthood. But when these variables were related to the interpersonal development of the child, again we detected no strong or consistent pattern of variation. On only one of the measures—self-esteem—was there any evidence that the children of more "rejecting" mothers display more signs of maladjustment. The offspring of the women whose initial reaction to becoming pregnant was positive had somewhat higher self-esteem at the five-year follow-up than the children of mothers who had reacted negatively, but this difference (35% versus 20%) was not statistically significant.

Moreover, when the young mother's post-delivery reaction to parenthood was considered, we found no evidence at all that these later attitudes were related to her child's social adjustment. Mothers who expressed low interest in parenthood at the five-year follow-up were not more likely to have children with low self-esteem. None of the other three measures of social development was related to maternal acceptance during the postpartum period.

It would seem, then, that preparation for parenthood does not have a pronounced effect on the social adjustment of the child. Especially in light of the negative findings presented in Chapter 9, it is important to emphasize that whatever the costs of early parenthood for the child, they are probably not the result of trauma or strains experienced by the young mother in adjusting to her role during or shortly after pregnancy.

### Parental Contact and Social Development

Earlier in this chapter we discovered that cognitive performance was related to the child's family experience during the follow-up period. In this section we consider whether social development was similarly affected by the child's relations with his or her parents and by early childhood socialization.

#### Marital Experience and Social Development

We have seen that early parenthood diminishes the child's chances of growing up in a two-parent family either because matrimony does not occur or because marital unions are quickly dissolved. Is there reason to believe that the child's social development is harmed as a result? Table 10.3A displays the child's performance on the four indices of social development cross-tabulated by the mother's marital situation at Time 4. Overall, the differences were relatively small, although they did show a consistent pattern. The children of the married women had the highest scores on all four indices; the offspring of broken marriages had the lowest on the four measures.

In our analysis of cognitive performance, we concluded that one of the reasons that children benefit from stable marital unions is that continuous contact with the father directly promotes achievement. The findings on the effect of father absence on a child's social development confirmed this conclusion. On three of the four measures, the children of parental couples outperformed those of nonparental couples. This pattern was especially evident

Table 10.3A. *Social Development of Study Children by Parents' Marital Status at Time 4*

| Criteria | Single | Married | Other |
|---|---|---|---|
| Deferral of Gratification (Percentage High) | 28 (97) | 31 (91) | 27 (81) |
| Efficacy (Percentage High) | 56 (55) | 62 (61) | 49 (51) |
| Trust (Percentage High) | 35 (79) | 43 (72) | 28 (64) |
| Self-Esteem (Percentage High) | 28 (88) | 30 (83) | 20 (74) |

Table 10.3B. *Social Development of Study Children by Parents' Marital History*

| Criteria | Married Father, Still Married | Married Other Male, Still Married | Married Father, Separated | Married Other Male, Separated | Never Married |
|---|---|---|---|---|---|
| Deferral of Gratification (Percentage High) | 27 (60) | 36 (25) | 33 (61) | 11 (19) | 28 (97) |
| Efficacy (Percentage High) | 73 (46) | 53 (40) | 47 (17) | 36 (11) | 56 (55) |
| Trust (Percentage High) | 51 (47) | 31 (49) | 26 (19) | 24 (14) | 35 (79) |
| Self-Esteem (Percentage High) | 32 (53) | 16 (57) | 25 (24) | 35 (47) | 28 (88) |

when we examined the intact families, but it held true for the children of separated parental couples as well (Table 10.3B). It would appear that we have additional evidence that family situations are more problematic for the child whose biological parents do not marry.

Again, whom the young mother had married turned out to be much more important than when she married. Children born out of wedlock suffered no special disadvantage as long as their parents eventually married and remained married. Of course, delayed marriage did have an adverse effect if it meant that the mother married someone other than the child's father or did not remain married. Only indirectly, then, did the timing of marriage affect the social development of the study children.

Looking again at Table 10.3B, we also learn that the children of women who remained single fell in the middle on the measures of adjustment. They did not do as well as the offspring of the women who entered a stable marriage with their child's father, but they performed as well as, if not better than, all other subgroups. Was this because many of these children were able to maintain stable and rewarding relationships with their fathers? It would seem that the answer is no. Among the children not residing with their fathers at Time 4, there was little evidence that paternal involvement was related to positive social development. Children who saw their fathers regularly did not score differently from those who had episodic or no relations with their fathers. When we looked more directly at measures of the quality of the father-child relationship, we were unable to discover any support for the proposition that children of unmarried mothers are better adjusted socially if they enjoy positive relations with their fathers (we relied on the mothers' assessments of father-child relations).

Finally, we considered the possibility that the effect of the father's participation depended on the sex of the child. Perhaps contact with the father was more critical for males than for females. The numbers dwindled when we introduced this additional variable, and the small size of the cells in the table makes it difficult to draw any definitive conclusion. However, no noticeable differences emerged when the effect of the father's absence was examined separately for boys and girls in families in which the young mother remained unmarried.

At most, then, the results supplied only partial support for the hypothesis that children who maintain stable and continuous relations with their fathers develop fewer personality problems. We did observe some signs that the study children did better when the parental couple married and remained married. The introduction of a stepfather into the family was invariably problematic. At the same time, there was little evidence that the children of the unmarried women benefited from frequent contact with their fathers.

### Relations with the Mother and Social Adjustment

No support was found in our earlier analysis of cognitive performance for our expectation that full-time mothers would be more effective in providing intellectual stimulation to their children. Indeed, for a variety of reasons, the children of full-time mothers were far less likely to develop cognitive skills at an early age than the children of mothers who shared child care responsibilities.

The findings on social adjustment did not parallel these results. On three of the four measures, no differences occurred among families with different child care arrangements. On only one item—efficacy—was a slight variation evident. Half the children of full-time mothers scored high on this measure as compared to two-thirds of the children of women who shared their child care duties. In light of the other negative results, we were not inclined to make much of this difference.

The mother's report on her childrearing practices and experiences provided another way of assessing her effect on the child's adjustment. Mothers who were more confident about their childrearing abilities were not more likely to raise children who were better adjusted socially. Similarly, we discovered no relationship between the mother's rating of her child's behavior and the child's performance on the doll-play test. Even when we used the presumably more objective index of the number of behavioral problems reported by the mother, we still found that the mother's portrait of the child was unrelated to the measures of interpersonal development.

This array of negative findings provides no confirmation of our expectation that the extent and style of the mother's involvement in the socialization process would influence the child's adjustment. Conceivably, the mother's influence is mitigated by the participation of other adults in the childrearing process. But we also cannot entirely dismiss the possibility that the explanation resides in the measures used; more reliable instruments might have produced different results. At least they would have provided a more convincing test of the mother's influence on the emotional development of the child.

### Economic Status and the Social Development of Children

One further potential link between early parenthood and the social development of children was examined. We considered the possibility that the adjustment of the child might be impaired only in families that had suffered severe economic deprivation as a result of premature parenthood. From the analysis of cognitive performance, in which we discovered that the economic status of the young mother was related to her child's score on the Preschool Inventory, there seemed to be some basis for exploring this hypothesis.

The results were not clear-cut, but there was some indication that on certain dimensions, economic disadvantage contributed to social maladjustment. On two of the indices—efficacy and trust—children in more economically secure families scored higher. On the other two indices, no relationship was evident (Table A.22).

Earlier we discovered that children in stable two-parent families tended to score higher on the measures of social adjustment. One reason for this finding stemmed from the fact that these households were better off economically; parents in such households were likely to be better educated and more regularly employed. Given the small size of our sample, it was difficult to explain the contribution of each of these factors to the child's scores on efficacy and trust. The results revealed that children from higher-status families were more likely to feel efficacious and trusting regardless of their parents' marital situation. However, the association between parental economic status and these indices of social adjustment was stronger for unmarried than for married women. In other words, the child of an unmarried mother was more likely to achieve higher scores on these measures if his or her parent had graduated, was not on welfare, and was employed. The child living in a two-parent household was less influenced by his mother's status. The father's presence had a salutory effect on adjustment whatever the mother's schooling or work experience.

Children of unmarried parents are more vulnerable to certain types of interpersonal problems when their mothers are in economically precarious positions. Conversely, single parenthood confers little disadvantage on the child as long as the young mother is able to complete school and enter the labor force. Naturally, there is some self-selection among the women in these two groups. Mothers who overcome the obstacles to remaining in school and are able to locate and retain a job tend to be more capable. Consequently, it is not altogether unexpected that their children should display a greater sense of efficacy and trust.

As we discovered in our analysis of cognitive development, the upwardly mobile segment of the sample seemed to have greater success in socializing their children. It is interesting to discover that marriage did little to improve the status of these women or the situation of their children. A father residing in the home enhanced the child's achievement if and only if the young mother had limited education or earning potential. In these circumstances, the presence of a father seemed to compensate for the mother's social limitations.


## CONCLUSION


The question posed in this chapter was whether the disruptive effects of early parenthood leave a lasting imprint on the unplanned child that may negatively affect his chances of success in later life. Two separate areas of potential disturbance were examined: the cognitive and interpersonal development of the study children at the five-year follow-up.

In each instance, we compared test scores of study children with results obtained from four different samples of preschool children. The analysis revealed that the children of adolescent mothers were less well equipped in terms of cognitive skills than their counterparts in the other samples. Their level of attainment was related strongly to their socioeconomic background, suggesting that the one important negative legacy of early parenthood is the economic disadvantage it brings to parent and child.

The results of the examination of the children's social adjustment were more complex. While certain differences among the various samples were evident, there was no clear indication that children of adolescent parents are more socially maladjusted. Even though the range of scores on the four measures of social development was rather small, in all instances the study children fell somewhere in the middle of the various groupings.

A more specific analysis was aimed at investigating whether a series of conditions associated with early parenthood—mother's age during pregnancy, mother's negative attitude about her first pregnancy, lack of contact between father and child, marital instability, separation of mother and child, and low economic status—had an adverse effect on the intellectual and interpersonal development of the child. Our findings are summarized in the following list.

1. The degree of preparation for parenthood was of little or no consequence. The age of the young mother and her reaction to her pregnancy were unrelated to the child's cognitive performance and social adjustment.

2. Family composition and contact between child and parents were associated with performance on the developmental tests. Children who had continuous contact with their fathers did better intellectually and socially. The effect of the young mother's involvement in the socialization process was ambiguous. Indeed, women who shared childrearing duties with others tended to have more success with their children.

3. There were several indications that these differences could be traced in part to the more favorable economic conditions enjoyed by children in stable two-parent families and by children of working single mothers. Intellectual achievement and certain interpersonal traits, namely, efficacy and trust, were related to the economic status of the family. In both instances, however, the advantage of growing up in a household headed by a couple showed up strongly only among those children whose mothers had not completed high school and were unemployed. If the socioeconomic status of mothers was high, children did relatively well on the tests regardless of the marital status of their parents.

All these findings must be regarded as provisional owing to the crudeness of the measures employed. Nevertheless, we find indications that the children of the young mothers are disadvantaged developmentally early in life. How pervasive and severe these disadvantages are is difficult to judge given the limitations of the instruments used in our study. We have been able to show that the deleterious effects are not borne equally by all the unplanned children. Certain children were severely handicapped, while others are not. In Chapter 11 we shall explore strategies of intervention that may lessen the detrimental impact of early childbearing for both the children and their parents.

# 11. Social Policy and the Teenage Parent

THIS BOOK HAS FOCUSED ON a question that at the outset seemed straightforward enough: what are the consequences of early childbearing for the later course of life of the young parent and her child? However, sometimes simple questions yield complex responses. Our aim has been not merely to analyze the costs of premature parenthood but also to consider in detail how and why these costs arise.

The purpose of this chapter is to assemble observations that have been scattered throughout the preceding analysis in order to draw some general conclusions about the social career of the adolescent parent and to identify a few focal issues that may have value for public policies and programs dealing with the teenage parent.

## EARLY CHILDBEARING AND SOCIAL DISADVANTAGE

This study began with an assumption shared by most theorists, practitioners, and citizens that precipitate parenthood creates social disadvantage by propelling the teenage mother into a role for which she is not adequately prepared. In the first chapter, it was alleged that early parenthood disrupts and disarranges the socially accepted sequence for establishing a family in our society. Accordingly, we anticipated that childbearing in adolescence would deprive the young mother of the necessary training, material resources, and social support that might have been forthcoming had she managed to delay the transition to motherhood.

This supposition was fairly well supported by the results of our investigation. We discovered a sharp and regular pattern of differences in the marital, childbearing, educational, and occupational careers of the adolescent mothers and their classmates. The young mothers consistently experienced greater difficulty in realizing life plans; a gaping disparity existed between the goals they articulated in the first interview and their experiences following delivery. In contrast, we found that the classmates, especially those who did not become pregnant premaritally during the five years of our study, had a far better record of achieving their immediate objectives in life.

While certain presumed effects of early pregnancy might in fact have stemmed from differences between the two samples, several findings appeared to challenge this possibility. In the first place, the similarity in the backgrounds of the young mothers and the classmates seemed to support the inference that the career patterns of the young mothers and their classmates diverged primarily as a result of unplanned pregnancy. Reinforcing this impression was the further discovery that even at the end of the study, the two samples held basically identical values and views about the desirability of marriage, ideal family size, educational attainment, economic independence, and childrearing. Given these similarities, it seems implausible that the unplanned birth was the by-product of initial cultural or personality differences between the young mothers and their classmates.

Finally, at different points throughout the analysis, we were able to show how the early pregnancy created a distinct set of problems for the adolescent parent that forced a redirection of her intended life course. In particular, we established a number of links connecting early childbearing to complications in marriage, to disruption of schooling, to economic problems, and to some extent to problems in family size regulation and childrearing as well.


## STEREOTYPING THE ADOLESCENT MOTHER


Despite the clarity and consistency of our findings, one cannot glibly conclude that parenthood in adolescence inevitably and irreversibly disrupts the life course of the female. We have pointed out that the negative consequences of an unplanned pregnancy can be rectified by certain actions and events. A sizable proportion of the young mothers in our study was able to cope successfully with the problems of early parenthood and, at least at the five-year follow-up, these women were making out just as well as their former classmates who did not become pregnant premaritally.

Certain atypical social occurrences such as early childbearing create an almost irresistible urge to construct sociological stereotypes, to characterize a diverse population as if it conformed to a single pattern. Tempting as it may be to refer to the teenage mother as a homogeneous category, our results advised extreme caution in this regard. One of the most impressive findings was the diversity of responses to a common event. Despite the fact that virtually all the participants in the study were low-income black females in their midteens who were premaritally pregnant for the first time, the outcome at the five-year follow-up was enormously varied. In fact, by the time of the last interview, the sample hardly could have been more diverse in every important area we explored. Whether it was the decision to wed, marital stability, subsequent child-bearing, work and welfare experiences, or methods of childrearing, the young mothers were extremely dissimilar.

Some women had been able to repair the disorder created by an untimely pregnancy by hastily marrying the father of the child. When these marriages were successful the situation of the young mothers closely resembled that of the former classmates who had delayed marriage and childbearing until their early twenties. Other young mothers developed innovative styles of coping with the problems created by early parenthood. Rather than repair their family careers, they rearranged them, putting off marriage indefinitely and resuming their education. When able to restrict further childbearing and make child care arrangements, these women often managed to achieve economic independence by the time the study ended. Still other participants were not so successful in coping with the problems caused by precipitate parenthood. Their prospects of achieving a stable marriage were damaged by the early pregnancy, and they were having great difficulty supporting a family on their own. Poorly educated, unskilled, often burdened by several small children, many of these women at age 20 or 21 had become resigned to a life of economic deprivation.

## EXPLAINING DIVERGENT CAREERS

While it is inevitable that we should try to characterize these diverse patterns along some dimension of success and failure—based either on the standards of the young mothers or on our own—at the same time it is important to recognize that every solution to adolescent parenthood has one element in common: each is an attempt to cope with the characteristic problems occasioned by early childbearing. Like all Monday morning quarterbacks, we are inclined to applaud the will, wisdom, and skills of those whose plans happen to succeed and to condemn the motives, judgment, and capabilities of those whose strategies fail, ignoring the extreme subjectivity involved in such hindsight evaluations. Consider the example of the pregnant woman who drops out of school to marry the father of her child. If the marriage works out, we infer that her policy was a good one. However, if the marriage breaks up and the young mother finds herself in an extremely vulnerable economic position, we are likely to arrive at the opposite conclusion. In either case, we usually ignore the fact that coping strategies simultaneously have the potential for both problem-producing and problem-solving.

Nevertheless, some coping strategies typically work out better than others. To put it in different words, some have more potential for resolving old problems than for raising new ones. For example, young mothers who married the father of their child, restricted their childbearing, and graduated from high school generally were able to minimize the disruptive effects of the unscheduled pregnancy. A higher proportion of these women had managed to achieve stable family relationships and attain some measure of economic security by the end of the study. No doubt in the minds of some readers this conclusion may arouse the suspicion that the participants in our study were being judged by middle-class standards. But it is presumptuous to argue that harmonious family relations and economic independence are goals exclusive to the middle class merely because its members have greater control over the means of attaining them.

It is clear that all but a very few of the young mothers had an image of the good life that included a stable marriage, economic security, and gratifying relations with their children. Moreover, those who had managed to achieve these objectives described themselves as much happier at the completion of the study than those whose life situations were less settled.[1] If standards of success were so widely shared by our respondents, how can we account for such diverse outcomes following the birth of the first child? There are several explanations, none of them mutually exclusive.

1. *Initial Differences within the Population.* Although we have pointed out that the women in our sample had many characteristics in common, nonetheless, it can be safely assumed that individual differences among the young mothers explained a certain amount of the divergence in their careers following the birth of the child. Educational achievement, family size limitation, marital stability, and childbearing patterns undoubtedly were affected by personality traits un-measured in this study as well as by differences, say, in aptitude. At various points in the analysis of our data, we were able to infer and sometimes to demonstrate that tastes, preferences, and commitments played a role in deciding career patterns and directions, such as the recruitment to sexual relations, the decision to marry, or the choice to continue in school.

While in no way denying the significance of psychological predisposition in shaping the career routes of the young mothers, it is important to recognize the links between these factors and the features of social structure to which we have been more attentive in our study. Without question, the women who over-came many of the problems created by an unplanned pregnancy were more capable and committed than those who negotiated less successfully the course of their later lives; but we must not fall into the trap of concluding that the personal limitations of the young mothers explained why so many had difficulty completing school, finding rewarding employment, maintaining stable marriages, or restricting childbearing. This reasoning is merely another version of what might be designated the "fallacy of supermotivation." When they possess *genuine* drive or a *real* desire to succeed, women/blacks/the blind/ex-cons/the

---

[1]Women who were married at Time 4 were far more likely to report that they were happier then than they had been during the past four or five years. When asked to rate themselves on a happiness scale of zero to 100, 52% of the married women assigned themselves a score of 90 or above as compared to 22% of the single women and only 15% of the previously married mothers. Subjective differences by economic status were less clear-cut although there was some indication that nonworking women on welfare were less content with their situation than those who had stable jobs.

mentally retarded are able to accomplish their goals. We can, after all, find individuals in all of these categories who have been able to overcome their handicaps and make use of existing opportunities, limited though they may be. The problem with this premise is that the disadvantaged individual must be extraordinarily committed to achievement in order to overcome the barriers created by limited opportunities, rigidities in the social structure, and discrimination. The socially advantaged need only be *motivated;* the disadvantaged must be *supermotivated.* Of course, only a few of them are.

Almost all the young mothers in our study wanted to complete high school but most were not so inspired to achieve educationally that they were prepared to remain in school whatever the difficulties might be or the sacrifices required. Similarly, with few exceptions, the young mothers wished to avoid a rapid repeat pregnancy but few were so anxious not to conceive that they continued to use birth control methods when events in their lives made contraceptive practice difficult or frightening. In short, the imperatives of everyday existence often eroded long-term commitments.

2. *Distribution of Social Resources.* Even if all the participants in the study had been "supermotivated," most would nonetheless have experienced severe difficulties in achieving their immediate life objectives. There was not a sufficient supply of highly eligible males to marry the young mothers; caretakers or day-care facilities were not available to care for the children of many of those who wished to return to school or to enter the labor market; and there was a shortage of stable and remunerative jobs whose benefits equalled the income received from public assistance. Given their limited access to these precious resources, a certain proportion of the young mothers was doomed—there are, in a manner of speaking, only so many seats at the table.

Those who are able to find a place are the persons who are ushered in as invited guests, those who push harder, or those who happen to be standing in the right spot. Very few of the women in our study fell into the category of invited guests—that is, people who occupy a privileged position in the competition for scarce resources. The few white women in our study, the adolescents from two-parent families, and the mothers in their late teens tended to be slightly favored when it came to marrying the father of the child, completing school, or obtaining work. However, these social attributes provided only a marginal advantage and seemed to have little more than a temporary influence on the life course of the adolescent mother.

We have already mentioned that determination and planning played an important role in the situation of the young mothers, as seen at the five-year follow-up. Chance, too, played a part. Fortuitously, some women found themselves in a relatively stronger position in the struggle for scarce resources. Of the adolescents who had been randomly assigned to the special Adolescent Family Clinic a greater percentage was able to prevent a second pregnancy merely because they happened to receive exposure to a better family planning program. Chance undoubtedly affected other areas of life as well: finding a job or a husband or adequate child care assitance. Interestingly, at the Time 4 interview, few of the young mothers attributed their career patterns to chance, but it is hard to ignore the fact that some were merely luckier than others.

3. *Career Contingencies.* Although there is undoubtedly a strong element of indeterminacy in the life course of the young mothers, clearly their career patterns take a predictable form too. Throughout the analysis, we observed that statuses were clustered together or arranged in regular sequences. For example, women who married were predisposed to drop out of school, to have additional children, and to become full-time mothers. Women who married the father of their child were more likely to remain wed, less likely to have several children, and less reliant on public assistance during the course of the study.

Becker and Strauss (1956) compared movement in social careers to riding an escalator. Initially there may be some choice as to which escalator one boards, but after the initial decision it may not be possible to control the direction or regulate the speed of passage. Of course, as Becker and Strauss pointed out, people can disembark and, on occasion, may switch escalators as well; however, they do so only with a certain amount of effort. In effect, voluntarily redirecting one's career may call for supermotivation if the course is one that is well established.

Initial decisions among the young mothers—for example, on adoption, marriage, and subsequent birth control use—took on added significance over time because they facilitated or constrained career maneuverability. These and other such choices influence the likelihood of future transitions because they establish or upset social routines, lay claim to, or deny access to, critical resources, and place the individual in a social network that makes the performance of certain roles possible and of others extremely difficult. Thus, for example, we became aware that the second pregnancy had an enormous impact on the career patterns of the young mothers. A second child swiftly and effectively removed the young mother from the school system or the labor market, drastically altering her chances of economic independence at least for a time.

## SOCIAL PROGRAMS AND THE REGULATION OF CAREER ROUTES

The distribution of individual and social resources and the arrangement of career sequences are not fixed features of the social system. Programs of social intervention attempt to alter these features by deliberately removing the constraints on certain types of career maneuvers and by creating incentives to encourage other movements. Returning to the metaphor of Becker and Strauss, action programs for the adolescent parent are intended to build connecting escalators to make transitions both more feasible and more likely. Although our investigation did not specifically assess such programs but only the impact and influence of the AFC on the young women in the study, certain conclusions about the nature of such efforts have nevertheless emerged.

1. The old saying that an ounce of prevention is worth a pound of cure may be hackneyed but it is also probably true. While the classmates who avoided an unplanned pregnancy were not necessarily destined to lead lives free of social and economic turmoil, their circumstances at the five-year follow-up were clearly better than those of the young mothers. Yet, there was when we began this study, and still is today, a conspicuous lack of programs designed to reduce the pool of recruits to early parenthood. The general approach to social problems in American society is reactive rather than preventive. This posture might be understandable if preventive strategies were difficult to devise, but this excuse hardly seems to apply in the case of adolescent parenthood. We possess both the know-how and the techniques to reduce the incidence of early pregnancy and limit the number of adolescent mothers. Family planning programs and abortion counseling, while imperfect strategies, can be effective preventive measures.

Despite some encouraging trends in recent years, one cannot help but be discouraged by the timidity of the approach toward prevention. Essentially, we still cling to the notion that provision of family planning services should be as cautious, unobtrusive, and inconspicuous as possible. Despite the fact that a clear majority of Americans favor birth control services for the sexually active teenager and endorse sex education in the schools, some institutional resistance and a great deal of institutional inertia have blocked the development of widespread and intensive sex education and family planning service programs for teenagers. Few populations are as potentially accessible to these services as are school-age youth. Yet school systems have been avoided, bypassed, and ignored as sites for pregnancy prevention programs.

In our discussion of the process of unplanned parenthood, we observed that potential recruits to early parenthood are reluctant to plan for sexuality or to take measures to avoid conception once they become sexually active; often they are tacitly encouraged to deny the possibility that their sexual actions may have negative consequences. Although a more open and accepting view of premarital sexual behavior is developing in American society, vestiges of the puritanical past persist. Family planners are still hesitant to reach out aggressively to the population they purport to serve.[2]

What we have said about the need for publicizing contraceptive information applies as well to abortion counseling (recently, feminist groups have been effective in promoting the use of abortion). Although we have reason to believe that many of the young mothers in our study were equivocal in their attitudes about abortion, if not opposed outright to it as a solution to an unplanned

[2]The approach in our country stands in sharp contrast, for example, to that in Scandinavia, where there is an active campaign to promote and provide birth control for teenagers: television ads, T-shirt emblems, and subway posters carry the message that contraception is a safe and easy way to prevent unwanted conceptions (Linnér, 1967).

pregnancy, they seemed poorly acquainted, even in the 1972 interview, with the specific procedures for arranging an abortion. Education about the alternatives to adolescent parenthood must be part of any realistic prevention program. In order to exercise these options, the teenager who becomes pregnant must have easy access to counseling. Here again, the school is a potential site for pregnancy testing and counseling programs—and school health personnel should be trained for these purposes.

2. Perhaps the most prominent feature of existing intervention programs is their crisis orientation. Most programs are designed to supply emergency aid to help the young mother get through the prenatal or early postpartum period. As should be obvious from our analysis, such programs are based on an ill-conceived notion that early parenthood is an affliction from which one recovers in time. The young mothers in our study were aided during pregnancy but abandoned when they became parents. And they were by no means unique (Klerman and Jekel, 1973). Most programs cease to offer services at the point that many of the gravest problems arise for the adolescent mother.

Educational, vocational, medical, or contraceptive programs are certain to fail unless they continue to provide services for as long as the need for services exists. In discussing the weakness of the contraceptive program provided by Sinai Hospital, we made reference to the ideology of inoculation. Most programs for the adolescent parent are based on the premise that short-term assistance will have a long-term impact. We discovered that short-term services produce short-term effects.

If we are to have any hope of influencing the career directions of adolescent parents, it is not enough to be present when plans are formed at important junctures in the life course; we must be available to ensure that these aims are implemented. Career plans are not binding contracts; they are subject to constant renegotiation as new considerations arise. It is far less critical to convince the young mother to stay in school, to use contraception, or to look for a job than to help her to realize these objectives. As the young mother encounters unforeseen obstacles, it may be necessary or convenient for her to reevaluate her initial goals. The formerly firm decision not to have a second child may weaken when she enters a new relationship, loses her job, or merely has difficulty practicing contraception. It is not simply that commitments lose strength over time, but that people's ability to act on their commitments may vary as circumstances in their lives change. Accordingly, unless programs for the adolescent mother extend past the early postpartum period, they are bound to have disappointing results.

3. Regrettably, the delivery of services often is better suited to the convenience of the professional than to the needs of the client. For example, the trend toward specialization among professionals has led to a high degree of fragmentation in service programs. While there has been some encouraging movement toward the creation of comprehensive programs for the adolescent parent, the fact remains that segmentation of services continues to be more the

rule than the exception. Educational programs typically do not offer day-care facilities, contraceptive clinics, job counseling and employment placement, or pediatric and medical care. At best, several forms of assistance are provided under one roof, and weak ties are formed with agencies that can provide supplementary services.

To eliminate completely the fragmentation in services may be both inefficient and expensive for it can involve a certain amount of duplication in assistance programs. Yet, unless programs make it easy for clients to avail themselves of their services, it is certain that they will be used by only a small portion of the population they are intended to reach. One solution to the problem of service fragmentation is to make the assistance program mobile, as has been done with some family planning clinics. Many other services also could be designed to be set up as they are needed. If art and music programs can rotate within the school system, so, too, can medical clinics and job placement or welfare assistance programs. If these programs do remain stationary, then at least transportation should be provided from schools and/or day-care facilities to them.

Besides the fragmentation of services, there is fragmentation of target populations. Day-care facilities all too often separate parent and child; educational programs typically isolate the young mother from the father of the child; parent education programs train the young mother but neglect her parent, who may have a central role in rearing the child; job training may be available to the female who bears the child but not to the male who would be willing to marry her if he had a steady job. Programs are oriented to serve individuals because our conception of social problems is highly individualistic.

There can be little doubt from our results that the fate of the young mother and her child hinges partly on the situation of the child's father. If existing services do not actively discourage his participation, they provide few incentives to attract him. Practitioners are continually amazed by the interest unwed fathers show in their children. If programs were predicated on that interest, they might witness even more of it.

4. Even worse than the fragmentation of services is the paucity of aid provided by programs for the teenage parent. We can point to few programs that come close to reaching a majority of the population in need of services, and those that do usually offer only token assistance. Educational programs reach at most one-third of school-age mothers; family planning programs are broader based but have only brief contact with participants and their influence is usually temporary. The two services most needed—day-care facilities and job placement programs—are in short supply.

Without greatly expanding the scope of services, we are not likely to counter successfully the adverse effects of early parenthood. Limited programs can produce only limited results. In particular, we cannot expect to modify the life course of the adolescent parent without providing substantial economic assistance, preferably in the form of stable employment for one or both parents;

child care in order to promote educational and economic advancement; and family planning services to prevent other unplanned pregnancies. By singling out these core components, we do not mean to imply that services such as medical care, psychological counseling, and parent education are not important as well. However, it is unrealistic to think that these auxiliary services are going to have much effect unless economic problems are addressed first.

In view of the problems adolescent parents face and the paucity of services available to them, the outcomes we observed were to be expected. Early parenthood impairs the prospect of a successful economic and family career not because most young parents are determined to deviate from accepted avenues of success or because they are indifferent to, or unaware of, the costs of early parenthood. The principal reason that so many young mothers encounter problems is that they lack the resources to repair the damage done by a poorly timed birth. We have suggested that those women who managed to overcome the problems associated with early pregnancy had unusual personal qualities, good fortune, and/or the ability to avail themselves of the limited opportunities that existed.

What would happen if service programs made it easy, not difficult, for women to restore order in their lives following an unplanned pregnancy? Let us imagine that instead of the short-term, fragmented, and partial assistance that currently exists, there were comprehensive and extended services for young parents and their children. Suppose, for example, that family planning programs to prevent unplanned pregnancies and to counsel women who did have unwanted conceptions were established in the schools. Suppose that a woman who elected to bring her pregnancy to term would be granted a child care allowance to purchase day-care services or to pay a relative or friend to care for her child while she completed her education or entered the labor force. And regardless of whether or not she remained in school, took a job, or assumed full-time child care responsibilities, the young mother would receive an income sufficient to meet the needs of her family. Furthermore, suppose the father were invited to join special educational or job training programs or were provided with a steady job. How many parental couples would elect to marry under these circumstances is a matter of speculation. This question aside, our results indicated that under conditions of economic security most fathers would contribute to the support of the family and willingly maintain a relationship with their children.

If the limited family planning program such as the one offered to the participants in our study had a modest degree of success, consider the possible effects of a more extensive service that maintained regular contact with participants over a period of years. While we cannot assume that such a program would completely eliminate unwanted conceptions, we can feel certain that a clinic that made more vigorous efforts to anticipate problems before they occurred, that reached out to participants when they encountered difficulties in using contraception, and that was prepared to establish a long-standing relationship with its clients, would appreciably help to reduce the number of unplanned births.

Providing easy access to social resources means that such resources will be used more readily. When services are difficult to utilize, they assist primarily the relatively privileged and the supermotivated. The privileged are in the best position to use them; the supermotivated are able to overcome barriers that normally discourage use. Making programs easy to use inevitably means that personal advantage plays a lesser part in determining who benefits from the provision of services.

## PROSPECTS FOR THE FUTURE

Doubtless some readers will regard our proposed reforms as irresponsible and unrealistic, but a strong case can be made that current policies for dealing with early parenthood are neither responsible nor realistic. Although we do not maintain that modest programs are totally ineffectual or undesirable, we cannot hold out much hope for their success. On the other hand, the results of our study have persuaded us that certain measures—the extension of day-care assistance, the provision of guaranteed employment and income assistance, and the expansion of family planning services—would substantially limit the deleterious effects of early parenthood.

Is there any reason to expect that the sort of program we advocate is likely to emerge in the near future? Regrettably, we think not. The course of action we urge requires increased government spending, which is hardly a popular call these days. In recent years it has become fashionable to speak of the limits of federal intervention, and efforts are under way to curtail the expansion of social services. The late surge of interest in the problems of the adolescent parent has declined in the last few years. New programs are less in evidence, and some established ones are being dismantled or cut back for lack of funds. What happened to the program in Baltimore was not unusual. When government funding ceases, interest in the problem of adolescent parenthood all but vanishes. Legislation calling for an expansion of comprehensive service programs for the teenage parent was introduced in Congress in 1975, but no serious observer expects these bills to result in additional funds in the immediate future. For the present it seems far more likely that we will witness a further reduction in the already inadequate range of services.

There is, we might conclude, a natural history to social programs just as there is a natural history to social problems. Since this study commenced, government action has been taken and then terminated in several areas: drug abuse was once the hot issue; today, child abuse is a popular focus of attention; next year, no doubt, some other social problem will be in vogue.

It is ironic that we are inclined to question the willingness of the disadvantaged to avail themselves of public services when the commitment of our society to such programs is so tentative. If our study offers any indication, a substantial majority of adolescent parents are willing and able to use social and economic resources when they are made available. Moreover, such programs can have an important impact on redirecting the life course of teenage mothers. But the assistance we are prepared to offer is woefully inadequate and often temporary as well. Is it possible that we owe the vicious cycle of poverty not to the poor themselves but to the vicious cycle of social inaction?

QUESTIONNAIRES

TIME BEGUN _____          INTERVIEW # _____

Good (morning/afternoon/evening), I'm Mrs. _____

As you know, during the past few years, Sinai Hospital has been trying to learn more about its patients and their families in order to improve its medical services. It has been some time since we talked to you and we would like to find out how you and your family have been doing.

1a. First, let me ask you if you have moved anytime in the past two years since we last talked to you?

☐ MOVED [CONTINUE]          ☐ NOT MOVED [SKIP TO QUESTION 2]

b. Do you find that the place you are living in now is nicer, not as nice, or about the same as the place you lived in last?

☐ NICER          ☐ NOT AS NICE          ☐ SAME

2. How many close friends do you have who live around here—many, a few, one or two, or no one whom you are close to?

☐ MANY          ☐ A FEW          ☐ ONE OR TWO          ☐ NO ONE

3. At the present time who besides yourself lives here?

[ASK RELATIONSHIP AND AGE OF EACH PERSON LIVING IN THE HOUSEHOLD AND DETERMINE BIRTH DATE OF ALL RESPONDENT'S CHILDREN]

| First and Last Name of Person | Relation to Respondent | Age and Date of Birth |
|---|---|---|
| | | |

4. And how old are you now? _____

5. What is the highest grade that you have completed in school? _____

6a. Since your first child [NAME OF CHILD] was born, have you been able to return to school even if only for a short time?

☐ YES [ASK]     b. How many times? _____

c. For how long?

FIRST TIME _____

SECOND TIME _____

THIRD TIME _____

☐ NO

7a. Are you attending school at the present time or not? Will you be attending school in September?

☐ YES [ASCERTAIN]          ☐ DAY SCHOOL          ☐ NIGHT SCHOOL

☐ NO [ASK]     b. Do you have any immediate plans to return to school?

☐ YES [CONTINUE]          ☐ NO [SKIP TO QUESTION 8]

c. What are your plans? _____

8. How far do you plan to go in school? _____

9. Now, I'd like to ask you some questions about what you are doing at the present time. Are you working at all or are you not employed at the present time?

☐ WORKING [CONTINUE]          ☐ NOT EMPLOYED [SKIP TO QUESTION 16]

10. What type of work do you do? [PROBE FOR KIND OF WORK]

_____

11.  How many hours a week do you work? _____HOURS/WEEK

12.  How long have you been working at your present job? _____

13.  What is your rate of pay? _____ PER HOUR

14.  What was your rate of pay when you first started this job? _____ PER HOUR

15.  How satisfied are you with your present job—very satisfied, fairly satisfied, somewhat satisfied, or not at all satisfied?

     □ VERY SATISFIED    □ FAIRLY SATISFIED    □ SOMEWHAT SATISFIED

     □ NOT AT ALL SATISFIED

[SKIP TO QUESTION 24]

16.  Have you worked at all in the past year?

     □ YES [CONTINUE]        □ NO [SKIP TO QUESTION 20]

17.  What type of work did you do? [PROBE FOR KIND OF WORK]

     _____

18.  What was your rate of pay? _____ PER HOUR

19.  What caused you to stop working? [PROBE] What other reasons?

     _____

     □ DON'T WANT TO WORK [SKIP TO QUESTION 26]

20.  What are the things that keep you from working at the present time?
     [PROBE] What else keeps you from working?

     _____

     □ IN SCHOOL [SKIP TO QUESTION 24]

     □ DON'T WANT TO WORK [SKIP TO QUESTION 26]

21.  If it weren't for that, would you want to take a job right now or would you prefer to wait awhile?

     □ WORK NOW      □ WAIT AWHILE      □ DON'T KNOW/NOT SURE

22.  What kind of job would you expect to get? _____

23.  How much money a week would you need to take home to make it worthwhile for you to work? _____ PER _____

24a. Have you discussed finding a (new) job with anyone in the past few months or hasn't the subject come up?

     □ YES [ASK]   b.  Who did you talk to? _____

     □ NO

25.  Could you use advice about employment opportunities or do you think you have as much information as you need at the present time?

     □ COULD USE ADVICE   □ HAVE INFORMATION   □ DON'T KNOW/NOT SURE

26.  Do you think that finding a job is mostly a matter of luck or does it depend more on how hard you look for one?

     □ MATTER OF LUCK   □ HOW HARD YOU LOOK   □ DON'T KNOW/NOT SURE

     □ OTHER [SPECIFY] _____

27a. There are people who say there is not much point in working when you can make about as much by going on welfare. Do you ever feel that it's just as good to go on welfare as it is to work?

     □ YES, JUST AS GOOD TO GO ON WELFARE   □ NO, RATHER WORK

     □ DON'T KNOW/NOT SURE

b.  Why do you feel that way? _____

28a.  If you had a choice between a job that paid $80 a week and you could get, say, $60 by going on welfare, which would you choose—the job or welfare?

☐ JOB  [ASK]   b.  Suppose you got the same amount from either the job or welfare, would you still choose to work or would you prefer to get welfare in that case?

☐ STILL CHOOSE TO WORK

☐ PREFER WELFARE IN THAT CASE

☐ WELFARE

29.  Some people have criticized the city for making it too easy to go on welfare. Others say that it is too difficult to get on welfare when you need it. How do you feel—do you think it's too easy or too difficult to get on welfare?

☐ TOO EASY    ☐ TOO DIFFICULT    ☐ OK AS IS    ☐ DON'T KNOW/NOT SURE

30a.  Suppose that you had enough money to live comfortably so that you really didn't have to work unless you wanted to. Would you choose to not work at all, to work part-time, or to work full time?

☐ NOT WORK AT ALL    ☐ WORK PART-TIME    ☐ WORK FULL-TIME

b.  Whey do you feel that way? _____

31.  To be really comfortable, about how much money
a week, take-home, does a family like yours need?   $ _____ PER _____

32.  What is the least amount that you could get along on? $ _____ PER _____

33a.  [HAND WHITE CARD] Here is a list of ways many people get money to live on. Can you tell me how much you get from each?

☐ YOUR EMPLOYMENT                                   $ _____ PER _____

☐ HUSBAND'S EMPLOYMENT                          $ _____ PER _____

☐ WELFARE                                                      $ _____ PER _____

☐ ASSISTANCE FROM FATHER OF CHILD[REN]  $ _____ PER _____

☐ ASSISTANCE FROM PARENTS                      $ _____ PER _____

☐ ASSISTANCE FROM OTHER RELATIVES         $ _____ PER _____

☐ UNEMPLOYMENT COMPENSATION               $ _____ PER _____

☐ VETERANS' BENEFITS                                 $ _____ PER _____

☐ SOCIAL SECURITY                                      $ _____ PER _____

[PROBE]  Are there any other sources from which you get money to live on?

How much? _____ $ _____ PER _____

b.  [IF WELFARE NOT MENTIONED, ASK] At the present time are you receiving any money from welfare?

☐ YES [ASCERTAIN AMOUNT AND RECORD ABOVE]

☐ NO  [SKIP TO QUESTION 35]

34a.  How long have you been receiving money from welfare? _____

b.  Do you get full or partial support?   ☐ FULL    ☐ PARTIAL

[IF RECEIVING MONEY FROM WELFARE, SKIP TO QUESTION 36]

[IF NOT RECEIVING MONEY FROM WELFARE, CONTINUE]

35a.  How about in the past five or six years—since your oldest child was born—have you received financial help from welfare anytime?

☐ YES [ASK]   b.  For how long? _____

[ASCERTAIN TYPE OF SUPPORT] ☐ FULL    ☐ PARTIAL

☐ NO

36a. When you were growing up, before [NAME OF CHILD] was born, did you or your family ever receive help from welfare?

☐ YES [ASK]    b. For how long? _____

[ASCERTAIN TYPE OF SUPPORT]

☐ FULL        ☐ PARTIAL        ☐ DON'T KNOW

☐ NO

37. Now I would like to ask your views on marriage. Some women feel they might be better off if they never got married. Do you ever feel that way or not?

☐ YES        ☐ NO        ☐ SOMETIMES/DEPENDS        ☐ NOT SURE

38. Why do you think most women decide to marry?

_____

39. If a woman does decide to marry, what do you think is the best age for her to marry?

_____

40. When you think of people you know who get married, how many have successful marriages—nearly all, most, about half, less than half, or very few?

☐ NEARLY ALL        ☐ MOST        ☐ ABOUT HALF

☐ LESS THAN HALF        ☐ VERY FEW        ☐ DON'T KNOW

41. What are the main reasons why a marriage does not work out?

_____

42. Do you think that having a good marriage is mostly a matter of luck or does it depend more on how hard you work to make things go right?

☐ MATTER OF LUCK        ☐ HOW HARD YOU WORK TO MAKE THINGS GO RIGHT

☐ DON'T KNOW        ☐ DEPENDS [SPECIFY] _____

43a. Here are some things that people sometimes say help or hurt a marriage. Do you think it helps or hurts a marriage if the couple lives with relatives after they're married?

☐ HELPS  ☐ HURTS  ☐ DON'T KNOW/NOT SURE  ☐ MAKES NO DIFFERENCE

[COMMENTS] _____

b. If the woman has a job after they marry does that help or hurt a marriage?

☐ HELPS  ☐ HURTS  ☐ DON'T KNOW/NOT SURE  ☐ MAKES NO DIFFERENCE

[COMMENTS] _____

c. Does it help or hurt a marriage if the woman has had sexual relations with her husband before they marry?

☐ HELPS  ☐ HURTS  ☐ DON'T KNOW/NOT SURE  ☐ MAKES NO DIFFERENCE

[COMMENTS] _____

d. If they wait for two or three years to have children does that help or hurt a marriage?

☐ HELPS  ☐ HURTS  ☐ DON'T KNOW/NOT SURE  ☐ MAKES NO DIFFERENCE

[COMMENTS] _____

e. Does it help or hurt a marriage if she is pregnant when they marry?

☐ HELPS  ☐ HURTS  ☐ DON'T KNOW/NOT SURE  ☐ MAKES NO DIFFERENCE

[COMMENTS] _____

f. Does it help or hurt if she has had a child by another man before getting married?

☐ HELPS  ☐ HURTS  ☐ DON'T KNOW/NOT SURE  ☐ MAKES NO DIFFERENCE

[COMMENTS] _____

44a. Who do you think should have most to say about the following matters—the husband or wife or should they have equal say. First, about the number of children to have, who should have more to say about that—the husband or the wife?

☐ HUSBAND ☐ WIFE ☐ EQUAL ☐ DON'T KNOW/NOT SURE

☐ MAKES NO DIFFERENCE

[COMMENTS] _____

b. Which one should have more to say about how to furnish the house?

☐ HUSBAND ☐ WIFE ☐ EQUAL ☐ DON'T KNOW/NOT SURE

☐ MAKES NO DIFFERENCE

[COMMENTS] _____

c. Where to go when they go out for the evening?

☐ HUSBAND ☐ WIFE ☐ EQUAL ☐ DON'T KNOW/NOT SURE

☐ MAKES NO DIFFERENCE

[COMMENTS] _____

d. Which one should have more to say about how to bring up the children?

☐ HUSBAND ☐ WIFE ☐ EQUAL ☐ DON'T KNOW/NOT SURE

☐ MAKES NO DIFFERENCE

[COMMENTS] _____

e. How to spend money?

☐ HUSBAND ☐ WIFE ☐ EQUAL ☐ DON'T KNOW/NOT SURE

☐ MAKES NO DIFFERENCE

[COMMENTS] _____

[IF <u>MARITAL STATUS UNKNOWN</u>, ASK QUESTION 45. IF KNOWN, CODE WITHOUT ASKING QUESTION.]

45a. At the present time are you single, married, separated, or divorced?

☐ SINGLE [ASK] b. Have you been married before at any time or have you always been single?

[IF MARRIED BEFORE, CHECK CURRENT STATUS]

☐ ALWAYS SINGLE [SKIP TO QUESTION 67]

☐ MARRIED/HUSBAND LIVING IN HOUSEHOLD [CONTINUE]

☐ SEPARATED

☐ DIVORCED  } [SKIP TO QUESTION 55]

☐ WIDOWED

46a. In your family who actually <u>does</u> have most to say about each of these things—like the number of children to have, do you or your husband have the most to say about that?

☐ RESPONDENT ☐ HUSBAND ☐ EQUAL ☐ DON'T KNOW/NOT SURE

☐ DEPENDS [SPECIFY] _____

b. Which one of you has most to say about how to furnish the house?

☐ RESPONDENT ☐ HUSBAND ☐ EQUAL ☐ DON'T KNOW/NOT SURE

☐ DEPENDS [SPECIFY] _____

c. Where to go when you go out for the evening?

☐ RESPONDENT ☐ HUSBAND ☐ EQUAL ☐ DON'T KNOW/NOT SURE

☐ DEPENDS [SPECIFY] _____

d. How to bring up the children?

☐ RESPONDENT    ☐ HUSBAND    ☐ EQUAL    ☐ DON'T KNOW/NOT SURE

☐ DEPENDS [SPECIFY] _____

e. How to spend money?

☐ RESPONDENT    ☐ HUSBAND    ☐ EQUAL    ☐ DON'T KNOW/NOT SURE

☐ DEPENDS [SPECIFY] _____

47a. Do you and your husband usually agree or usually disagree on how to bring up the children?

☐ USUALLY AGREE    ☐ USUALLY DISAGREE    ☐ DON'T KNOW/NOT SURE

☐ 50-50/EQUAL [ASK] Why do you feel that way? _____

b. What about the number of children to have, do you and your husband agree on that or not?

☐ USUALLY AGREE    ☐ USUALLY DISAGREE    ☐ DON'T KNOW/NOT SURE

☐ 50-50/EQUAL [ASK] Why do you feel that way? _____

c. What about how to furnish the house?

☐ USUALLY AGREE    ☐ USUALLY DISAGREE    ☐ DON'T KNOW/NOT SURE

☐ 50-50/EQUAL [ASK] Why do you feel that way? _____

d. Where to go when you go out for the evening—do you usually agree or usually disagree?

☐ USUALLY AGREE    ☐ USUALLY DISAGREE    ☐ DON'T KNOW/NOT SURE

☐ 50-50/EQUAL [ASK] Why do you feel that way? _____

e. How to spend money—do you usually agree or usually disagree?

☐ USUALLY AGREE    ☐ USUALLY DISAGREE    ☐ DON'T KNOW/NOT SURE

☐ 50-50/EQUAL [ASK] Why do you feel that way? _____

48. When you do disagree, who usually wins out—you or your husband?

☐ RESPONDENT    ☐ HUSBAND    ☐ 50-50/EQUAL    ☐ DON'T KNOW/NOT SURE

49. When you have a fight, how does it usually end—do you usually stop being angry or do you often go on feeling mad even after the fight is over?

☐ STOP BEING ANGRY    ☐ GO ON FEELING MAD    ☐ NOT SURE/DEPENDS

50. How often do you and your husband go out together in the evening—would you say several times a week, about once a week, one or two times a month, or less than that?

☐ SEVERAL TIMES A WEEK          ☐ ONCE A WEEK

☐ ONE OR TWO TIMES A MONTH      ☐ LESS THAN THAT

51. How about doing something together at home like watching TV—about how often do you do that with your husband?

☐ SEVERAL TIMES A WEEK          ☐ ONCE A WEEK

☐ ONE OR TWO TIMES A MONTH      ☐ LESS THAN THAT

52. How often do you have a chance to talk over together something that happened during the day?

☐ SEVERAL TIMES A WEEK          ☐ ONCE A WEEK

☐ ONE OR TWO TIMES A MONTH      ☐ LESS THAN THAT

53. [HAND BUFF CARD]

On this card is a scale from zero to 100. I'd like you to rate your marriage on this scale. If you are not at all satisfied with your marriage, you would rate it zero. If you are very satisfied, you would rate it 100. Or you may give a score anywhere in between, depending on how satisfied you are. All things considered, how would you rate your marriage from zero to 100?

NOT AT ALL SATISFIED   □ □ □ □ □ □ □ □ □ □ □   VERY SATISFIED

             0  10  20  30  40  50  60  70  80  90  100

54. If you could change one thing about your marriage, what do you think it would be?

_____

55a. Have you been married more than once?

□ YES [ASK]   b. How many times?_____

□ NO, MARRIED ONLY ONCE

56a. What was the month and year of your (first) marriage? MONTH_____ YEAR_____

b. About how long did you know your (first) husband before you were married? _____

[IF MARRIED ONLY ONCE AND STILL MARRIED, SKIP TO QUESTION 58]

c. [IF MARRIED ONLY ONCE AND SEPARATED OR DIVORCED, ASK]

When did your marriage break up? MONTH _____ YEAR _____

Was that the date of your separation or divorce? □ SEPARATION □ DIVORCE

[IF MARRIED ONLY ONCE AND WIDOWED, ASK]

When were you widowed? MONTH _____ YEAR ._____

[SKIP TO QUESTION 58]

57. [FOR EACH MARRIAGE ASK]
a. What was the month and year of your (second/third) marriage?
b. About how long did you know your (second/third) husband before you were married?
c. How did that marriage end?
d. What month and year was that?
e. Was that the date of your separation or your divorce?

SECOND.   MARRIED   MONTH _____ YEAR _____

              HOW LONG KNEW HUSBAND BEFORE MARRIAGE _____

              □ STILL MARRIED   □ SEPARATED   □ DIVORCED   □ WIDOWED

              ENDED   MONTH _____ YEAR _____

              DATE OF   □ SEPARATION   □ DIVORCE

THIRD   MARRIED   MONTH _____ YEAR _____

              HOW LONG KNEW HUSBAND BEFORE MARRIAGE _____

              □ STILL MARRIED   □ SEPARATED   □ DIVORCED   □ WIDOWED

              ENDED   MONTH _____ YEAR _____

              DATE OF   □ SEPARATION   □ DIVORCE

[IF CURRENTLY WIDOW, SKIP TO QUESTION 63]

[ASK ABOUT PRESENT OR MOST RECENT HUSBAND]

58. How old is your (former) husband now? _____

59. What is the highest grade your (former) husband completed in school? _____

60. Is he working at the present time, unemployed, or still in school?

☐ WORKING

☐ WORKING AND IN SCHOOL  } [CONTINUE]

☐ UNEMPLOYED

☐ IN SCHOOL  } [SKIP TO QUESTION 63]

☐ DON'T KNOW

61. What kind of work does he do? [PROBE FOR <u>KIND</u> OF WORK]

62. How satisfied would you say he is with his present job—very satisfied, fairly satisfied, not so satisfied, or not at all satisfied?

☐ VERY SATISFIED    ☐ FAIRLY SATISFIED    ☐ NOT SO SATISFIED    ☐ NOT AT ALL SATISFIED    ☐ DON'T KNOW

63. When you compare yourself to friends who are still unmarried, how do you think it happened that you got married and they did not?

64. In the year or so before you got married, about how often were you seeing your husband—every day, several times a week, about once a week, once or twice a month, or less than that?

☐ EVERY DAY            ☐ ONCE A WEEK            ☐ LESS THAN THAT

☐ SEVERAL TIMES A WEEK    ☐ ONCE OR TWICE A MONTH

65. During this time, about how often did you have sexual relations—every day, several times a week, about once a week, once or twice a month, or less than that?

☐ EVERY DAY            ☐ ONCE A WEEK            ☐ LESS THAN THAT

☐ SEVERAL TIMES A WEEK    ☐ ONCE OR TWICE A MONTH        ☐ NEVER

[IF WIDOW/SEPARATED/DIVORCED, SKIP TO QUESTION 68]

66a. [IF CURRENTLY MARRIED ASK]

About how often do you have sexual relations now—every day, several times a week, about once a week, once or twice a month, or less than that?

☐ EVERY DAY            ☐ ONCE A WEEK

☐ SEVERAL TIMES A WEEK    ☐ ONCE OR TWICE A MONTH

☐ LESS THAN THAT [SKIP TO QUESTION 74]

b. In the past few months, have you ever gone for two or three weeks without having relations fairly regularly?

☐ YES, GONE FOR TWO OR THREE WEEKS    ☐ HAVE RELATIONS REGULARLY

[SKIP TO QUESTION 74]

67. When you compare yourself to your friends who have gotten married, how did it happen that they got married and you did not?

68a. Do you have any definite marriage plans in the near future

☐ YES [ASK]  b. When do you plan to marry? _____

☐ NO

69. Thinking back over the past year or so, about how often do you get a chance to go out with men—every day, several times a week, about once a week, once or twice a month or less often than that?

☐ EVERY DAY            ☐ ONCE OR TWICE A MONTH

☐ SEVERAL TIMES A WEEK    ☐ LESS THAN THAT

☐ ONCE A WEEK          ☐ NOT AT ALL [SKIP TO QUESTION 71]

70. Is there one person in particular that you go out with or do you go out with several different men?

☐ ONE PERSON      ☐ SEVERAL

71. About how often have you had sexual relations when you are going out or at other times—every day, several times a week, about once a week, once or twice a month, or less than that?

☐ EVERY DAY

☐ SEVERAL TIMES A WEEK    } [CONTINUE]

☐ ONCE A WEEK

☐ ONCE OR TWICE A MONTH

☐ LESS THAN THAT    } [SKIP TO QUESTION 73]

☐ NOT AT ALL [SKIP TO QUESTION 74]

72. In the past few months, have you ever gone for two or three weeks without having relations or do you have relations fairly regularly?

☐ GONE TWO OR THREE WEEKS     ☐ HAVE RELATIONS REGULARLY

73. In the past few months, about how many men have you had relations with at least once? _____

74. How many times have you gotten pregnant, including times when the pregnancy ended before the child was born? _____ TIMES

75. Please tell me the age of each child you have who is living at the present time. [PROBE] Do you have any children who are not living with you whom you did not mention?

[ASCERTAIN NAME, DATE OF BIRTH, AGE IN MONTHS, AND SEX]

| | | | SEX | |
| --- | --- | --- | --- | --- |
| NAME | DATE OF BIRTH | AGE IN MONTHS | MALE | FEMALE |
| _____ | _____ | _____ | ☐ | ☐ |
| _____ | _____ | _____ | ☐ | ☐ |

76a. Did you give birth to any children who were born live but who have died?

☐ YES [CONTINUE]     ☐ NO [SKIP TO QUESTION 77]

b. How many of your children have died? _____

[ASCERTAIN NAME, DATE OF BIRTH, AGE AT DEATH, AND SEX]

| NAME | DATE OF BIRTH | AGE AT DEATH | MALE | FEMALE |
| --- | --- | --- | --- | --- |
| _____ | _____ | _____ | ☐ | ☐ |
| _____ | _____ | _____ | ☐ | ☐ |

77a. Many women have pregnancies that do not produce a live baby because of miscarriage, accidental loss, or other reasons. Have you ever lost a pregnancy accidentally? This includes pregnancies that may have lasted only a very short time and it also includes babies born dead.

☐ YES [ASK]    b. How many pregnancies have you lost that way? _____

         c. When did [EACH] occur? YEAR _____ MONTH _____

☐ NO

78a. Many women who get pregnant when they do not want another baby right then will do something to end the pregnancy or will have an abortion performed. Have you ever had a pregnancy end this way?

☐ YES [CONTINUE]     ☐ NO [SKIP TO QUESTION 79]

b. How many times have you had pregnancies interrupted this way? _____

c. When did [EACH] occur?

| YEAR | MONTH | SELF | DOCTOR | SOMEONE ELSE | OTHER |
|------|-------|------|--------|--------------|-------|
| ____ | ____ | ☐ | ☐ | ☐ | ____ |

d. When your pregnancy ended this way did you do it yourself, did a doctor do it, someone else you know, or what? [RECORD ABOVE]

[SKIP TO QUESTION 80]

79. Do you think that you <u>might</u> ever decide to have an abortion?

☐ YES, DEFINITELY      ☐ NO, PROBABLY NOT

☐ YES, PERHAPS      ☐ NO, DEFINITELY NOT      ☐ CAN'T SAY

[COMMENTS] _____

80a. [HAND YELLOW CARD] Which of the following statements best describes how you feel about abortion?

☐ I STRONGLY APPROVE OF IT.

☐ I MOSTLY APPROVE OF IT BUT SOME THINGS ABOUT IT I DO NOT LIKE.

☐ I AM NOT SURE WHETHER I APPROVE OR DISAPPROVE OF IT.

☐ I DISAPPROVE OF IT BUT THERE ARE SOME THINGS ABOUT IT I LIKE.

☐ I STRONGLY DISAPPROVE OF IT.

b. Why do you feel that way? _____

[TAKE BACK CARD]

81a. Are you pregnant now?

☐ YES [ASK]   b. When you became pregnant this time, were you regularly using contraception, that is, nearly every time you had sexual relations?

☐ YES   ☐ NO

☐ NO

82. Thinking about (this/your most recent) pregnancy—how did you feel when you <u>first</u> discovered that you were pregnant?

_____

[IF <u>CURRENTLY PREGNANT</u>, SKIP TO QUESTION 91]

[IF <u>NOT</u> CURRENTLY PREGNANT, CONTINUE]

83a. [HAND GREEN CARD] Suppose you became pregnant in the next few months. Which of the following statements on this card would best describe the way you would feel?

☐ I AM HOPING TO BECOME PREGNANT AND WOULD BE VERY HAPPY. [SKIP TO QUESTION 84]

☐ I AM NOT PLANNING TO BECOME PREGNANT BUT WOULD BE HAPPY ANYHOW.

☐ I WOULD RATHER NOT BECOME PREGNANT BUT WOULD NOT BE TOO UPSET.

☐ I DON'T WANT TO BECOME PREGNANT AND WOULD BE RATHER UPSET.

☐ I DON'T WANT TO BECOME PREGNANT AND WOULD BE VERY UPSET.

b. When would you like to become pregnant again?

_____   ☐ YEARS

FROM NOW   ☐ NEVER   ☐ DON'T KNOW

☐ MONTHS

☐ DEPENDS [SPECIFY] _____

[TAKE BACK CARD]

84. How many children in all do you think you would like to have? _____

85.    How many children do you think you will actually end up having? _____

86a.    Are you using any method to keep from getting pregnant at the present time?

    ☐ YES [CONTINUE]    ☐ NO [SKIP TO QUESTION 92]

  b.    [HAND PINK CARD] What methods are you using?  [CHECK ALL THAT APPLY]

    ☐ DIAPHRAGM  ☐ RHYTHM SYSTEM  ☐ COIL    ☐ TUBES TIED

    ☐ DOUCHE      ☐ PILL         ☐ CONDOM  ☐ OTHER [SPECIFY]

    ☐ FOAM        ☐ RING         ☐ IUD      _____

[TAKE BACK CARD]

  c.    Since your last pregnancy, when did you begin?  DATE _____

87a.    Did you use another method before you started using [TYPE USING]?

    ☐ YES [ASK]  b.    What method was that? _____

                c.    How long did you use that method? _____

    ☐ NO

[IF RING , COIL, IUD, OR TUBES TIED METHOD CURRENTLY USED, SKIP TO QUESTION 90]

88a.    When you have sex relations do you use [TYPE USING] or some method of birth control or contraception absolutely every time or do you sometimes not?

    ☐ EVERY TIME [CONTINUE]    ☐ SOMETIMES NOT [SKIP TO QUESTION 89]

  b.    [IF PILL USED, ASK] From time to time do you ever forget to take the pill?

    ☐ YES [CONTINUE]    ☐ NO [SKIP TO QUESTION 90]

89a.    About how much of the time do you not use some kind of birth control?  Think back, out of the last ten times you had sex relations, about how many of those times did you not use any birth control method?

    _____ TIMES [CONTINUE]    ☐ USED EVERY TIME IN LAST TEN
                                            [SKIP TO QUESTION 90]

  b.    How does it happen that you sometimes use birth control and sometimes not?

    [PROBE] _____

90a.    Many women who start using birth control often find one reason or another to stop using it altogether for a period of time.  In the last few years has there been a period of time when you were not using birth control?

    ☐ YES [CONTINUE]    ☐ NO [SKIP TO QUESTION 96]

  b.    How long a time did you go without using birth control? _____

  c.    How did it happen that you stopped using birth control?
    [PROBE] Were there any other reasons that made you stop?

    _____

[SKIP TO QUESTION 96]

91a.    How many children in all do you think you would like to have? _____

  b.    How many children do you think you will actually end up having? _____

92a.    Have you ever used any method to keep from having babies?

    ☐ YES [CONTINUE]    ☐ NO [SKIP TO QUESTION 96]

  b.    [HAND PINK CARD] What methods were you using before you stopped? [CHECK ALL THAT APPLY

    ☐ DIAPHRAGM  ☐ RHYTHM SYSTEM  ☐ COIL  ☐ PILL  ☐ RING  ☐ IUD
    ☐ DOUCHE      ☐ CONDOM    ☐ FOAM  ☐ OTHER [SPECIFY]_____

[TAKE BACK CARD]

93. How did it happen that you stopped?

_____

94. How long has it been since you stopped using any kind of birth control?____ MONTHS

95. Before you stopped, how long had you been using some kind of birth control?
_____ MONTHS

96. If you did not use birth control, how likely would you feel that you might become
pregnant? Thinking of the last time you did not use birth control, how likely did you
feel that you mgith become pregnant?  [SHOW BLUE CARD]

☐ I FELT ALMOST CERTAIN THAT I WOULD BECOME PREGNANT.

☐ I FELT THAT THERE WAS A GOOD CHANCE THAT I MIGHT BECOME
PREGNANT.

☐ I FELT THAT MY CHANCES OF BECOMING PREGNANT WERE ABOUT
FIFTY-FIFTY.

☐ I FELT THAT THERE WAS SOME CHANCE OF BECOMING PREGNANT BUT IT
PROBABLY WOULD NOT HAPPEN.

☐ I FELT THAT THERE WAS ALMOST NO CHANCE OF BECOMING PREGNANT.

[COMMENTS] _____

97. Do you think that not getting pregnant is mostly a matter of luck or does it depend
more on how careful you are?

☐ LUCK    ☐ HOW CAREFUL YOU ARE    ☐ DON'T KNOW/NOT SURE

Now let me ask you a few questions about you and your family.  First about [NAME OF
FIRST CHILD]

98. How old is (he/she) now? _____    ☐ DIED [SKIP TO QUESTION 163]
[CODER RECORD DATE OF BIRTH] _____

[IF NO MALE LISTED IN QUESTION 3, SKIP TO QUESTION 100]

[IF HUSBAND OR MALE COMPANION LISTED IN QUESTION 3, CONTINUE]

99. Is [NAME OF MALE LISTED IN QUESTION 3] [CHILD]'s own father or (his/her)
stepfather?

☐ YES, OWN FATHER IN HOME  [SKIP TO QUESTION 109]

☐ NO, OWN FATHER NOT IN HOME  [CONTINUE]

100. [ASCERTAIN FOR FATHER NOT IN HOME]  NAME _____

ADDRESS _____

PHONE NUMBER _____

101a. During the past year has [CHILD] ever gotten a chance to spend time with [NAME OF
FATHER]?

☐ YES  [SKIP TO QUESTION 102]

☐ NO  [ASK]   b.  How does it happen [CHILD] doesn't get a chance to spend time
with (his/her) father?

_____

[SKIP TO QUESTION 104]

102a. About how often do [CHILD] and (his/her) own father spend time together—every day,
several times a week, once a week, on weekends, or less than that?

☐ EVERY DAY    ☐ SEVERAL TIMES A WEEK    ☐ ONCE A WEEK

☐ ON WEEKENDS    ☐ LESS THAN THAT

b. How much do you think that [CHILD]'s father enjoys playing with (him/her)—very
much, somewhat, or not so much?

☐ VERY MUCH  ☐ SOMEWHAT  ☐ NOT SO MUCH   ☐ DON'T KNOW/NOT SURE/
DEPENDS

c. How much does [CHILD] like to play with (his/her) father—very much, somewhat, or not so much?

☐ VERY MUCH   ☐ SOMEWHAT   ☐ NOT SO MUCH   ☐ DON'T KNOW/NOT SURE/ DEPENDS

d. Do you think they spend too little time together, too much, or about the right amount?

☐ TOO LITTLE   ☐ TOO MUCH   ☐ RIGHT AMOUNT

103. In matters concerning [CHILD], who usually makes the important decisions—you, (his/her) own father, both of you together, or someone else?

☐ RESPONDENT   ☐ FATHER   ☐ BOTH   ☐ SOMEONE ELSE

104a. Does [CHILD]'s father pay any expenses in bringing up [CHILD] or not?

☐ YES [ASK]   b. About how much each month?

     ☐ LESS THAN $10   ☐ $20 TO $29   ☐ $40 TO $49

     ☐ $10 TO $19     ☐ $30 TO $39   ☐ $50 AND OVER

     ☐ DON'T KNOW

☐ FATHER IS MOST RECENT HUSBAND [QUESTIONS 58-62, SKIP TO QUESTION 108]

105. What is the highest grade that [NAME OF FATHER] completed? _____

106. How old is he now? _____

107a. Do you know whether [NAME OF FATHER] is working at present, unemployed, or still in school?

☐ WORKING [CONTINUE]     ☐ UNEMPLOYED

                             ☐ IN SCHOOL     [SKIP TO QUESTION 108]

                             ☐ DON'T KNOW

b. What exactly does he do? [PROBE FOR <u>KIND</u> OF WORK]

_____

c. How satisfied would you say he is with his present job—very satisfied, fairly satisfied, not so satisfied, or not at all satisfied?

☐ VERY SATISFIED   ☐ FAIRLY SATISFIED   ☐ NOT SO SATISFIED   ☐ NOT AT ALL SATISFIED   ☐ DON'T KNOW

108. [IF RESPONDENT IS SINGLE OR DIVORCED FROM FATHER OF CHILD]
Is he single or married now?

☐ SINGLE   ☐ MARRIED   ☐ MARRIED BUT SEPARATED

☐ MARRIED SINCE BUT DIVORCED NOW    ☐ DON'T KNOW

109a. Who spends most of the time caring for [NAME OF FIRST CHILD]? Is it you or someone else?

☐ RESPONDENT [SKIP TO QUESTION 111]    ☐ SOMEONE ELSE [CONTINUE]

b. Who is that? _____

☐ CHILD DOES NOT LIVE WITH MOTHER [SKIP TO QUESTION 110]

c. Does she care for [CHILD] in your home or somewhere else?

☐ IN HOME     ☐ SOMEWHERE ELSE

d. How many hours a week does [PERSON] stay with [CHILD]? _____

110. How does [CHILD] feel about staying with [PERSON]?

_____

111a. [IF NOT WORKING ASK QUESTION 8] Could you make satisfactory arrangements for caring for your child(ren) if you were able to find a job you wanted?

    ☐ YES [ASK]  b.  What arrangements would you make?

    ☐ NO

---

c. [IF WORKING ASK QUESTION 8] Is [PERSON IN 109] able to take care of your child(ren) all the time when you're working or do you have some other arrangement in addition?

    ☐ YES, TAKES CARE OF CHILD(REN) ALL THE TIME

    ☐ NO, MAKE ADDITIONAL ARRANGEMENTS [ASK]

        d.  What other arrangement do you have?

---

112. Suppose you didn't have the arrangement you have now. Which of the following child care arrangements would you be willing to use? Would you leave your child

| | YES | NO | NOT SURE | BEST |
|---|---|---|---|---|
| a. With a relative or close friend in your home? | ☐ | ☐ | ☐ | ☐ |
| b. With a babysitter in your home? | ☐ | ☐ | ☐ | ☐ |
| c. At a day-care center in your neighborhood? | ☐ | ☐ | ☐ | ☐ |
| d. With a relative or close friend in their home? | ☐ | ☐ | ☐ | ☐ |
| e. With a babysitter in your home? | ☐ | ☐ | ☐ | ☐ |

113. Which of these is the best possible arrangement? [RECORD ABOVE] Why do you feel that way?

---

114. [IF NO TO DAY-CARE CENTER]

Why do you feel unwilling to have your child go to a day-care center in your neighborhood?

---

115a. [IF CHILD DOES NOT LIVE WITH MOTHER] Why is [CHILD] living with [NAME OF PERSON]?

---

b. Do you have any plans for (him/her) to stay with you?

    ☐ YES [ASK]  c. What plans _____

    ☐ NO

116a. During most weeks, about how many hours a day do you spend with [CHILD], that is, when you are doing things together? [NUMBER OF HOURS EACH WEEK] _____

b. Do you think you spend too little time together, too much, or about the right amount?

    ☐ TOO LITTLE    ☐ TOO MUCH    ☐ RIGHT AMOUNT

117a. Did you name [CHILD] after any member of the family?

    ☐ YES [ASK]  b.  Who did you name him/her after?

        [SPECIFY RELATIONSHIP TO MOTHER] _____

                               [SKIP TO QUESTION 118]

    ☐ NO [CONTINUE]

c. What made you decide to call (him/her) [NAME]?

---

118a. What about (his/her) middle name—was that after any member of the family?

    □ YES [ASK]   b.  Who?

           [SPECIFY RELATIONSHIP TO MOTHER] _____

                                         [SKIP TO QUESTION 119]

    □ NO [CONTINUE]

   c. What made you decide to give (him/her) [NAME] as a middle name?

_____

119a. [HAND LARGE WHITE CARD] Which three qualities listed on this card would you say are the most desirable for a (boy/girl) of [CHILD]'s age to have? [NUMBER IN ORDER MENTIONED]

| THREE MOST DESIRABLE | | THREE LEAST IMPORTANT |
|---|---|---|
| _____ | Has good manners | _____ |
| _____ | Tries hard to succeed | _____ |
| _____ | Is honest | _____ |
| _____ | Is neat and clean | _____ |
| _____ | Has good sense and sound judgment | _____ |
| _____ | Has self-control | _____ |
| _____ | Acts like a (boy/girl) should | _____ |
| _____ | Gets along well with other children | _____ |
| _____ | Obeys parents well | _____ |
| _____ | Is responsible | _____ |
| _____ | Is considerate of others | _____ |
| _____ | Is interested in how and why things happen | _____ |
| _____ | Is a good student | _____ |

   b. All of these may be desirable, but could you tell me which three you consider <u>least</u> important? [RECORD ABOVE]

120a. Some mothers feel that it is important for their children to understand why they make certain rules. Others say the important thing is that the child learn to obey. How do you feel about this—should parents have to explain a rule or should they teach their child to obey?

    □ TRY TO EXPLAIN   □ TEACH THEM TO OBEY   □ BOTH

    □ DON'T KNOW/NOT SURE/DEPENDS

   b. Do you usually try to explain or does (he/she) do as told without an explanation?

    □ DOES AS TOLD   □ GIVES EXPLANATION   □ BOTH

   c. It is sometimes said that certain children are <u>born</u> to be bad and parents can't do much to change them. Do you think that there are certain children <u>born</u> to be bad?

    □ YES                       □ NO [SKIP TO QUESTION 121]

    □ DON'T KNOW/NOT SURE   } [CONTINUE]

   d. Do you wonder whether (your child/any of your children) have been born to be bad?

    □ YES [IF MORE THAN ONE CHILD ASK]   e.  Which one? _____

    □ NO

    □ DON'T KNOW/NOT SURE

121. Parents describe their children in different ways. Suppose you were giving [CHILD] a score on the way (he/she) behaves. On this card is a list of things that describe children—and for each one I'd like you to give me a score from zero to 100. [HAND LARGE YELLOW CARD] For instance, the first one is <u>uncooperative</u> or <u>cooperative</u>. If (he/she) is totally uncooperative, you would give a score of zero. If (he/she) were the opposite—perfectly cooperative, you would give a score of 100.

Or you may give (him/her) a score anywhere in between zero and 100.  Where would (he/she) actually belong?

|  | | SCORE |
|---|---|---|
| a. | UNCOOPERATIVE/COOPERATIVE | _____ |
| b. | SHY/OUTGOING | _____ |
| c. | MESSY/CLEAN | _____ |
| d. | SLOW/SMART | _____ |
| e. | BABYISH/GROWN UP | _____ |
| f. | RUDE/POLITE | _____ |
| g. | BORED/EAGER TO LEARN | _____ |
| h. | SAD/HAPPY | _____ |
| i. | DISOBEDIENT/OBEDIENT | _____ |

[TAKE BACK CARD]

122.  A lot of talk goes on about the way children behave.  What kinds of behavior problems do you worry about the most?

_____

123a. [HAND BUFF CARD] Which three problems on this card would make you most worried if they should occur with [CHILD]?  [NUMBER IN ORDER MENTIONED]

_____ GETTING INTO FIGHTS WITH OTHER CHILDREN

_____ NOT WANTING TO GO TO SCHOOL

_____ HAVING TROUBLE GETTING TO SLEEP AT NIGHT

_____ KEEPING TO [HIM/HER]SELF ALL THE TIME

_____ REFUSING TO EAT AT MEALTIMES

_____ TAKING THINGS THAT DON'T BELONG TO [HIM/HER]

_____ WETTING [HIS/HER] BED

_____ NOT BEING ABLE TO CONTROL [HIS/HER] TEMPER

_____ TALKING BACK TO GROWN-UPS

_____ NOT WANTING TO PLAY WITH OTHER CHILDREN

_____ NOT TELLING THE TRUTH

b. Suppose you did have a problem like [REPEAT THREE MOST SERIOUS], is there anyone in particular you might go to for advice?

☐ NO ONE   ☐ FAMILY   ☐ FRIEND   ☐ OTHER [SPECIFY] _____

c. [IF ONLY FAMILY MEMBER OR FRIEND MENTIONED, ASK]
Do you think there is any point in getting advice from someone else like a doctor or social worker, or do you think people like that really can't help that much?

☐ YES, CAN HELP   ☐ NO POINT, CAN'T HELP   ☐ DON'T KNOW/NOT SURE
☐ DEPENDS [SPECIFY] _____

124a. Looking at the list again, could you tell me whether any of these is a problem with [CHILD]?  First, getting into fights with other children?

☐ YES [CONTINUE]     ☐ NO [SKIP TO QUESTION 125]

b. How often does that occur—several times a week, once a week, once a month, or less often than that?

☐ SEVERAL TIMES A WEEK   ☐ ONCE A WEEK   ☐ ONCE A MONTH
☐ LESS OFTEN

c. What do you do about it?

_____

125. [IF MORE THAN ONE CHILD] Does [CHILD] fight much with (his/her)
     brother(s)/sister(s)?

   □ YES    □ NO    □ DEPENDS    □ DON'T KNOW/NOT SURE

126a. Not wanting to go to school—is that a problem?

   □ NOT YET IN SCHOOL [SKIP TO QUESTION 127]

   □ NO [SKIP TO QUESTION 127]           □ YES [CONTINUE]

   b. How often does that occur—several times a week, once a week, once a month, or
      less often than that?

   □ SEVERAL TIMES A WEEK    □ ONCE A WEEK    □ ONCE A MONTH

   □ LESS OFTEN

   c. What do you do about it?

   _____

127a. Having trouble getting to sleep at night?

   □ YES [CONTINUE]      □ NO [SKIP TO QUESTION 128]

   b. How often does that occur?

   □ SEVERAL TIMES A WEEK    □ ONCE A WEEK    □ ONCE A MONTH

   □ LESS OFTEN

   c. What do you do about it?

   _____

128a. Keeping to (him/her)self all the time?

   □ YES [CONTINUE]      □ NO [SKIP TO QUESTION 129]

   b. How often does that occur?

   □ SEVERAL TIMES A WEEK    □ ONCE A WEEK    □ ONCE A MONTH    □ LESS OFTEN

   c. What do you do about it?

   _____

129a. Refusing to eat at mealtimes?

   □ YES [CONTINUE]      □ NO [SKIP TO QUESTION 130]

   b. How often does that occur?

   □ SEVERAL TIMES A WEEK    □ ONCE A WEEK    □ ONCE A MONTH    □ LESS OFTEN

   c. What do you do about it?

   _____

130a. Taking things that don't belong to (him/her)?

   □ YES [CONTINUE]      □ NO [SKIP TO QUESTION 131]

   b. How often does that occur?

   □ SEVERAL TIMES A WEEK    □ ONCE A WEEK    □ ONCE A MONTH    □ LESS OFTEN

   c. What do you do about it?

   _____

131a. Wetting (his/her) bed?

   □ YES [CONTINUE]      □ NO [SKIP TO QUESTION 132]

   b. How often does that occur?

   □ SEVERAL TIMES A WEEK    □ ONCE A WEEK    □ ONCE A MONTH    □ LESS OFTEN

   c. What do you do about it?

132a. Not being able to control (his/her) temper?

☐ YES [CONTINUE]        ☐ NO [SKIP TO QUESTION 133]

b. How often does that occur?

☐ SEVERAL TIMES A WEEK    ☐ ONCE A WEEK    ☐ ONCE A MONTH    ☐ LESS OFTEN

c. What do you do about it?

_____

133a. Talking back to grown-ups?

☐ YES [CONTINUE]        ☐ NO [SKIP TO QUESTION 134]

b. How often does that occur?

☐ SEVERAL TIMES A WEEK    ☐ ONCE A WEEK    ☐ ONCE A MONTH    ☐ LESS OFTEN

c. What do you do about it?

_____

134a. Not wanting to play with other children?

☐ YES [CONTINUE]        ☐ NO [SKIP TO QUESTION 135]

b. How often does that occur?

☐ SEVERAL TIMES A WEEK    ☐ ONCE A WEEK    ☐ ONCE A MONTH    ☐ LESS OFTEN

c. What do you do about it?

_____

135a. Not telling the truth?

☐ YES [CONTINUE]        ☐ NO [SKIP TO QUESTION 136]

b. How often does that occur?

☐ SEVERAL TIMES A WEEK    ☐ ONCE A WEEK    ☐ ONCE A MONTH    ☐ LESS OFTEN

c. What do you do about it?

_____

[TAKE BACK CARD]

136. Many people feel that the best way to handle problems is just not to think about them too much. Are you that kind of person?

☐ YES        ☐ NO        ☐ NOT SURE/DEPENDS

137a. Have you read any articles or books that deal with the subject of how to raise your children?

☐ YES [ASK]  b. What were they? _____

☐ NO

☐ DON'T KNOW/DON'T REMEMBER

138. Children start to do things at different ages.
Can you tell me whether [CHILD]

|  | YES | NO |
|---|---|---|
| a. Is able to dress (him/her)self alone? | ☐ | ☐ |
| b. Walk to the corner on an errand by (him/her)self? | ☐ | ☐ |
| c. Say the alphabet correctly? | ☐ | ☐ |
| d. Count to twenty? | ☐ | ☐ |

139a. Has [CHILD] started school?

☐ YES [ASK]  b. What school? _____

c. Is that kindergarten or first grade?  ☐ KINDERGARTEN

☐ FIRST GRADE

☐ NO

140. Did [CHILD] attend any preschool program such as Get Set, Head Start, or any nursery school?

☐ YES [SPECIFY NAME OF PROGRAM, LOCATION, AND ASCERTAIN DATES ATTENDED]

PROGRAM _____ ADDRESS _____ DATES _____

☐ NO

[IF NOT IN KINDERGARTEN OR FIRST GRADE, SKIP TO QUESTION 147]

141. How does [CHILD] seem to be doing in school?

_____

142. Does (he/she) seem to get along with (his/her) classmates or do you think (he/she) might be having trouble making friends at school?

☐ GETS ALONG   ☐ HAVING TROUBLE   ☐ DEPENDS   ☐ DON'T KNOW/NOT SURE

143. Do you know whether or not (he/she) likes (his/her) teacher?

☐ YES, LIKES      ☐ NO, DOESN'T      ☐ DON'T KNOW

144a. Do you happen to recall her name?

☐ YES [ASK]   b.  What is her name? _____

☐ NO

145. Have you had a chance to meet [CHILD]'s teacher yet?   ☐ YES   ☐ NO

146a. Have you had an opportunity to attend any meetings at the school yet?

☐ YES   ☐ NO [ASK]   b.  Do you expect to be able to go to meetings at school?

☐ YES   ☐ NO

147a. If you could have your wish, what grade in school would you like (him/her) to complete?

_____

b. How far do you think (he/she) will actually go in school?

_____

148. Here is a picture of a child watching TV with (his/her) mother.

a. About how often do you get a chance to watch TV with [CHILD]—almost every day, several times a week, about once a week, or less than that?

☐ ALMOST EVERY DAY   ☐ SEVERAL TIMES A WEEK   ☐ ABOUT ONCE A WEEK

☐ LESS THAN THAT

b. When you are watching TV together do you usually talk a lot about what you are seeing?

☐ YES   ☐ NO   ☐ DEPENDS   ☐ DON'T WATCH TOGETHER

c. Do you have definite rules about (his/her) watching TV?

☐ YES [ASK]   d.  What are they? _____

☐ NO

149a. What are (his/her) favorite TV programs?

☐ SESAME STREET _____       ☐ OTHER [SPECIFY] _____

☐ ELECTRIC COMPANY _____       _____

b. [IF SESAME STREET OR ELECTRIC COMPANY MENTIONED, ASK]

About how often does (he/she) watch [EACH]?   [RECORD ABOVE]

150a.  [IF SESAME STREET OR ELECTRIC COMPANY <u>NOT</u> MENTIONED, ASK]

Does [CHILD] get a chance to watch either Sesame Street or Electric Company?

□ YES [ASK]   b. About how often does (he/she) watch [EACH]? [RECORD ABOVE]

□ NO   [ASK]   c. Do you get UHF channels on your TV set? □ YES □ NO

151.  Here is a picture of a mother reading to her child.

a. About how often do you get a chance to read to [CHILD]?

□ ALMOST EVERY DAY   □ SEVERAL TIMES A WEEK   □ ABOUT ONCE A WEEK
□ LESS THAN THAT

b. Does anyone else in the family read to (him/her)?

□ YES       □ NO

c. Has [CHILD] been taught to read any words by (him/her)self?

□ YES       □ NO       □ DON'T KNOW

d. If you heard [CHILD] try to read a story on (his/her) own, what do you think you would say to (him/her)?

_____

152.  Here is a picture of a child helping mother around the house.

a. About how often does [CHILD] help you around the house?

□ ALMOST EVERY DAY   □ SEVERAL TIMES A WEEK   □ ABOUT ONCE A WEEK
□ LESS THAN THAT

b. Do you have any rules about the jobs (he/she) is supposed to do?

□ YES [CONTINUE]       □ NO [SKIP TO QUESTION 153]

c. What are they? _____

d. Does [CHILD] do this on (his/her) own or do you find it helps to encourage (him/her)?

□ DOES ON OWN       □ IT HELPS TO ENCOURAGE

e. What do you say or do when [CHILD] doesn't follow these rules?

_____

153.  Here is a picture of a child sticking close to (his/her) mother and wanting to be with her all the time.

a. How often does [CHILD] act this way?

□ ALMOST EVERY DAY   □ SEVERAL TIMES A WEEK   □ ABOUT ONCE A WEEK
□ LESS THAN THAT

b. Suppose your child asks you to help out with something like getting dressed that you know (he/she) can do (him/her)self, will you help (him/her) out or do you insist that (he/she) do it by (him/her)self?

□ WILL HELP OUT   □ INSIST HE DO IT (HIM/HER)SELF   □ DEPENDS
□ DON'T KNOW/NOT SURE

154.  Here is a picture of a child playing outside.

a. How often does [CHILD] get a chance to play outside, either alone or with other children?

□ ALMOST EVERY DAY   □ SEVERAL TIMES A WEEK   □ ABOUT ONCE A WEEK
□ LESS THAN THAT

b. How far is [CHILD] allowed to go from home by (him/her)self? _____

c. Can you give me an idea of about how many friends [CHILD] has to play with? _____

d. How many do you know by name? _____

155. Here is a picture of a child eating (his/her) supper. Imagine that [CHILD] is the child in the picture.

    a. Do you have any rules for [CHILD] about eating?

        □ YES [CONTINUE]      □ NO [SKIP TO QUESTION 156]

    b. What are they? _____

    c. Tell me what you do when [CHILD] doesn't do what (he/she)'s supposed to.

    _____

156. How often do you usually get a chance to eat supper with [CHILD]—almost every day, several times a week, once a week or so, or less often than that?

        □ ALMOST EVERY DAY  □ SEVERAL TIMES A WEEK  □ ONCE A WEEK OR SO

        □ LESS OFTEN

157. Here is a picture of a mother and child at a playground.

    a. About how often do you go to a playground with [CHILD]?

        □ ALMOST EVERY DAY     □ ABOUT ONCE A WEEK   □ ON WEEKENDS

        □ SEVERAL TIMES A WEEK   □ LESS OFTEN

    b. Suppose you have been there for about an hour and you are ready to go home but [CHILD] isn't—what do you think you might say or do?

    _____

158. Here is a picture of two adults talking to each other and a child trying to get (his/her) mother's attention.

    a. About how often does [CHILD] act that way—almost every day, several times a week, about once a week, or less often than that?

        □ ALMOST EVERY DAY  □ SEVERAL TIMES A WEEK  □ ABOUT ONCE A WEEK

        □ LESS OFTEN

    b. Tell me what you (might) do when this happens.

    _____

[IF NO FATHER OR STEPFATHER LIVING IN HOME, SKIP TO QUESTION 160]

159. Here is a picture of a father and child playing together.

    a. About how often does [CHILD] get a chance to play with (his/her) father?

        □ ALMOST EVERY DAY     □ ABOUT ONCE A WEEK   □ ON WEEKENDS

        □ SEVERAL TIMES A WEEK   □ LESS OFTEN

    b. How much do you think that [CHILD]'s father enjoys playing with (him/her)—very much, somewhat, or not so much?

        □ VERY MUCH  □ SOMEWHAT  □ NOT SO MUCH  □ DEPENDS  □ DON'T KNOW/ NOT SURE

    c. How much does [CHILD] like to play with (his/her) father—very much, somewhat, or not so much?

        □ VERY MUCH  □ SOMEWHAT  □ NOT SO MUCH  □ DEPENDS  □ DON'T KNOW/ NOT SURE

    d. Do you think they spend too little time together, too much, or about the right amount?

        □ TOO LITTLE     □ TOO MUCH     □ RIGHT AMOUNT

160. What kinds of things does [CHILD] do that make you happy?

    _____

161a. Do you do anything in particular when (he/she) acts this way?

        □ YES [ASK]  b. What do you do? _____

        □ NO

162. On this card are words to describe parents. I'd like you to give yourself a score on each of these things, from zero to 100, or anywhere in between, depending on how you would describe yourself as a parent. [HAND LARGE BLUE CARD]
For example, the first one is <u>strict</u> or <u>easy</u>. If you are completely strict you would score zero, and if you are the opposite—totally easy—you would score 100. Or you may score anywhere in between. Where would you actually belong on each of these things?

SCORE

    a. STRICT/EASY     _____

    b. IMPATIENT/PATIENT     _____

    c. CRITICIZING/PRAISING     _____

    d. DEMANDING/EASYGOING     _____

    e. WORRIED/CONFIDENT     _____

    f. UNSYMPATHETIC/UNDERSTANDING     _____

    g. BORED/INTERESTED     _____

    h. CONTROLLING/ENCOURAGE FREEDOM     _____

163. Now just a few final questions about yourself. [HAND LARGE PINK CARD] I'd like you to give a score rating on how happy you are these days. If you are completely happy, you would give a score of 100; if you are completely unhappy, you would give a score of zero. Or you may give a score anywhere in between, depending on how happy you are these days. All things considered, how would you rate yourself?

COMPLETELY UNHAPPY   ☐ ☐ ☐ ☐ ☐ ☐ ☐ ☐ ☐ ☐ ☐   COMPLETELY HAPPY
    0  10  20  30  40  50  60  70  80  90  100

164a. Thinking back to four or five years ago, would you say that you were happier then, happier now, or just about the same?

☐ HAPPIER THEN     ☐ ABOUT THE SAME [SKIP TO
☐ HAPPIER NOW   [CONTINUE]     QUESTION 165]

  b. Why do you feel that way? _____

165. If there was one thing that you <u>could</u> change as you think back over the past few years, what would that be?

_____

166. [HAND LARGE GREEN CARD] On this card is a list of things people often want to change about themselves. Again, using the scale from zero to 100, give me a score depending on how much you would like to change each of these things. If you want <u>no</u> change, you would rate the thing zero; if you'd like a <u>complete</u> change, you would rate it 100. Or you may score each thing anywhere in between. For instance, the first one is <u>the way you look</u>—how would you rate that, from zero for <u>no</u> change in the way you look, to 100 for a <u>complete</u> change.

SCORE

    a. THE WAY YOU LOOK     _____

    b. HOW OLD YOU ARE     _____

    c. THE FACT THAT YOU ARE (MARRIED/ SINGLE/SEPARATED/DIVORCED/WIDOWED)     _____

    d. THE NUMBER OF CHILDREN YOU HAVE     _____

    e. HOW YOU FEEL ABOUT YOURSELF     _____

    f. YOUR RELIGION     _____

    g. YOUR RACE     _____

    h. THE KIND OF PARENT YOU ARE     _____

[IF SCORE ABOVE ZERO FOR <u>KIND OF PARENT</u>, ASK]

In regard to the kind of parent you are, what changes would you make?

_____

167a. That's really all the questions I have, except I'm curious about your reactions to the interview. Were there any parts of this interview you minded answering?

    □ YES [ASK]  b.  What parts? _____

    □ NO

168a. If we asked these questions of your friends, do you think they would hesitate to tell the truth about any of them?

    □ YES [ASK]  b.  Which questions? _____

    □ NO

169a. Were there any questions you were reluctant to tell the truth about?

    □ YES [ASK]  b.  Which questions? _____

    □ NO

[IF NO LIVING FATHER, OR IF FATHER LIVES IN HOUSEHOLD, TERMINATE]

Thank you.

We feel it's important to find out how the men feel and we are going to send a young man to talk to [FATHER OF CHILD] just like I've talked to you. Do you know where his mother lives?

NAME _____       TIME ENDED _____

ADDRESS _____    INTERVIEWER _____ DATE _____

PHONE _____    EDITED BY ___ . ___  VERIFIED BY _____ DATE _____

## OBSERVATION

CHILD'S NAME _____    DATE OF INTERVIEW _____

I. Environment

    A.  Behavior with sibling(s) _____

    B.  Behavior with adult(s) _____

    C.  Physical environment

        Obvious play areas _____

        Condition of home _____

        Freedom of movement in home _____

II. Physical Characteristics

    A.  Appearance of child        C.  Hearing

    _____        _____

    B.  Obvious medical problems    D.  Vision

    _____        _____

                         E.  Motor activity

                         _____

III. Verbal Behavior

    A.  Elaborate _____

    B.  Quality of speech

        Descriptive _____

        Monosyllabic _____

        Speech defects _____

IV. Method of controlling behavior during visit

    A. Punishment _____

    B. Reward _____

V. Acceptance of child



INTERVIEW # _____

### CHILD INTERVIEW

CHILD'S NAME _____    MOTHER'S NAME _____

ADDRESS _____    DATE OF INTERVIEW _____

PHONE NUMBER _____    CHILD INTERVIEWED BY _____

BIRTH DATE _____    MOTHER INTERVIEWED BY _____

☐ BOY    ☐ GIRL

TIME BEGUN _____

INITIAL INTERACTION. MOTHER AND CHILD PLAY WITH PUZZLE.
[OBSERVE, MAKE DETAILED NOTES]

TIME ENDED _____



1. Pick the one that looks most like you. [PRESENT TWO DOLLS SAME SEX AS CHILD'S, ONE WHITE, ONE BLACK]

    ☐ WHITE    ☐ BLACK

2. Which do you want to be like when you grow up? [PRESENT ADULT MALE AND FEMALE DOLLS SAME RACE AS CHILD'S]

    ☐ MALE    ☐ FEMALE

3. PEABODY INVENTORY.    TIME BEGUN _____    TIME ENDED _____

4. HOME STORY.    TIME BEGUN _____

Now, we're going to make up a TV show. We're going to make up a story for our TV show about a child who's just exactly like you. Which one will be just like you in our story? [TWO DOLLS SAME RACE AND SEX AS CHILD'S BUT DRESSED DIFFERENTLY FROM EACH OTHER] OK, so this is you. Let's even give (him/her) your name. We'll call (him/her) _____. [CHILD'S NAME] Let's call this other one your friend. What would you like to name (him/her)? [IF CHILD SELECTS OWN NAME AGAIN, SAY, NO, THAT'S YOUR NAME: LET'S PICK ANOTHER NAME]

FRIEND'S NAME _____

Now _____ [CHILD] is in (his/her) house today and (he's/she's) playing with (his/her) mommy. (His/Her) friend _____ comes over and says, "Come and play with me." What does [CHILD] do? Does (he/she) keep playing with (his/her) mommy or go play with (his/her) friend? Which one? [SHOW MOTHER AND FRIEND AND ASK CHILD TO POINT]

☐ MOTHER    ☐ FRIEND

Why did (he/she) choose _____?

_____

[IF CHILD CHOOSES MOTHER, CONTINUE]     [IF CHILD CHOOSES FRIEND, CONTINUE]

What do (he/she) and (his/her) mommy do?     What do (he/she) and (his/her) friend do?

_____     _____

Then (his/her) friend goes home and [CHILD] is playing by (himself/herself). Mommy comes in and she has two candy bars. She says, "[CHILD], you can have either this one [SHOW PICTURE OF LITTLE BAR] right now or this one [SHOW PICTURE OF BIGGER ONE] later, before bedtime." Which one does [CHILD] choose, this one [POINT TO LITTLE BAR] <u>now</u> or this one [POINT TO BIG BAR] <u>later, before bed</u>?

☐ LITTLE BAR          ☐ BIG BAR

Why does (he/she) choose this one?

_____

Then someone knocks at the door. It's [CHILD]'s friend _____ again and (he/she) wants to play. [CHILD] and (his/her) friend are playing in the house for awhile, but they're not having very much fun because one of them feels angry and not very nice. Which one feels angry and is not very nice? [SHOW DOLLS, CHILD AND FRIEND]

☐ CHILD          ☐ FRIEND

Why does _____ fell angry and not very nice?

_____

(His/Her) friend goes home and [CHILD]'s mother decides to go to the store and takes [CHILD] with her. [CHILD] gets hungry and wants something to eat. [CHILD]'s mommy says, "You can choose something to eat or I'll choose it for you." Who chooses what to eat—[CHILD] or (his/her) mommy? [SHOW DOLLS]

☐ CHILD          ☐ MOTHER

Why does _____ choose?

_____

They come home from the store, and [CHILD] plays while mommy talks to her friend. After awhile, mommy looks at the table and sees that the milk has spilled. She thinks that maybe [CHILD] was the one who spilled the milk but [CHILD] <u>really didn't do it</u>. She comes over and says she's going to hit [CHILD]. What does [CHILD] do? [LET CHILD RESPOND SPONTANEOUSLY]

☐ SPONTANEOUS RESPONSE          ☐ NONSPONTANEOUS RESPONSE

_____

Does (he/she) run away or tell her (he/she) didn't do it?

☐ RUN AWAY          ☐ TELL HER (HE/SHE) DIDN'T DO IT

[CHILD] decides to tell (his/her) mommy that (he/she) really didn't spill the milk. When (he/she) tells her, what does mommy say?

☐ SPONTANEOUS RESPONSE          ☐ NONSPONTANEOUS RESPONSE

_____

Does she still think that [CHILD] did it?

☐ YES          ☐ NO

TIME ENDED _____

PRESCHOOL INVENTORY. [DO FIRST HALF]          TIME BEGUN _____
                                               TIME ENDED _____

5. SCHOOL STORY.          TIME BEGUN _____

Now, let's make up another story, this time about school. Do you go to school?

☐ YES          ☐ NO

Do you like school? _____

Well, we're going to make up another story about a (boy/girl) just like you. Let's even give the (boy/girl) your name again. Now, which one will be you in the story? [SHOW DIFFERENT SET OF SAME SEX DOLLS] Let this one be (his/her) friend. What shall we name (his/her) friend? _____ OK, now [CHILD AND FRIEND] are in school and the teacher asks them to build a house with some blocks. One of them says, "I don't know how to build a very good house." Which one says that—[CHILD] or (his/her) friend _____ ? [SHOW DOLLS]

☐ CHILD          ☐ FRIEND

Why does _____ say it? _____

They play some more in school with the other kids, and then the teacher brings in some toys for the children to take home. She lets the children choose. When it's [CHILD]'s turn, she says, "[CHILD], you can take this box [SHOW SMALL BOX OF CRAYONS] home today or that box [SHOW LARGE BOX OF CRAYONS] home tomorrow." Which does [CHILD] choose? This box for today or that box for tomorrow?

☐ SMALL BOX          ☐ BIG BOX

Why does (he/she) choose that one? _____

Do you have crayons at home?

☐ YES          ☐ NO

Now let's pretend that you were choosing some toys to take home.

Which of these toys would you most like to play with? [SHOW PICTURES]

☐ TRUCK          ☐ DOLL          ☐ BLOCKS          ☐ MAGIC MARKERS          ☐ BOOKS
☐ BASKETBALL          ☐ JUMP ROPE          ☐ PUZZLE

Which is your next favorite?

☐ TRUCK          ☐ DOLL          ☐ BLOCKS          ☐ MAGIC MARKERS          ☐ BOOKS
☐ BASKETBALL          ☐ JUMP ROPE          ☐ PUZZLE

Are there any you wouldn't want to play with? [MORE THAN ONE ALLOWED]

☐ TRUCK          ☐ DOLL          ☐ BLOCKS          ☐ MAGIC MARKERS          ☐ BOOKS
☐ BASKETBALL          ☐ JUMP ROPE          ☐ PUZZLE          ☐ NONE

If you could play with most of these toys but had to give one away to another child, which one would you give to another child?

☐ TRUCK          ☐ DOLL          ☐ BLOCKS          ☐ MAGIC MARKERS          ☐ BOOKS
☐ BASKETBALL          ☐ JUMP ROPE          ☐ PUZZLE

Do you have any toys like these at home? [RECORD YES OR NO FOR EACH TOY]

|  | YES | NO |
|---|---|---|
| TRUCK | ☐ | ☐ |
| DOLL | ☐ | ☐ |
| BLOCKS | ☐ | ☐ |
| MAGIC MARKERS | ☐ | ☐ |
| BOOKS | ☐ | ☐ |
| BASKETBALL | ☐ | ☐ |
| JUMP ROPE | ☐ | ☐ |
| PUZZLE | ☐ | ☐ |

If you were choosing some toys to take home, would you choose this one or this one?

☐ TRUCK ☐ DOLL

Would you choose this one or this one?

☐ BASKETBALL ☐ JUMP ROPE

Now, remember, we made up a TV show about a (boy/girl) just like you named [CHILD'S NAME], and we're making up a show about school. [CHILD] is still in school and the teacher is asking a question. She looks for the child who knows the right answer. Which one knows the right answer—[CHILD] or (his/her) friend _____?

☐ CHILD ☐ FRIEND

Why do you think _____ knows the right answer?

_____

Then the teacher decides to play another game with the children. She shows every child some pictures and asks them to pick the one that's just like them. It's [CHILD]'s turn. Which one does (he/she) pick, this one or this one? Which is most like (him/her)? [SHOW PORTERFIELD ITEMS]

a. ☐ FIGURE FALLING ☐ FIGURE SITTING ☐ FIGURE RUNNING

b. ☐ FIGURE DEPENDENT ☐ FIGURE SELF-SUFFICIENT

c. ☐ FIGURE DEPENDENT ☐ FIGURE SELF-SUFFICIENT

d. ☐ FIGURE WITH ADULT ☐ END FIGURE FRONT ☐ TALL FIGURE BACK

e. ☐ FIGURE ALONE ☐ FIGURE RIGHT ☐ FIGURE LEFT ☐ FIGURE CENTER

f. ☐ FIGURE SCOLDED ☐ FIGURE AMONG GROUP

g. ☐ FIGURE TEARING ☐ FIGURE HITTING ☐ FIGURE OBSERVING

h. ☐ FIGURE ALONE ☐ BOY BACK ☐ GIRL BACK ☐ FRONT FIGURE

i. ☐ FIGURE ALONE ☐ MIDDLE GROUP ☐ LINE LEADER

j. ☐ FIGURE ALONE ☐ FIGURE BACK ☐ FIGURE PROFILE

Then, after that the kids all have some time to play. Some of them are going to play a game, and they are going to choose the person they like the best to play the game with them. Who will the kids choose—[CHILD] or (his/her) friend _____?

☐ CHILD ☐ FRIEND

Why do they choose _____?

_____

What game do they play?

_____

What's your favorite game?

_____

After they are playing for awhile, the teacher sees that one of the children is crying. She thinks someone has hit him. She thinks maybe [CHILD] did it. Well, [CHILD] really did do it, (he/she) was really the one, but the other child hit (him/her) first. The reacher says, "[CHILD] go sit in the corner because you hit that boy." What does [CHILD] do?

☐ SPONTANEOUS RESPONSE ☐ NONSPONTANEOUS RESPONSE

[COMMENTS] _____

Does (he/she) sit in the corner or tell the teacher that the other child hit (him/her) first?

_____

Let's say (he/she) tells the teacher that the other kid hit (him/her) first. What does the teacher do? Does she think (he's/she's) lying or does she believe (him/her)?

_____

TIME ENDED _____

TIME BEGUN _____

The kids all go into the classroom and it's time for drawing. The teacher tells each kid to draw a picture of himself. Let's pretend you're in a class. Draw a picture of yourself. You can use any of this paper and these crayons. [LET CHILD DRAW]

Who is that a picture of? _____

TIME ENDED _____

6. FINISH PRESCHOOL INVENTORY.  TIME BEGUN_____TIME ENDED_____

TIME BEGUN _____

7. SELF-PORTRAIT STORY.

This is a picture of you. Will you tell me a story about you in the picture? [PROBE, IF NECESSARY] Tell me about what the child in the picture can do or knows how to do.

TIME ENDED _____

TIME BEGUN _____

8. FREE PLAY

[GIVE CHILD ALL DOLLS] Here are all the dolls. Why don't you make up a story now?

TIME ENDED _____

9. DELAYED GRATIFICATION.

Suppose you had the choice of getting a small candy bar like this one right now or a big candy bar like that after dinner. Which would you take?

☐ SMALL         ☐ BIG

10. FINAL INTERACTION.

CHILD CHOOSES

☐ DRAWING TOYS

☐ TINKER TOYS

TIME ENDED _____

Appendix B

SUPPLEMENTARY TABLES

Table A.1A

Adolescents' Contraceptive Experience and Birth Control Instruction[1]

| Adolescents' Experience | Neither Reports Instruction | Mother Yes, Daughter No | Daughter Yes, Mother No | Both Report Instruction |
|---|---|---|---|---|
| Have Used Contraceptives | 23% | 38% | 42% | 52% |
| Never Used Contraceptives | 77 (83) | 62 (37) | 58 (88) | 48 (98) |

[1] The respondents include only adolescent mothers who were single at Time 1 as a full sexual history was not collected from the women who were married since their parents often were not interviewed.

Table A.1B

Adolescents' Contraceptive Experience and Mothers' Knowledge of Daughters' Sexual Activity

| Adolescents' Experience | Neither Report Mother Aware | Mother Aware, Daughter Thinks She Is Not | Mother Unaware, Daughter Thinks She Is | Both Report Mother Aware |
|---|---|---|---|---|
| Have Used Contraceptives | 34% | 44% | 50% | 58% |
| Never Used Contraceptives | 67 (155) | 56 (32) | 50 (52) | 42 (36) |

Table A.1C

Adolescents' Contraceptive Experience and Mothers' Attitude toward Premarital Sex

| Adolescents' Experience | Both Regard Mother as Restrictive | Mother Restrictive, Daughter Regards Her as Permissive | Mother Permissive, Daughter Regards Her as Restrictive | Both Regard Mother as Permissive |
|---|---|---|---|---|
| Have Used Contraceptives | 19% | 46% | 41% | 59% |
| Never Used Contraceptives | 81 (80) | 54 (50) | 59 (78) | 41 (87) . |

Table A.2

Adolescents' Contraceptive Experience by Birth Control Instruction
and Relationship with Father of Child[1]

|  | Temporary Relationship | | Stable Relationship | |
|---|---|---|---|---|
|  | Low Sexual Activity | High Sexual Activity | Low Sexual Activity | High Sexual Activity |
| Birth Control Instruction |  |  |  |  |
| Both Report Instruction | 0 (10) | 47 (19) | 46 (13) | 69 (45) |
| Mother No, Daughter Yes | * | 32 (22) | 33 (15) | 52 (44) |
| Mother Yes, Daughter No | * | * | * | 42 (19) |
| Neither Reports Instruction | 7 (14) | 22 (18) | 26 (19) | 22 (27) |
| Percentage Difference | −7 | +25 | +20 | +47 |

[1] Cells contain percentage with contraceptive experience.

* Percentage not calculated when base is under 10.

Table A.3

Probability of Marriage among Adolescent Mothers
from Point of Delivery

| Months | Total | Number Marrying | Monthly Probability of Marriage | Cumulative Probability of Remaining Single | Cumulative Probability of Marrying | Lost to Follow-up |
|---|---|---|---|---|---|---|
| −6 | 384 | 84 | .22 | .78 | .22 | 0 |
| 0 | 300 | 5 | .02 | .76 | .24 | 0 |
| 6 | 295 | 30 | .10 | .68 | .32 | 0 |
| 12 | 265 | 25 | .09 | .62 | .38 | 5 |
| 18 | 235 | 26 | .11 | .55 | .45 | 5 |
| 24 | 204 | 13 | .06 | .52 | .48 | 1 |
| 30 | 190 | 17 | .09 | .47 | .53 | 6 |
| 36 | 167 | 12 | .07 | .44 | .56 | 2 |
| 42 | 153 | 8 | .05 | .42 | .58 | 5 |
| 48 | 140 | 7 | .05 | .40 | .60 | 23 |
| 54 | 110 | 8 | .07 | .37 | .63 | 31 |
| 60 | 71 | 2 | .03 | .36 | .64 | 34 |
| 66 | 35 | 1 | .03 | .35 | .65 | 16 |
| 72 | 18 | 1 | .06 | .33 | .67 | 14 |

Table A.4

Marital Timing by Age of Adolescent Parents at Time 1

| | Age of Mother | | | Age of Father | | | |
|---|---|---|---|---|---|---|---|
| Marital Status | 15 and Under | 16 | 17 | 18 and Under | 19 | 20 | 21+ |
| Married before Delivery | 12% | 21% | 33% | 5% | 15% | 25% | 36% |
| Ever Married | 56 (84) | 61 (105) | 72 (132) | 48 (58) | 60 (68) | 64 (61) | 72 (91) |

| | Percentage Married at Delivery by Age of Father | | | | Percentage Ever Married by Age of Father | | | |
|---|---|---|---|---|---|---|---|---|
| Age of Mother | 18 and Under | 19 | 20 | 21+ | 18 and Under | 19 | 20 | 21+ |
| 15 and under | 4 (27) | 7 (14) | 20 (20) | 25 (12) | 37 (27) | 50 (14) | 75 (20) | 67 (12) |
| 16 | 8 (25) | 13 (24) | 33 (18) | 31 (26) | 48 (25) | 58 (24) | 67 (18) | 65 (26) |
| 17+ | * | 20 (30) | 22 (23) | 42 (53) | * | 67 (30) | 52 (23) | 77 (53) |

* Percentage not calculated when base is under 10.

Table A.5

Marital Timing by Sexual Standards
of Adolescent Mothers and Their Mothers[1]

| Marital Status | Daughter P[2], Mother P | Daughter P, Mother R | Daughter R, Mother P | Daughter R, Mother R |
|---|---|---|---|---|
| Married before Delivery | 4% | 6% | 7% | 17% |
| Married after Delivery | 39 | 50 | 47 | 55 |
| Never Married | 57 | 44 | 45 | 28 |
| | (74) | (32) | (84) | (76) |

[1] This table excludes women already married at Time 1 interview and women not interviewed at Time 4.

[2] P = permissive; R = restrictive.

Table A.6

Cumulative Probability of Separation
by Marital Timing and Marriage Partner

| Months from Marriage Date | Married Father of Child before Delivery | Married Father of Child after Delivery | Married Other Man after Delivery[1] |
|---|---|---|---|
| 12 | .10 | .23 | .22 |
| 24 | .25 | .33 | .45 |
| 36 | .36 | .47 | .65 |
| 48 | .41 | .57 | * |

[1] Not included are two women who married a man not the child's father before delivery.

* Base is under 10 at beginning of month.

Table A.7

Probability of Separation by Courtship Pattern

Length of Relationship

| Months from Marriage Date | Brief Duration prior to Marriage[1] (43) | Extensive Duration prior to Marriage (138) |
|---|---|---|
| 12 | .30 | .17 |
| 24 | .51 | .29 |
| 36 | .51 | .43 |

[1] Brief duration is defined as under two years.

Table A.8

Sexual History of Relationship

| Months from Marriage Date | Infrequent Relations with One Male (77) | Frequent Relations with One Male (46) | Infrequent Relations with Several Males (14) | Frequent Relations with Several Males (16) |
|---|---|---|---|---|
| 12 | .16 | .25 | .38 | .42 |
| 24 | .28 | .39 | * | * |
| 36 | .43 | .64 | * | * |

* Probability not reported when base is under 10.

Table A.9

Cumulative Probability of Pregnancy
by Ambition and Marital Status at Time 4

|  | Single | | | Ever Married | | |
|---|---|---|---|---|---|---|
|  | Low (18) | Medium (67) | High (34) | Low (50) | Medium (111) | High (37) |
| Month |  |  |  |  |  |  |
| 12 | .22 | .18 | .03 | .48 | .28 | .22 |
| 24 | .39 | .31 | .12 | .56 | .50 | .51 |
| 36 | .44 | .40 | .26 | .66 | .65 | .65 |
| 48 | * | .48 | .32 | .76 | .71 | * |
| 60 | * | .61 | .36 | * | * | * |

* Base under 10 at the beginning of the month.

Table A.10

Cumulative Probability of Second Pregnancy by Educational Career

Total

|  | Never Returned (80) | Returned, No Longer In School (62) | Returned, Still In School (21) | Graduated Before Delivery (27) | Returned, Graduated (106) | Graduated, Still Attending (25) |
|---|---|---|---|---|---|---|
| Month |  |  |  |  |  |  |
| 12 | .35 | .27 | .29 | .37 | .12 | .12 |
| 24 | .64 | .52 | .43 | .48 | .25 | .28 |
| 36 | .73 | .63 | * | .67 | .40 | .36 |
| 48 | .80 | .69 | * | * | .46 | .40 |

|  | Single | | | Married | | |
|---|---|---|---|---|---|---|
|  | Never Returned | Returned[1] Not Graduated | Returned,[2] Graduated | Never Returned | Returned[1] Not Graduated | Returned,[2] Graduated |
| Month |  |  |  |  |  |  |
| 12 | .38 | .19 | .05 | .36 | .33 | .19 |
| 24 | .63 | .31 | .11 | .58 | .59 | .40 |
| 36 | * | .44 | .18 | .67 | .71 | .59 |
| 48 | * | .50 | .23 | .74 | * | .65 |

* Base is under 10 at the beginning of the month.

[1] Includes those still attending school who have not graduated.

[2] Includes those who graduated before delivery.

Table A.11

Attitudes toward Birth Control among Adolescents before and after Delivery[1]

| Attitudes | Family Prenatal Interview | Clinic Postpartum Interview (226) | Percentage Change | Control Prenatal Interview | Group Postpartum Interview (149) | Percentage Change |
|---|---|---|---|---|---|---|
| 1. Birth control often doesn't work even if you are careful. (% disagree) | 55 | 85 | +30 | 55 | 82 | +27 |
| 2. The best kind of birth control is the kind the boy uses. (% disagree) | 63 | 89 | +26 | 61 | 79 | +18 |
| 3. The kind of birth control that a woman has to put inside of herself makes me feel a little sick. (% disagree) | 30 | 33 | +3 | 30 | 34 | +4 |
| 4. Even if I could, I don't think I would want to use birth control every time I had sexual relations. (% disagree) | 71 | 92 | +21 | 62 | 93 | +21 |
| 5. Using birth control sometimes keeps girls from enjoying sexual relations. (% disagree) | 50 | 83 | +33 | 51 | 84 | +33 |
| 6. Birth control pills are not harmful even if you take them regularly. (% agree) | 44 | 70 | +32 | 40 | 67 | +27 |
| 7. I don't think I know enough about birth control. (% disagree) | 8 | 76 | +68 | 14 | 54 | +40 |

[1] Seven of the 382 respondents interviewed elected not to participate in the AFC and were assigned to the regular prenatal program. Consequently, their responses were excluded for purposes of this analysis.

Table A.12

Cumulative Probability of Birth Control Continuation by
Program Experience and Marital Status at Time 4

### Total

| Month | Before Delivery (113) | After Delivery (116) | Never Married (99) |
|---|---|---|---|
| 12 | .58 | .58 · | .80 |
| 24 | .31 | .29 | .58 |
| 36 | .24 | .22 | .43 |
| 48 | .16 | .21 | .34 |
| 60 | .16 | .19 | .32 |

| | AFC Group | | | Control | | |
|---|---|---|---|---|---|---|
| Month | Before Delivery (72) | After Delivery (72) | Never Married (62) | Before Delivery (41) | After Delivery (44) | Never Married (37) |
| 12 | .58 | .60 | .84 | .58 | .55 | .73 |
| 24 | .33 | .33 | .60 | .28 | .28 | .53 |
| 36 | .23 | .23 | .48 | .25 | .20 | .36 |
| 48 | .18 | .23 | .39 | .12 | .17 | .25 |
| 60 | .18 | .23 | .39 | * | .11 | .21 |

* Base is under 10.

Table A.13

Educational Achievement of Adolescent Mothers by
Family Characteristics prior to First Pregnancy

| Family Profile | Dropouts | Nongraduates Still in School | High School Graduate | |
|---|---|---|---|---|
| Education of Parents | | | | |
| Neither High School Graduate | 42% | 9 | 49 | (231) |
| One or Both High School Graduates | 32% | 8 | 61 | (51) |
| Occupational Status of Parents | | | | |
| Head of Household Employed at Skilled Job | 39% | 9 | 52 | (132) |
| Head of Household Employed at Unskilled Job | 40% | 7 | 53 | (107) |
| Head of Household Unemployed | 42% | 10 | 48 | (48) |
| Per Capita Family Income | | | | |
| Under 500 | 58% | 9 | 33 | (70) |
| 500-750 | 38% | 8 | 54 | (63) |
| 751-1499 | 33% | 12 | 54 | (57) |
| 1500+ | 26% | 7 | 67 | (46) |
| Head of Household | | | | |
| Couple | 41% | 6 | 43 | (201) |
| Female | 46% | 13 | 47 | (100) |
| History of Illegitimacy | | | | |
| Mother | 43% | 6 | 51 | (67) |
| Other Relative | 45% | 7 | 47 | (95) |
| None | 21% | 13 | 65 | (75) |

Table A.14

Educational Achievement of Adolescent Mothers by Ambition

| Education | Low Ambition | Medium Ambition | High Ambition |
|---|---|---|---|
| Less Than High School | 92% | 48% | 15% |
| Never Returned | 55 | 18 | 3 |
| Returned, No Longer in School | 28 | 19 | 11 |
| Returned, Still in School | 9 | 11 | 1 |
| High School Graduate | 8 | 51 | 85 |
| Never Returned | 0 | 9 | 10 |
| Returned, No Longer in School | 7 | 37 | 48 |
| Returned, Still in School | 1 | 5 | 27 |
| | (71) | (181) | (71) |

Table A.15

Educational Achievement of Adolescent Mothers by Timing of Second Pregnancy and Marital Status

| Educational Status | Single | | | | | Ever Married | | | | |
|---|---|---|---|---|---|---|---|---|---|---|
| | Pregnant within 11 Months | 12-23 Months | 24-35 Months | 36 Months or More | No Second Pregnancy | Pregnant within 11 Months | 12-23 Months | 24-35 Months | 36 Months or More | No Second Pregnancy |
| Dropout | 78% | 72% | 61% | 23% | 27% | 63% | 76% | 46% | 41% | 45% |
| Graduate | 22 | 28 | 39 | 77 | 73 | 37 | 24 | 54 | 59 | 55 |
| | (14) | (18) | (13) | (13) | (62) | (32) | (50) | (28) | (27) | (53) |

Table A.16A

Educational Achievement of Adolescent Mothers by
School Attendance during Pregnancy

|  | Number of Months during Pregnancy Remained in School | | |
|---|---|---|---|
| Education | 4 Months or under | 5-9 Months | Never Dropped Out |
| Less Than High School | | | |
| Never Returned | 36% | 13% | 10% |
| Returned, No Longer in School | 29 | 17 | 13 |
| Returned, Still in School | 8 | 15 | 3 |
| High School Graduate | | | |
| Never Returned | 7 | 10 | 10 |
| Returned, No Longer in School | 18 | 39 | 49 |
| Returned, Still in School | 3 | 7 | 19 |
|  | (103) | (72) | (104) |

Table A.16B

Educational Achievement of Adolescent Mothers by
School Attendance during Pregnancy, Controlling for Ambition

|  | Low | | | Medium | | | High | | |
|---|---|---|---|---|---|---|---|---|---|
| Level of Ambition | 4 | 5-9 | Never | 4 | 5-9 | Never | 4 | 5-9 | Never |
| Did Not Graduate | 88 | * | * | 73 | 45 | 29 | 36 | 6 | 11 |
| High School Graduate | 12 | * | * | 27 | 55 | 71 | 64 | 94 | 89 |
|  | (33) | (5) | (7) | (56) | (44) | (66) | (14) | (16) | (38) |

* Percentage not calculated when base is under 10.

Table A.17

Sources of Income for Adolescent Mothers and Classmates

| Income Source | Adolescent Mothers | | | Classmates with a Premarital Pregnancy | | | Classmates without a Premarital Pregnancy | | |
|---|---|---|---|---|---|---|---|---|---|
| | Under 20% | 20-79% | 80% and Over | Under 20% | 20-79% | 80% and Over | Under 20% | 20-79% | 80% and Over |
| Income from Employment | 55 | 20 | 25 | 46 | 19 | 35 | 30 | 27 | 43 |
| Income from Welfare | 65 | 17 | 18 | 78 | 14 | 8 | 96 | 2 | 2 |
| Income from Husband | 69 | 15 | 16 | 74 | 14 | 22 | 67 | 21 | 12 |
| Income from Father of Child | 89 | 10 | 1 | 83 | 13 | 4 | — | — | — |
| Income from Family | 95 | 3 | 2 | 94 | 6 | — | 88 | 6 | 6 |
| Other Income | 95 | 5 | — | 99 | 1 | — | 97 | 2 | 1 |

Table A.18

Welfare Patterns of Adolescent Mothers by Marital History

| Welfare Experience | Married before Delivery, Still Married | Married after Delivery, Still Married | Married before Delivery, Separated | Married after Delivery, Separated | Always Single |
|---|---|---|---|---|---|
| Never on Welfare during Study | 53% | 57% | 36% | 9% | 34% |
| On Welfare before,[1] Not at Time 4 | 44 | 29 | 24 | 13 | 18 |
| Still on Welfare | 3 | 14 | 39 | 78 | 49 |

[1] Respondent indicates that she was on welfare since becoming pregnant but is not on welfare at Time 4.

Table A.19

Welfare Patterns of Adolescent Mothers by Parity and Marital Status

| Welfare Experience | Single | | Married | | Other | |
|---|---|---|---|---|---|---|
| | One Child[1] | Two or More Children | One Child[1] | Two or More Children | One Child[1] | Two or More Children |
| Never on Welfare during Study | 43% | 13% | 81% | 41% | 38% | 11% |
| On Welfare But Not at Time 4 | 22 | 5 | 19 | 43 | 28 | 15 |
| Still on Welfare | 35 | 82 | — | 16 | 34 | 74 |
| | (79) | (39) | (36) | (68) | (29) | (66) |

[1] Includes cases of women who have no children living at home.

Table A.20

Support Patterns by Paternal Involvement and Marital Status[1]

| Amount of Support | Adolescent Mother Married Not to Father | | | | Father Previously Married to Adolescent Mother | | | | Adolescent Mother Unmarried | | | |
|---|---|---|---|---|---|---|---|---|---|---|---|---|
| | Total (29) | Regular Contact (0) | Irregular Contact (2) | No Contact (27) | Total (64) | Regular Contact (22) | Irregular Contact (19) | No Contact (23) | Total (103) | Regular Contact (27) | Irregular Contact (38) | No Contact (5) |
| None | 93 | * | * | 96 | 63 | 36 | 74 | 78 | 57 | 22 | 53 | * |
| Gifts/No Money | — | * | * | — | 2 | 5 | — | — | 5 | 11 | 5 | * |
| Under $50 per Month | 7 | * | * | 4 | 8 | 9 | 10 | 4 | 22 | 41 | 21 | * |
| $50 and over per Month | — | * | * | — | 28 | 50 | 16 | 17 | 16 | 26 | 21 | * |

[1] Excludes cases for which complete information was not available, including 23 cases of women who did not marry the father of the child and whose marriages were no longer intact at Time 4.

Table A.21A

Median Preschool Inventory Score
by Marital History of Adolescent Mothers[1]

| Time of Marriage | Total | Married Father of Child | Married Other Man | Separated from Father of Child |
|---|---|---|---|---|
| Married before Delivery | 76 (82) | 82 (27) | * | 74 (26) |
| Married after Delivery | 69 (107) | 80 (28) | 60 (25) | 64 (32) |

[1] Cells contain median percentile scores.

* Score not calculated when base is under 10.

Table A.21B

Median Preschool Inventory Score by Marital Experience

| Married Father of Child | Married Other Man | Separated from Father of Child | Separated from (Other Man) Husband | Single |
|---|---|---|---|---|
| 81 (55) | 60 (25) | 74 (58) | 65 (19) | 63 (95) |

Table A.21C

Median Preschool Inventory Score
by Amount of Contact Between Father and Child

| Living with Father | Regular Contact | Irregular Contact | No Contact |
|---|---|---|---|
| 81 (55) | 71 (49) | 63 (59) | 59 (61) |

Table A.22

Social Development of Study Children and Economic Status of Their Parents

| Profile of Parents | Deferral of Gratification[1] | Efficacy[1] | Trust[1] | Self-Esteem[1] |
|---|---|---|---|---|
| Education of Mother | | | | |
| High School Dropout | 30 (135) | 49 (82) | 32 (107) | 27 (124) |
| High School Graduate | 28 (134) | 64 (95) | 40 (108) | 26 (121) |
| Welfare Status | | | | |
| Currently on Welfare | 32 (107) | 48 (63) | 32 (85) | 33 (89) |
| Past Welfare Experience | 27 (63) | 54 (41) | 34 (50) | 16 (56) |
| Never on Welfare | 25 (96) | 68 (62) | 40 (77) | 27 (98) |
| Work Status | | | | |
| Unemployed for at Least Two Years | 28 (144) | 52 (69) | 30 (187) | 33 (107) |
| Recently Employed | 36 (53) | 56 (41) | 45 (47) | 17 (52) |
| At Least Two Years of Work Experience | 25 (72) | 75 (47) | 39 (61) | 32 (66) |
| Socioeconomic Status of Mother | | | | |
| Low | 26 (144) | 50 (84) | 29 (111) | 31 (129) |
| High | 32 (124) | 63 (83) | 43 (104) | 22 (115) |

[1] Cells contain the percentage in the high category.

# Bibliography

Atkyns, Glenn C. 1968. "Trends in the Retention of Married and Pregnant Students in American Public Schools." *Sociology of Education* 41 (1):57-65.

Bachman, Jerald, et al. 1971. *Youth in Transition*. Vol. 3, *Dropping Out—Problem or Symptom?* Ann Arbor: Institute for Social Research, University of Michigan.

Baizerman, Michael, et al. 1971. *Pregnant Adolescents: A Review of Literature with Abstracts 1960-1970*. Washington, D.C.: Consortium on Early Childbearing and Childrearing, Research Utilization and Information Sharing Project.

Baizerman, Michael, et al. 1974. "A Critique of the Research Literature Concerning Pregnant Adolescents, 1960-1970." *Journal of Youth and Adolescence* 3 (1):61-75.

Bakke, E. W. 1940. *The Unemployed Worker*. New Haven: Yale University Press.

Baldwin, Alfred L. 1960. "The Study of Child Behavior and Development." In *Handbook of Research Methods in Child Development*, ed. Paul H. Mussen. New York: Wiley.

Banfield, Edward C. 1970. *The Unheavenly City: The Nature and the Future of Our Urban Crisis*. Boston: Little, Brown. Revised in 1974.

Bartz, Karen Winch, and F. Ivan Nye. 1970. "Early Marriage: A Propositional Formulation." *Journal of Marriage and the Family* 32 (2):258-268.

Becker, Howard S. 1963. *Outsiders—Studies in the Sociology of Deviance*. New York: Free Press.

———. 1970. *Sociological Work: Method and Substance*. Chicago: Aldine.

Becker, Howard S., and Anselm L. Strauss. 1956. "Careers, Personality, and Adult Socialization." *American Journal of Sociology* 62 (3):253-263.

Bell, Robert R. 1965. "Lower Class Negro Mothers' Aspirations for Their Children." *Social Forces* 43 (4):493-500.

———. 1966. *Premarital Sex in a Changing Society*. Englewood Cliffs, N.J.: Prentice-Hall.

Bell, Robert R., and Jay B. Chaskes. 1970. "Premarital Sexual Experience among Coeds, 1958 and 1968." *Journal of Marriage and the Family* 32 (1):81-84.

Berg, Ivar. 1971. *Education and Jobs: The Great Training Robbery.* Boston: Beacon Press.

Bernard, Jessie. 1966. *Marriage and Family among Negroes.* Englewood Cliffs, N.J.: Prentice-Hall.

Bernstein, Rose. 1963. "Gaps in Services to Unmarried Mothers." *Children* 10 (2):49-54.

Bettleheim, Bruno. 1969. *The Children of the Dream.* New York: Macmillan.

Biderman, Albert D., and Albert J. Reiss, Jr. 1967. "On Exploring the Dark Figure of Crime." *Annals of the American Academy of Political and Social Science* 374 (November):1-15.

Biller, Henry B. 1970. "Father Absence and the Personality Development of the Male Child." *Developmental Psychology* 2:181-201.

Blake, Judith. 1961. *Family Structure in Jamaica.* New York: Free Press of Glencoe.

———. 1974. "The Teenage Birth Control Dilemma and Public Opinion." *Science* 180:708-712.

Blumer, Herbert. 1962. "Society as Symbolic Interaction." In *Human Behavior and Social Processes,* ed. Arnold M. Rose. Boston: Houghton Mifflin.

Bott, Elizabeth. 1971. *Family and Social Network.* 2d ed. New York: Free Press.

Bowerman, Charles E., et al. 1966. *Unwed Motherhood: Personal and Social Consequences.* Chapel Hill, N.C.: Institute for Research in Social Science, University of North Carolina.

Braen, Bernard B., and Janet Bell Forbush. 1975. "School-age Parenthood—A National Overview." *Journal of School Health* 45 (5):256-262.

Bright, Margaret. 1966. "Social Indications and Implications for Family Planning Services." Mimeographed.

Broderick, Carlfred B. 1965. "Social Heterosexual Development among Urban Negroes and Whites." *Journal of Marriage and the Family* 27 (2):200-203.

———. 1966. "Sexual Behavior among Preadolescents." *Journal of Social Issues* 22 (1):6-21.

Bumpass, Larry L., and James A. Sweet. 1972. "Differentials in Marital Instability." *American Sociological Review* 37 (6):754-766.

Burchinal, Lee G. 1960. "Research on Young Marriage: Implications for Family Life Education." *Family Life Coordinator* 9:6-24.

———. 1965. "Trends and Prospects for Young Marriages in the United States." *Journal of Marriage and the Family* 27 (2):243-254.

Burr, Wesley R. 1972. "Role Transition: A Reformulation of Theory." *Journal of Marriage and the Family* 34 (3):407-416.

Calhoun, Arthur W. 1960. *A Social History of the American Family:* Vol. 1, *Colonial Period.* New York: Barnes & Noble.

Campbell, Arthur A. 1968. "The Role of Family Planning in the Reduction of Poverty." *Journal of Marriage and the Family* 30 (2):236-245.

Cannon, Kenneth L., and Richard Long. 1971. "Premarital Sexual Behavior in the Sixties." *Journal of Marriage and the Family* 33 (1):36-49.

Carter, Genevieve W. 1968. "The Employment Potential of AFDC Mothers: Some Questions and Some Answers." *Welfare in Review* 6 (4):1-11.

Carter, Hugh, and Paul C. Glick. 1970. *Marriage and Divorce: A Social and Economic Study.* Cambridge: Harvard University Press.

Caulfield, Mina Davis. 1974. "Imperialism, the Family, and Cultures of Resistance." *Socialist Revolution* 4 (2):67-86.

Cavan, Ruth S. 1959. "Unemployment: Crisis of the Common Man." *Journal of Marriage and the Family* 21 (2):139-146.

–––. 1964. "Subcultural Variations and Mobility." In *Handbook of Marriage and the Family,* ed. Harold T. Christensen. Chicago: Rand McNally.

Children's Defense Fund. 1974. *Children Out of School in America.* Cambridge: Children's Defense Fund.

Chilman, Catherine S. 1966. *Growing Up Poor.* Washington, D.C.: U.S. Government Printing Office.

Christensen, Harold T. 1953. "New Approaches in Family Research: The Method of Record Linkage." *Marriage and Family Living* 20 (1):38-42.

–––. 1960. "Cultural Relativism and Premarital Sex Norms." *American Sociological Review* 25 (1):31-39.

–––. 1963. "Timing of First Pregnancy as a Factor in Divorce: A Cross-cultural Analysis." *Eugenics Quarterly* 10 (1):119-130.

Christensen, Harold T., and Christina Gregg. 1970. "Changing Sex Norms in America and Scandinavia." *Journal of Marriage and the Family* 32 (4):616-627.

Clague, Alice J., and Stephanie J. Ventura. 1968. *Trends in Illegitimacy: United States–1940-1965.* Washington, D.C. National Center for Health Statistics, Series 21, No. 15.

Clark, Kenneth, and Mamie Clark. 1939. "The Development of Consciousness of Self and the Emergence of Racial Identity in Negro Preschool Children." *Journal of Social Psychology* 10:591-599.

Clark, Monna G., and Suzanne Berstein Salsburg. 1974. *The Legal Rights of Women in Marriage and Divorce in Maryland.* Baltimore: Women's Law Center.

Clausen, John A. 1965. "Family Structure, Socialization, and Personality." In *Review of Child Development Research,* ed. Martin L. Hoffman and Lois Wladis Hoffman. New York: Russell Sage Foundation.

–––. 1972. "The Life Course of Individuals." In *Aging and Society.* Vol. 3, *A Sociology of Age Stratification,* ed. Matilda White Riley, Marilyn Johnson, and Anne Foner. New York: Russell Sage Foundation.

Clausen, John A. (ed.). 1968. *Socialization and Society.* Boston: Little, Brown.

Cohen, Albert K. 1955. *Delinquent Boys: The Culture of the Gang.* Glencoe, Ill.: Free Press.

Cohen, Elizabeth G. 1965. "Parental Factors in Educational Mobility." *Sociology of Education* 38 (5):404-425.

Cohen, Sarah Betsy, and James A. Sweet. 1974. "The Impact of Marital Disruption and Remarriage on Fertility." *Journal of Marriage and the Family* 36 (1):87-96.

Coleman, James S. 1974. *Youth: Transition to Adulthood.* Chicago: University of Chicago Press.

Coleman, James S., et al. 1966. *Equality of Educational Opportunity.* Washington, D.C.: U.S. Government Printing Office.

Coombs, Janet, and William W. Cooley. 1968. "Dropouts: In High School and after School." *American Educational Research Journal* 5:343-363.

Coombs, Lolagene C., and Zena Zumeta. 1970. "Correlates of Marital Dissolution in a Prospective Fertility Study: A Research Note." *Social Problems* 18 (1):92-101.

Coombs, Lolagene C., et al. 1970. "Premarital Pregnancy and Status before and after Marriage." *American Journal of Sociology* 75 (5):800-820.

Coser, Rose Laub. 1964. "Authority and Structural Ambivalence in the Middle-Class Family." In *The Family: Its Structure and Functions,* ed. Rose Coser. New York: St. Martin's Press.

Cutright, Phillips. 1971a. "Illegitimacy: Myths, Causes and Cures." *Family Planning Perspectives* 3 (1):25-48.

———. 1971b. "Illegitimacy in the United States: 1920-1968." Unpublished monograph.

———. 1971c. "Income and Family Events: Marital Stability." *Journal of Marriage and the Family* 33 (2):291-306.

———. 1973. "Timing the First Birth: Does It Matter?" *Journal of Marriage and the Family* 35 (4):585-596.

———. 1974. "Teenage Illegitimacy: An Exchange." Letters from readers. *Family Planning Perspectives* 6 (3):132-133.

Davis, Fred. 1963. *Passage through Crisis.* New York: Bobbs-Merrill.

Davis, Kingsley, and Judith Blake. 1956. "Social Structure and Fertility: An Analytic Framework." *Economic Development and Cultural Change* 4:211.

Deutsch, Martin, et al. (eds.). 1968. *Social Class, Race, and Psychological Development.* New York: Holt, Rinehart and Winston.

Deutscher, Irwin. 1973. *What We Say/What We Do.* Glenview, Ill.: Scott, Foresman.

Dickens, Helen O., et al. 1973. "One Hundred Pregnant Adolescents: Treatment Approaches in a University Hospital." *American Journal of Public Health* 63 (9):794-800.

Dixon, Ruth B. 1971. "Explaining Cross-cultural Variations in Age at Marriage and Proportions Never Marrying." *Population Studies* 25 (2):215-233.

Duncan, Beverly, and Otis Dudley Duncan. 1969. "Family Stability and Occupational Success." *Social Problems* 16 (3):273-285.

Duncan, Otis Dudley, et al. 1965. "Marital Fertility and Size of Family Orientation." *Demography* 2 (2):508-515.

Duncan, Otis Dudley, et al. 1972. *Socioeconomic Background and Achievement.* New York: Seminar Press.

Dyer, Everett D. 1963. "Parenthood as Crisis: A Re-Study." *Marriage and Family Living* 25:196-201.

Ehrmann, Winston. 1964. "Marital and Nonmarital Sexual Behavior." In *Handbook of Marriage and the Family,* ed. Harold T. Christensen. Chicago: Rand McNally.

Elder, Glen H., Jr. 1968. *Adolescent Socialization and Personality Development.* Chicago: Rand McNally.

———. 1973. "On Linking Social Structure and Personality." *American Behavioral Scientist* 16 (6):785-800.

———. 1974. *Children of the Great Depression.* Chicago: University of Chicago Press.

———. 1976. "Family History and the Life Course." *Journal of Family History* 1 (1) in press.

Elkin, Frederick, and Gerald Handel. 1972. *The Child and Society: The Process of Socialization.* 2d ed. New York: Random House.

Erlanger, Howard S. 1974. "Social Class and Corporal Punishment in Childrearing: A Reassessment." *American Sociological Review* 39 (1):68-85.

Figley, Charles R. 1973. "Child Density and the Marital Relationship." *Journal of Marriage and the Family* 35 (2):272-282.

Fuller, Richard K., and Richard Myers. 1941. "The Natural History of a Social Problem." *American Sociological Review* 6 (3):320-329.

Freedman, Ronald, and Lolagene C. Coombs. 1970. "Pre-marital Pregnancy, Child-spacing, and Later Economic Achievement." *Population Studies* 24 (3):389-412.

Furstenberg, Frank F., Jr. 1969. "Birth Control Knowledge and Attitudes among Unmarried Pregnant Adolescents: A Preliminary Report." *Journal of Marriage and the Family* 31 (1):34-42.

———. 1971a. "Birth Control Experience among Pregnant Adolescents: The Process of Unplanned Parenthood." *Social Problems* 19 (2):192-203.

———. 1971b. "Preventing Unwanted Pregnancies among Adolescents." *Journal of Health and Social Behavior* 12:340-347.

———. 1971c. "The Transmission of Mobility Orientation in the Family." *Social Forces* 49 (4):595-603.

———. 1972. "Attitudes toward Abortion among Young Blacks." *Studies in Family Planning* 4:66-69.

———. 1974a. "Teenage Illegitimacy: An Exchange." Letters from readers. *Family Planning Perspectives* 6 (3):133-134.

———. 1974b. "Work Experience and Family Life." In *Work and the Quality of Life: Resource Papers for Work in America,* ed. James O'Toole. Cambridge: MIT Press.

———. 1975. *Unplanned Parenthood: The Social Consequences of Teenage Childbearing.* Final report. Washington: Maternal and Child Health Service.

Furstenberg, Frank F., Jr., et al. 1972. "How Can Family Planning Programs Delay Repeat Teenage Pregnancies?" *Family Planning Perspectives* 4 (3):54-60.

Furstenberg, Frank F., Jr., and Charles A. Thrall. 1975. "Counting the Jobless: The Impact of Job Rationing on the Measurement of Unemployment." *Annals of the American Academy of Political and Social Science* 418 (March):45-49.

Gebhard, Paul H., et al. 1958. *Pregnancy, Birth and Abortion.* New York: Harper & Brothers.

Glasser, Paul, and Elizabeth Navarre. 1965. "Structural Problems of the One-Parent Family." *Journal of Social Issues* 21 (1):98-109.

Glazer, Nona Y., and Carol F. Creedon (eds.). 1969. *Children and Poverty: Some Sociological and Psychological Perspectives.* Chicago: Rand McNally.

Glidewell, John C. (ed.). 1961. *Parental Attitudes and Child Behavior.* Springfield, Ill.: Charles C. Thomas.

Goffman, Erving. 1959. *The Presentation of Self in Everyday Life.* New York: Doubleday.

———. 1963. *Stigma: Notes on the Management of Spoiled Identity.* Englewood Cliffs, N.J.: Prentice-Hall.

Goode, William J. 1956. *After Divorce.* Glencoe, Ill.: Free Press.

———. 1960. "Illegitimacy in the Caribbean Social Structure." *American Sociological Review* 25 (1):21-30.

———. 1961. "Illegitimacy, Anomie, and Cultural Penetration." *American Sociological Review* 26 (4):319-925.

———. 1963. *World Revolution and Family Patterns.* New York: Free Press.

Goode, William J. (ed.). 1964a. *Readings on the Family and Society.* Englewood Cliffs, N.J.: Prentice-Hall.

———. 1964b. *The Family.* Foundations of Modern Sociology Series. Englewood Cliffs, N.J.: Prentice-Hall.

Goodwin, Leonard. 1972. *Do the Poor Want to Work?: Studies in the Work Orientations of the Poor and the Nonpoor.* Washington, D.C.: Brookings Institution.

Gordon, David M. 1972. *Theories of Poverty and Underemployment.* Lexington, Mass.: Heath, Lexington Books.

Gottlieb, David. 1964. "Goal Aspirations and Goal Fulfillments: Differences between Deprived and Affluent American Adolescents." *American Journal of Orthopsychiatry* 34:934-941.

Graves, William L. 1972. "Who Gets Married? A Study of Black Teenage Girls Who Conceived Out of Wedlock." Paper presented at the Southern Sociological Society Annual Meetings.

Green, Arnold W. 1941. "The Cult of Personality and Sexual Relations." *Psychiatry* 4:343-348.

Greenleigh Associates. 1960. *Facts, Fallacies and Future.* New York: Greenleigh Associates.

Greven, Philip J., Jr. 1966. "Family Structure in Seventeenth-Century Andover, Massachusetts." *William and Mary Quarterly* 23:234-256.

Gustavus, Susan. 1973. "The Family Size Preferences of Young People: A Replication and Longitudinal Follow-up Study." *Studies in Family Planning* 4 (12):335-342.

———. 1975. "Fertility Socialization Research in the United States: A Progress Report." *Papers of the East-West Population Institute* 35 (July).

Gustavus, Susan, and Charles B. Nam. 1970. "The Formation and Stability of Ideal Family Size among Young People." *Demography* 7:43-51.

Alan Guttmacher Institute. 1975. "The Unmet Need for Legal Abortion Services in the United States." *Family Planning Perspectives* 5 (7):224-230.

Hammond, Phillip E. (ed.). 1964. *Sociologists at Work: Essays on the Craft of Social Research.* New York: Basic Books.

Hannerz, Ulf. 1969. *Soulside: Inquiries into Ghetto Culture and Community.* New York: Columbia University Press.

Hartley, Shirley. 1975. *Illegitimacy.* Berkeley: University of California Press.

Haselkorn, Florence. 1966. *Mothers-At-Risk.* New York: Adelphi University School of Social Work Publications.

Havighurst, Robert J. 1961. "Early Marriage and the Schools." *School Review* (Spring):36-47.

Heise, David R. 1972. *Personality and Socialization.* Chicago: Rand McNally.

Heiss, Jerold. 1972. "On the Transmission of Marital Instability in Black Families." *American Sociological Review* 37 (1):82-92.

Herzog, Elizabeth. 1967. *About the Poor: Some Facts and Some Fictions.* Washington, D.C.: U.S. Government Printing Office.

Herzog, Elizabeth, and Cecelia E. Sudia. 1970. *Boys in Fatherless Families.* Washington, D.C.: Government Printing Office.

Hetzel, Alice M., and Marlene Cappetta. 1973. "Teenagers: Marriages, Divorces, Parenthood, and Mortality." Vital and Health Statistics. U.S. Department of Health, Education, and Welfare, Series 21:23.

Hill, Reuben, and Joan Aldous. 1969. "Socialization for Marriage and Parenthood." In *Handbook of Socialization Theory and Research,* ed. David A. Goslin. Chicago: Rand McNally.

Hobbs, Daniel F., Jr. 1965. "Parenthood as Crisis: A Third Study." *Journal of Marriage and the Family* 27 (3):367-372.

———. 1968. "Transition to Parenthood: A Replication and an Extension." *Journal of Marriage and the Family* 30 (3):413-417.

Hoeft, Douglas, L. 1968. "A Study of the Unwed Mother in the Public School." *Journal of Educational Research* 61 (5):226-229.

Horan, Patrick M., and Patricia Lee Austin. 1974. "The Social Bases of Welfare Stigma." *Social Problems* 21 (5):648-657.

Horowitz, Eugene, and Ruth Horowitz. 1938. "Development of Social Attitudes in Children." *Sociometry* 1:301-338.

Howard, Marion. 1968. *Multi-Service Programs for Pregnant School Girls.* Washington, D.C.: Children's Bureau.

———. 1972. "The Task Ahead . . ." *Sharing* (August).

Hughes, Everett C. 1972. *The Sociological Eye: Selected Papers on Work, Self, and the Study of Society.* Chicago: Aldine-Atherton.

Hunt, Morton M. 1966. *The World of the Formerly Married.* New York: McGraw-Hill.

Hurley, John R., and Donna P. Palonen. 1967. "Marital Satisfaction and Child Density among University Student Parents." *Journal of Marriage and the Family* 29 (3):483-484.

Hyman, Herbert H. 1959. *Political Socialization.* Glencoe, Ill.: Free Press.

Hyman, Herbert H., et al. 1954. *Interviewing in Social Research.* Chicago: University of Chicago Press.

Jacobson, Paul. 1959. *American Marriage and Divorce.* New York: Rinehart.

Jaffe, Frederick S. and Steven Polgar. "Family Planning and Public Policy: Is the Culture of Poverty the New Cop-Out?" *Journal of Marriage and the Family* 30 (2):228-235.

Jeffers, Camille. 1967. *Living Poor: A Participant Observer Study of Priorities and Choices.* Ann Arbor: Ann Arbor Publishers.

Jencks, Christopher, et al. 1972. *Inequality: A Reassessment of the Effect of Family and Schooling in America.* New York: Basic Books.

Jenstrom, Linda L., and Tannis M. Williams. 1975. "Improving Care for Infants of School-age Parents." *Sharing* (spec. supp.).

Jorgensen, Valerie. 1973. "One-Year Contraceptive Follow-up of Adolescent Patients." *American Journal of Obstetrics and Gynecology* 115 (4):483-486.

Kantner, John F., and Melvin Zelnik, 1972. "Sexual Experience of Young Unmarried Women in the United States." *Family Planning Perspectives* 4 (4):9-18.

———. 1973. "Contraception and Pregnancy: Experience of Young Unmarried Women in the United States." *Family Planning Perspectives* 5 (1):21-35.

Katz, Elihu, and Paul F. Lazarsfeld. 1955. *Personal Influence.* New York: Free Press.

Keeve, J. P. 1965. "Selected Social, Educational and Medical Characteristics of Primiparous 12-16 Year Old Girls." Part 1. *Pediatrics* 36 (3):394-401.

Kephart, William M. 1964. "Legal and Procedural Aspects of Marriage and Divorce." In *Handbook of Marriage and the Family,* ed. Harold T. Christensen. Chicago: Rand McNally.

Kerckhoff, Alan C. 1972. *Socialization and Social Class.* Englewood Cliffs, N.J.: Prentice-Hall.

Kerckhoff, Alan C., and Keith E. Davis. 1962. "Value Consensus and Need Complementarity in Mate Selection." *American Sociological Review* 27 (3):295-302.

Kett, Joseph F. 1974. "History of Age Grouping in America." In *Youth: Transition to Adulthood*, ed. James S. Coleman. Chicago: University of Chicago Press.

Kinsey, Alfred C., et al. 1948. *Sexual Behavior in the Human Male*. Philadelphia: Saunders.

Klausner, Samuel Z. 1972. *The Work Incentive Program: Making Adults Economically Independent*. Report prepared for Office of Research and Development, Manpower Administration, U.S. Department of Labor. Philadelphia: University of Pennsylvania.

Klerman, Lorraine V., and James F. Jekel. 1973. *School-age Mothers: Problems, Programs, and Policy*. Hamden, Conn.: Linnet Books.

Kohn, Melvin. 1969. *Class and Conformity: A Study in Values*. Homewood, Ill.: Dorsey Press.

Kohn, Melvin L., and Carmi Schooler. 1969. "Class, Occupation, and Orientation." *American Sociological Review* 34 (5):659-678.

Komarovsky, Mirra. 1964. *Blue-Collar Marriage*. New York: Random House.

Kreps, Juanita. 1971. *Sex in the Marketplace: American Women at Work*. Baltimore: Johns Hopkins Press.

Kriesberg, Louis. 1970. *Mothers in Poverty: A Study of Fatherless Families*. Chicago: Aldine.

Kuvelsky, William P., and Angelita S. Obordo. 1972. "Projections for Marriage and Procreation." *Journal of Marriage and the Family* 34 (1):75-84.

LaBarre, Maurine, and Weston LaBarre. 1969. *The Double Jeopardy, the Triple Crisis—Illegitimacy Today*. New York: National Council on Illegitimacy.

Ladner, Joyce A. 1971. *Tomorrow's Tomorrow: The Black Woman*. Garden City, N.Y.: Doubleday.

Leacock, Eleanor Burke. 1971. *The Culture of Poverty: A Critique*. New York: Simon and Schuster.

LeMasters, E. E. 1957. "Parenthood as Crisis." *Marriage and Family Living* 19:353-355.

Lewis, Hylan. 1967. "Culture, Class and Family Life among Low-Income Urban Negroes." In *Employment, Race and Poverty*, ed. Arthur M. Ross and Herbert Hill. New York: Harcourt, Brace & World.

Lewis, Oscar. 1968. *The Study of Slum Culture—Backgrounds for La Vida*. New York: Random House.

Liebow, Elliot. 1967. *Tally's Corner*. Boston: Little, Brown.

Linner, Birgitta. 1967. *Sex and Society in Sweden*. New York: Harper & Row, Colophon Books.

Lipset, Seymour Martin. 1960. *Political Man: The Social Bases of Politics*. New York: Doubleday.

Locke, Harvey. 1951. *Predicting Adjustment in Marriage: A Comparison of a Divorced and Happily Married Group*. New York: Holt, Rinehart and Winston.

Lopata, Helena Z. 1971. *Occupation Housewife.* New York: Oxford University Press.

Lowrie, Samuel H. 1965. "Early Marriage: Premarital Pregnancy and Associated Factors." *Journal of Marriage and the Family* 27 (1):49-56.

Maccoby, Eleanor E. 1961. "The Development of Moral Values and Behavior in Childhood." In *Socialization and Society,* ed. John A. Clausen. Boston: Little, Brown.

Malinowski, Bronislaw. 1930. "The Principle of Legitimacy." In *The Family: Its Structure and Functions,* ed. Rose L. Coser. New York: St. Martin's Press.

Marland, S. P., Jr. 1972. "U.S. Commissioner of Education's Statement on Comprehensive Programs for School-age Parents." *Sharing* (March).

Martz, Helen E. 1963. "Illegitimacy and Dependency." Health, Education, and Welfare Indicators. Bureau of Family Services, Welfare Administration, U.S. Department of Health, Education, and Welfare (September).

Matza, David. 1964. *Delinquency and Drift.* New York: Wiley.

Menken, Jane. 1972. "The Health and Social Consequences of Teenage Child-bearing." *Family Planning Perspectives* 4 (3):45-53.

Miller, S. M. 1969. "The American Lower Class: A Typological Approach." In *Children and Poverty: Some Sociological and Psychological Perspectives,* ed. Nona Y. Glazer and Carol F. Creedon. Chicago: Rand McNally.

Miller, Warren B. 1973. "Psychological Vulnerability to Unwanted Pregnancy." *Family Planning Perspectives* 5 (4):199-201.

Modell, John, et al. 1976. "Social Change and Life Course Development in Historical Perspective." Paper. *Journal of Family History.* (1), in press.

———. "The Timing of Marriage in the Transition to Adulthood: Continuity and Change, 1860-1975." Special issue of the *American Journal of Sociology* on History and the Family, forthcoming.

Moles, Oliver C., Jr. 1965. "Child Training Practices among Low-Income Families: An Empirical Study." *Welfare in Review* 3 (12):1-20.

———. 1969. "Predicting Use of Public Assistance: An Empirical Study." *Welfare in Review* 7 (6):13-19.

Monahan, Thomas P. 1951. *The Pattern of Age at Marriage in the United States: A Dissertation in Sociology.* Philadelphia: Stephenson-Brothers.

———. 1960. "Premarital Pregnancy in the United States." *Eugenics Quarterly* 7 (3):140.

Moss, Joel J. 1964. "Teenage Marriage: Crossnational Trends and Sociological Factors in the Decision of When to Marry." *Acta Sociologica* 8:98-117.

Moss, Joel J., et al. 1971. "The Premarital Dyad during the Sixties." *Journal of Marriage and the Family* 33 (1):50-69.

Moynihan, Daniel P. 1968. "The Crisis in Welfare." *Public Interest* 10:3-29.

National Center for Health Statistics. 1970. "Interval between First Marriage and Legitimate First Birth, United States, 1964-66." *Monthly Vital Statistics Report* 18 (12).

Neugarten, Bernice L. (ed.). 1968. *Middle Age and Aging: A Reader in Social Psychology.* Chicago: University of Chicago Press.

Neugarten, Bernice L., and Joan W. Moore. 1968. "The Changing Age-Status System." In *Middle Age and Aging,* Bernice L. Neugarten. Chicago: University of Chicago Press.

Noland, R., and C. Sherry. 1967. "Educator Attitudes and Practices Regarding the Pregnant High School Girl." *Mental Hygiene* 51 (1):49-54.

Nolte, M. Chester. 1973. "Why Your Board Should Review and (Probably) Remake Its Policy toward Pregnant Schoolgirls." *American School Board Journal* (March):23-27.

Nortman, Dorothy. 1974. "Parental Age as a Factor in Pregnancy Outcome and Child Development." *Reports on Population/Family Planning* 16:1-51.

Nye, Ivan F., and Lois W. Hoffman. 1963. *The Employed Mother in America.* Chicago: Rand McNally.

Osofsky, Howard J. 1968. *The Pregnant Teenager.* Springfield, Ill.: Charles C. Thomas.

Parsons, Talcott, and Renee C. Fox. 1952. "Illness, Therapy, and the Modern Urban American Family." *Journal of Social Issues* 13 (4):31-44.

Paulker, Jerome D. 1969. "Girls Pregnant Out of Wedlock." In *The Double Jeopardy, the Triple Crisis—Illegitimacy Today.* ed. Maurine LaBarre and Weston LaBarre. New York: National Council on Illegitimacy.

Perkins, Barbara Bridgman. 1974. *Adolescent Birth Planning and Sexuality: Abstracts of the Literature.* Washington, D.C.: Consortium on Early Childbearing and Childrearing.

Phillips, Derek L. 1972. *Knowledge from What?: Theories and Methods in Social Research.* Chicago: Rand McNally.

Piven, Frances Fox, and Richard A. Cloward. 1971. *Regulating the Poor: The Functions of Public Welfare.* New York: Random House, Vintage Books.

Placek, Paul J., and Gerry E. Hendershot. 1974. "Public Welfare and Family Planning: An Empirical Study of the 'Brood Sow' Myth." *Social Problems* 21 (5):658-673.

Podell, Lawrence. 1967. *Women, with and without Husbands, on Welfare.* Preliminary Report No. 1. New York: Center for Social Research, City University of New York.

Pohlman, Edward H. 1969. *Psychology of Birth Planning.* Cambridge: Schenkman.

Pope, Hallowell. 1967. "Unwed Mothers and Their Sex Partners." *Journal of Marriage and the Family* 29 (3):555-567.

———. 1969. "Negro-White Differences in Decisions Regarding Illegitimate Children." *Journal of Marriage and the Family* 31 (4):756-764.

Pope, Hallowell, and Charles W. Mueller. 1975. *The Intergenerational Transmission of Marital Instability: Comparisons by Race and Sex.* Sociology Working Paper Series, Iowa City: University of Iowa, No. 75-1.

Porter, Judith D. R. 1971. *Black Child, White Child.* Cambridge: Harvard

Pratt, William F. 1965. "Premarital Pregnancies and Illegitimate Births in a Metropolitan Community—An Analysis of Age and Color Differentials." Paper presented at the Meetings of the Population Association of America, April.

*Preschool Inventory.* 1970. Rev. ed. Princeton: Educational Testing Service.

Presser, Harriet B. 1971. "The Timing of the First Birth, Female Roles and Black Fertility." Part 1. *Milbank Memorial Fund Quarterly* 3:329-361.

———. 1975 (October). "Social Consequences of Teenage Childbearing." Paper presented at the Conference on the Consequences of Adolescent Pregnancy and Childbearing, Bethesda, Maryland.

Radin, Norma, and Constance K. Kamii. 1965. "The Child-rearing Attitudes of Disadvantaged Negro Mothers and Some Educational Implications." *Journal of Negro Education* 34 (Spring):138-46.

Rains, Prudence Mors. 1971. *Becoming an Unwed Mother.* Chicago: Aldine-Atherton.

Rainwater, Lee. 1960. *And the Poor Get Children.* Chicago: Quadrangle Books.

———. 1965. *Family Design: Marital Sexuality, Family Size and Contraception.* Chicago: Aldine.

———. 1966. "Crucible of Identity: The Negro Lower-Class Family." In *The Negro American,* ed. Talcott Parsons and Kenneth Clark. Boston: Houghton Mifflin.

———. 1970. *Behind Ghetto Walls.* Chicago: Aldine.

Rainwater, Lee, and William L. Yancey (eds.). 1967. *The Moynihan Report and the Politics of Controversy.* Cambridge: MIT Press.

Rapaport, Robert N. 1964. "The Male's Occupation in Relation to His Decision to Marry." *Acta Sociologica* 8:68-82.

Ravacon, Patricia B., and John J. Dempsey. 1972. "An Annotated Bibliography on Married and Pregnant Students in Education Journals of the 1960's." *Perspectives in Maternal and Child Health* 4:1-6.

Rein, Mildred. 1972. "Determinants of the Work-Welfare Choice in AFDC." *Social Service Review* 46 (December):539-566.

Reiss, Ira L. 1967. *The Social Context of Premarital Sexual Permissiveness.* New York: Holt, Rinehart and Winston.

Reiss, Ira L., et al. 1974. "Premarital Contraceptive Usage: A Study and Some Theoretical Explorations." Unpublished paper.

Ricketts, Susan Austin. 1973. *Contraceptive Use among Teenage Mothers: Evaluation of a Family Planning Program.* Ph.D. dissertation, University of Pennsylvania.

Riessman, Frank. 1962. *The Culturally Deprived Child.* New York: Harper & Brothers.

Riley, Matilda White, et al. 1969. "Socialization for the Middle and Later Years." In *Handbook of Socialization Theory and Research,* ed. David A. Goslin. Chicago: Rand McNally.

Riley, Matilda White, Marilyn Johnson, and Anne Foner (eds.). 1972. *Aging and Society*. Vol. 3, *A Sociology of Age Stratification*. New York: Russell Sage Foundation.

Roberts, Robert W. 1966. (ed.) *The Unwed Mother*. New York: Harper & Row.

Rodman, Hyman. 1963. "The Lower-Class Value Stretch." *Social Forces* 42 (3):205-215.

———. 1971. *Lower-Class Families: The Culture of Poverty in Negro Trinidad*. London: Oxford University Press.

Rosen, Bernard C., et al. 1969. (eds.) *Achievement in American Society*. Cambridge: Schenkman.

Rosenberg, Morris, and Roberta G. Simmons. 1971. *Black and White Self-Esteem: The Urban School Child*. Washington, D.C.: American Sociological Association.

Ross, Heather L. and Isabel V. Sawhill. 1975. *Time of Transition: The Growth of Families Headed by Women*. Washington, D.C.: The Urban Institute.

Ross, Jane. 1970. "The Pill Hearings: Major Side Effects." *Family Planning Perspectives* 2 (2):6-7.

Rossi, Alice S. 1964. "Equality between the Sexes: An Immodest Proposal." In *Life Cycle and Achievement in America*, ed. Rose Coser. New York: Harper & Row, Torchbooks.

———. 1968. "Transition to Parenthood." *Journal of Marriage and the Family* 20 (1):26-39.

———. 1972. "Family Development in a Changing World." *American Journal of Psychiatry* 128 (9):1057-1066.

Rossi, Peter H., and Zahava D. Blum. 1969. "Class, Status, and Poverty." In *On Understanding Poverty: Perspectives from the Social Sciences*, ed. Daniel P. Moynihan. New York: Basic Books.

Roth, Julius A. 1963. *Timetables: Structuring the Passage of Time in Hospital Treatment and Other Careers*. New York: Bobbs-Merrill.

Ryan, William. 1971. *Blaming the Victim*. New York: Random House, Vintage Books.

Ryder, Norman B. 1965. "The Cohort as a Concept in the Study of Social Change." *American Sociological Review* 30 (6):843-861.

———. 1974. "The Demography of Youth." In *Youth: Transition to Adulthood*, ed. James S. Coleman. Chicago: University of Chicago Press.

Sarrel, Philip M. 1967. "The University Hospital and the Teenage Unwed Mother." *American Journal of Public Health* 57 (8):308-313.

Sauber, Mignon, and Eileen M. Corrigan. 1970. *The Six-Year Experience of Unwed Mothers as Parents*. New York: Community Council of Greater New York.

Sauber, Mignon, and Elaine Rubinstein. 1965. *Experiences of the Unwed Mother as a Parent*. New York: Community Council of Greater New York.

Scanzoni, John H. 1970. *Opportunity and the Family*. New York: Free Press.

―――. 1972. *Sexual Bargaining: Power Politics in the American Marriage.* Englewood Cliffs, N.J.: Prentice-Hall.

Scanzoni, Letha, and John Scanzoni. 1975. *Men, Women and Change.* New York: McGraw-Hill.

Scheff, Thomas J. 1966. *Being Mentally Ill.* Chicago: Aldine.

Schorr, Alvin L. 1965. "The Family Cycle and Income Development." *Social Security Bulletin* 29:14-25.

Schulz, David A. 1969. *Coming Up Black: Patterns of Ghetto Socialization.* Englewood Cliffs, N.J.: Prentice-Hall.

Sears, Robert R., Eleanor E. Maccoby, and Harry Levin. 1957. *Patterns of Child Rearing.* Evanston, Ill.: Row, Peterson.

Sewell, William H., and Vimal P. Shah. 1968. "Social Class, Parental Encouragement, and Educational Aspirations." *American Journal of Sociology* 73 (5):559-572.

Shah, Farida, et al. 1975. "Unprotected Intercourse among Unwed Teenagers." *Family Planning Perspectives* (1):39-44.

Shea, John R. 1973. "Welfare Mothers: Barriers to Labor Force Entry." *Journal of Human Resources* 7:90-102.

Sheppard, Harold L., and Herbert E. Striner. 1968. "Family Structure and Employment Problems." In *Negroes and Jobs: A Book of Readings,* ed. Louis A. Ferman, Joyce L. Kornblush, and J. A. Miller. Ann Arbor: University of Michigan Press.

Shereshefsky, Pauline M., and Leon J. Yarrow. 1973. *Psychological Aspects of a First Pregnancy and Early Postnatal Adaptation.* New York: Raven Press.

Siegal, E., et al. 1971. "Continuation of Contraception by Low Income Women: A One-Year Follow-up." *American Journal of Public Health* 61 (9):1886-1898.

Simpson, Richard L. 1962. "Parental Influence, Anticipatory Socialization and Social Mobility." *American Sociological Review* 27 (4):517-522.

Skard, Aase Gruda. 1965. "Maternal Deprivation: The Research and Its Implications." *Journal of Marriage and the Family* 27 (2):333-343.

Sklar, June, and Beth Berkov. 1973. "The Effects of Legal Abortion on Legitimate and Illegitimate Birth Rates: The California Experience." *Studies in Family Planning* 4 (11):281-292.

―――. 1974. "Teenage Family Formation in Postwar America." *Family Planning Perspectives* 6 (2):80-90.

Smigel, Erwin O., and Rita Seiden. 1968. "The Decline and Fall of the Double Standard." *Annals of the American Academy of Political and Social Science* 376 (March):6-17.

Smith, Daniel Scott. 1973. "The Dating of the American Sexual Revolution: Evidence and Interpretation." In *The American Family in Social-Historical Perspective,* ed. Michael Gordon. New York: St. Martin's Press.

Stack, Carol. 1974. *All Our Kin.* Chicago: Aldine.

Staples, Robert (ed.). 1971. *The Black Family: Essays and Studies.* Belmont, Calif.: Wadsworth.

―――. 1973. *The Black Woman in America.* Chicago: Nelson-Hall.

Stine, O. C., et al. 1964. "School Leaving Due to Pregnancy in an Urban Adolescent Population." *American Journal of Public Health* 54 (1):1-6.

Sullerot, Evelyne. 1971. *Woman, Society and Change.* New York: McGraw-Hill.

Sweet, James A. 1973. *Women in the Labor Force.* New York: Seminar Press.

―――. 1974. "Marital Disruption and Fertility: Some Evidence from U.S. Census Data." Working paper 74-13, Center for Demography and Ecology, University of Wisconsin, Madison.

Sykes, Gresham M., and David Matza. 1957. "Techniques of Neutralization: A Theory of Delinquency." *American Sociological Review* 22 (6):664-673.

Taeuber, Conrad, and Irene B. Taeuber. 1958. *The Changing Population of the United States.* New York: Wiley.

Taeuber, Irene B., and Conrad Taeuber. 1971. *People of the United States in the 20th Century.* Washington, D.C.: U.S. Government Printing Office.

Thomas, William I. 1967. *The Unadjusted Girl.* New York: Harper & Row.

Thomas, William I., and Florian Znaniecki. 1958. *The Polish Peasant in Europe and America.* 2 vols. New York: Dover (first pub. 1923).

Toby, Jackson. 1957. "Orientation to Education as a Factor in the School Maladjustment of Lower-Class Children." *Social Forces* 35 (1):259-266.

Trussell, T. James. 1975 (October). "Economic Consequences of Teenage Childbearing." Paper presented at the Conference on the Consequences of Adolescent Pregnancy and Childbearing, Bethesda, Maryland.

Twentieth Century Fund Task Force on Employment Problems of Black Youth. 1971. *The Job Crisis for Black Youth.* New York: Praeger.

U.S. Bureau of the Census. 1970a. *Census of Population: 1970, Detailed Characteristics, Final Report* PC(1)-D22 Maryland. Washington, D.C.: U.S. Government Printing Office.

―――. 1970b. *Census of Population and Housing: 1970, Census Tracts, Final Report* PHC(1)-19 Baltimore, Maryland. SMSA. Washington, D.C.: U.S. Government Printing Office.

―――. 1972a. *Current Population Reports,* Series P-60, No. 88, "Characteristics of the Low-Income Population: 1972 (Advance Data from March 1973 Current Population Survey)." Washington, D.C.: U.S. Government Printing Office.

―――. 1972b. *Current Population Reports,* Series P-20, No. 242, "Educational Attainment: March 1972." Washington, D.C.: U.S. Government Printing Office.

Vincent, Clark E. 1961. *Unmarried Mothers.* New York: Free Press of Glencoe.

Vital Statistics of the United States. 1970. Public Health Service. National Center for Health Statistics. Washington, D.C.: U.S. Government Printing Office.

Volkart, Edmund H. (ed.). 1951. *Social Behavior and Personality: Contributions of W. I. Thomas to Theory and Social Research.* New York: Social Science Research Council.

Waller, Willard W. 1930. *The Old Love and the New: Divorce and Readjustment.* Philadelphia: Liveright.

———. 1938. *The Family: A Dynamic Interpretation.* New York: Cordon.

———. 1940. *War and the Family.* New York: Dryden Press.

Weiss, Carol H. 1972. *Evaluation Research: Methods of Assessing Program Effectiveness.* Englewood Cliffs, N.J.: Prentice-Hall.

Weissberg, Norman C. 1970. "Intergenerational Welfare Dependency: A Critical Review." *Social Problems* 18 (2):257-274.

Westoff, Charles F., and Richard H. Potvin. 1966. "Higher Education, Religion, and Women's Family Size Orientations." *American Sociological Review* 31 (3):489-496.

Whelan, Elizabeth Murphy. 1972. "Estimates of the Ultimate Family Status of Children Born Out-of-Wedlock in Massachusetts, 1961-1968." *Journal of Marriage and the Family* 34 (4):635-646.

Whyte, William F. 1949. "A Slum Sex Code." *American Journal of Sociology* 49 (1):24-31.

Winch, Robert F., and Scott A. Greer. 1964. "The Uncertain Relation between Early Marriage and Marital Stability: A Quest for Relevant Data." *Acta Sociologica* 8:83-97.

Yarrow, Leon J. 1960. "Interviewing Children." In *Handbook of Research Methods in Child Development,* ed. Paul H. Mussen. New York: Wiley.

Yarrow, Marian Radke. 1960. "The Measurement of Children's Attitudes and Values." In *Handbook of Research Methods in Child Development,* ed. Paul H. Mussen. New York: Wiley.

Yarrow, Marian Radke, et al. 1968. *Child Rearing: An Inquiry into Research and Methods.* San Francisco: Jossey-Bass.

Young, Leontine R. 1954. *Out of Wedlock.* New York: McGraw-Hill.

Zelnik, Melvin, and John F. Kantner. 1972. "Sexuality, Contraception and Pregnancy among Young Unwed Females in the United States." In *Demographic and Social Aspects of Population Growth,* ed. C. F. Westoff and R. Parke, Jr. Vol. 1 of Commission Research Reports. Washington, D.C.: U.S. Government Printing Office.

———. 1974. "The Resolution of Teenage First Pregnancies." *Family Planning Perspectives* 6 (2):74-90.

Zivin, Gail. 1973. "Locating a Behavioral Index of Children's Capacity to Cope." Paper presented at Advanced Behavior Seminar, University of Pennsylvania.

# Index

Ms. Lynne D. Diggs